MYANMAR'S BUDDHIST-MUSLIM CRISIS

Myanmar's Buddhist-Muslim Crisis

Rohingya, Arakanese, and Burmese Narratives of Siege and Fear

JOHN CLIFFORD HOLT

University of Hawai'i Press ◈ Honolulu

Printed in the United States of America
24 23 22 21 20 19 6 5 4 3 2 1

Library of Congress Cataloging-in-Publication Data

Names: Holt, John, author.
Title: Myanmar's Buddhist-Muslim crisis : Rohingya, Arakanese, and Burmese narratives of siege and fear / John Clifford Holt.
Description: Honolulu : University of Hawai'i Press, [2019] | Includes bibliographical references and index.
Identifiers: LCCN 2019007822 | ISBN 9780824881795 (cloth : alk. paper) | ISBN 9780824882112 (pbk. : alk. paper)
Subjects: LCSH: Rohingya (Burmese people)—Violence against. | Violence—Burma—Rakhine State. | Islam—Relations—Theravāda Buddhism. | Theravāda Buddhism—Relations—Islam. | Buddhism and state—Burma.
Classification: LCC DS528.2.R64 H65 2019 | DDC 959.105/3—dc23
LC record available at https://lccn.loc.gov/2019007822

University of Hawai'i Press books are printed on acid-free paper and meet the guidelines for permanence and durability of the Council on Library Resources.

Cover photo: Central Mosque, Sittwe. Built in the late nineteenth century, it was abandoned in 2012 after forcible removal of the Rohingyas. Photo by author.

For June Carla Holt

CONTENTS

This has been a very difficult book project, perhaps the most challenging I have undertaken as a professional academician, because of the heart-wrenching nature of the tragedy that forms a focal point of the book—the ruined or shortened lives of so many innocent people at the hands of morally challenged forces of the Myanmar state, forces that have brooked no fair contestations of their diabolical methods and aims, denying their culpability to the very end. I have been affected emotionally, politically, and professionally by the task of ferreting out and then attempting to understand what has occurred in Myanmar in the recent past, the deleterious state of affairs that developed between segments of its Buddhist majority and Muslim minority communities. The more I came to understand, the more I was troubled. At the very least, the experience has underscored the reality that religion is a double-edged sword, capable of generating either the most sublime or the most hideous of what it can mean to be human. An understanding of what has occurred recently between Buddhists and Muslims in Myanmar, but also in Sri Lanka and Thailand, upends stereotypes, especially persistent in the West, of Buddhists as essentially peaceful, nonviolent religious sojourners and Muslims as regular fomenters of aggressive hostility against nonbelievers.[1]

The experience also raised important questions for me related to theory and method in the study of religion. After briefly explaining the original impetus for this project, I will make a few prefacing comments regarding methodological implications that arose for me in the process of researching and writing this book.

As I reflect upon it now, the catalytic moment for the project began when, in late June of 2014, I gave a keynote address at a conference on Buddhism and its relations with other religions in South and Southeast Asia at the International Centre for Ethnic Studies in Kandy, Sri Lanka, a presentation in which I talked about how the communist Pathet Lao takeover in Laos, the spectacular economic transformation in Thailand, the devastating period of cruelty inflicted by the Khmer Rouge regime in Cambodia, fifty years of military dictatorship in Myanmar, and the twenty-six years of civil war in Sri Lanka had impacted the ethos of some sections of the Theravada Buddhist community in each country, respectively. My thesis was actually quite simple and straightforward: significant social, economic, and political changes directly impact the evolving nature and character of religious culture so that a reflexive relation obtains between the two. In the Sri Lankan context, I referred specifically to how tensions among communities produced by the long civil war between the Liberation Tigers of Tamil Eelam and the security forces of the Sinhala-dominated Sri Lankan government had abetted the rise of the ultranationalist Bodu Bala Sena

(BBS; Buddhist Power Force). My primary and specific illustration for how militancy was continuing to arise in Buddhist quarters was a recent serious attack of violence that BBS leaders had inspired on the predominantly Muslim areas of Alutgama (a town fifty kilometers south of Colombo) in June 2014, just a week before my presentation.[2] I had been made aware—though not until eleven p.m. on the night before the conference commenced—that the so-called lay CEO of the BBS would be in attendance. Unfortunately, at the last minute the organizers of the conference had not only decided to invite a leader of the BBS to attend what I and other scholar-participants had assumed would be an academic conference, but also provided him with a platform of some forty-five minutes at the end of the proceedings to respond, a chance for him to air his objections to the views espoused in my talk and the talks presented by other academics in attendance. I felt, as did other scholars at the meeting, that the academic and intellectual ethos of the conference had been compromised by this political imposition and that the organizers had been intimidated by the repressive climate for public discourse in Sri Lanka that had then prevailed and, in effect, had made a gratuitous capitulation to Buddhist militants, who at that time enjoyed at least the tacit support of the nationalist government in power.

On the night following the conclusion of the conference, an old and trusted Sinhalese friend of mine forwarded an e-mail to me that had been circulated to many of the sixty to seventy people who had attended the conference, a message in which I had been identified as an unsympathetic outside observer typical of the misled international community, one who had failed to understand the dangerous predicament that Buddhism then faced in Sri Lanka. Because of my earlier positive academic experiences in Sri Lanka (among other distinctions, I had been awarded an honorary doctorate from the University of Peradeniya in 2002, and three of my historically oriented books had been translated into Sinhala and sometimes read as part of syllabi in university-level courses), I was saddened to read that I had been labeled as a someone who ought to know better than to write things that threaten the well-being of future Buddhist interests on the island. The e-mail had been created and distributed by a longtime acquaintance of mine, of more than thirty years, a retired professor in the social sciences whom I had hosted many years earlier as visiting faculty at my home college in America. I became despondent. I worried that this might be indicative of how formerly insightful and apparently liberal-minded people had hardened their perspectives in sympathy with the militant stance taken by Buddhist nationalists now dominating public discourse about Buddhism's relation to other religions in Sri Lanka. In the days following, I pondered a decision to undertake a further study of the unfolding phenomenon of Buddhist militancy in Sri Lanka, an effort that eventually resulted in the publication of *Buddhist Extremists and Muslim Minorities: Religious Conflict in Contemporary Sri Lanka* (Holt 2016).

Meanwhile, I formulated a proposal for consideration by the John Simon Guggenheim Foundation to undertake a study of Buddhist militancy in the Theravada contexts of Sri Lanka, Myanmar, and Thailand, because I could recognize, especially in the rhetoric of Burmese nationalist monks, a very similar xenophobia being articulated against Muslims in Myanmar. The proposal was favorably received and funded, for which I am greatly indebted. Immediately I began the daily routine of scouring internet news digests for updates about the continuing and deteriorating situations in Myanmar and Thailand. I began to develop a multiyear plan of study. I had not anticipated that I would spend much of the next four years focused almost exclusively on the Myanmar dimension of the project.

Myanmar's religious culture and history were not entirely new to me, but compared to what I had come to know about Sri Lanka, where I had lived for many years and studied in some considerable depth, my knowledge of Myanmar made me a relative neophyte. I began reading in depth. I would make eight separate trips to Myanmar and interview some thirty different individuals, settling on fourteen with whom I would develop extended conversations, the accounts of which, following a contextualizing introduction, form the heart of this book: five with Muslims (three men and two women, four Rohingya and one Kaman), two Arakanese Buddhists from Rakhine State, seven Burmese Buddhists (four laymen and three monks), and four Bengali Hindu/Buddhists (which I count as one since they were part of the same family and complemented one another in what they had to say). Four of these conversations took place in Arakan (Rakhine State), another three in Mandalay, and seven in Yangon.

I have no doubt that if someone else had decided to undertake this type of project, the results would have been quite different. First, my initial interests followed from my own personal experiences while studying religious change in Theravada Buddhist cultures over the past four decades, mostly, but not exclusively, in Sri Lanka and to a lesser extent in Laos.[3] In those earlier historical studies, while it was not a predominant focus, there had always been some attention given to the relation between Buddhist religious culture and political power. What I was observing in the present was but another powerful iteration of that general pattern, but now in the contemporary context. I was under no illusion that the history of Buddhist cultures and society was innocent of aggressive political machinations and periodic campaigns of violence. So this study sustains a trajectory of my previous research interests.

Second, how I managed serendipitously to meet the people with whom I developed dialogues largely determined the substance and scope of the discussions that emerged and, therefore, how the unfolding dimensions of the problem in contemporary Myanmar would be understood more specifically. I became acutely sensitive to the insightful observation made by the noted political scientist Paul Brass that "publicized versions of many so-called . . . riots . . . , like many aspects of ethnic identity itself, are constructions upon events that are usually open to a multiplicity of interpretations" (Brass 1997, 6). In other words, how an event is reported, and its consequent significance understood, depends largely on the vantage point of the individual (which may be intimately local, regional, national, or international, and conditionally dependent upon religio-ethnic–cum–political interests and prerogatives). Context became an overriding issue in fielding the observations and perspectives that I received from my variegated interlocutors. Moreover, nothing short of serendipity was responsible for whom I eventually encountered and cultivated in these extended conversations. Two people in particular, journalist Wai Moe and scholar Jacques Leider, abetted my introductions to no less than nine of my eventual interlocutors. The noted Norwegian scholar Iselin Frydenlund, the Rohingya political activist Abu Tahay, and my former student Shawn Bose initially facilitated another three, while I managed to impose myself on two others without benefit of an intermediary. On occasion, I had to rely on translators, as two of the people with whom I conversed had only a modicum of English capabilities.

Third, and related to the issue of English, the fact that the vast bulk of my interchanges occurred in English meant that my conversation partners were all very well-educated individuals, and therefore not especially representative of most Rohingya, Arakanese, and Burmese. My Rohingya partners informed me that the literacy rate among Rohingya in Arakan (Rakhine State) is about 20 percent and that literacy among Arakanese Buddhists would not be very much higher, and one of my Burmese partners pointed out that the poverty level in the rural Myanmar countryside is about 70 percent. The fact that twelve of my fourteen conversation partners were fluent in English also emphasizes the educated elite profile of the perspectives I engaged. A much broader sample and scope, or more representative set of interviews, has been provided expertly by Matthew Schissler, Matthew J. Walton, and Phyu Phyu Thi (2015), who analyzed the interviews of seventy-eight people in six different locales across Myanmar in 2015 to ascertain the nature and function of hate speech and rumor in the construction of "narratives of threat and self-defence" from Islam. The basis for some of the conclusions they reached can also be found in segments of conversations in this book. By comparison, my conversations were not onetime encounters but were occasioned over several meetings while the on-the-ground situation in the country continued to evolve over the course of three or four years. Moreover, my "informants" were especially well informed and thoughtful, invested leaders in their communities, and critical observers of the political culture of the country. They were all genuinely worried for Myanmar's future.

Some of the conundrums that I often faced in my conversations, especially with Buddhist monks, but also with Rohingya political leaders, involved how to respond to assertions that I knew were patently false or partly untrue, though knowing that they were proffered in complete sincerity and understandably conditioned by the interlocutors' locations and direct experiences. Sometimes the statements I listened to were historically problematic in nature or, much worse, simply fabrications that had become part and parcel of the manner in which people from one of these communities were viewing the "other." In other words, stereotypes often abounded because of how they had earlier proliferated in uncontested fashion, especially through the Myanmar Burmese conventional and social media. Among Buddhists, especially monks, this was often the case with the manner in which Islam and Muslims in general were being understood and portrayed. I often had to resist the temptation to insist on correcting my partners, but as the conversations evolved over time, I decided to push back a bit because these experiences had led to my own questions about the role of an academic and the boundary, if there should be one, between activism and scholasticism. I ultimately came to the conclusion that good scholarly work can be regarded as activist in nature, and I felt a growing responsibility to at least comment upon what I knew to be either closer to the truth or completely erroneous, while at the same time, as Brass avers, realizing that "objective" accounts are illusive if not impossible, that we have to ultimately settle for "more or less persuasive and unpersuasive, more or less scrupulous or self-serving, more or less dispassionate or prejudiced accounts, some of which contained elements of a whole 'truth' of the event, but none that could explain the whole" (Brass 1997, 8). Increasingly, I came to respect even more deeply the work of my friend Jacques Leider, who has persisted in his insistence on historical accuracy amid a welter of criticism from some within the Rohingya community, and some within the Burmese and Arakanese communities as well. As scholars, we cannot abscond from a responsibility of asserting what we know to be the case; we cannot simply remain quiet for politically expedient reasons or out of sympathy for the oppressed. In that way, good scholarship can be constructive, even if its substance is not always congenial to an individual's political aims. At the beginning my work, I had a tendency to simply listen in an attempt to garner and then to re-present a given perspective. I was collecting voices, as it were, to garner the spectrum of opinions. I still think that is an important initial and necessary task in a project such as this. But as I got to know my interlocutors better, and we gained a measure of trust and comfort with each other, I was far more apt to challenge what I knew to be false or unfounded. These patterns can be observed in several of the following conversations, especially after the autumn of 2017, when the Tatmadaw (the Myanmar military) and government unleashed a tide of propaganda to discredit the reports of the UN, international NGOs, and the international media, who had the benefit of listening firsthand to the narratives of Rohingya refugees who had escaped to Bangladesh from the atrocities occurring in northern Arakan. In part, I came to think of the project in its later stages perhaps in a way similar to how one of my teachers, S. J. Tambiah, had regarded a couple of his own works, as "engaged tracts."[4] I came to see my side of the conversations as attempts, first, to understand, and then, if necessary or possible, to inform, and in some cases even instruct. That is, at times, my part of the conversations became something of an intervention. I felt that, given the circumstances, I had been forced into that role, one that I only reluctantly embraced. I had read reports from trusted sources and had seen videos that were not contrived, so I could not in good conscience bury the uncomfortable truths that they revealed when confronted with their spirited denial. I hasten to add that I remained on very cordial terms with all of my interlocutors throughout, even with one of my discussants whom I found almost totally deluded and beyond the pale of rehabilitation.[5] I want to emphasize, however, that I am not among those who would argue that Burmese and Arakanese are not really Buddhist because of how they view the Rohingya. If they are not Buddhist, then what are they? A Buddhist conceptual canopy houses the worldviews through which they interpret.

With further regard to my Buddhist interlocutors, I came to see how Buddhist thought and cosmology functioned precisely as a type of conceptual canopy that would not be transcended easily. By this, I am trying to point to how, because of Myanmar's isolation and the concomitant dismantling of its system of higher education from 1962 through 2010, there seemed to be almost a total lack of conceptual apparatus in public play to field the kinds of complex problems intrinsic to the dynamics of a fledgling democracy in a socially pluralistic or multicultural context. While the populace as a whole has been especially keen to embrace a democratic form of government after fifty years of military dictatorship, the values and concepts that undergird the democratic process have not yet been developed or understood widely. Primordial claims to the country by one religio-ethnic community (Burmese) or to parts of the country by another (Arakanese) are routinely cited as legitimation for fearing or excluding the presence of others. For many, majoritarianism is synonymous with democracy. Even if an ethic of tolerance was cited in conversation, its rationale would be articulated firmly within the ambit of Buddhist rhetoric. I encountered very little in terms of a transcendence of a Buddhist conceptual canopy, a transcendence that might embrace an understanding of the universality of human rights regardless of religious orientation, or the given nature of citizenship to those who are born within the country, or the ideal of a shared equality of belonging for all communities. Rather, values such as tolerance of difference or an ethic of modified inclusivity were articulated as instances of *karuna* (compassion), *metta* (loving-kindness), or *karma* (action producing consequences). I came away feeling as if the rhetorical pattern established by Prime Minister U Nu back in the 1950s, in which he had used Buddhist concepts to explain the virtues of socialism, was still the predominant pattern in play. For example, U Nu had explained the eventual utopian socialist ideal aim as *lokanibbana* (nirvana in this world). Buddhist ideas were the prism through which political conceptions were articulated and thereby embraced. Moreover, the military governments of the past fifty years had increasingly pandered to the imagery of Buddhist kingship by posturing as merit makers par excellence to sell their legitimacy to a pious populace. Or Buddhist ideas were the measure by which aspects of any imported ideology would be tested and legitimated. For the Bamar (Burmans), therefore, this is how Myanmar remains essentially a Buddhist country. Buddhist thought and practice are often the measure of all things. As for the Arakanese, Arakan is primordially and essentially Arakanese Buddhist. Many Arakanese regard themselves as descendants of the original occupants of the land, descendants of the Buddha's own Sakya clan who accompanied him on his alleged visit to Arakan to spread the *dhamma* (dharma). How are people from other religious persuasions to understand their places in a conceptual context like this? This situation led me to ask some of my interlocutors, in the end, whether they would favor a new secular constitution. If and when a sorely needed new constitution is chartered, how this decision is taken will be of eminent importance for the future of intercommunal relations in the country.

Myanmar is a naturally beautiful and resplendent country with a long and rich cultural history. When I first visited Burma in 1990, I came away feeling as if it was the most religious society I had ever encountered. That may still be the case, for reasons I have just explained, but also because Buddhists continue to heap whatever margins of their incomes that they can afford in support of the sangha and its material culture. Some twenty-eight years after I first visited the country, it is clear to me that Myanmar is now at a critical crossroads in terms of stepping up to the crisis that its military and Buddhist nationalists have created. I am unsure that appeals to the Buddhist canopy can provide the kind of ideological superstructure necessary for all peoples in the union to fully belong.

While these comments indicate something of the theoretical challenges I faced, I also faced some very practical, or methodological, challenges. First, gaining access to a few of my conversation partners was very difficult indeed and required some creativity in circumnavigating normal procedures whose effects would have imposed problematical outcomes for my interlocutors, insofar as they might have become further suspect in the eyes of authorities with vested interests. I had to learn to be especially discreet. Freedom of inquiry is still a largely contested issue in Myanmar. Investigative scholars or journalists can be seriously harassed and in some cases jailed on trumped-up charges of betraying the interests of the state. Second, because of the sensitivity of a number of the issues I discussed with my counterparts, I did not record our conversations by audio. I feared that recording might lead to more stilted conversations, and one of my main aims was always to encourage them to be more relaxed and therefore less calculated in what they had to say. Instead, I relied upon my ability to multitask, to type as feverishly at the computer keyboard as I could while my interlocutors spoke, often checking with them to make sure that I had recorded their comments accurately. I was abetted by the fact that in almost all instances, we met on multiple occasions. After reviewing what I had recorded from one occasion, I would begin the next session by trying to clarify whatever I might be somewhat unsure about from the previous conversation. I found the dimensions of this method exhausting at times, for it required all of my powers of concentration to focus on what was being said at the moment, recording that, and then thinking ahead to where the discussion could next head profitably.

The plan of this book is straightforward. In the introduction, I have tried to accomplish a number of tasks to contextualize the next three parts of the book. In the first instance, I have provided a backdrop in the Sri Lankan context for the emergence of militant Buddhist activism that has focused its aim on the Muslim community. The substantial claims of the Sri Lankan monks are a mirror image of what monastic Buddhist nationalists in Myanmar eventually came to aver. I have also sketched out in general the nature of the Buddhist-Muslim conflict in southern Thailand, in the process providing comparative comments where apt to signal similarities and differences. I have then proceeded to outline respective "narratives of siege" that Bamar and Rakhine Buddhists articulate, noting some of the historical and religious roots of these collective self-understandings of decline and fear. I have stressed that the nature of the imbroglio in northern Arakan is not simply Buddhist versus Muslim but actually entails a triangular set of reflexive relations obtaining between Rohingya and Rakhine Buddhists, Rohingya and Bamar Buddhists, and Rakhine Buddhists and Bamar Buddhists. Finally, I have provided a detailed account of the major events germane to the conflict since the 2012 riot in Sittwe, the major watershed moment that set off the current direction of strife and deepened alienation between communities. I have also tried to include an account of international diplomatic and nongovernmental organization responses to the worsening conditions. This chronological account informs many of the specific discussions addressed in the conversations constituting parts 1, 2, and 3 of the book.

Parts 1, 2, and 3 are organized according to the geographical locale of the conversations. I made this decision because many of the referents within the discussions are local, and my conversational partners were steeped in those specific concerns. It so happens that conversations with progressive activists all took place within Yangon (part 1), which is most likely the only venue in Myanmar, with the exception perhaps of Mandalay, where one can engage many individuals of that political persuasion. In more than one way, Yangon, especially downtown Yangon, proves to be an exception to the rest of the country by virtue of the representative kaleidoscopic presence of so many different religio-ethnic communities. It happened that all three conversations with Buddhist monks took place in Mandalay (part 3), which is the site of the greatest concentration of teaching monasteries in the country, by no means an accident since it also served as the last of the capitals of the long line of Bamar kings. I felt it was only fitting that the three conversations with Buddhist monks should form the final part of the book, as I tried to ask tough questions about how Buddhism formed a piece of the problem at hand. Finally, the section on Arakan (part 2) grounds the conversations within the current context of Rohingya and Kaman discrimination at the hands of the Rakhine and Bamar with an attempt to unpack the rationale of the former's hostile dispositions toward both the Rohingya and Bamar.

As I previously noted, a fellowship from the John Simon Guggenheim Foundation made this work possible, in addition to small but timely research stipends provided by the Faculty Development Committee at Bowdoin College. Additional supporting funds from my endowed faculty chair derived from the William R. Kenan, Jr. Foundation. I had the opportunity to frame various sections of this book after being invited to make presentations in several academic venues. The interest that colleagues took in my work, and the questions that they and their audiences raised, stimulated me to persevere. Professor Juliane Schober of Arizona State University asked me to address the Theravada Studies Group at an annual meeting of the Association for Asian Studies in 2017, and also to address a conference focused on Buddhist/Muslim Tensions in the Bay of Bengal at Arizona State in 2014; Juliane also generously encouraged me during the earliest stages of this project when I was plagued with moments of self-doubt about whether I was up to the task; Bénédicte Brac de la Perrière and Nicolas

Sihlé invited me to address colleagues at Le Centre d'Études Interdisciplinaires sur le Bouddhisme (CEIB) at the Sorbonne in Paris; Bénédicte's comments on three occasions helped to provide me with a fundamental orientation to Burmese religious culture; Iselin Frydenlund brought me to Norway for a lecture at the Peace Research Institute Oslo and has generously shared with me her own research on Buddhist-Muslim conflicts in Myanmar and Sri Lanka throughout the years; Professor Christoph Emmerich included me in a panel of presentations, along with Juliane Schober and Bénédicte Brac de la Perrière, on the plight of the Rohingya at the University of Toronto; Professor Phyllis Granoff invited me to speak at Yale; and Professor Alex von Rospatt arranged for me to be included in the University of California, Berkeley, Buddhist Studies lecture series; it was also at Alex's instigation that I was invited as the Ruby Lord Visiting Professor of South and Southeast Asian Studies at the University of California, Berkeley, in the spring of 2018, during which time a significant amount of work germane to this project was completed. I also gave relevant talks on the topic at the Harvard Buddhist Studies Forum, to the Theravada Civilizations Project, funded by the Henry Luce Foundation, and at Amherst College. I am grateful for all of these opportunities that gave me a chance to think through material that ultimately has been included in this book, to field questions, and to ponder feedback on these occasions.

Finally, I thank all of my conversation partners for their time, patience, and encouragement. It is their contributions that make this book worthy of publication. There were also many individuals in Myanmar who assisted me in times of need. Because of the sensitive manner in which this book may be received, if it is received at all in Myanmar, I have chosen not to invoke their names within this context. In three instances, I have also not used the names of my conversation partners.

Pamela Kelley, executive editor at the University of Hawai'i Press, consistently pushed me, even when I proved recalcitrant at times, to make additions and several revisions that, in the end, enhanced the quality of the manuscript immensely. This is the third book on which we've worked together, and she has proved to be the consummate editor each time. Jennifer Snow, an academic technology consultant at Bowdoin, made the maps. I am also very grateful to Patcharin Malairat for advice and support provided throughout much of the project. Finally, my spouse, Sree Padma, listened to many of my attempts to make sense out of what I had experienced and heard. Her reactions were usually timely and insightful.

Notes

1. A particularly articulate and concise assessment of these perspectives on Buddhism and Islam is given by Dan Arnold and Alicia Turner, "Why Are We Surprised When Buddhists Are Violent?" *New York Times,* March 6, 2018.

2. The presentation was revised and published as "Militant Buddhists and Minority Others: Ethnic Conflict in South and Southeast Asia" (Holt 2015).

3. In addition to my Sri Lankan book-length studies, I researched and wrote *Spirits of the Place: Buddhism and Lao Religious Culture* (Honolulu: University of Hawai'i Press, 2009).

4. Here, I am referring to Tambiah 1986 and 1992. I am comfortable to be part of Tambiah's *parampara* (lineage). (Though I could never claim the kind of intimacy he owned with his native Sri Lankan religious culture, I could, however, claim an intimacy with the study of Buddhist thought and practice and the construction of normative Buddhist worldviews.)

5. I am referring to the infamous national Burmese Buddhist monk Ashin Wirathu, with whom I met three times.

ABBREVIATIONS

ANP	Arakan National Party
ARSA	Arakan Rohingya Salvation Army
ASEAN	Association of Southeast Asian Nations
BBS	Bodu Bala Sena
CRPP	Committee Representing People's Parliament
EU	European Union
ICC	International Criminal Court
ICRC	International Committee of the Red Cross
IDP	internally displaced persons
INGO	international nongovernmental organization
ISIS	Islamic State in Iraq and Syria
JHU	Jatika Hela Urumaya
LTTE	Liberation Tigers of Tamil Eelam
Ma Ba Tha	Association for the Preservation of Society and Religion
Ma Ha Na	government sangha administrative commission
NGO	nongovernmental organization
NIC	national identity card
NLD	National League for Democracy
NRC	national registration card
NVC	national verification card
RSO	Rohingya Solidarity Organization
OHCHR	Office of the High Commissioner for Human Rights (United Nations)
OIC	Organization of Islamic Cooperation
SLORC	State Law and Order Restoration Council (Myanmar government)
UCC	Union Certificate of Citizenship
UN	United Nations
UNDP	Union National Development Party; Rohingya political party
UNICEF	United Nations Children's Fund
USDP	Union Solidarity and Development Party; military-dominated party in control of Myanmar from 2010 to 2015
VOA	Voice of America
8888	uprising led by student activists against Ne Win's government that began on August 8, 1988
969	9 virtues of the Buddha, 6 virtues of the *dhamma,* and 9 virtues of the sangha; a Buddhist nationalist monastic organization aiming to boycott Muslim businesses

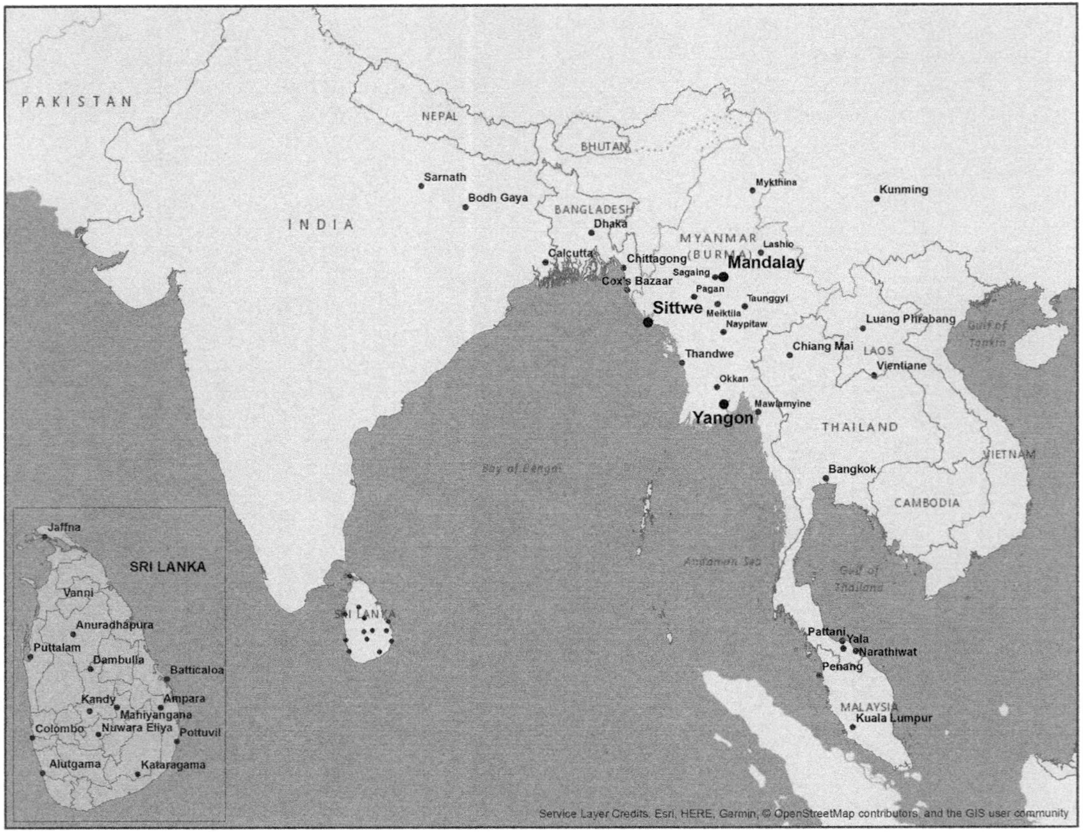
PAKISTAN
NEPAL
BHUTAN
INDIA
Sarnath
Bodh Gaya
BANGLADESH
Dhaka
Calcutta
Chittagong
Cox's Bazaar
Mykthina
Kunming
MYANMAR (BURMA)
Lashio
Mandalay
Sagaing
Pagan
Taunggyi
Sittwe
Meiktila
Naypitaw
Luang Phrabang
Chiang Mai
LAOS
Vientiane
Thandwe
Okkan
Mawlamyine
Yangon
THAILAND
VIETNAM
Bangkok
CAMBODIA
SRI LANKA
Jaffna
Vanni
Anuradhapura
Puttalam
Dambulla
Batticaloa
Kandy
Ampara
Mahiyangana
Colombo
Nuwara Eliya
Pottuvil
Alutgama
Kataragama
Pattani
Yala
Narathiwat
Penang
MALAYSIA
Kuala Lumpur
Service Layer Credits. Esri, HERE, Garmin, © OpenStreetMap contributors, and the GIS user community

Map of Asia

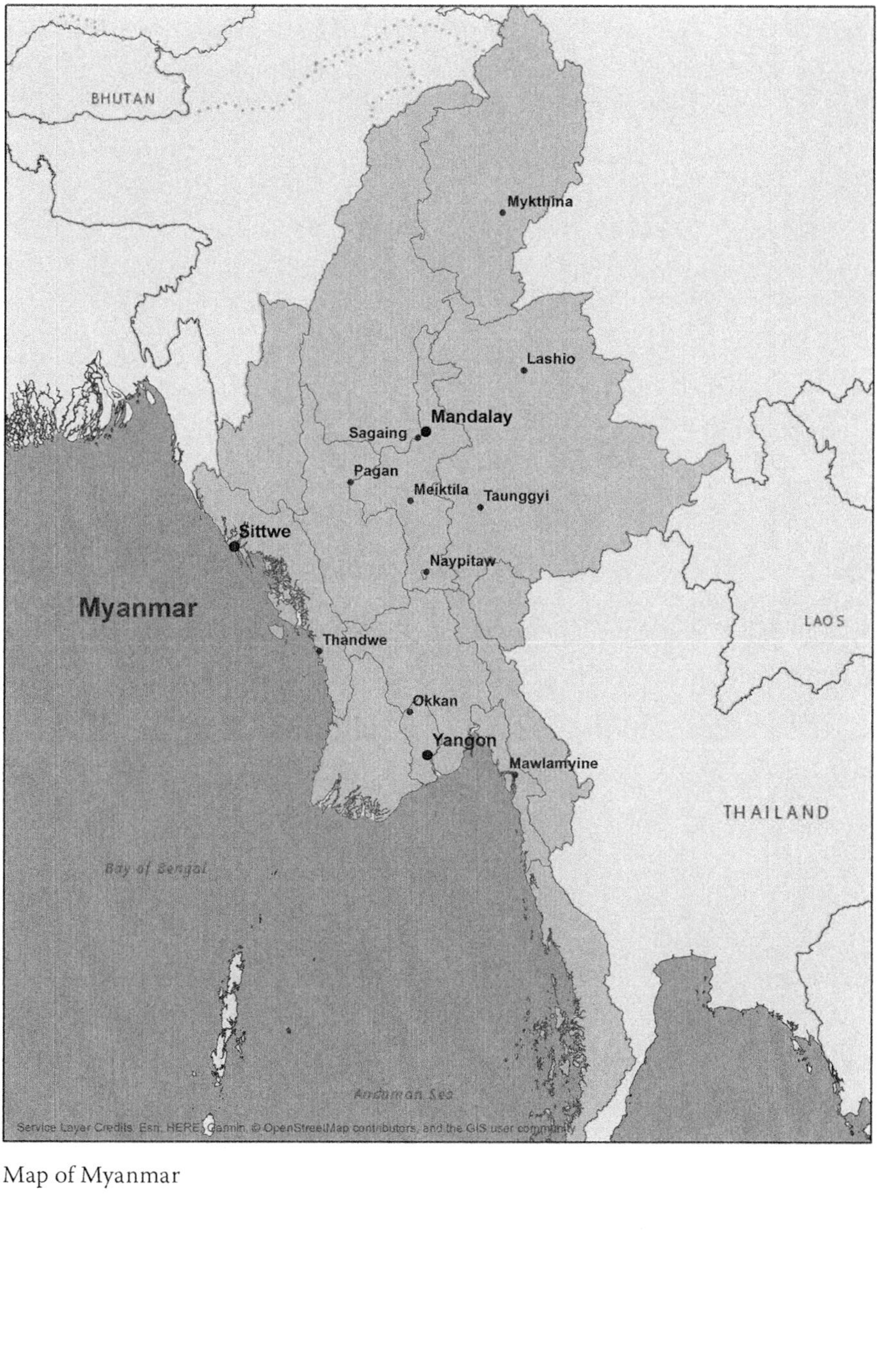

Map of Myanmar

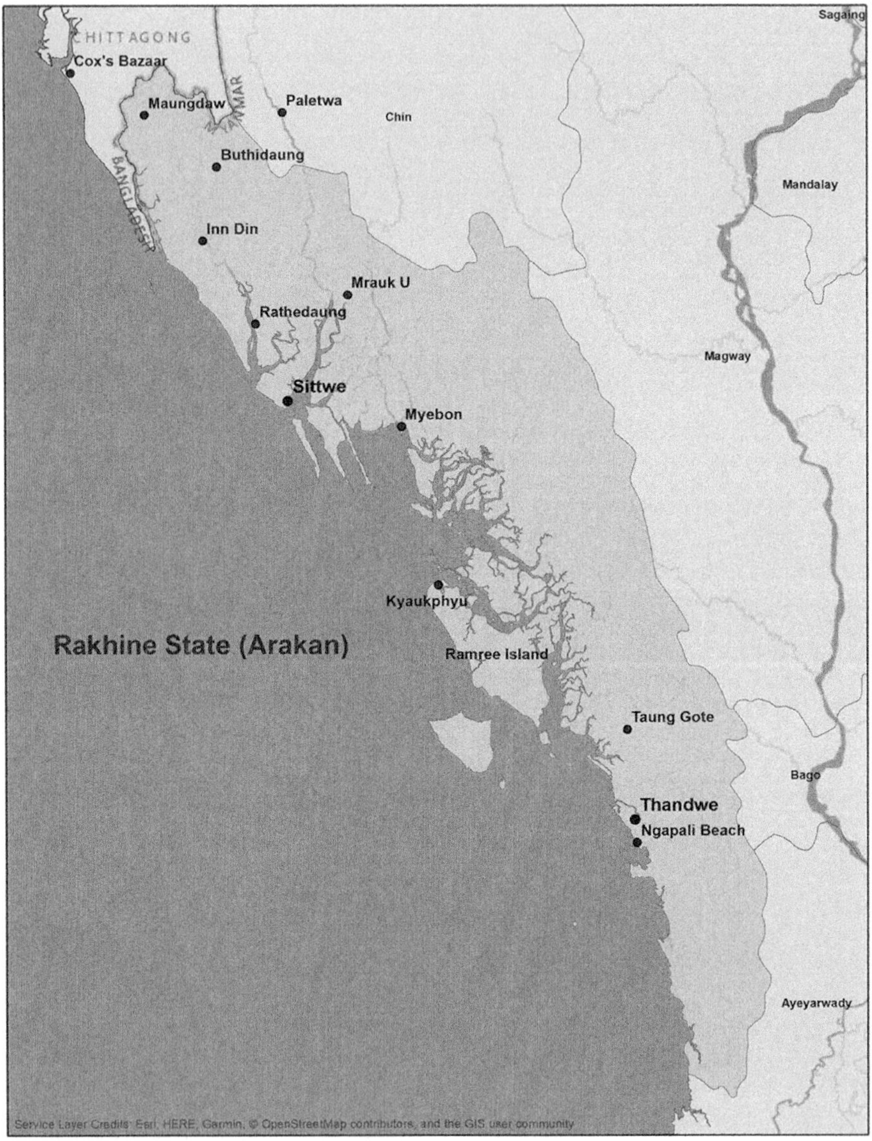

Map of Rakhine State

Introduction

Problems, Narratives, and Backgrounds

> [Our] epoch has witnessed the rise in many countries of repressive authoritarianism in both military and democratic guises, equipped with Western weaponry, inflamed by populist slogans and fundamentalist doctrines, and assisted by a flagrant manipulation of the mass media, which have vastly expanded their reach. The optimism of the sociologists, political scientists, and anthropologists who naively foretold an "integrative revolution" and the inevitable decline of "primordial loyalties" such as kinship, caste, and ethnicity in third world countries, has by now waned and dimmed. The introduction of constitutions and democratic institutions, enshrining human rights, universal franchise, the party system, elected legislatures, majority rule, and so on, has often resulted in strange malformations that are far removed from the goals of liberty, justice, and tolerance that were the ideological supports of Western European and North American liberal-democratic syntheses. Something has gone awry in center-periphery relations throughout the world, and a manifestation of widespread ethnic conflict, accompanied in many instances by collective violence among people who are not aliens but enemies intimately known.
>
> —S. J. Tambiah, *Leveling Crowds*

S. J. Tambiah's general assessment of South Asian sociopolitical calamities fits uncannily well with the dynamics of interethnic struggle now being experienced in Myanmar. The analyses that comprised Tambiah's masterful study were based on eight case studies of collective violence throughout the various countries of South Asia. In each of these instances, Tambiah tracked the dynamics of how particular ethnic communities had engaged in struggles not only with other ethnic communities, but also with the powers of the state. In the particular case of Myanmar that is the focus of this book, however, what is different is that the state, and not a minority ethnic group, has been the preponderantly attacking protagonist exacerbating the tensions at hand. That is, in Myanmar, the pattern of violence has been efficiently carried out as a strategic policy by a heavily armed state against a thoroughly outmanned and almost defenseless minority population. In the opinions of many critical observers, including a United Nations fact-finding mission, what has transpired in Myanmar may be characterized accurately as an instance of state-sponsored ethnic cleansing or genocide.

Sri Lanka, Myanmar, and Thailand have each experienced a grave intercommunal conflict between Theravada Buddhist and Muslim communities in the recent past, though the roots of these conflicts go back many generations. This is a book primarily about the conflict in Myanmar, but in this introduction and in the fourteen conversations that follow, I have made comparisons among all three of these national contexts when they are apt, in order to draw attention to distinctions and particularities on the one hand, and to similarities on the other.

My scholarly focus of inquiry over the years has been the dynamics of historical change within Theravada Buddhist religious cultures, and my theoretical touchstones still lie within the conceptual horizons of the history of religions discipline, so my analytical emphases are often on the religious dimensions of these conflicts, despite the fact that social, economic, and political realities intrinsic to each are often the predominant causes for particular moments of conflict. In ferreting out the various dynamics in play, I have avoided placing blame for the conflicts onto the abstract constructs labeled Theravada Buddhism or Islam, as I think that such blunt and imprecise reifications are perhaps one of the best ways in which the current conflicts can become either further inflamed or reduced in a way that camouflages complexity. Euro-Americans, in particular, often assume that Buddhism is *essentially* a religion of peace, while Islam is *essentially* prone to violent aggressions against outsiders. The conflicts in each of these Theravada-dominated cultures reveal very different realities that these kinds of essentialized stereotypes cannot camouflage.

The narrative of this book is not an inspiring one; it is, in the final analysis, a rather complex and depressing story. The situation in Myanmar is not simply that Buddhist racists have attacked innocent Muslims, as many reports in the international media have had a tendency to portray. Nor is it simply a matter, as some Buddhist nationalists aver, of a tidal wave of Bengali immigrants and insurgent radical Muslim terrorists seeking to first overtake Rakhine State (formerly Arakan), in western Myanmar, before they set their sights on taking over the whole of the country and then Southeast Asia in its entirety. I would also not want to make the facile suggestion that the truth lies somewhere between these two thorough misconceptions. My primary aim in the chapters following this introduction is to give voice to representative understandings of people in Myanmar who have been affected by, are close to, or are vitally concerned with the violence of intercommunal conflict. From their personal testimonies, rooted as they are in specific vantage points conditioned by location, religion, and vocation, some of the nuances and complexities intrinsic to these tragic developments will arise. The conflicts also continue to evolve, as do their representative understandings, thereby requiring renewed assessments. Following this introduction, which serves as background and context, the substance of fourteen conversations, some of them continuing over almost four years, are presented.

In this introduction, I have tried to do two things: (1) to sketch out in general Rohingya, Arakanese, and Burmese perspectives concerning the recent conflict and (2) to provide a general historical backdrop of the major events of the past five years as a context within which to situate the conversations. With regard to the first, people in each of these three communities in question see themselves as aggrieved parties and articulate a narrative of siege.

Before attending to these two tasks, I will also allude briefly and comparatively to the dynamics of Buddhist-Muslim conflicts in Sri Lanka and Thailand. I do this especially with regard to Sri Lanka, as there are significant links between the Buddhist monastic communities of these two countries that have affected the manner in which ultranationalist Buddhist positions have been articulated. I hasten to add at the outset that these extreme nationalist positions are by no means normative for, or representative of, the entirety of these respective Theravada Buddhist communities. Indeed, there are significant monastic moves being made in contemporary Myanmar and Sri Lanka to counter the extremist positions loudly proclaimed by nationalist monks. In the chapters that follow, the views of progressive Buddhist monks and laymen in Myanmar will be articulated in some detail, in addition to the perspectives of Burmese nationalist monk U Wirathu, widely regarded as the vanguard of Burmese ultranationalist Buddhist aspirations, and Sitagu, one of Myanmar's most popular and respected monks.

Comparative Contexts of Conflict: Sri Lanka, Myanmar, and Thailand

My interests in the problem of Buddhist-Muslim conflicts was first generated by my observations of the rise of the Bodu Bala Sena (BBS; Buddhist Power Force) in the era following Sri Lanka's civil war (1983–2009), that is, since 2012. Because there are clear ideological and political links between the BBS and U Wirathu's 969 (a Buddhist nationalist organization promoting boycott of Muslim businesses) and then Ma Ba Tha (acronym for Association for the Preservation of Society and Religion) Movements in Myanmar, I will begin by providing an overview of what transpired earlier in Sri Lanka, since it seems to have been a harbinger for what eventuated in Myanmar, and since monks from the Sinhala and Burmese sanghas have cooperated with one another in advancing Buddhist nationalist agendas. Because there are some parallels and instructive contrasts with neighboring Thailand, I shall also give a brief overview of the dynamics in play there before proceeding to a detailed reprise of the events that have unfolded in Myanmar since 2012.

During Sri Lanka's ethnic pogrom of July 1983 (some of which I witnessed personally), between three thousand and four thousand Tamils were murdered and thousands of homes and businesses torched by Sinhalese thugs, many of whom had been organized by members of the Buddhist-dominated Sri Lankan government. Known colloquially as "Black July," the 1983 pogrom is regarded as the watershed that galvanized Tamil and Sinhala ethnopolitical forces into a civil war that lasted some twenty-six years before Sri Lankan government military forces decisively decimated the cadres of the Liberation Tigers of Tamil Eelam (LTTE) in 2009 and many thousands of Tamil people, who, unfortunately, were simply in the path of the Sri Lankan army's final advancing onslaught. Following Black July and many years of war, an avalanche of scholarship emerged to ascertain the causes that generated what often came to be regarded in the international media, and in some scholarly circles, as a Sinhala Buddhist–Tamil Hindu conflict. Early on, I argued that reasons for the war were primarily economic and only secondarily religious, but no one disagrees that the civil war escalated a surge of Sinhala Buddhist nationalism.[1]

Fifteen years into the civil war and after several sensational terrorist bombings inflicted by the LTTE on the Sinhala public, including religiously traumatic assaults on revered sites of Buddhist worship,[2] many Sinhalese were increasingly drawn to the militant and chauvinistic political views espoused by a "modern" charismatic monk, the Venerable Gangodawila Soma, an articulate master of rhetoric who exploited effectively virtually all forms of media to convey his vision of a Buddhist country under siege by Hindu, Muslim, and Christian conspiracies. Soma's message, resonating with a wide cross section of the Sinhala Buddhist public (about 65 percent of the Sri Lankan population), was cloaked within erudite, persuasive sermons lending legitimacy to hard-line reactionary political perspectives, perspectives that countered moderate quarters of Sinhala and Tamil opinion affirming the pluralist bases or multicultural dimensions of Sri Lankan society. For Soma, Sri Lanka has always been essentially a Buddhist country. During the civil war, many Sinhala people who shared Soma's perspective felt that they were struggling to maintain the sovereignty of the country for the sake of the religion. Thus, many Sinhala Buddhists saw the efforts of Soma as a spirited defense of the nation to save the Buddhist religion. When Soma died unexpectedly on a visit to Russia in late 2003, rumors of his demise at the hands of Christians were spread so vigorously and ubiquitously throughout the island that then president Chandrika Kumaratunga had to appoint a committee of experts to inquire into the precise cause of his death. No foul play was ever proved. However, in the wake of these rumors and Soma's emotion-filled funeral, purportedly the largest funeral attended in Sri Lanka's history, a new monastic political party, the Jatika Hela Urumaya (the Sinhala People's Heritage), or JHU, was established with fanfare, promoted by some as a legacy of Soma's life, and rationalized with the view that the Buddhist sangha had often played a supervisory role for political authority in traditional Sri Lankan regimes of political power before the long, 450-year era of colonization by Western powers that ended only in 1948 with independence from Great Britain. The JHU won nine seats in parliament in the general election that followed in 2004. That election set a historical precedent: monks of the Buddhist sangha were formally institutionalized into the official governing structure of the country, an unprecedented development in the Theravada Buddhist world of

Sri Lanka and Southeast Asia. Monastic participation in the political life of the country had been institutionalized by democratic enfranchisement. (Buddhist monks in Thailand are not even allowed to vote, and no monks in Burma, Laos, and Cambodia are known to have ever pursued public office.) Whether or not monks should engage in political activity has been a long-debated issue in all Theravada societies, a debate prefigured in discussions within the sangha itself about whether the monastic vocation is best realized by an orientation to working for the welfare of the lay village people (*gamavasi*) by helping to assuage their experiences of *dukkha* (suffering, unsatisfactoriness), or by retiring to the forest (*vanavasi*) to pursue the quietude of meditation leading to the realization of *nibbana* (final extinction from samsara, the wheel of rebirth).

With the rise of Soma's popularity and the subsequent founding of the JHU, attacks of vandalism on Christian churches, in all cases of the Protestant evangelical missionary type, escalated in number. Roman Catholics were largely left alone. As these attacks spread in 2004, JHU monks introduced a bill into parliament to ban "unethical conversions." There was widespread concern that aggressive evangelical proselytizing would soon lead to a decline in the Buddhist demography and represented a serious threat to the future of the Buddhasasana (Buddhist tradition or teaching). These many years later, this controversial bill has yet to be taken up for a formal vote, but it stimulated a heated public debate that further sharpened the religious boundaries between Buddhists and Christians. Sporadic attacks on churches have continued since.

Soma had also taken aim at Muslims (approximately 9 to 10 percent of the Sri Lankan population), especially during the final five years of his public "ministry," charging that huge swaths of land now belonging to Muslims in the country's southeast region had been stolen from historic Buddhist temples. He warned against the influx of new Muslim wealth coming into the country from the Middle East, where many Muslims have sought employment, and prophesied about impending demographic shifts due to the absence of birth control practices among Muslims. He pointed to the increasing number of mosques being constructed as material evidence of Islam's expansion. With public attention more riveted on the civil war and increasing tensions between Buddhists and Christians, not much recognition was given to the concomitant rising tensions between Buddhists and Muslims that Soma had helped to foment. This eclipse in focus occurred in part because the LTTE had become an inveterate enemy of the Muslim community as well. They had evicted more than one hundred thousand Muslims from the northern Jaffna Peninsula in 1990 and had perpetrated provocative massacres in killing hundreds of Muslims on the east coast, some while worshiping within their mosques. LTTE victimization of Muslims thereby pitted the geopolitical interests of the Muslims with the Sinhala Buddhists, for they shared a common enemy.

Three years after the civil war ended (in June 2012), monks and laity from the historic Dambulla Rajamahavihara temple in the Central Province converged on a small nearby mosque to demand its removal from allegedly temple-owned land. After protests from local Muslims, the government sided with the

Buddhists' claims and ordered the mosque relocated, a harbinger of events to follow. More than six hundred documented incidents in the following years exacerbated relations. In February 2013, a new Buddhist extremist group led by monks, the Bodu Bala Sena (BBS; Buddhist Power Force), engaged in public agitations condemning the production of halal food, not because it involves the slaughter of animals and contravenes the Buddhist precept of not to kill, but because it directly causes Sinhala Buddhists to pay more for their food for reasons that they do not subscribe to and cannot control. The BBS proposed another ban too: that Muslim women should stop wearing the burka, chiefly citing security reasons. Meanwhile, a second extremist Buddhist group, the Ravana Balaya (Ravana's Power)[3] launched a two-week, 250-kilometer pilgrimage from the sacred shrine at Kataragama in the rural southeast of the country to the capital, Colombo, concluding with a high-profile presentation of a petition to then president Mahinda Rajapaksa, formally demanding the ban on halal food. Then on the first night of Ramadan, thugs broke into a mosque near Mahiyangana, about fifty kilometers east of Kandy, smeared it with pig intestines, and left a pig's severed head reportedly facing the direction of Mecca. In the Grandpass neighborhood of Colombo on the night of Eid at the end of Ramadan in August, a mob of Buddhist outsiders attacked Muslims in prayer within a newly built mosque, seriously injuring the incumbent imam. A disturbing pattern in these attacks was government culpability: few perpetrators of violence were apprehended and few significant steps taken to assure Muslims of their safety during their ritual observances. Indeed, it was reported that the powerful secretary to the Ministry of Defense (the brother of the president) was a featured speaker at the BBS's "leadership academy" in March of that year. Finally, in June of 2014, after a rally at which the general secretary of the BBS, Ven. Gnanasara Attha Thero, stoked a crowd of seven thousand Sinhala Buddhist supporters to a frenzy with a genuine hate speech in which he confessed to the racist nature of his BBS perspective,[4] the adjacent predominantly Muslim town of Alutgama was set to siege with more than sixty homes torched, three mosques ransacked, and three Muslims murdered.[5]

While the election of President Maithripala Sirisena and his coalition government in January 2015 seemed to have acted as a mitigating force on militant Buddhists further terrorizing Muslims and Christians, two more significant instances of violence in Ampara (extreme southeast region of the island) and Digana (just northeast of Kandy in the central highlands) occurred in March 2018, signaling that the BBS and its ultranationalist allies[6] are not dormant forces but remain active and ready to reassert their violent provocations against Muslims if opportunities arise. What has been disturbing about this latest violence is that it has become clear that the Sri Lanka Police Special Task Force, along with politicians related to former president Mahinda Rajapaksa's new political party, were likely complicit in these attacks. As I mentioned, attacks against Muslims have now numbered about six hundred since the recent trouble began to flare in 2012 and 2013, according to the Muslim Secretariat in Sri Lanka (Reuters, March 26, 2018).

I have provided this extended backdrop of the Buddhist-Muslim problem in contemporary Sri Lanka because, while undertaking a study of the rise of Buddhist militancy in Sri Lanka, I was struck immediately by how a similar pattern of ideology and conflict had flared in Myanmar. Indeed, the ideology of the Bodu Bala Sena in Sri Lanka and the 969 and Ma Ba Tha Movements in Myanmar were remarkably similar in tone and substance. In both contexts, Muslims were scapegoated for roughly the same reasons despite the fact that the two Muslim communities in these respective countries are very different in nature. Even within each national context, the Muslim communities are quite diverse, ranging economically from successful urban businessmen to poor rural agricultural workers. Moreover, in Myanmar, as in Sri Lanka, the Muslim community has a number of separate origins, ranging from the Chinese Panthay in Mandalay to the Bengali-speaking Rohingya Muslims in Arakan.[7] In Sri Lanka, while it is common for many Muslims to assert an Arabic origin, most have South Indian historical roots, while a few others are of Malay descent.[8] In both national contexts, the collective Muslim communities are quite diverse in nature.

In Myanmar, a very serious outbreak of violence occurred between Arakanese Buddhists and Rohingya Muslims in June of 2012, a riotous and fiery imbroglio claiming the lives of about two hundred Muslims and leaving more than 120,000 people homeless in Sittwe, the capital of Rakhine State (Arakan), bordering Bangladesh in western Myanmar. Violence then spread to other parts of the country over the course of the next year: forty-three Muslims were killed in March 2013, in the central Burmese town of Meiktila in three days of communal havoc. Other attacks on Muslims occurred periodically throughout the country in places like Lashio in Shan State and then in Mandalay, the former royal capital and putative center of Burmese Buddhist monasticism. Thus, Buddhist-Muslim tensions had flared simultaneously in Sri Lanka and Myanmar and also had continued apace in Thailand's most southern three provinces. Before I proceed to introduce the situation in Myanmar in greater detail, I will first provide a thumbnail sketch of what has transpired in neighboring Thailand, since there are some parallels to be noted in that context as well.

There has been, and continues to be, a violent insurgency mounted by militant ethnic Malay Muslims that has been severely repressed by Thai military forces in the deep south of Thailand in its three provinces of Pattani, Yala, and Narathiwat, a confrontation in which at least sixty-five hundred people have been killed since the early 2000s. While the situation in Thailand has cooled just a bit at this time, at least in terms of the number of violent deaths during the past three years, the root problems of the conflict have yet to be addressed practically. Talks with an umbrella group observed by the Malay government are ongoing, but the leading militant group, the Barisan Revolusi Nasional, has yet to join the peace talks and probably won't until the military-controlled Thai government turns power over to an elected civilian regime, a prospect at the moment that seems to be likely only in 2019, if the junta's often postponed promises hold then. And still at that time, the base question will need to be tackled: how does a community that defines itself primarily in terms of language, religion, and history (Malay, Muslim, and a distant historical memory of autonomy) accommodate itself or not to a country that identifies itself essentially with the Thai language, Buddhist religion, and almost a thousand years of political independence, which it marks summarily by lineages of Buddhist kingship? This fundamental structural problem, the issue of how a minority people can fully belong within a state that has insisted, for more than a century, on religious, cultural, and linguistic homogenization—on what it calls "Thainess"—is the fundamental issue at hand.[9] In Myanmar, "Burmanization" has functioned in a similar manner.

On the Thai Buddhist side of the problem, there is an unsettling question about whether Thais can eventually summon a political will to embrace a more pluralistic conception of their society or national political culture, so that regional and ethnic tensions might abate. As in Myanmar among the Burmese, there remains the assumption that Thai Buddhist culture is the norm for the country and that other minority people need to either integrate or conform to this religio-cultural-political default position. There is little sign that a conception of pluralism or multiculturalism will be translated into public policy in the near future. The link between religion and the state, embodied by the symbolism of Buddhist kingship and the state's formal administration of the Buddhist sangha, an administrative feature of Myanmar as well but not of Sri Lanka, is thoroughly entrenched and embraced, enthusiastically so, by a vast, overwhelming majority of the Thai Buddhist demographic. Thai Buddhist people outside the deep south often display little in the way of understanding sympathetically the perspective and aspirations of their minority Muslim population.

Thailand remains "the most Buddhist" of all Theravada-dominated countries, with 95 percent of its citizens regarding themselves as nominally Buddhist in identity. A formula for peaceful coexistence with Malay Muslims continues to seem a distant reality at the moment, one that will take many years of goodwill at the negotiation table to accomplish, and then a good effort at selling it to the rank and file of both sides. What is unique about the Muslim situation in the deep south of Thailand, when compared to Myanmar, is that Pattani, Narathiwat, and Yala have very developed educational infrastructures, including Muslim primary- and secondary-level institutions per se, as well as universities. There are many Muslim and non-Muslim NGOs hard at work to help ameliorate the problem on the ground, an abundance of goodwill to see this thorny situation through. Moreover, the Muslims of these provinces remain secure in their own culturally Malay Muslim identity. Unlike Muslims in Myanmar, they are not derided for choosing how to be known collectively. Many families move back and forth across the Malaysian border for educational reasons, for job opportunities, or for prospective marriages. The border is not regarded as a barrier. Unlike the Rohingya of Myanmar and the Muslims of Sri Lanka, they continue to have other more convenient options besides the homeland into which they have been born. Crucially, and unlike most Rohingya in Myanmar, Malay Muslims are citizens of the state. In addition, as I have mentioned, there is actually a formal political discussion taking place between Malay Muslim representatives and the Thai state. That kind of eventuality seems a far distant and unlikely hope for the Rohingya of Myanmar, who have yet to begin to find a unified voice or political representation. A fundamental problem for the Rohingya is not only that they are not politically organized to speak with one voice, but also that they are not even allowed to participate in the political process at all. Moreover, unlike in southern Thailand and Sri Lanka, where there are many nongovernmental organizations hard at work in efforts to ameliorate conditions on the ground, there are comparatively few present by comparison in contemporary Myanmar.

In any case, what is common between the Myanmar context and the Sri Lankan and Thai contexts is that many people in the majoritarian Buddhist communities of each identify their countries as *essentially Buddhist*. Democracy has often come to mean majoritarianism in practice. This identification of Buddhist nations with the state has been institutionalized in different ways within each country, but the problem of belonging remains fundamentally the same for minority peoples in each of these countries, respectively.

Burmese Buddhist Nationalism and the "Bengali" Problem

Having provided these introductory remarks about the simmering conflicts between Buddhists and Muslims in Sri Lanka and Thailand, I will now proceed to focus on the problem in Myanmar by first sketching out some general trajectories indicative of the problem at hand before providing a more specifically historical chronological account that functions as a backdrop to the contemporary scene and the substantive conversations that constitute the heart of this book. Parallels with what has happened in Sri Lanka will become more apparent.

Similar to Sri Lanka's Soma, a charismatic monk, Ashin Wirathu, had surfaced in Myanmar by 2013 as the mouthpiece of Burmese Buddhist militancy. A sensational caption to his photo on the cover of the international edition of *Time* magazine (July 1, 2013) read "The Face of Buddhist Terror," and the article unfortunately referred to him as a "Buddhist Bin Laden" articulating a "mantra of hate." It was an explosive and I felt not altogether fair exposé, sensationalist as it was, though Wirathu managed with his characteristic bravado to utter some outlandish and unfounded claims about Muslims during the interview. When it was published, the magazine's issue was banned (unsurprisingly) in Myanmar and Sri Lanka for being inflammatory. Skepticism of the international media surged in the aftermath of this publication.

Wirathu was released from prison in February 2012, after serving eight years of a twenty-five-year sentence imposed in 2003 for inciting hatred for Muslims. He says he was regalvanized by the riots in Rakhine State, and so he helped to establish the 969, a movement aimed at boycotting Muslim businesses and patronizing Buddhist establishments only. Like Soma in Sri Lanka, he publicly preached sermons in which he warned against the lack of birth control among the Muslims and the loss of Buddhist lands to them. And like Soma, he was particularly concerned with the conversion of Buddhist women to Islam, especially those who had married Muslim men. He organized the circulation of a petition, receiving more than 5 million signatures, supporting four legislative bills placing severe restrictions on Buddhist-Muslim marriages, making conversion from one religion to another extremely difficult, limiting the number of children who might be born to women under certain demographic circumstances, and formally banning polygamy. These bills, known collectively as the "four race and religion laws," were eventually passed in 2015 by the Union Solidarity and Development Party (USDP), the military proxy political party that dominated Myanmar's parliament before the general elections of November 2015, which swept Aung San Suu Kyii and the National League for Democracy (NLD) into quasi-power in March 2016. Wirathu also inspired the establishment of hundreds of "Buddhist Sunday schools," modeled after those earlier established in Sri Lanka. Within the context of sermons, he typically emphasized, as he did in the *Time* cover article, that "Muslims are breeding so fast, and they are stealing our women, raping them. They would like to occupy our country, but we won't let them. . . . We must keep Myanmar Buddhist! If we are weak, our land will become Muslim. . . . We'll end up like Afghanistan or Indonesia." Wirathu portrayed the Rohingya Muslims of Arakan as recent illegal Bengali interlopers, pandering to a widespread misconception, earlier especially prevalent among Arakanese Buddhists but now widely believed throughout Buddhist Myanmar, including among the military (Tatmadaw), that the Rohingya had arrived in this western borderland region of Burma mostly in postindependence times (1948). But historically, in fact, many Muslims had lived in the region for generations, some even before British colonial rule beginning in the early nineteenth century. Moreover, we know from a variety of sources (see especially Leider 2005) that Muslims were a significant presence in the Arakanese Buddhist kingdom of Mrauk U from the fifteenth to the late eighteenth century. Many had been brought from Bengal to Mrauk U by Buddhist kings to work in agriculture. There are also Portuguese sources from the sixteenth and seventeenth centuries that contain derisive comments about Muslims of this area being fierce competitors in trade; therefore, a different type of Muslim community was probably in place even before the farmworkers were imported. From Burmese sources, it is also evident that many Muslims were living in the region when the Burmese king Bodawpaya conquered Arakan in 1785. Indeed, Kaman Muslims are said to have assisted in the removal of the famous Mahamuni Buddha image from Arakan to Mandalay, where it had been "invited" following the Burmese invasion. So, the Muslim presence is by no means as recent as Wirathu and many others, especially leading generals of the Myanmar Tatmadaw and some National League for Democracy government officials, now claim, and it is likely that one form or another of Muslim settlement has been part of the Arakan social mosaic for many centuries, since Arab traders first settled on the Arakan coast plying their vocations more than a thousand years ago. Questions regarding the historicity of Rohingya Muslims per se raise yet a different set of issues. There is no doubt that the period of

British rule from the early nineteenth to the mid-twentieth century facilitated the migration of many more Muslims from Bengal. Unfortunately, the understanding of the Rohingya Muslims as recent illegal border jumpers has now become somewhat standard in many current Burmese and Arakanese narratives.

A prominent Buddhist monk-scholar in Thailand, Phra Paisal Visalo, has said that Burmese monks were quite isolated until recently but have come under the influence of Sri Lanka's militant monks. Indeed, the similarities in ideology shared by Wirathu and Soma are starkly evident. Moreover, each context has been exacerbated because Buddhist-dominated governments did little to protect the Muslim minorities in their midst. But Burma's Muslims have been in an even more precarious bind. The 1982 Citizenship Law, which is still the law of the land, though originally promulgated by military dictator Ne Win, excluded Rohingya Muslims from among 135 other ethnic groups deemed "indigenous" and thereby eligible for full citizenship. The Rohingya are, therefore, now largely a "stateless" people, despite the fact that they were allowed to vote in the parliamentary elections of 1990, 2010, and 2012, not to mention the elections held during U Nu's democratic period from 1948 until 1962. Their variously issued identification cards over the years have now been expropriated.

The most recent "verification process" requires that Arakanese Muslims register as "Bengalis," therein giving up their self-identification as "Rohingya" and consequently forfeiting any claims to full citizenship that they might legitimately advance as members of that minority. Many non-Rohingya Muslims, even those who consider themselves fully acculturated "Burmese Muslims," are also being told that they must register as Bengalis (*Frontier,* January 11, 2018). If Rohingya or other Muslims register as Bengalis—and very few have opted for this—they have to provide documentation to trace their lineages back for three generations of residency in Myanmar, and all of their parents and grandparents must have been full citizens. Some who have met these requirements have been issued "pink cards," which entitle them to full citizenship. In a pilot program run in Myebon township in 2014, only 40 people out of 1,200 who applied as Bengalis were granted pink cards. Another 169 were granted green cards, which is a "naturalized citizenship" designation, a status that gives full rights except the right to run for parliament or serve in the military. And then there was the white card, for "temporary residents," which was vetted by parliament to allow noncitizens like the Rohingya to vote, which, as I mentioned, they did in the first quasi-democratic elections in 2010. The white-card scheme met with vitriolic protests in February 2015, especially in Rakhine State among Arakanese Buddhists, and ultimately the idea was scrapped in May of that year, leaving most Rohingya without any formal identification.

The resistance among Rohingya against registering as Bengalis is based on the fact that many simply don't want to identify themselves as Bengalis when their families have lived in Myanmar for generations and they have regarded their country of birth as their own; there is also the fear that in the future the Myanmar government could decide to send all people who have claimed to be Bengalis to Bangladesh (*The Irrawaddy,* October 10, 2014; Reuters, September 27, 2014) since, as "Bengalis," they would certainly not be regarded as "Burmese nationals."[10] In fact, most of them, about 1 million out of 1.5 million, have now fled to Bangladesh, and the issues involved in their repatriation to Myanmar are turning out to be quite complicated. So, a basic problem clouding the situation stems from the fact since "Rohingya" is a term in the eastern Bengali dialect that means "Arakanese," the Myanmar government is asking Rohingya to renounce their identities of belonging to Rakhine State. In addition, Bangladesh has consistently refused to consider "repatriation" of these so-called Bengalis (though how to manage some 1 million Rohingya refugees has become their immediate burden). This renders the Rohingya as a people caught between two states that refuse to accept them as citizens.

Following the 2012 riots in Sittwe, Rohingya were segregated into apartheid-like conditions, restricted to no more than two children per family, left without medical or educational facilities, bereft of legal counsel, and denied freedom of movement. This left most without any opportunity to seek gainful employment, and consequently, many have become almost totally dependent for survival on aid from international nongovernmental organizations. It is often noted in the international media that the Rohingya Muslims are among the world's "most vulnerable" people. Even the very few Rohingya who have successfully passed through the verification process and thereby been given green cards have not yet been allowed to travel freely. Moreover, some Kaman Muslims, a community of some forty-five thousand who are distinct from Rohingya Muslims and who are included in the list of 135 indigenous communities, have been put into the isolation of internally displaced persons (IDP) camps and have been asked to go through the verification process, registering as Bengalis (*The Irrawaddy,* October 10, 2014). As I mentioned earlier, other Muslims in Yangon have been asked to register as Bengalis despite the fact that they are thoroughly acculturated "Burmese Muslims."

Meanwhile the lion's share of Rohingya, those who dwelled in the surrounding villages of Maungdaw, Buthidaung, and Rathedaung in the northern regions of Rakhine State bordering Bangladesh, were also confined in their movements to their domiciles or villages and, like their kin who had been placed in IDP camps around Sittwe, denied mobility and access to education, medicine, and outside jobs. This situation simmered and festered until October 9, 2016, when a ragtag group of militants, armed basically with little more than farm implements and a few stolen guns, attacked Myanmar border stations and killed nine Burmese security guards. In response, the Myanmar army, under the leadership of Senior General Min Aung Hlaing, unleashed a brutal "clearance operation," sending more than seventy thousand traumatized Rohingya refugees fleeing into Bangladesh. The UN High Commissioner for Refugees accepted a report in February of 2017 based on interviews with some 220 of these refugees that concluded that rape and murder had become the methodologies by which the Burmese military (Tatmadaw) seemed to be pursuing a policy of ethnic cleansing (see OHCHR 2017). An even more brutal and much more extensive crackdown got under way after August 25, 2017, following a second so-called Rohingya terrorist attack, for which a group with the newly coined name of Arakan Rohingya Salvation Army (ARSA) claimed responsibility. This attack, also the work of a less-than-well-armed, ill-disciplined collection of inexperienced fighters, the origins of which are discussed at length in the conversations that follow, was orchestrated against twenty-nine border guard positions and just one army installation. ARSA was spectacularly unsuccessful in its aggression and has earned ignominy for a massacre of its own that claimed the lives of at least ninety-nine Hindus living in two villages of rural Maungdaw, according to a carefully documented investigation conducted by Amnesty International (BBC, May 22, 2018). ARSA denied responsibility. But this time, in the aftermath of the ARSA attacks, around 690,000 Rohingya fled to Bangladesh in late 2017, in fear of what they call the Buddhist militias,[11] meaning Rakhine Buddhists, and the "Buddhist army," or the Tatmadaw. Hundreds of Rohingya villages, approximately 350 of them, were completely burned down, and untold numbers of men, women, and children were raped and murdered in a horrific campaign that, if the survivors are to be believed, veritably constituted what the United States and the United Nations have now called a "textbook case of ethnic cleansing." In September 2018, a UN fact-finding mission concluded that the Tatmadaw's actions constituted genocide and recommended that the International Criminal Court (ICC) in the Netherlands bring the leading generals of the army to trial. Aung Sang Suu Kyii and her NLD government were also cited as complicit. The US Department of State reached a similar conclusion in its detailed eight-month study.[12] The Myanmar government has rejected these allegations.

The governments of Myanmar and Bangladesh quickly agreed on a repatriation plan by November 2017, to be launched by the third week of January 2018—perhaps too quickly, as UN officials familiar with the scene on the ground publicly worried about safety conditions for the return of Rohingya and insisted that no Rohingya be coerced into returning. The Bangladeshi government seemed to understand this position and invited the UN to be part of the repatriation process to ensure that no returns were coercive. On the Myanmar side, there has been a consistently strong resistance to allowing outsiders (read, any foreigners) to be involved in helping to facilitate Rohingya transitions back to northern Arakan, or to provide much-needed humanitarian assistance in the affected northern regions of the state. There is some evidence to suggest that Rohingya may never be allowed to return to their villages of origin, as some of these have already been bulldozed and "model national villages" are being erected for Rakhine and Burmese Buddhists in the vicinities formerly inhabited predominantly by Rohingya.

In late April 2018, a group of fifteen UN officials representing the UN Security Council visited refugees in Cox's Bazaar in Bangladesh before proceeding to Myanmar to meet Senior General Min Aung Hlaing and Aung San Suu Kyii. The general denied that his troops had been involved in rape and murder, and Aung San Suu Kyii said her government was working toward the repatriation of refugees and was now open to considering the UN's participation in that process (*Frontier,* May 17, 2018). In early May, the Myanmar government announced that it had cleared eleven hundred refugees now in Bangladesh to return to Arakan. In September, the first representatives from the United Nations High Commissioner for Refugees were finally allowed into northern Arakan to begin surveying the current situation with an eye for making initial recommendations to proceed with the return of willing Rohingya.

In the rest of Myanmar itself, it is difficult to find much sympathy for the Rohingya. As far as I can ascertain, only a Karen[13] women's group has publicly spoken out in sympathy with their plight, largely on account of their own previous experiences with the Tatmadaw. There is the sense among many in Myanmar that the Rohingya have played victimization to the hilt in their attempt to gain the support and sympathy of the international community. Jacques Leider, the most well-informed European scholar on the history of Arakan (see Leider 2005), believes that such appeals to victimization make it difficult to understand more precisely the vicissitudes of history that contextualize the current problem (Leider 2018).

I will try to illustrate why there is little sympathy for the Rohingya in Myanmar through recounting continuing conversations that I pursued over more than three and half years and eight separate trips to Myanmar. As I mentioned at the outset, I have tried to give voice to Muslims, Bamar (Burmese) Buddhists, and Arakanese Buddhists, to men and women, and to laity and clerics. At the outset, I think it is especially important to give attention to the little-known Arakanese perspective, because almost all of the international media coverage of the conflict in Myanmar has focused on what has happened to the Rohingya at the hands of the Burmese military, on attacks condoned by the Buddhist monastic militant group known as the Ma Ba Tha or on the seemingly perplexing stance of silence taken by Nobel laureate and now state counselor Aung San Suu Kyii. In writing about the Arakanese Buddhists, my hope is that my presentation will contribute in some small degree to understanding the nature of the contemporary imbroglio in Arakan (Rakhine State) in western Myanmar.

Narratives of Siege

There are really three parties involved in the dynamics of violence and oppression now in play in Arakan, rather than only two (the Buddhist and the Muslim). That is, the basic structure of the problem over time has involved a triangle of reflexive relations obtaining between Arakanese Buddhists and Bamar Buddhists, Arakanese Buddhists and Rohingya Muslims, and Rohingya Muslims and Bamar Buddhists. It is very significant that all three parties articulate a "narrative of siege." Unfortunately, given the recent atrocities that have been inflicted by the Myanmar Tatmadaw upon the Rohingya, the Rohingya narrative has now been made painfully quite evident in the international media. And Burmese narratives about decline and siege have been documented by a number of scholars in the fields of Buddhist studies and history during the past fifty years, discussions that highlight Buddhist temporal conceptions of decline on the one hand and reflections on the deleterious significance of British colonial domination on the other.[14] But apart from what can be learned from Jacques Leider's careful fifteenth- to eighteenth-century historical study, the perspective and history of Arakanese Buddhists remains largely unfamiliar to many observers. So I will include in this introduction an emphasis on current Arakanese Buddhist perspectives in general. In addition to their fear that Rohingya Muslims will overrun them in Rakhine State, Arakanese Buddhists remain leery—better, consummately suspicious—of Burmese political power, particularly as it is articulated through Buddhistic rhetoric. And here is why:

Every December 31 marks the commemoration of a watershed moment in Arakan history. It seems poignant, if not enormously significant, that one of the most feted public holidays of the calendar year in Arakan marks a moment of great loss, the fall of the Mrauk U Empire, which flourished from the fifteenth through the eighteenth century as the most powerful political and economic regime in the Bay of Bengal region. Mrauk U commanded much of what is now western and upper Burma and the eastern Indian states, as well as some of what is now Bangladesh, including the important seaport of Chittagong.[15] Indeed, historic tensions between the Arakanese and Bamar since the fall of Mrauk U and the subsequent theft and transport of the famous Mahamuni Buddha image, linked to the likeness of the Buddha himself in Arakanese memory, an image that had functioned as the palladium for Arakanese Buddhists, reflects the symbolic heart of a continuing narrative of loss and siege. The Mahamuni image now, of course, is ensconced in a grand temple in Mandalay and is regarded, next to the Shwedagon Pagoda, as perhaps the most sacred place of pilgrimage for Burmese

Mahamuni image, Mandalay

Buddhists in Myanmar. In Arakan, a "new Mahamuni" image has been enshrined some twenty-five kilometers north of Mrauk U, and its reproduction, in either sculpted or photographic form, is seen ubiquitously in Sittwe and in other Arakanese-dominated towns and temples throughout Rakhine State.

The French anthropologist Alexandra de Mersan has written an incisive article on the significance of making Buddha images in Arakan (de Mersan 2012). In discussing how Buddha images are thought to be invested with power, and how the Mahamuni image came to be regarded as the palladium of Arakan kingship and thereby "the founding myth of Arakanese society for at least the last two centuries," she summarizes the many versions of the Mahamuni legend as follows:

> King Candasuriya, founder of Dhannawati, the first capital of Arakan, was honored by the visit of the Buddha Gautama who taught his law (*dhamma*). The king, his family and all inhabitants were overjoyed, and then converted enthusiastically to this new teaching. Before leaving the country, the Lord Buddha accepted the king's request, to make an effigy of him in remembrance of his teaching. Metal was collected, and with the help of celestial beings, the image was cast over a period of seven days. This image was believed to be an original likeness of Gautama Buddha, enlivened by the Buddha himself and reflecting his features as if it were his "younger brother." Due to the likeness of the historical Buddha, as a "living-double" or a twin, the statue was thought as endowed with great powers. These powers are conceived as "power protection." The image and shrine were thus greatly revered for centuries. It functioned as the palladium of the Arakanese kings until the Burmese seized the statue and brought it back to their capital after their conquest of the kingdom of Arakan.
>
> (De Mersan 2012, 98–99)

De Mersan proceeds to describe how and why the creation of Buddha images are invested with power in relation to specific localities, the process by which images are consecrated, and so on, before concluding with this remarkably Durkheimian analytical statement:

> The making of a Buddhist bronze image in a monastery is a collective contribution, which allows a precious and powerful statue to be constructed from all individual contributions melted in the crucible. In doing so, the statue materializes and strengthens what constitutes Arakanese society, in reference to the Mahamuni image, namely, *a specific moral and spiritual community*. The notion of power seems to be essential in many contemporary discourses at the "symbolic level," reflecting also the confrontation or competition between inhabitants and the [Burmese] political regime. Thus, through the production of its characteristic Buddha statuary, the Arakanese society is perpetuated by means of Buddhist iconography expressive of its Mahamuni image palladium and the reenactment of its myth. In the context of nation-building inside of Burma today, this is the only way the Arakanese

> can freely express their "specificity" without fearing repression from the military regime claiming the primacy of "national unity" as opposed to "localized particularity."
>
> (De Mersan 2012, 109; italics mine)

In mid-January 2018, police canceled a commemoration of the fall of Mrauk U and the loss of the Mahamuni image at which Aye Maung, a previous leader of the Arakan National Party (ANP), was scheduled to speak. Aye Maung had delivered an "incendiary" public speech the day before in Rathedaung urging greater autonomy and even armed struggle if necessary in an apparent appeal for support for the Arakan Army, which since its inception in 2009 has engaged the Tatmadaw on numerous occasions. When a protest formed at news of the cancellation, police opened fire and seven Arakanese were killed and several more injured. Months later, people in Mrauk U were reportedly still seething with anger against Burmese repression (*Frontier*, April 24, 2018), a repression that has to be understood within the backdrop of de Mersan's discussion about power and national identity.

What has also been lost, since the Burmese invasion and subjugation, is the regular deployment of the written Arakanese language, though spoken Arakanese remains the first language for virtually all Arakanese Buddhists. Consequently, Arakanese culture per se has become profoundly oral in orientation, meaning that a chief means of disseminating information and knowledge, and how knowledge's meaning is shaped, is communicated by means of the oral, which is now pasted into social media. What has also been lost for two centuries is any sense of a sustainable economy driven by anything other than subsistence farming and fishing, and mining for minerals in Arakan's rivers, where working conditions border on the desperate. The extensive trade networks that historically vitalized this geographic and cultural region during the Mrauk U era are now completely gone. At present, Arakan is economically the second-least-developed state in Myanmar. If the tourist area around Ngapali Beach near Thandwe and the nascent tourist scene in Mrauk U are excluded, then Arakan may be the most impoverished region of Myanmar. And since the southern regions of Arakan border on more agriculturally developed areas of the Irrawaddy delta, this also points to how it is that northern Arakan, the site of intense communal conflict, is possibly the poorest region of contemporary Myanmar. Grinding poverty is an aspect of life for the vast majority of northern Arakan's population, whether Muslim or Buddhist, Rohingya or Rakhine.

Fifty years following the Burmese subjugation, Sittwe, now the capital of Rakhine State, became a British administrative center for what became 124 years of colonial subordination. In the Arakanese perspective, the current Muslim "threat" posed by Rohingya is but the latest invasion of their land, actually the fourth wave of invasion as it were, following the Burmese, British, and again the Burmese at the time of independence. I was told repeatedly by Arakanese Buddhists that the Muslim population of Rakhine State is now more than half, though the most reliable estimates I have seen put the Muslim population at perhaps 30 percent before about 65 percent of those people recently fled to Bangladesh as refugees in response to the onslaughts of the Myanmar army and their Arakanese militia cohorts. Given the recent exodus, therefore, the Rohingya population is now likely only 10 or 15 percent of Rakhine State at present. Before the recent refugee flood to Bangladesh, though, Rohingya Muslims formed less than half of the total Muslim population in the country as a whole. However, in fact, Rohingya did form a solid overwhelming majority in northern Arakan around the townships of Maungdaw, Buthidaung, and Rathedaung, and for a brief period from 1961 to 1964 enjoyed a slight measure of distinctive recognition before the central Burmese government, under the military dictator General Ne Win, abolished a nascent rudimentary administrative structure that had been put into place by the earlier government of democratically elected prime minister U Nu. At this time, radio programming in the Rohingya language on state media, initiated by the U Nu government, was also abolished by Ne Win.

Muslims in northern Arakan had agitated against being a part of the formation of the Union of Burma at independence in 1948, along with many other minorities at that time, and in the 1950s some armed skirmishes had occurred between Burmese government forces and mujahideen. It was not until the early 1960s that the term "Rohingya" was coined in print by community leaders as signaling a separate Muslim political identity. This historical fact is routinely ignored in some recent Rohingya constructions, and Mrauk U is even understood by some Rohingya activists today as having been essentially a Muslim kingdom, based on the fact that an impressive mosque had been built in the vicinity of the royal palace, some courtiers had indeed been Muslim, some elegant poetry from the period in Arabic and Urdu has survived, and Mrauk U kings also had Arabic names, because much of their kingdom occupied what is now Chittagong and the eastern frontier of Bangladesh. This Rohingya perspective of Muslims having dominated the Mrauk U kingdom really unnerves the Arakanese. It is also a historical exaggeration. The very term "Rohingya" also angers them because in the eastern Bengali dialect in which Rohingya speak, the term can actually be translated as "Arakanese." For Arakanese Buddhists, this is a usurpation of Arakan identity.

While renderings of history help contextualize the perspectives informing Buddhist-Muslim tensions in Arakan—and I shall lay out more of this history in a later section of this introduction—there is another possible reality in play: the contemporary tensions in Arakan between Muslims and Arakanese Buddhists are, in part, the result of the recent political reforms that have provided for limited or more liberal means of political expression, after some fifty years of severe suppression by a succession of three Burmese military juntas. Long-repressed competitive tensions between Arakanese Buddhists and Rohingya exploded, it is said, when the lid of government suppression on both was loosened in 2012. Tensions over land—who is gaining it and who is losing it in northern Arakan—figure centrally in the bedrock layers of tensions between the communities. The Arakanese have felt that they have been continuously moved out of the northern part of their state. This is problematic insofar as their primordial vision for the state includes all of it.

A centrally important narrative now current among the Arakanese captures something of the narrative of siege now so profoundly gripping them, a perspective I found relatively easy to surface in conversations with monks and laity alike about how the recent violence began. The narrative recounting how the current trouble between Arakanese Buddhists and Muslims began usually commences with an emphasis on the rape of an Arakanese Buddhist woman by three "Bengali, Muslim" men and, as such, seems to function as a kind of trope for how some Arakanese understand the long-standing penetration of Muslims into their midst. The rape of Buddhist women has also been cited in at least two other contexts in Burma subsequently, in Meiktila and in Mandalay as well. The latter instance, which turned out to be a lie, was spread efficiently on social media by U Wirathu and his followers but was counteracted quickly by moderate Buddhists and Muslims in Mandalay, leading to a relatively short-lived day of chaos with "only" two people left dead from the mayhem. (The same strategy of using the rape of or harm to women has also been practiced several times in Sri Lanka by the Bodu Bala Sena.) Regardless of whether the rapes actually have occurred, it is not only a metaphor for Muslim penetration, but also an assertion that Buddhists are responding from a position of the moral high ground. Reports about the harming of monks are also flashpoints for inciting passions undergirded by moral imperatives to defend the bases of Buddhist culture and society. Buddhist women and the saffron robe are the markers of culture that need to be defended at all costs. I have written elsewhere about a religious syntax to the perpetrated violence by Buddhists against Muslims, especially in Sri Lanka (see Holt 2016, pp. 194–212). That syntax is partly constituted by the importance of ritual time and ritual space, how collisions of ritual cultures are often the moments leading to the outbreak of violence. The violation of women and the desacralization of Buddhist monastic robes are two symbolic tropes frequently woven into this syntax.

Another perspective that has recently gained some traction in Arakan, due to the concomitant strains caused by heavy-handed military administration, is that the military actually has an interest in seeing these two communities (the Arakanese Buddhist and the Rohingya Muslim) at odds with each other, insofar as the conflict provides it with an opportunity to play one faction off against the other to prevent the emergence of a regional resistance to centralized hegemony. Or, to frame it differently, the continuing trouble between the Arakanese and Rohingya legitimates the presence of a heavily armed military presence. One can even hear occasional not-so-whispered rumors in Arakan that goons recruited by the government actually instigated a good deal of the trouble in 2012 in order to further drive a wedge between the two communities and to ensure its continued role as "peacekeeper." Most recently, the army has postured as the defender of the nation against a "Muslim radical terrorist insurgency." I was struck in January 2018 by how attitudes toward the Tatmadaw had recently changed, and seemingly dramatically: the extent to which the previously almost ubiquitous disdain for the Tatmadaw had now morphed into support, especially among many Burmese Buddhists, for the erstwhile "defenders of the nation." This, of course, was less true among Arakanese, who are now becoming more ambivalent about the Tatmadaw. In the past, it was not unusual to see large signs in conspicuous public places stating that "the Tatmadaw will never betray the nation." It seems that many in the Burmese public now actually believe this adage. (Tangentially, I was struck as well in early 2018 by how military camouflage pants and shirts had become stylistically fashionable among many Burmese youth in Yangon and Mandalay. This would have been unimaginable until recently.) This brings me to a very important point about the current situation in Arakan.

Unfortunately, there is a fantastic amount of disinformation that continues to be disseminated on social media among the Arakanese and a patent sense among many Arakanese Buddhists that the outside world, meaning the world beyond Arakan, simply doesn't understand their plight, doesn't understand their experiences of oppression and siege. This feeling was telescoped in the relatively massive and vitriolic 2014 protests in Sittwe against NGO assistance to the Rohingya, which led to the withdrawal of Médecins Sans Frontières (Doctors Without Borders) and other NGOs, and an angry demonstration against UN secretary-general Ban Ki-moon as well. As early as July 2013, Ban Ki-moon, in formally prepared comments to diplomats at the UN, had warned Myanmar of "dangerous polarization." He added that "if it is not addressed urgently and firmly, underlying tensions could provoke more upheaval, undermining the reform process and triggering negative regional repercussions" (*New York Times,* July 11, 2013). A militant monk in Sittwe told me bluntly that with these demonstrations, his community had sent a clear message with a plan to both Barack Obama and Ban Ki-moon when they visited Myanmar: that all Rohingya in Arakan should be deported to Bangladesh. Ban Ki-moon and Barack Obama were locally seen in Arakan as siding with the Muslims because of their lack of understanding of the local reality, of the Muslim demographic invasion. Indeed, there is a great deal of resentment and suspicion about "the international media" because of the way in which Arakanese Buddhists have been portrayed as simply villainous perpetrators of violence against innocent Rohingya. At the same time, anachronistic renderings of history continue, and here the current American perspective was understood and attacked by this militant monk, who asserted that when World War II ended, the Americans gave their weapons over to the "Bengali Muslims," who are still using them to attack Arakanese![16] I also heard from two other reasonably intelligent monks that Americans continue to supply weapons to Muslim jihadists. When I asked why the Americans would do this, both told me that it is common knowledge that Barack Obama is a Muslim! (At that time, I recalled to myself an adage that I think has been sometimes attributed to Winston Churchill or Mark Twain, though I cannot be sure of its origins: "A lie makes its way half way around the world before the truth gets its pants on.")

When I asked well-informed activists back in Yangon, a number of whom had been released from prison only in the past two to three years at that time, why such disinformation so patently false is so prevalent among the Arakanese, the consistent answer was that the army and government continue to wage a vigorous campaign of "psychological warfare." They averred that the conduit for dissemination not only consists of the state-run newspaper (*New Light of Myanmar*), state-regulated television, and social media (especially Facebook), but also runs through various Buddhist monks who promote these views within the context of local sermons. According to these activists, it is in the government's interest to stoke the fear of a Muslim menace in order to posture as the defender of a primarily Burmese Buddhist state. This, of course, plays conveniently into the Burmese's own narrative of siege. It is likely that these perpetrated rumors are the source for claiming that more than half of the population in Rakhine State has become Muslim.

Indeed, there is a consensus among progressives in Yangon that the rise of the Muslim problem beyond Arakan to other parts of Burma was aided and abetted by Buddhist nationalists in the government led by then president Thein Sein. Activists in Yangon point out that one of the early consequences of the conflict was a deflection of attention away from the Chinese, who had increasingly drawn unfavorable attention for the past several years as they moved aggressively to dominate the business community in Mandalay in the north, and also began the construction of controversial oil and gas pipelines from Ramree Island on the Arakan coast all the way through Burma and finally to Kunming. According to these sources, the Muslim problem deflected attention away from "the Chinese problem," thus to the advantage of the government, so their speculative thinking goes. There are others in Yangon who perceived that the recent exodus of Rohingya from northern Arakan is part of a grand scheme to grab land and develop it anew. After a recent trip to China by Aung San Suu Kyii, a spokesperson for the Chinese government announced a rather facile "three-point plan" for the situation in Arakan: (1) solve the problem; (2) promote the peace; and (3) with Chinese assistance, economically develop the region. The government's continued close cooperation with the Chinese ensures that Myanmar will continue to receive Chinese backing and will benefit from Chinese vetoes in the UN Security Council whenever almost all of the rest of the members are seeking to take direct action to provide for some accountability for the worsening problems in Arakan.

Most of the Arakanese Buddhist refugees from the 2012 fiery imbroglio in Sittwe who were first settled into camps around Sittwe have now been resettled. The government has also announced plans to build "national villages," a plan that would seem to be aimed at benefiting Rakhine Buddhists and other indigenous peoples of the region. However, there is still no clearly articulated action plan yet for the Rohingya still languishing in the massive IDP camp holding more than one hundred thousand people just north of Sittwe; this despite the fact that most of these Muslims were longtime local residents of Sittwe before the trouble began, and not recent border jumpers as they now tend to be portrayed. Their properties in Sittwe have now been confiscated. They do not seriously entertain the option of declaring themselves as "Bengali" in order to be "verified"—very few have opted for that path. Also, under the 1982 Citizenship Law, if they could prove third-generation residency, they could become second-class citizens with the green card as "Bengalis."

Meanwhile, Arakanese Buddhists feel powerless too. I interviewed two leaders of the Arakan National Party while in Mrauk U and Sittwe in late 2014, the first of whom had spent twenty years in prison under the military junta and was released only in 2012. (Fearing recriminations, they preferred to remain anonymous.) Their party, the ANP, was the most successful of the minority ethnic parties in the November 2015 national elections, gaining some forty-four seats in the lower and upper houses of parliament and also gaining a majority in the Rakhine State assembly. The first ANP leader said to me: "We have no power, because the military has 25 percent at every level in both national houses and also the state. I've never heard of this kind of constitution. We are only a colony under this government. This is Burmese neocolonialism. Whenever there is any meeting in Kachin, Chin, or Mon State, I go to represent our people in these meetings. We all want majority democracy, democracy like the British, like the USA. We are in opposition to the almost total Bamar centralization that has been in play since 1962's military coup. Right now, our party leader cannot represent the interests of Arakan [Rakhine State]. This is wrong. We have no right to promote the interests of our people. We want decentralization. Every state should be able to administrate its own affairs. We don't have any choice in choosing our leader for our state, as the 'premier' is appointed by the president. We'd like to have constitutional change but I don't believe that will happen."

But then in commenting on the Muslim problem in the midst of Arakan, he stated erroneously that "Rohingya" is an Arakanese word meaning "'jobless, homeless, gipsy or stateless.' They don't speak a Rohingya language [which seems to be definitive for ethnicity as it has been framed in Burma]. They are Bengalis who came to do some contract jobs and go back home from time to time. They are not a national community of Myanmar. Those who keep crossing into Myanmar by giving bribes to the military border guards should not get citizenship." He went on to say, as if to soften his rhetoric of opposition to the "Bengali Muslims," that he employs a lot of Muslims on his farm outside of Mrauk U and that Muslims and Arakanese have lived and worked together peacefully in this region for a "very long time."

Indeed, when one travels by river north of Mrauk U, one passes alongside a patchwork of riverbank villages, some Arakanese Buddhist, some Rohingya Muslim, some Chin Buddhist, and some Chin Christian.[17] One can see Muslim men working as porters on the docks of some of these villages, unloading rocks to be used in the construction of new roads, or working in one of the several sifting or mining operations along the river. In an odd way, the demographic landscape is both differentiated (in terms of separate villages) and integrated (in terms of simultaneous coexistence and cross-community contributions to the local economy).

The Rakhine perspective in terms of their relation to the Rohingya gained increasing sympathy among Burmese over the course of the next three years, from 2014 to 2017. One evening while eating dinner in an upscale restaurant down on the Yangon waterfront, I had occasion to glance through the July 2017 issue of *Myanmar Insider,* a slickly produced monthly magazine intended for the edification of the expatriate community living in Yangon. The magazine contains "analyses" covering contemporary economic/business and political and diplomatic news, as well as reviews of restaurants and cultural events. It is intended to be a sophisticated digest of what is current in Yangon. I read through an extensive "analysis" article entitled "Talking about the Pot Calling the Kettle Black" by one Mark (Ramree), possibly a pen name, in which the interim report of the Kofi Annan Commission was not so subtly criticized for recommending changes to the 1982 Citizenship Law. After providing a highly skewed historical reprise of Arakan in which the original presence of "Bengalis" was blamed on "British slave trade," the article proceeded in advancing the following profile of the Rohingya from an Arakanese perspective, before it shifted voice to add its own commentary. I provide an excerpt below to give a sense of what had become a commonly articulated public perspective in the summer of 2017. Quoting "an ethnic Rakhine,"

> There is a well-planned strategy by Bangladesh Muslim terrorists together with other power Islamic countries to in one way or another destabilize Myanmar. Rakhine people do not like illegal immigrants' bad behavior and terrorism. They do not want them to stay in Rakhine State because they are trying to riot and destroy a peaceful environment by using well-planned strategies. Rakhine people have a kind heart to allow them to stay in the past. . . . Now Bengalis want to drive away Rakhine people. . . . Openly we say that they are stealing not just our land; they are stealing our fatherland, our forests, and all of our other resources. They are also stealing our honor, dignity and sense of being one Rakhine State. And their aim is to destroy our nation and religion with [an] unlimited birth rate, after that they will try to form an Islamic state in our own land.

Then, under the heading of "Aggressive Aliens," the article shifted voice with this commentary: "The word 'Rohingya' is utterly hostile to our nation, our people, our ethnicity, and especially to Arakan (Rakhine) people, who live peacefully under the Buddha's teachings. The usage of this hostile word is agitating the communal conflicts to become bigger. . . . It creates more hatred and tension between the two communities. Rakhine people know the meaning of so-called 'Rohingya' is invader. . . . [W]e can accept the true name 'Bengali,' because the word 'Bengali' is a real word. One cannot create a fake ethnic race." The article proceeds to describe previous instances of "Muslim invasions," in particular citing the border guard attacks of October 9, 2016, as continuing evidence for the current wave of "insurgency." It also contains several fuzzy photos of "Bengali terrorists" toting firearms, before closing with a mention of the constitutional mandate given to the Tatmadaw for securing the nation, and an affirmation of Aung San Suu Kyii's position of advocating a verification process within the confines of the 1982 Citizenship Law.

The phrase "narratives of siege" indicates the importance of a national memory of loss and lack, or more specifically, how the exigencies of time are understood to bear witness to a people's identity and contribute to the formation of a historical consciousness. For the vast majority of Burmese Buddhists, particularly those who are not the modern Westernized "socially engaged" or neo-orientalist Buddhist types, or those whose focus is exclusively upon the Abhidhamma portion of the Tripitaka (Buddhist canon) and *vipassana* meditation as their sole religious preoccupations, civilizational time or historical memory begins with the life and teachings of the Buddha and will begin anew with the coming of Metteyya (Pali) or Maitreya (Sanskrit), the future Buddha of the next "Buddha cycle." This is as true of Burmese as it is of Arakanese. For the Arakanese, the Mahamuni image is regarded as an actual likeness of the Buddha, and members of the Buddha's Sakya clan who allegedly accompanied him to visit Arakan are the primordial people from whom the Arakanese descend. In other words, civilization and time begin with the Buddha. The notion that the Buddha was a prototypical Burmese is also held by many Bamars.

E. Sarkisyanz masterfully outlined, some fifty years ago, the conceptuality of time within traditional Burmese Buddhist circles, particularly among rural folk (Sarkisyanz 1965). In this conceptual schema, time assumes a trajectory of decline, especially during the second half of a projected five-thousand-year era between the appearances of the buddhas Gotama and Metteyya (Skt. Maitreya). Consistent with Pali *Digha Nikaya* suttas, such as the *Agganna* and *Cakkavatti Sihanada*, as well as the postcanonical Pali and Sinhala versions of the *Anagatavamsa Desana* (see Holt 1992), the material and moral quality of life are measured by the efficacious presence or observance of the Buddha's *dhamma* (dharma; teaching or truth of the Buddha). With the decline in the *dhamma*'s observance, as time marches ever further away from the *dhamma*'s original dispensation propagated by the Buddha, not only does it become progressively more difficult to realize the truth of *nibbana*, but the actual quality of life and moral observance, each related to the other in tandem, karmicly decline. Insofar as upholding the norms of *dhamma* in society and maintaining the health of the sangha were requisite for Buddhist kingship, the disestablishment of Buddhist kingship per se, which is what happened in 1885 in Burma when the British arrested and deported Thibaw, the last of the Burmese kings in Mandalay, signals nothing short of a catastrophe for the Buddhasasana and has consequently wrought a transformation in the religion's ethos by intensifying the sense of decline. Various studies since Sarkisyanz's have mapped out the transformation of this subsequent ethos emphasizing the manner in which merit-making-conscious lay organizations, meditation lineages, and sangha reformations have attempted to regain and retain the Buddhist vigor of Burmese society in the absence of kingship and in the face of the *dhamma*'s deleterious decline.[18] Moreover, other studies have pointed out how in the past fifty years of postindependent Burma, military juntas have attempted to posture, in a manner in which they liken themselves to the kings of the past, as the protectors and purifiers of the religion in the face of hostilities that have resulted from a relatively constant condition of civil war waged against an array of ethnic minority groups with aspirations for separate states or greater autonomy.[19] But perhaps the most indicative movements signaling the stress of siege mentality are to be found in the defiant political aspirations articulated by the academically accomplished and linguistically erudite Buddhist monk U Ottama in the 1920s and the truly millenarian-based rebellion led by the ex-monk and royal pretender Saya San during the economic desperation of the 1930s, both aimed at freeing Burma and its decline from the power and control of the colonial British, whose presence was interpreted as consummately detrimental to the continued longevity and health of the *sasana* (tradition or lineage of the Buddha's teaching). In short, it is this historical self-understanding of decline and defeat, decline from the politically halcyon days of Burmese kingship in Pagan and Mandalay in the eleventh through thirteenth and seventeenth through nineteenth centuries, coupled with the belief that Burma's national purpose is none other than to perpetuate the original and purest forms of the Buddhasasana, that continues to inform Burmese memory. The purported or perceived rise (or threat, as it has been seen by monastic extremists such as U Wirathu) of Islamic prosperity or expansionism fits neatly as another chapter within this scenario of perceived decline, this mentality of a religion and nation, the two inseparable to most Burmese, under siege. The Arakanese share in this mentality, reinforced by the vicissitudes of their own deleterious political historical experience of the past 235 years.

There is another dimension contributing to the narrative of siege among the Burmese Buddhists that I should also mention, particularly for the purpose of noting a possible historical inflection of the manner in which the presence of Muslim communities is understood by many Burmese. Most Indians were asked to leave the country in 1962 by General Ne Win (though many others had left previously, following the end of World War II and the British colonial departure). In each case, all of their properties were confiscated. The conventional narrative often repeated by Burmese is that Indians had been brought by the colonial British in the late nineteenth and early twentieth centuries to cultivate lands and to assist in civil administration. Indeed, since Burma was part of the British Raj, there were no boundaries dividing India and Burma from each other, a fact that needs to be emphasized in understanding why so many "Bengali Muslims" were readily settled in Rakhine State, or Arakan. That is, Burma was administered as part of the British Raj as just another province, like Bengal, Gujerat, or the Madras Presidency. So travel between the regions of what is now Bangladesh and what is now Burma, especially Arakan, or Rakhine State, was quite fluid and unimpeded.[20]

In another part of Burma, there is a region southeast of Moulmein (now Mawlamyine) in Mon State that today remains dominated by Muslim farmers who came from India in the wake of the First Anglo-Burmese War (1824–1826), some say even earlier, after which Moulmein and Akyab (now Sittwe) in Arakan became chief operating ports and administrative seats for the colonial British.

Very significantly, it is the main mosque in Moulmein that the ancestors of these farmers helped to build that was one of the original flash points generating the beginnings of the anti-Muslim Buddhist 969 and Ma Ba Tha Movements, the leaders of which claimed that the mosque was built on top of a Buddhist sangha *sima*, or consecrated space where the *patimokkha* (monastic discipline) and *upasampada* (ordination) rites, which sustain the behavioral purity and lineage of the sangha, are regularly held.

In any case, many Indians (including Hindus, Christians, and Muslims) also engaged in commerce, particularly in larger cities such as Mandalay and Rangoon [Yangon],[21] which, by the late nineteenth and early twentieth centuries, had become essentially "Indian cities." Indian Chettiars are particularly singled out in this account of Burmese remembrance, as they have been in other contexts in South Asia, as aggressive moneylenders who foreclosed on Bamar small landholders especially during the years of great economic depression in the 1930s, or, even worse but probably not very common, accepted daughters for payments on land indebtedness. The legacy of the Chettiars is often mentioned within the rationalizations of Bamar-dominated governments for having asked Indians to leave, making it clear that Indian days of "privilege" under the British had ended. Compounding the sense of grievance, if not alienation, between Bamars and Indians, there also was an Indian disposition not to intermarry with Bamars and to remain a separate subcommunity, a penchant not shared by other "interlopers," such as the Chinese. Rather than going out of the Indian community to marry, Indians instead often chose to marry on an intercaste basis, a factor that shows the extent to which they sought to remain within the larger Indian communal fold in a way that would have created considerable controversy back home in India, and in the process sustained their sociocultural and religious differences with the Burmese in Myanmar. Moreover, this subnarrative about the alien "Indian other" within the Bamar midst seems to support the general sense of a people under duress due to outside international pressures. This notion is a complementary part of the discourse on decline. To be clear, there is not a simple equation made in the Bamar mind between Indians, Indian Muslims, and "Rohingya" or "Bengali Muslims," but all three categories share in the sense of a related yet relatively foreign intrusive "other," though not as radically "other" historically as the British or other Europeans. However, all three would be referred to in derogatory fashion as *kalar* (basically, "foreigners from South Asian origins"), a term discussed at length in later conversations.

It also needs to be noted that ancient India looms large in the Buddhist religious imaginations of both Arakanese and Bamar Buddhists. Indeed, an NLD politician and information officer was arrested in December 2015 for asserting (correctly) that the Buddha cannot be regarded as having been Burmese. A case was brought against him for injuring the religious feelings of Buddhists (*The Irrawaddy*, June 2, 2015). So it is not so much India per se that constitutes the "other," but rather Hindus, Muslims, and Christians of Indian background. Whatever the case may be, the distinction of "otherness" is made primarily on religious grounds. Christians, particularly Chin, Kachin, and some Karen, lament today that they are still regularly discriminated against by Burmese Buddhist government officials as well.

It may well be that this consciousness of the "other," which broadly includes "Bengali Muslims," was a factor in why any Indian subcommunity as a whole, including the "Bengali Muslims" or "Rohingya," were not to be included in the official list of 135 peoples who have a stake in Myanmar, at least in terms of the 1982 law promulgated under General Ne Win's military dictatorship.

While one can find many people who will say that Rohingya and Rakhine Buddhists managed to live comfortably, or without great tension, in many locales throughout Arakan over long periods of time, there is quite an involved and sometimes acrimonious history behind the current problem that needs to be recognized and acknowledged. One of the reasons that Rakhine Buddhists have long felt as if they are being overwhelmed is that as early as the period between 1871 and 1911, according to the British census, the population of Muslims grew to three times what it had been, while the Rakhine increased by only 20 percent. The Burmese population also grew exponentially, so that Arakanese were then outnumbered in what they regarded as their own land. It is no surprise, then, that the Arakanese came to feel a squeeze between the growth of both the Muslim and Burmese communities.

At the same time in the rest of Burma, migrants from many parts of India became a significant part of the Burmese economy, not just as agricultural workers, but also as professionals, shopkeepers, and moneymen. As I mentioned earlier, by the time of the worldwide economic depression of the 1930s, many Burmese farmers went into debt with Indian Chettiars, which resulted in many Indians eventually controlling great swaths of land.

In Lee Jones's (2017) critical essay about the political economy of Myanmar published online on the *New Mandala* website, the consequences of these developments are parsed in this way:

> The reaction to this rapid influx was a racially inflected form of economic nationalism which still persists today. This is not entirely dissimilar to the xenophobic nationalism that has sometimes accompanied mass immigration in straitened economic circumstances in many Western countries. There were anti-Indian riots in 1930–31 and specifically anti-Muslim riots in 1926 and 1938. These were led by the majority ethnic Bamar and did not spread into Rakhine itself. It was not until Britain's defeat by invading Japanese forces in 1942 that communal violence erupted there, with Rakhine militias exploiting the war to wreak bloody vengeance on their Muslim rivals, prompting tens of thousands to flee into India.
>
> To make matters worse, the British then armed Rohingya volunteer forces, ostensibly to attack the occupying Japanese, but instead these groups often raided Rakhine settlements and Buddhist monasteries and pagodas. These forces also accompanied Britain's reconquest of Rakhine, after which armed Rakhine groups were forcibly suppressed. Understandably, some of the returning Muslims feared being incorporated into the postcolonial Burmese

> state, launching a "Mujahit" rebellion to press for the incorporation of northern Rakhine into East Pakistan, prompting counterinsurgency operations by the Burmese army through the 1950s.
>
> An important legacy of this WWII-induced displacement, and the subsequent unrest, is that Muslims gradually returning to Rakhine were thereafter often depicted as "illegal Bengali immigrants." This complex, unhappy history is what lies behind the subsequent rejection of the Rohingya—a term used commonly only after Burma's independence—as one of Myanmar's 135 official "national races," and their designation instead as "Bengalis."

In his remarkably cogent and concise historical summary, which serves as an effective backdrop to current Burmese and Rakhine dispositions toward the South Asians in their midst, Jones notes how the process of

> Burmanisation culminated in the nationalisation of 15,000 businesses after the 1962 military coup, prompting 125,000 to 300,000 ethnic Indians to flee the country. They followed the more than 400,000 Indians, British and Anglo-Burmese who had already left following decolonization. The post-2011 "969" movement, which encouraged Buddhists to boycott Muslim businesses, is arguably just the latest instantiation of this form of xenophobic economic nationalism. . . .
>
> This history explains why there is widespread support today for Ma Ba Tha, for the Protection of Race and Religion Laws (which discriminate against Muslims) and for the ethnic cleansing currently being perpetrated by the Myanmar military. It also explains why, politically, Aung San Suu Kyi has such limited room for manoeuvre—though it must be stressed that she has done virtually nothing to challenge these dangerous myths or to foster intercommunal harmony. Indeed, her own office's use of the term "Bengali," her past remarks about "global Muslim power," and her purging of Muslims from the ranks of NLD parliamentary candidates in 2015, all suggest that she may even personally share anti-Muslim prejudices.

As early as 1962, the Tatmadaw began to cull Muslims out of its ranks. By 1977–1978, it launched Operation Dragon King, that is, "clearance operations" ahead of a national census, thereby forcing 200,000 Muslims to flee into Bangladesh. The military junta's 1982 Citizenship Law left the Rohingya in a legal and political void. In 1988, the Rohingya in northern Arakan backed the prodemocracy movement but faced another brutal suppression in 1992, with yet another 250,000 fleeing to Bangladesh.

Setting the Recent Context: A Résumé of Conflict since 2012

Following the destabilizing imbroglio[22] in Sittwe of June 2012,[23] the scope and intensity of Buddhist-Muslim conflict increased dramatically across Myanmar in 2013, marked especially by a serious riot that broke out in Meiktila, about two hours south of Mandalay in central Burma. More than forty Muslims lost their lives and an entire area of Meiktila's downtown was torched. More than twelve thousand Muslims were displaced (BBC, April 4, 2013). The precipitous moment of the riot, which began as a dispute in a jewelry shop, was the alleged attack by Muslims on a Buddhist monk. One of my interlocutors in Mandalay (3: "The Anti-Nationalists"), a truly heroic monk, provided safe haven for around a thousand Muslims fleeing the badly afflicted downtown area and dramatically defied a group of unruly would-be mayhem makers. Other subsequent outbreaks, including one three weeks later in Okkan, a small town one hundred kilometers north of Yangon, again involving a monk who was allegedly knocked down by a Muslim woman on a bicycle (*The Irrawaddy,* April 30, 2013), and another outbreak in Lashio in Shan State in May (during which another Buddhist monk magnanimously sheltered hundreds of fleeing Muslims at his monastery) signified that the conflict was no longer between only Rohingya Muslims and Arakanese Buddhists, but had been nationalized, owing in part to the xenophobic rhetoric of militant Buddhist monks, including, of course, U Wirathu, one of my Mandalay monastic conversationalists (3: "The Nationalist"). Now it was not only the Rohingya, who form less than half of the nation's Muslim community, but nearly all Muslims in Myanmar who began to fear. In both the Sittwe and Meiktila riots, as in Sri Lanka at the same time, security forces could not be counted upon to protect Muslims and their properties.

In October 2013, another serious riot broke out in Thandwe, midway down the Arakan coast. This time, the targets were Kaman Muslims, not Rohingya. More than 150 homes were burned to the ground, and nearly 500 people were left homeless. Five Muslims were killed, including an eighty-nine-year-old man and a ninety-four-year-old woman, both too infirm to flee, and both stabbed to death. One of my interlocutors wistfully recalled the personal impact of this riot on her own sense of well-being and how it affected the local Kaman Muslim community (2: "The Teacher").

In December 2013, Reuters (December 4, 2013) published the results of extensive investigative reporting that took their reporters to Myanmar, Thailand, and Malaysia, where they uncovered a network of human traffickers preying on Rohingya seeking to flee Myanmar by boat and hoping to reach Malaysia (see also *New York Times,* March 14, 2014). Various estimates claimed that as of 2015, about eighty-seven thousand Rohingya had left Arakan by boat and that around two thousand had died at sea or under harsh conditions, usually in the deep south of Thailand, while attempting to reach Malaysia. Thai authorities were implicated in this human trafficking and racketeering.

By mid-2014, the four "race and religion laws" aimed at Muslims and advocated by U Wirathu and the Ma Ba Tha were vetted in parliament. One of the laws pertaining to conversion from one religion to another requires the consent of local authorities; the other laws restrict marriage between people of different religions, outlaw polygamy, and give regional governments the prerogative to enforce birth control rates. Ko Ni, a constitutional expert and Muslim lawyer working with the NLD, was highly critical of the race and religion laws when interviewed by *The Irrawaddy* (September 2, 2015). He was assassinated three months later at Yangon's international airport. Many expected Aung San Suu

Kyii's National League for Democracy to repeal these laws once elected, but it has not done so.

Also, in mid-2014, communal violence broke out in Mandalay, Myanmar's second city and former capital of the last line of Burmese Buddhist kings. This clash had the potential to become a major conflagration, but religious leaders from both communities and the timely intervention of riot police prevented the mayhem from getting out of control beyond two days. Again, the flash point was the alleged rape of a young Buddhist woman by two Muslim brothers. Two of my Buddhist monastic interlocutors (3: "The Anti-Nationalists" and "The Rector") would comment directly on the fracas and its aborted ending.

By August 2014, plans were being proposed for all undocumented Rohingya to be vetted by a "citizenship verification process" (*The Irrawaddy,* August 22, 2014). The verification process has essentially been a failed policy since it was first put into play. The vast majority of Rohingya refused to register as "Bengalis," as, in their view, they would forfeit their claims to be Rohingya who deserve citizenship (*The Irrawaddy,* September 23, 2014).

In November 2014, on the eve of President Obama's second visit to Myanmar, the *New York Times* (November 12, 2014) ran an article indicating how, for some, Aung San Suu Kyii had "fallen short of expectations" because "she has refused to admonish the government for its harsh policies against the Rohingya Muslim majority, policies that Obama criticized last week." But when Obama visited Yangon again in mid-November, he steered clear of any direct criticism of Aung San Suu Kyii. He did, however, make a note about violence against Muslims by saying that "discrimination toward the Rohingya or any other religious minority does not express the kind of country, over the long term, that Burma wants to be" (*New York Times,* November 14, 2014). But by using the term "Rohingya," Obama touched a local nerve, one that UN secretary-general Ban Ki-moon would also aggravate a few days later when he, too, referred to the Muslim minority in Arakan as "Rohingya," thereby eliciting a statement by the Burmese government expressing its "deep disappointment" and concern about how references such as these could "inflame local sentiment." A year and half later, Aung San Suu Kyii would admonish a new American ambassador for using the term "Rohingya" on his arrival in Yangon.

As the campaign for the much-anticipated November national general election began to gather steam during the summer months of 2015, Muslim political parties, including the Democracy and Human Rights Party headed by U Kyaw Min, one of my primary Rohingya interlocutors (1: "The Elder Statesman"), the National Development and Peace Party, and the National Democratic Party for Development, all had their candidates for parliament disqualified on citizenship-related issues. As the political field became clear, and out of expedience (fear of the Ma Ba Tha's influence and the charge that the NLD was "pro-Muslim"), the NLD decided not to field any Muslim candidates at all (*Myanmar Now,* October 16, 2015).

The November election saw Aung San Suu Kyii's National League for Democracy win 80 percent of the vote, hailed in the international media as a great moment for democracy. Many Muslims, despite the fact that her party had not fielded a single Muslim candidate, still held out a fading hope that their issues would receive a much fairer hearing. Just days after the new NLD government took office, its new religious affairs minister, Aung Ko, a former Tatmadaw general and ex–Union Solidarity and Development Party lawmaker, in an interview with Voice of America, stated that in Myanmar, while Buddhists were "full citizens," "Muslims made up the majority of Burma's 'associate citizens,' implying that those who practice Islam are classified as partial citizens or foreigners." Abu Tahay, one of my most faithful interlocutors (1: "The Historian"), said publicly, "Citizenship cannot be based on religion. Therefore, it was not appropriate [for the minister of religious affairs] to talk like this" (*The Irrawaddy*, April 4, 2016).

Three weeks later a demonstration of about two hundred people led by a dozen militant nationalist Ma Ba Tha monks outside of the American embassy in Yangon protested in vitriolic fashion the use of the term "Rohingya," which had been posted on the embassy's Facebook page, a post in which sadness had been expressed for the deaths of several Rohingya who had drowned in a boat accident off of Sittwe as they were trying to travel by sea to buy goods because of restrictions against their traveling on land (*Myanmar Now*, April 28, 2016). Aung San Suu Kyii declared that using "emotive" terms was not constructive in addressing the complexities of the situation and that her government needed "space" to solve this difficult problem. American ambassador Scot Marciel's reaction was blunt: "They [Rohingya] get to choose what they want to be called. . . . That's a fundamental international practice and we respect that. That's been our approach and it will continue to be our approach" (*The Irrawaddy* May 12, 2016). Wai Wai Nu, one of my female Rohingya interlocutors (1: "The Gadfly"), made the case publicly that the government should begin to address the issue by consulting with ethnic minorities. She asked the government: "Why are you denying us our identity and not taking a feasible, constructive and inclusive step to move forward?" (Reuters, June 23, 2016).

Attacks by a motley assemblage of ill-equipped Rohingya on border posts on October 9, 2016, which met with a brutal Tatmadaw response, drastically changed the calculus of the situation in Arakan and seemed at first to validate Burmese and Arakanese fears about terrorist attacks led by jihadist Muslim militants. The UN proposed a fact-finding mission composed of three eminent international experts on human rights to travel to Myanmar, but this proposal was rebuffed by the NLD government. Suu Kyii did set up a commission to investigate what had happened, but it was led by Vice President Myint Swe, a former Tatmadaw general, and produced nothing but an unconvincing whitewash. The army had also conducted its own probe earlier, in which it had announced that its troops had not acted beyond the bounds of its codes of discipline. On April 25, 2017, the UN published its own detailed report based on more than two hundred interviews with refugees in Bangladesh indicating how murder, rape, and arson were the methodologies used by the Tatmadaw that resulted in seventy-five thousand Rohingya fleeing the country.

In late May, the government's Buddhist sangha authority, the Ma Ha Na, which weeks earlier had announced a one-year public preaching ban on U Wirathu, declared that the Ma Ba Tha, responsible for much anti-Muslim propaganda, was now to be banned from operating under its present name and must take down all signboards across the country by July 15 (*The Irrawaddy,* May 23, 2017; *Frontier,* May 23, 2017).

Since its appointment by Aung San Suu Kyii in September 2016, just weeks before the October 9 attacks on Burmese border posts, much anticipation awaited the announcement of the so-called Kofi Annan Commission. Though the constituency of the committee did not necessary augur well for their interests,[24] Rohingya leaders remained somewhat hopeful, based on the reputation of Kofi Annan's integrity as the former secretary-general of the United Nations. The commission's interim report was issued in March 2017 and urged the Myanmar government to form a joint committee with Bangladeshi authorities to oversee the return of refugees and to prevent human trafficking, to close all internally displaced persons (IDP) camps while specifying a timeframe for completion of a citizenship verification process, and to grant freedom of movement and access to education and health facilities for all people equally, regardless of ethnic or religious origins. On August 24, 2017, the much-anticipated final report of the commission was made public amid an increasing sense of urgency, owing to the fact that the Tatmadaw had recently begun another round of "clearance operations," this time in the vicinity of Rathedaung. (Just before leaving Myanmar earlier in August, I had seen photos taken at the Sittwe airport of the arrival of a cadre of new, rugged-looking Tatmadaw troops, perhaps 150 or so in number, who were being brought in, ominously I thought at the time, to help search out the presence of "Muslim terrorists" purportedly training in the hills of northern Arakan. This group of cadres was later identified as members of the Tatmadaw's Thirty-Third Light Infantry, notorious for earlier brutal attacks on other ethnic minority groups in Myanmar, including civilians [*Frontier,* August 24, 2017].)

The issues identified in the Kofi Annan interim report about the need to close the IDP camps and to provide freedom of movement regardless of citizenship status as well as access to health and education were again emphasized in the final report, but several other important matters were stressed as well. First, the commission noted that a highly militarized response to the Rohingya problem (i.e., what had transpired following October 9, 2016) "is highly unlikely to bring peace to the area" (Reuters, May 24, 2017). "The commission warned that if human rights were not respected and 'the population remain politically and economically marginalized—northern Rakhine State may provide fertile ground for radicalization, as local communities may become increasingly vulnerable to recruitment by extremists.'" More pointedly, the commission criticized in detail several aspects of the 1982 Citizenship Law and the 2008 military-introduced constitution as failing to meet international standards, especially by establishing the notion of different levels of citizenship that betrayed principles of discrimination (*The Irrawaddy,* May 24, 2017; AFP, May 24, 2017).

The commission also urged the government to issue birth certificates to those whose documents had been lost in the chaos of earlier instances of violence.

The Tatmadaw's response to the Kofi Annan Commission's report was harsh. Commander in Chief Senior General Min Aung Hlaing questioned the "impartiality" of the commission and asserted that many of its points were "factually wrong." He warned that the issue of citizenship would remain a matter of adjudication according to the 1982 Citizenship Law. He lamented that when journalists had been given access to northern Arakan (another recommendation made in the commission's report), they had created news that "lacked accuracy." Finally, he said that "the commission needs to understand the perspective of the military, the government, and local Arakanese . . . [or] it will be tough to address the issues" (*The Irrawaddy*, May 24, 2017; *Frontier*, May 24, 2017; Reuters, May 24, 2017).

Eight hours after this critically important report was issued, violence broke out in northern Arakan in the form of attacks on twenty-nine police and border posts and one army installation. Also attacked was the Hindu village previously mentioned, where ninety-nine people lost their lives. An immediate claim for its instigation was made by the Arakan Rohingya Salvation Army (ARSA). If defending Rohingya was its intended effect, ARSA badly miscalculated, as its attack unleashed an onslaught of violence visited upon Rohingya civilians throughout northern Arakan villages that has resulted in a catastrophe—the deaths of thousands, alleged sexual assaults on hundreds of women, the burning down of 354 villages, and the creation of what became the world's largest refugee camp (in Cox's Bazaar, Bangladesh, just across the Myanmar border). The Tatmadaw easily routed many of the young and poorly equipped Rohingya. Various reports in the press noted that after a few days, while 13 Myanmar soldiers or police had been killed, some 370 Rohingya had been killed as well (Reuters, September 1, 2017), a ratio of nearly 30 to 1. The attackers, many of whom were not armed with guns, but instead with hoes, machetes, and poles, were no match for the Tatmadaw.

The violence in northern Arakan was matched by an ascendant war of propaganda on various social media platforms. A dramatic upsurge from more than fifteen hundred Twitter accounts created between August 25 and 30 began spilling out messages declaring that the country was under attack by Bengali Muslim terrorists and that the Tatmadaw was valiantly defending the nation (Reuters, September 2, 2017). The *New York Times* (October 15, 2018) eventually published an investigative piece made possible by one of my interlocutors (1: "The Stringer") in which evidence was produced indicating that as many as seven hundred Tatmadaw soldiers, mostly trained in Russia, had been for years creating as many as fifteen hundred bogus pages on Facebook to disseminate patently false reports about Muslim jihadist activities and clearly contrived hate speech.

Meanwhile, international pressure on Aung San Suu Kyii continued to mount. Nobel Peace laureate Malala Yousafzai said to Aung San Suu Kyii that "the world is waiting and the Rohingya Muslims are waiting" (BBC, September 4, 2017).

On September 9, Archbishop Desmond Tutu, the eighty-five-year-old Nobel Peace laureate who said he was breaking a vow of silence on public affairs, issued an impassioned plea to Aung San Suu Kyii: "The images we are seeing of the suffering of the Rohingya fill us with pain and dread. . . . My dear sister, if the political price for your ascension to the highest office in Myanmar is your silence, the price is surely too steep. . . . A country that is not at peace with itself, that fails to acknowledge and protect the dignity and worth of all its people, is not a free country. It is incongruous for a symbol of righteousness to lead such a country; it is adding to our pain" (*Frontier,* September 9, 2017). At the same time, the *New York Times* (September 9, 2017) published a powerful condemnation stating that "Aung San Suu Kyii is presiding over ethnic cleansing in which villages are burned, women raped, and children butchered."

As expectations for her to act constructively built, Aung San Suu Kyii delivered a much-anticipated speech in mid-September in which she tried to address issues related to the events occurring in northern Arakan. The *New York Times* (September 18, 2017) characterized her speech generally in this way: "She steadfastly refused to criticize the country's military, which has been accused of a vast campaign of killing, rape and village burning." She was quoted as saying, "'The security forces have been instructed to adhere strictly to the code of conduct in carrying out security operations, to exercise all due restraint and to take full measures to avoid collateral damage and the harming of innocent civilians. . . . We condemn all human rights violations and unlawful violence. We feel deeply for the suffering of all the people caught up in the conflict.' But, asking why the world did not acknowledge the progress made in her country, she also boasted that Muslims living in the violence-torn area had ample access to health care and radio broadcasts. And she expressed uncertainty about why Muslims might be fleeing the country, even as she sidestepped evidence of widespread abuses by the security forces by saying there had been 'allegations and counter-allegations.'" The BBC (September 19, 2017) also published a very critical article in which many of Aung San Suu Kyii's stated claims were assessed and then rebutted with evidence, including: that there had been no armed conflicts since September 5, that action would be taken against those who go against the laws of the land, and that all people in Rakhine have access to education and health care without discrimination. On September 15, *The New Yorker* magazine published a story with the headline "Aung San Suu Kyi, the Ignoble Laureate," while the UK's *Telegraph* ran an article entitled "Aung San Suu Kyi: Burmese Military Prisoner or Monster?" Even her biographer, Peter Popham, on September 8 published an article in the UK's *Independent* that read: "As Aung San Suu Kyi's biographer, I have to say that the only good thing she can do now is resign." *The New Yorker* (October 2, 2017) published a provocative "Letter from Myanmar" entitled "What Happened to Myanmar's Human-Rights Icon?" in which Aung San Suu Kyii was portrayed as a symbol of human rights without ever having to say very much about the issue itself and that stated that her admirers, international and domestic, over the years read a lot into that inchoate symbolism. The profile of Suu Kyii was the evolution of a sheltered, narrow, and often petulant person of privilege who has a problem fielding criticism, delegating authority, or transcending a sense of entitlement deriving from her identification with her father, a mythic-origins hero of the nation and the army.

The intense international criticism and media reporting on the atrocities occurring in Arakan and the avalanche of critical articles about Aung San Suu Kyii soon drew a sharp reaction from Myanmar journalists. It was clear that many in Myanmar had been insulted by these severe attacks on Suu Kyii. *The Irrawaddy* published a long article that gave voice to several prominent Myanmar journalists who complained bitterly about how the international media had been publishing accounts that were entirely one-sided and biased, often lacking verification and in some cases sensationalized in order to make good profitable copy in places like the Middle East. A remarkable "closing of the ranks" had begun to settle in.

During the first two weeks of October 2017, Myanmar government and military officials went on a further media offensive seeking to complicate the dominant narrative articulated by the mainstream international press. U Zaw Htay, the spokesperson for Aung San Suu Kyii's State Counsellor Office, asserted, "We believe that the Bengalis are plotting against the government by misleading the [the international community] that there is a mass migration. . . . It is not honest. [Self-identifying Rohingya Muslims] are fleeing even as we have told them that nobody would cause harm to them, and [the government] would provide security and social assistance" (*The Irrawaddy,* October 6, 2017).

That the Burmese public would be lining up in support of the military and Aung San Suu Kyii seemed to be a consequence of dispositions and values signaled by research undertaken by the Asian Barometer Survey. Its findings suggested that while the Burmese public affirmed a very high support for democracy, "the liberal political values that undergird democratic processes" were not supported very strongly at all. Some 80 percent of those surveyed stated that religious authorities should play a significant role in lawmaking and that the question of citizenship should be linked to religious affiliation. Nearly two-thirds opposed any restraints on the executive branch, while pluralism was regarded as a dangerous social phenomenon. Seven in ten said that students should not question teachers.

Meanwhile, the first signs that Myanmar and Bangladesh were seriously discussing ways in which Rohingya might be repatriated surfaced on November 2 when the government announced that an agreement was nearly in place with Bangladesh (*Frontier,* November 2, 2017). This would be the beginning of announcements that would involve fits and starts to the process of repatriation, which, as of January 2019, had not yet begun.

On November 6, the UN Security Council issued a formal statement in which it expressed "grave concern over reports of human rights violations and abuses in Rakhine State, including by the Myanmar security forces, in particular against persons belonging to the Rohingya community." The genre of "statement" was significant on a number of fronts, insofar as it was clear that Russia and China would have vetoed the genre of "resolution" that had been put forward by France and Britain. The statement also addressed the problem of Myanmar's unwillingness to allow a UN fact-finding team into northern Arakan (Reuters, November 7, 2017).

As of early December 2017, the number of refugees in Bangladesh had climbed to 640,000. The numbers continued to increase in part because of the lack of aid reaching the remaining Rohingya (about 150,000) in northern Arakan, coupled with the impossibility of Rohingya engaging in their usual agricultural and marine vocations (Reuters, November 23, 2017; *Frontier*, December 11, 2017).

In early December, controversy swirled around the visit of Pope Francis to Myanmar. Specifically, a debate centered around whether or not the pope would use the term "Rohingya" in his public addresses. Though the pope had a history of referring publicly to compassion needed for the Rohingya, he had been advised by local church authorities in Yangon to avoid using the term out of concern for a backlash against Christian minority people in Myanmar. Francis did avoid the term publicly. But when he traveled to Bangladesh in the following days and visited with about twenty Rohingya refugees who had been brought to Dhaka, he said that "God's presence is within the Rohingya community." Moreover, he said he was crying and tried to hide his tears when hearing the desperate stories from Rohingya regarding their ordeals (Reuters, December 2, 2017).

In mid-December, Médecins Sans Frontières, on the basis of surveys of 2,434 households in Rohingya refugee camps conducted over a period of one month, said, "At least 6,700 Rohingya, in the most conservative estimations, are estimated to have been killed, including at least 730 children below the age of five" (AFP, December 14, 2017). Two weeks later, Save the Children issued a report cited in the *New York Times* (December 31, 2017) declaring that a third of the 650,000 refugees in Cox's Bazaar were minors, and 30 percent of those were under five years old.

On December 18, the UN high commissioner for human rights, Zeid Ra'ad Al Hussein, granted interviews first to the BBC and then to American National Public Radio. He said in the BBC interview, reported by Reuters (December 18, 2017), that the violence perpetrated on the Rohingya by the Tatmadaw was "well thought out and planned." Moreover, he said, "The elements suggest that you cannot rule out the possibility that acts of genocide have been committed." He added that "it wouldn't surprise me in the future if the court were to make a finding on the basis of what we see." But Myanmar is not a member of the International Criminal Court, so a referral to that court would have to be made by the UN Security Council, unlikely insofar as China could and probably Russia would veto such a move. On National Public Radio, Al Hussein said that both Senior General Min Aung Hlaing and Aung San Suu Kyii could possibly face genocide charges. In April 2018, a prosecutor at the ICC asked a three-judge panel to allow her to begin proceedings in the case, arguing that since the refugees are now in Bangladesh, a signatory to the creation of the ICC, the court has jurisdiction despite the fact that Myanmar is not a member. In September 2018, the judges ruled that the ICC did, indeed, have jurisdiction, insofar as the Rohingya refugees had been forced to cross the border into Bangladesh, a signatory to the court's convention.

On December 20, the government of Myanmar announced that UN special rapporteur on Myanmar Yanghee Lee would be barred from returning to the country and that the government's cooperation with the UN would be suspended during her tenure.

After months of ranting about "fake news" and following the arrest of Reuters journalists Wa Lone and Kyaw Soe Oo (who had been investigating the murders of ten Rohingya in an Arakan village) on charges of possessing classified documents, Senior General Min Aung Hlaing's office admitted for the first time that Tatmadaw troops were involved in murderous activities (AFP, January 11, 2018). Weeks later it would be revealed that soldiers involved in the killing of the ten men were sentenced to ten years in prison. Meanwhile, Wa Lone and Kyaw So Oo, who had been investigating this case, were arrested and ultimately convicted of making reports deleterious to national security. In an article about declining press freedom in Myanmar and the consequent fears being experienced by journalists, Reuters (December 22, 2017) noted that the Myanmar government had incarcerated twenty-nine journalists in the twenty months since the NLD came to power and that Myanmar had been ranked 131 out of 180 nations for press freedom by Reporters Without Borders.

In one of the conversations that follow, my Rohingya interlocutor (1: "The Historian") complained in January 2018 that Facebook had frozen his account because he had been posting videos to document Tatmadaw violence in northern Arakan while the government and Buddhist nationalists continued to post blatantly false statements and propaganda without hindrance. In April of 2018, *The Irrawaddy* (April 20, 2018) published an investigative article in which it asserted that Facebook had been very slow to respond to media abuse from all parts of the spectrum. But it particularly focused on how the Tatmadaw had sought to game the social media platform. The article asserted that between 1993 and 2013, four thousand Tatmadaw soldiers had studied cyberwarfare, aviation, and nuclear technology in Russia, more than any other Southeast Asian nation. At present, some six hundred soldiers were in "Russian military higher education." It further averred that the Tatmadaw was behind a spate of cyberattacks leading up to the November 2015 elections. Moreover, "Many government officials with [Facebook] accounts have used them to post hate speech and violent threats. . . . The Myanmar military's psychological warfare department is believed to have hundreds of trained officers running multiple Facebook accounts posting sexy pictures and using female names to attract followers and then spread fake news whenever [needed]." In response, Facebook announced that it was hiring dozens of Burmese-language workers and would do its best to monitor the platform to prevent abuse as much as possible, but admitted that the task was daunting. In August 2018 Facebook suspended General Min Aung Hlaing's account.

On May 31, 2018, the Myanmar government finally signed a memorandum of understanding with two UN agencies, the United Nations Development Program and the Office of the United Nations High Commissioner for Refugees, to help facilitate the return of Rohingya refugees from Myanmar. As part of the memorandum, a three-person independent investigatory commission consisting of two Myanmar nationals and one foreigner would be appointed, apparently in line with the recommendations of the Kofi Annan commission and in response to the concerns expressed by the UN Security Council representatives weeks earlier.

In late January, 2019, Aung San Suu Kyii announced the intention to form a committee in parliament to formulate plans for a revision of the constitution.

Notes

1. Through a study of the history of the ceremonial veneration of the Dalada ("tooth-relic" of the Buddha), especially in the form of the *asala perahara* processions now performed annually in Kandy, Sri Lanka, I have attempted to show how the changing nature of this centrally important ritual is an index to increasing nationalistic sentiments among Sinhala Buddhists during the past half century. See "*Asala Perahara:* Powers of the Buddha's Tooth-Relic in Sri Lanka," in Holt 2017.

2. For a study of how religious times and places were often the occasions and venues for violent intercommunal attacks in Sri Lanka, see my chapter "A Religious Syntax to Recent Communal Violence in Sri Lanka," pp. 194–212 in Holt 2016.

3. The curious name of this group requires some explanation. In most versions of the Hindu epic Ramayana, Ravana is the antagonist who has abducted the epic's heroine, Sita, the wife of the dharma-minded heroic king Rama, and transported her as his captive to his kingdom in Lanka. Recently, the veneration of Ravana as an indigenous power to Sri Lanka has arisen within reactionary sections of the Sinhala community. In part, this development can be seen as a resistance to the presence of outside influences on Sinhala culture and society, particularly those emanating from neighboring India. The aims of this group are not only to resist outside influences and interventions, but also to foster those aspects of religion, culture and society understood as native to Sri Lanka.

4. See a video recording of portions of this speech (partially translated into English): "Hated speech by BBS secretary Galabodatthe Nanasara Tero (With English Subtitels)," YouTube video, 6:30, posted by "Sri Lankan Expat," June 16, 2014, https://www.youtube.com/watch?v=-fPMWD8f9lE.

5. For a detailed account of this attack and its significance for locals in the aftermath, see Farzana Haniffa, "Stories in the Aftermath of Alutgama," pp. 164–193 in Holt 2016.

6. A new group of violent vigilantes calling itself the Mahasona Balakaya appears to have been involved in this mayhem, and perhaps it is associated with the BBS. "Mahasona" is the name of the fierce chief *yakkha* (demon) in Sinhala folklore, and *balakaya* can be translated as "body force."

7. An excellent overview of the Muslim community in Myanmar has been written by Melissa Crouch, "Myanmar's Muslim Mosaic and the Politics of Belonging" (Crouch 2016).

8. For an overview, see Nuhman 2007.

9. Two detailed and insightful analyses of the conflict in southern Thailand have been written by Duncan McCargo: *Tearing Apart the Land* (McCargo 2008) and *Mapping National Anxieties* (McCargo 2011). On how Muslims have dealt with "Thainess," see Nilsen 2012.

10. "Burmese" is a more inclusive term than "Burman," as the latter refers specifically to the Bamar language and people, the term from which "Burma" was derived by the colonial British.

11. Deputy Minister for Home Affairs and Tatmadaw Major General Aung Soe told the upper house of parliament in January that the Tatmadaw had trained thirty armed Rakhine militias in Maungdaw beginning in February and March of 2017 (*The Irrawaddy,* January 30, 2018).

12. US Department of State, *Documentation of Atrocities in Northern Rakhine State,* August 2018, https://www.state.gov/documents/organization/286307.pdf.

13. The Karen, sometimes referred to as Kayin, are a very significant non-Burmese Buddhist and Christian ethnic group with their own state in central eastern Myanmar bordering Thailand. They have for decades experienced tensions with the Burmese Tatmadaw and have organized two militant groups to counteract the Burmese Tatmadaw's repressions. Periodically, there have been aspirations for independence. Consistently, there have been aspirations for more autonomy.

14. Relevant discussions of these themes can be found in Sarkisyanz 1965; Schober 2011; Charney 2009; Mendelson 1975; Walton 2016; and Fuller 2018.

15. See Leider 2005 for a most comprehensive treatment of the Mrauk U Empire.

16. This is likely a case of mistaken identity insofar as it was the British who had armed Muslims in the waning months of World War II as they sought to repossess Arakan. Muslims were known to have raided Rakhine militia positions at this time.

17. The Chin are an ethnic group forming the preponderant population in Chin State, located to the north of Rahkine State.

18. See, for instance, Turner 2014.

19. Perhaps the most salient of these studies is Schober 2011.

20. An efficient overview of the coming of both Indian and Chinese immigrants to colonial Rangoon is given by Michael Charney (2009, pp. 22–26).

21. Rangoon is what the British called this city. The Burmese have always called the city Yangon.

22. I have written a far more detailed account of events, which can be found at https://www.uhpress.hawaii.edu/title/myanmars-buddhist-muslim-crisis.

23. An extended journalistic and analytical account of the riots in Sittwe and Meiktila has been written by Francis Wade (2017, pp. 98–122).

24. The commission was comprised of three members from the international community, including Kofi Annan, and six from Myanmar—two Rakhine Buddhists, two Yangon-based Muslims, and two government representatives.

PART ONE

Yangon (Rangoon)

Shwedagon Pagoda, Yangon

Shwedagon Pagoda auxiliary shrines and meditation rooms, Yangon

Abu Tahay, “The Historian”

U Kyaw Min, “The Elder Statesman”

Khin Zaw Win with John Holt, “The Activist”

I first visited Burma in 1990, just months before the National League for Democracy (NLD; led by Aung San Suu Kyii) won the national election, an election that the Tatmadaw subsequently refused to recognize. At that time, I had been fortunate to secure a visit visa from the Burmese embassy in Colombo, Sri Lanka, as a professor of Buddhism, so I was granted the maximum amount of time allowed in the country: one week. From the moment of my arrival at the Yangon airport, I was chaperoned by government tourist officials for the entire week, and except for a day coming and going in Rangoon, I spent all of my time in Pagan and Mount Popa becoming familiar with Pagan's eleventh- through thirteenth-century temple architecture: painting and sculpture at the former and contemporary iterations of popular Buddhist ritual at the latter. It would be twenty years before I visited Burma again, in 2010.

On two visits in 2010, over a period collectively of two months, I spent several weeks in Yangon mostly under the direction of U Myo Myint, who had just retired as the government's director of religious affairs. Through Myo Myint, I gained access to an important monastery in northwest Yangon and conducted fieldwork there on the annual *kathina* (robe and gift giving) rite.[1] My initial reactions to Yangon after an absence of twenty years were really very unfavorable. The streets and sidewalks were in an even more decrepit state of dangerous deterioration than I remembered from 1990. Buildings seemed more ramshackle than ever. Sanitation was not an obvious value. I felt somehow disgusted at how the city had been entirely neglected while the Tatmadaw had decamped to their newly built capital of Naypitaw and had continued to skim off the economy with little allocation for maintaining and improving the welfare of the people living in the country's most important city. Yangon in 2010 was in a sorry state of disrepair and physically reflected the terrible economic condition of the country at large, a condition that had forced the Tatmadaw to figure out a new approach to the country's economy, which was perhaps the real reason behind their decision to allow for some political liberalization.

I didn't return again to Myanmar until early 2014. By this time, dramatic social and cultural changes were under way in an accelerated fashion. Many construction cranes hovered over ascending high-rise buildings dominating the Yangon skyline, signaling the advent of a new urban lifestyle. Recently reconditioned automobiles from Japan had been imported by the thousands, many of which had become taxis, and now choked arterial routes not designed to carry such a heavy load of traffic. Traffic lights had been installed. A major grant from Japan had allowed for the reconstruction of sidewalks, and so it became relatively safe and easy to pace the streets of downtown Yangon. Western music could be heard in new restaurants and cafés catering to an emerging middle class. Foreign tourists were seen in significant numbers at the Shwedagon Pagoda. Some women had eschewed wearing *thanaka,* the paste of a softwood tree similar in appearance to sandalwood paste and used cosmetically,

1. See my *Theravada Traditions* (Holt 2017), pp. 189–238.

and had begun to wear their hair in stylish Western fashions. Some younger women had donned knee-length rather than ankle-length skirts and joined many men who had begun to opt for pants rather than the lungyi or sarong. Supermarkets in remodeled colonial-era buildings had begun to replace the ubiquitous street or sidewalk markets. Change was in the air culturally, complementing the political expectation for an enhanced democratic government after the November 2015 elections. At that moment, social and cultural change seemed to herald an impending political change. While still relatively sleepy in comparison to other Southeast Asian cities like Bangkok and Singapore, Yangon was now on the move in many ways for perhaps the first time in fifty years. And it was in Yangon that the Rohingya political elite were now ensconced.

I came to love Yangon. It was exciting to see the rapid transformation occurring each time I arrived. I was often caught up in the street scenes, of South Indian goddess processions, of Buddhist monks delivering sermons over loudspeaker systems on closed-off downtown street blocks, of hearing the Muslim call to prayer, of watching families linger and picnic in Mahabandoola Park, of bantering with businessmen out for an evening stroll down by the riverbank at twilight. New restaurants were sprouting up in every direction of downtown, and I never missed a chance each time I passed through to spend some hours at the Shwedagon Pagoda, what for me is one of the most spectacular sacred Buddhist sites in Southeast Asia, if not in the entire Buddhist world of Asia. Eventually, I came to feel somewhat at home in Yangon and developed a grateful feeling that the Tatmadaw had decamped for Naypitaw.

The Historian

July 2015. When I first started working on this project, Jacques Leider, my good friend who is a specialist in the history of Arakan, provided me with contact information for Abu Tahay, indicating that he was a political leader among the Rohingya now living in Yangon. I'm not sure that Jacques had actually met Abu Tahay before he gave me his reference. If they had met, they would have engaged in long historical discussions, with Jacques gently trying to contextualize some of Abu Tahay's historical claims about the differences between the Muslim and Rohingya historical presence in Arakan. For Abu Tahay, the presence of Islam in Arakan is an important part of the lineage of contemporary Rohingya identity. For Jacques, the term "Rohingya" came into political currency only in the 1950s, even though it may have been used in different contexts earlier (see Leider 2013, pp. 204–255).

I decided to begin the heart of this book with my extended conversations over three years with Abu Tahay, in part because his historical arguments, whether or not they stand up to verification, help us to see how history looms so importantly as a factor in trying to understand the current communal problem, and how versions of it inform the claims of Rohingya, Arakanese, and Burmese.

I found Abu Tahay to be very earnest and committed. From the outset, I was very impressed with his awareness of the gravity of the contemporary crossroads facing the Rohingya community. All of his work on researching the history of his people related directly to his hopes about their future. Abu Tahay is on the younger side of the same generation politically as U Kyaw Min and U Kyaw Hla Aung (two other elderly Rohingya political figures of some note who became very important interlocutors for me). He is probably at least twenty years younger than either. Both Abu Tahay and U Kyaw Min had been elected to parliament from the Buthidaung region of northern Arakan, Kyaw Min back in 1990 in the election that was never honored by the Tatmadaw and Abu Tahay in 2010. Neither was ever allowed to take up his seat in parliament. I sensed a bit of a rivalry and yet mutual respect between the two men. Abu Tahay joined U Kyaw Min and Kyaw Min's daughter Wai Wai Nu on a trip to Norway in May 2015 for a conference focused on the plight of the Rohingya, sponsored in part by the Norwegian Nobel Institute and the Parliament of the World's Religions. On that trip Abu Tahay had met the Venerable Jotika, a progressive Buddhist monk from Mandalay who was being given a special award in Oslo by the Parliament of the World's Religions for promoting peace between religions, specifically his initiative to found the University of Global Peace in Mandalay. It was through Abu Tahay's recommendation that I was able to meet Ven. Jotika in Mandalay, weeks later, during the summer of 2015. I thought it was ironic that it was through a leading Rohingya activist/politician that I had been able to meet one of Myanmar's most progressive Buddhist monks and then proceeded to develop an extensive conversation with this monk over the course of the next three-plus years.

In any case, I was to meet Abu Tahay in Yangon at a luxury hotel near Kandawgyi Lake, a hotel obviously frequented by successful international business and diplomatic types. It was said that Barack Obama stayed here during his two visits to Yangon. Though I was dressed in slacks and a dress shirt (sans tie), I felt that my apparel was distinctly understated for the venue. I waited in the lobby directly across from the registration desk for about twenty minutes past our agreed-upon time. Finally, I asked for and received a user name and password for the hotel's Wi-Fi and discovered a fresh e-mail from Abu Tahay asking me to leave the lobby area and to meet him outside in the lovely garden area around the corner of the building and to the side of the hotel. There he was waiting at an out-of-the-way table sipping coffee and smoking cigarettes with a friend. Above and beyond a beautifully crafted pond, there was a lovely long view to the west of the Shwedagon Pagoda. We would speak here at this spot each time we met during the next three years.

After I introduced myself, Abu Tahay immediately seized the initiative and launched into what seemed to be a prepared lecture, with the help of his iPad, to which he frequently referred in documenting or illustrating his bevy of continuous assertions. He proceeded confidently, point by point, in a rather formal fashion, and I had virtually no time to intervene with my own questions. I became simply a captive audience of one, and so I dutifully took notes on my computer as extensively as I could. I reproduce the substance of these notes immediately below as they were asserted. (It was only during my third meeting with Abu Tahay that I was able to intervene and to learn much of anything about his personal history.) His presentations provide a historical contextualization from a more-than-interested Rohingya point of view.

Abu Tahay begins by referring to the 1982 Citizenship Law promulgated by Tatmadaw dictator Ne Win regarding indigenous people and their claims on citizenship. Indigenous people entitled to citizenship are those whose communities were deemed present in Myanmar before 1823, the year before the British established their colonial presence in lower Burma. One hundred thirty-five different communities were so identified, but not the Rohingya. Abu Tahay wants to argue that the Rohingya's Muslim ancestors have been in Myanmar as early as the ninth century CE and perhaps even before that. This historical fact, if substantiated, would obviate the need to prove anew their presence as an ethnic group before 1823 and render his community eligible for citizenship, the legal pressing need of the day. He says that he has spent a lot of time looking for primary documents to establish this pre-1823 Muslim presence. But instead of primary sources, his first reference is to a book published with the title *The*

Light of Sasana by the Directorate of Resettlement, Ministry of Defence, in 1997. He shows me a sentence on a page he has scanned, which states that "Islam was introduced to Arakan in Myanmar 1000 to 1200 years ago." This book, published by the Myanmar government, also refers to Arab shipwrecks, and thereby the coastal presence of Muslim Arab traders, and a permanent Muslim settlement dating to the reign of King Mahataing Sandra (788–810 CE). Abu Tahay has deliberately begun his argument by citing a Myanmar government publication released during the height of military dictatorship, ironic given the fact that it is the Burmese army, who tightly controlled the government between 1962 and 2015, that is perhaps the most nationalistic force currently opposing citizenship for the Rohingya people.

The second point that Abu Tahay promulgates is that the Rohingya language is similar to Vesali, the dialect spoken during King Mahataing Sandra's time and the language of an illustrative inscription dating to this reign. The inscription is a very famous one and is found at the Ananda Sandra Stone Monument, or Shittaung Temple Pillar, in Mrauk U. Abu Tahay argues that the Rohingya language is actually more similar to Vesali than either Arakanese or Burmese. Again, this is his way of establishing the primordial presence of people who would later be called Rohingya back to the earliest days of the Mrauk U kingdom.

Abu Tahay then goes on to cite five old and dated academic observations confirming the presence of Rohingya ethnicity prior to 1823, including a 1799 edition of *Asiatic Researches* (vol. 5) containing a reference to "the Mohammedans of Arakan, who have long been settled in Arakan, and who call themselves Rooinga, or natives of *Arakan*." This is the famous reference attributed to Francis Buchanan, a classic article that contains comparisons of specific words between Bengali, Hindi, and Rohingya dialects, thereby confirming, according to Abu Tahay, that the languages are different. This is a key issue, of course, because it linguistically rebuts the contemporary charge by many Burmese and Arakanese Buddhists that the Rohingya are no different from Bengalis and are mostly people who have recently jumped the Bangladesh/Myanmar border. It also can be used to distinguish the language spoken by Rohingya from the Chittagong Bengali dialect. (A number of Burmese and Arakanese I subsequently met asserted that the Rohingya speak the Chittagong Bengali dialect.) Next in Abu Tahay's presentation follows a Latin book published in 1850 in Germany that also has a reference to the Rohingya language of Arakan. Then there comes the nineteenth-century work of Henry Glassford Bell, a compilation of observations on different tribes in the region, and here "the Mohammedans" are also mentioned, while Rakhine is noted as a language *not* originally spoken by the region's inhabitants. This point would be a devastating claim to the narrative of Arakanese Buddhists, who argue for their provenance in the region since the time of an alleged visit of the Buddha. Finally, Abu Tahay cites a recent Yangon University geography curriculum for the history specialization that contains a note about how the Rohingya have been present in northern Arakan "since early days."

As Abu Tahay works through this material, he does so with such dispatch that I struggle to keep up. He flashes scan after scan in front of me, and I am unable to stop him to get full bibliographic information. After each point he makes, he pauses only briefly to make sure I understand and agree with the implication. There is no interrupting Abu Tahay's determination to assail me with a convincing academic brief in rapid-fire style. Following this opening barrage, he refers to a report by one Charles Paton, an early administrative British subcommissioner of Arakan who penned "A Short Report on Arakan" in 1826, which Abu Tahay says he secured from Indian government sources stored in Delhi. This source notes a population of some thirty thousand Mohammedans, sixty thousand "Rakhine," and ten thousand Burmese. Abu Tahay says that this establishes the fact that Muslims were present in significant numbers at the *beginning* of British rule and therefore refutes the argument that Rohingya are simply people brought into Arakan by the British during their rule. These figures also represent percentages of the population that are not very different from what they are at present, another fact that directly contradicts the claims made by many Burmese, but especially Arakanese, that Rakhine State is on the verge of being overrun by increasing numbers of Rohingya, due not only to illegal immigration from Bangladesh but also to a high birthrate. Abu Tahay next furnishes data from an 1872 British census that notes about sixty-four thousand Muslims in Arakan some forty-five years later and goes on to say that they "may" be an indigenous people who "differ little" from the other Arakanese "except for the religion." He then cites information from the 1911 British census that documents a dramatic increase of Arakanese Buddhists arriving from Chittagong (now Bangladesh) who had originally fled when the Burmese conquered Arakan in December 1784. Other sources in this regard report that some two hundred thousand Arakanese Buddhists fled into what is now Bangladesh during the time of the Burmese conquest. The 1941 British census observes that Muslims are not necessarily regarded as "Indians" because they have been long settled and "for all intents and purposes [are] to be regarded as an indigenous race." Abu Tahay particularly relishes pointing out this last British notation because it reflects a historically "official" perspective on how his people were regarded before Burmese independence was established.

Finally, with regard to all of these numbers, Abu Tahay points out that if one were to apply the "incremental rate of normal population growth [2.4 percent] from the 1826 figures through to 2013, it is clear that many Muslims have fled or emigrated, evidenced by the fact that there are now only 1.2 million Muslims in Arakan when "normally" the population would have grown to 2.3 million. This again directly rebuts Burmese and Arakanese claims about how the Muslims are in the process of overrunning Rakhine State.

My way-too-expensive hotel coffee has now grown cold because I have been glued to my computer, scrambling to get down every important detail that my new friend puts forth. Abu Tahay is anxious to move on to more contemporary history, especially how the Rohingya were treated more equitably by U Nu's democratically elected and yet Buddhist-nationalist-dominated government during the mid-twentieth century. He begins by pointing to a government cabinet decision made in 1954 to identify Rohingya as "union nationals." At this time, 75 percent of all Muslims in the country were Rohingya living in northern Arakan. He cites another U Nu government decision on May 15, 1961, to provide official national radio broadcasts to the Rohingya in their own language. Tatmadaw dictator Ne Win would stop this practice in 1965. Summarizing, Abu Tahay states, "Four or five elected parliamentary governments between 1947 and 1965 recognized Rohingya as a distinctive community in a de facto manner as evidenced by various cabinet decisions." He also cites a court case in 1949 in which a subordinate judge in Buthidaung told one Abdul Zolil, who was applying for citizenship, that he didn't need to apply because "you already belong to one of the 'indigenous races.'" Finally, Abu Tahay notes a document from 1959 indicating that Rohingya university students were allowed to form their own student group and a Rangoon University history club from 1958 to 1962, confirming Rohingya as a distinct ethnic group.

By this time, after two hours of intense lecture and my frenzied note taking, I can see that Abu Tahay feels satisfied that I have now become a sympathetic, if not fully saturated, listener. I seize the opportunity of a slight lull created by a waiter who wants to know if we will have more coffee and cookies, though I haven't touched mine yet. I ask Abu Tahay when and why antipathy for the Rohingya surfaced so significantly in Arakan. I had been told by others that tensions had simmered beneath the surface for decades before the 2012 explosion in Sittwe and that the expression of these tensions had been mitigated earlier by the heavy-handed presence of the Burmese military, who had kept a tight lid on growing resentments. Abu Tahay nods in apparent agreement, or perhaps it is just a nod that he understands me, but he goes on to explain that he thinks that the real impetus for the present anti-Rohingya antipathy began in the early 1990s during a bid by the State Law and Order Restoration Council (SLORC) to centralize power. Unrest in Arakan, he feels, had been stoked by no less than the military government itself as a way to rationalize even tighter control over the northern regions of the state. The rationale here was also to legalize control over properties and natural resources to expropriate them from the local Muslims. I had heard this contention from others, including non-Rohingya activists in Yangon who had also gone so far as to stress that the 2012 fiery imbroglio between Rohingya and Arakanese Buddhists had been fed by outside agitators that included out-of-uniform military personnel. Moreover, the government's continued plans to build ports for oil and gas pipelines that would lead to China and sea trade between Sittwe and India had precluded almost entirely any participation by or benefit for the local population, be they Rakhine Buddhist or Rohingya Muslim. Following on this line, Abu Tahay goes on to assert that the radically extreme Buddhist 969 Movement, which inspired boycotts of Muslim businesses and later morphed into the Ma Ba Tha had essentially been encouraged by people in the Union Solidarity and Development Party (USDP) government (2010–2015).

This initial meeting with Abu Tahay was a dizzying experience for me. I was at first a bit dubious regarding some of his sources, but also impressed that he had taken the time and care to research as carefully as he had. I ask him if he has been able to make similar presentations to many others from the West. I am then astonished to see photos he produces of himself posturing first with David Cameron, then the British prime minister, and then with none other than President Barack Obama on the first of his two visits to Myanmar. Having seen these photos, I ask him why he would bother spending his time with someone like me. His response is that the history of the Rohingya is not well known either in Myanmar or in the West and he is determined to rectify this situation as best he can, hoping to convince reasonable people of the simple fact that Rohingya only want to be treated equally in Myanmar. He trusts that I am in a position to pass on the truth of the matter to people who count. I say I will try not to disappoint him.

January 2016. I meet Abu Tahay about four months later at the same luxury hotel venue. Meanwhile, I had met the Venerable Jotika up in Mandalay and other progressive monks through him. I was grateful to Abu Tahay for providing me with this breakthrough and for being willing to see me again. I am determined this time to learn more about him personally, but he stands ready with his arms loaded with documents and his iPad again! This time, again he frames his argument within the context of the 1982 Citizenship Law. Rather than working to abolish this law per se, which had been established during Ne Win's dictatorship and which was patently aimed at discriminating against the Rohingya, he believes his historical argument, when presented to reasonable people, will be understood and accepted if it can be offered in an accessible form. Here is a man who truly believes in speaking truth to power! Indeed, he thinks the best strategy now is to work to recruit some of the military-appointed people in parliament and, on the basis of a national reconciliation process, change the constitution itself, which would pave the way for wholesale transformation, including of the 1982 law. He is banking on the fact that some of these military-appointed parliamentarians are reasonable and that they can assess an argument with an independent critical mind. I marvel at his faith. Here is his basic argument as he presented it to me in January 2016.

The 2008 constitution and 1982 law—especially the 1982 law, which has three different levels of citizenship rights—leave no room for accommodating the Rohingya. In Abu Tahay's view, there should be only one level of citizenship, regardless of all contingencies. This is the same conclusion that the vaunted commission headed by former UN secretary-general Kofi Annan would recommend in August 2017. Abu Tahay says, "If the government does not amend this law, we need to ask for the reinstatement of our full citizenship. We want to amend just a few articles, which would basically guarantee Rohingya citizenship based on parents being citizens before 1982, but the government is focusing instead on claims that a person's family who was in Myanmar before 1948 and who opted for citizenship before then qualifies. These people who qualify according to this strict 1948 rubric must still apply to a central body [Ministries of Border, Home, Defense, Immigration, and Foreign Affairs]. Then a decision can be made about whether you are a citizen, associate citizen, or naturalized citizen. We can't accept this because to comply with this is basically to admit that our people are illegal migrants. There is no guarantee that you will be granted citizenship—associate or naturalized, or turned down completely [only full citizens can run for office]—which means proving your parents were citizens." The Rohingya were recognized by previous governments as an official community until 1965 and were granted the same documents other ethnic communities received at that time. "Does a current government have the right to deny the rights of people who were citizens under previous governments? Previously, other minorities [Chin, Kachin, Karen] held the same identity [national identity card—NIC] before the 1982 law went into effect."

I ask Abu Tahay, "What is the disposition of other minorities towards the Rohingya?" So far, he doesn't see any sympathy, and he says that the reason is primarily religious, because there is basically no difference in characteristics between Rohingya and these groups except for that factor. "For instance, the Kaman [another small Muslim group], who are recognized as one of the 135 ethnic groups enumerated in the 1982 law, are among those who are also now languishing in IDP camps, despite their indigenous status and therefore 'guarantee' of citizenship protection; those who are Christians face similar discriminatory problems in dealing with the government. Kachin, Chin, and Kayin [Karen] are also suffering at the hands of Burmese Buddhists. It is their Christian religion that is the reason that they are being subjected to discrimination. Religion is the deciding aspect.

"People born before 1982, who were already over twelve or eighteen years and were regarded as citizens, should not be disenfranchised. Moreover, given the issues of identity in the country before 1982, these people actually held national identity cards, including the Rohingya. The NIC was the only proof required for citizenship before 1982. These were issued under the 1948 citizenship act at the time of independence. The UCC [Union Certificate of Citizenship] was issued to people not born within the Myanmar Union but who had come to Myanmar under the British before 1942 and who lived for eight out of ten years before 1948 in the country. For those who had the UCC under the 1948 citizenship [election] law, they could elect whether they would become Myanmar citizens or retain their original citizenships. So, before 1982, we had two types of citizens: native NIC holders and non-native UCC cardholders. Rohingya were classified citizens under both."

This time Abu Tahay is under some time constraints and so we end our meeting much earlier than I would have liked. So I packed up and headed back to the little hotel where I was encamped and tried to recover as much as I could from our conversation. In a post-session e-mail exchange, we agreed to meet again when I traveled to Yangon the following summer.

July 2016. When we do meet again at the usual place and time, Abu Tahay is ready again with a historical argument, but this one is comprehensive. He truly believes that history is on his side. Fundamentally, he wants to argue that the introduction of Islam to Arakan was tantamount to the presence of Rohingya in Arakan, since Islam is the Rohingya historical heritage.

He begins this lecture by referring to "Persian sources" documenting how Mohammad Haniffa, fourth son of Ali (son-in-law to Muhammad himself) by a second wife, came to Maungdaw in northern Arakan around the year 800 CE and married Queen Kaiyapuri, an indigenous ruler who converted to Islam. This is significant to him because it antedates when, in fact, some scholars believe that the Arakanese began to settle in the area (though, of course, the Arakanese believe that their ancestors date to the time of the Buddha's alleged visit in the fifth century BCE). According to Abu Tahay, everyone in Maungdaw knows this story. I find it a fascinating colonization myth of great contemporary relevance insofar as one of the chief objectives of the Buddhist nationalists is to stop Buddhist women's conversion to Islam and intermarriage with Muslim men, a reversal of the process flagged in this primordial moment! And, of course, the 2012 fiery imbroglio that was the riot in Sittwe began on the basis of an alleged rape of a Buddhist woman by a Muslim man. Abu Tahay points out that near Maungdaw there are two mountains named after these two primordial parents of the land. Though this would appear to be a Shia story (of Persian origin), Abu Tahay believes that it is really pre-Shia. This colonization myth is supplemented by the belief that later Arabic traders came to settle during the time of Hindu dynasties, he says.

There are now about nineteen unrecognized minority peoples (Buddhist, Christian, and Muslim) in Myanmar's current national context. "The ultranationalists believe that they are safeguarding the nation. But what they are really doing is trying to cover up the 'real history.'" Abu Tahay argues that a third "wave" of Islam is described in the account referred to by G. H. Luce in his *Phases of Pre-Pagan Burma: Languages and History* (1985). Abu Tahay goes on to cite Luce's *Phases* (p. 95), in which he records that the Rohingya claim to have occupied the east bank of the Mayu River region for the past thousand years. Luce says that "this is an exaggeration" but that it is undeniable that Muslim invaders entered what is now Arakan in 1202. The local chiefs were converted at this time to Islam and yet owed allegiance to the Pagan kingdom. Yegar (1972, p. 25), the Israeli scholar who tried to write comprehensively about Muslims in Southeast Asia, argues that the Rohingya are indistinguishable from other Muslims in the region, and G. E. Harvey (*Outline of Burmese History* [1947], p. 91) notes that only under the Pagan regime was suzerainty established over Arakan, even though indigenous hereditary rulers actually ruled as governors not appointed by Pagan. Abu Tahay wants to argue that this indisputably proves that Muslims were then ruling in Arakan.

A fourth Islam phase (Mughal) occurred in the fifteenth century (1403), when the king of Arakan, Min Saw Mon (Narameikhla), fled to Bengal and took shelter there for twenty-four years. After twenty-four years, during which time he may have studied Islam, according to some sources (a controversial point), the Bengalis sent troops to Arakan to restore him to the throne. Twenty thousand military forces plus support staff accompanied General Wali Khan with

Min Saw Mon, but in the face of confusion, the king fled again to Bengal. Another thirty thousand troops were sent to Arakan to defeat an absconding and traitorous Wali Khan, who was captured and sent back to India, where he was executed. Min Saw Mon was thereby reestablished on the throne. Abu Tahay's point here is that at least fifty thousand Muslim troops, along with legions of supplemental support, entered Arakan at this time. The Kaman Muslims trace their own origins to these events.

A fifth phase, or Muslim wave, began with the Portuguese bringing Muslim slaves, perhaps as many as fifty thousand, during the early sixteenth century (from India and what is now Bangladesh).

Finally, a sixth phase occurred during the fifteenth- to eighteenth-century Mrauk U dynasty, when the Mughal king Shah Shuja took refuge in Arakan along with the many Turkish soldiers in his retinue.

In addition, from the fifteenth century, there was an active trade route between Java and central Asia that traversed the Arakan coast. So Islam and Muslims from central Asia also contributed to the Muslim presence in Arakan.

In light of all of this, Abu Tahay avers that there are two categories of Rohingya ancestry: one type of wave involves those who have converted to Islam—in other words, mostly Hindu people (maybe a few Buddhists); a second wave of Rohingya is made up of the racial mixtures of Arabs, Persians, Turkish, central Asians, and Bengalis. The 1982 law predicates 1823 as the time that establishes the presence of indigenous people, and Abu Tahay argues his position to satisfy this rubric. He deploys a theory of ethnic identity based not on racial considerations, but rather on religiocultural history. It is also his way of rebutting the claim that Rohingya are simply Bengali, a people to be identified solely in terms of race and language.

Abu Tahay closes by reasserting, as he did in a previous meeting, that before 1965, the Rohingya were recognized as citizens and had possession of national identity cards. Everyone had to surrender their national identity cards in the early 1990s, and all were given white cards (indicating temporary status). The government has the records of these cards at the township, state, and federal levels. Abu Tahay contends that if the government was honest and thorough in claiming to execute a verification process, these records could be utilized.

In this third meeting with Abu Tahay, I was frustrated again by my inability to seize the conversational initiative. As we parted I thanked him profusely but also told him that next time we would meet in the wintertime, that I would want to learn more about his personal history, and that if he wanted to prepare in advance, he should think what he would like to tell me about his own experiences of being a Rohingya in contemporary Myanmar. He smiled shyly and agreed. We bade each other farewell.

January 2017. I was in high anticipation of my fourth visit with Abu Tahay because the situation in northern Arakan had deteriorated drastically following the Tatmadaw's draconian response to the killing of nine border guards on October 9, 2016, by a group of less-than-well-armed insurgents, the identity of which turned out to be hotly contested. About seventy-five thousand Rohingya had fled across the border into Bangladesh as the Tatmadaw's disproportional brutality ensued. While my agenda was to learn more about Abu Tahay personally, I had just spoken with U Kyaw Min (1: "The Elder Statesman") a few days before and had heard his interesting surmises about what had transpired on October 9. How would Abu Tahay explain what had happened, the event that led to a dramatic spiraling downward of the Rohingya's situation in northern Arakan?

He begins, "There was a buildup of trucks ferrying supplies by the army in the days leading up to October 9, indicating some level of understanding regarding what was to transpire in terms of imminent attacks on Rohingya." The attack on the border guards probably came from a group first formed in 2006 by Abdul Hakin, a notorious drug lord from the southern side of Maungdaw. His group has morphed into a formidable drug-trafficking ring comprised of both Arakanese Buddhists and Rohingya Muslims and linked to Bangladeshi border guards and also certain Bangladeshi parliamentarians. Abu Tahay surmises that the attack on October 9 was a revenge attack on the Burmese border guards for not cooperating. "Earlier in September, they had attacked the Bangladesh guards apparently for the same reason. This group had also abducted Rohingya before October 9 and demanded ransoms. So my view is that the response to October 9 is that the Myanmar government acted opportunistically to attack Rohingya. The diaspora Rohingya also acted opportunistically in claiming responsibility for the attack in order to raise funds from other Muslim militant groups to further their movement. Then a third group of local opportunists began to loot. The drug group is still loose in the mountains today. But there is a shadowy group behind them who must be a Burmese-speaking group. A group of militants being shown in a video first speaking in Burmese for five minutes claims responsibility before switching into the Rohingya language. This becomes the ruse for the attack by the military on the Rohingya. The men shown in the video are clearly seen but they were never investigated. So it was a drug group who was attacking their previous partners [the border guards on both sides]."

Abu Tahay then takes out his phone and shows me videos of bodies of burned Rohingya who died when the government troops began their counteroffensive—"so how could they have set fire to their villages as the government claims?" He shows me more videos of army personnel looting in the villages and says he has 163 videos related to this violence. From what I see from the limited videos he shares, the February 2017 UN flash report drawn from 220 interviews of Rohingya refugees in Bangladesh (OHCHR 2017) could be easily substantiated, while at the same time the videos refute the Tatmadaw's response that the UN's report was filled with completely fallacious accounts. As of mid-2017, Aung San Suu Kyii was still backing the military's version of events, denying that any harsh treatment of the Rohingya had taken place. The UN report documented widespread rape, murder, arson, and torture, consistent with previous Tatmadaw behavior in relation to other ethnic groups in Myanmar over the years.

Aung San Suu Kyi was also refusing visas to a blue-ribbon panel of UN-appointed investigators who were to form a fact-finding committee.

With this brief discussion of the issue of the hour addressed quickly, I remind Abu Tahay that I want my visit this time to be focused on learning more about his personal background. I can tell he is prepared. And so he begins. "I was born in 1964 in a village on the outskirts of Buthidaung. I studied at middle school in Nyaung Chaung. In school, I stood first from kindergarten through eighth grade. I attended Buthidaung High School, where I also stood number one for ninth grade. All subjects were combined in an all-around development program. Matriculation from Sittwe came in the tenth grade. I studied science and math at Akyab Regional College in 1982–1983, then civil engineering from 1983 to 1987 at Yangon University. There was a strike that delayed my graduation. I also studied courses in political science. I faced no restrictions because I and my parents had full citizenship. In order to study for the three professional lines of engineering, medicine, and commerce, one's citizenship had to be established in order to be admitted. I then did a master's of engineering degree in water resources, development, and engineering at Rangoon Technological University, but I did not complete this degree because of a student boycott related to the 8888 Uprising [which eventually led to Ne Win's resignation and the identification of Aung San Suu Kyii as the leader of the newly formed National League for Democracy]. In 1989, we formed a political party, the Student League for Mayu Development, and I was the township [Buthidaung] chair of this party and I ran for the union parliament from this party in 1990. I ran second to U Kyaw Min. I married a girl from Buthidaung in 1989, on May 14, and before long I was detained by the police, on June 23, 1989, for six months. We had protested the treatment of Aung San Suu Kyii for discrimination against her on the basis of her marriage to a foreigner. A SLORC general, Lieutenant General Tin Oo, had slandered her. I was detained in a prison for six months because of my involvement with the spread of a letter of protest. After that I ran for election in 1990. Had I been guilty, I would not have been allowed to run.

"Our party was dismantled by SLORC after the elections. Everyone's party was dismantled. The NLD had some sense that this would happen so they retained their registration lists for the future.

"Meanwhile, I transferred my family to Yangon, and there we had three children. My older son is becoming a medical doctor now by receiving his degree from an Indonesian university. He stood sixth in all of Burma in the matriculation exam and so he was allowed to study medicine at Rangoon [Yangon] Medical University. After two years, he got accepted to an Indonesian university. The second boy will sit the matriculation this year, in 2017. The third is my daughter, who is now in class five in Yangon. Now I am a senior licensed engineer for the municipals and an ASEAN [Association of Southeast Asian Nations] registered engineer. Currently I am also doing construction for Prestige Myanmar Construction Group. I have been to Malaysia, Saudi Arabia, and Indonesia to practice engineering but also took the opportunity from 1991 to 1996 to study the history of Islam and how it reached Myanmar.

"I have been to Norway in 2016 and have been to Hiroshima in connection with the Asia Pacific Intellectual (API) conference. I submitted two papers at the State University of Yogyakarta and at Indonesia University on 'No Place for Rohingyas' and 'Islam and Minority Religion in Myanmar.' Last year I gave a paper at Chulalongkorn University in Bangkok on 'Refugees, Migrants and Displacement.' We need to concentrate on why people are displaced because without that there would not be any migration. In 2013, I went on the International Visitor Leadership Program sponsored by the US Department of State to Washington, DC, Boston, Los Angeles, and New Orleans. Recently I have been to New Delhi, India, and visited six refugee camps for Rohingya there. I submitted a paper to the Indian Home Ministry about how to solve the Rohingya issue [since a border is shared with India]. We've done a lot of conferences here locally on the history and legal status of Rohingya. Rohingya are not illegal immigrants! In 2010, I sought election representing Buthidaung. I won that election, but the Union Election Commission dismissed me even though I actually won the most votes. I sued against the ruling USDP party in Naypitaw. I requested a recount. It took a year for the recount to be done and I won by 4,792 more votes than the USDP candidate. Though I got the vote, the government charged I had breached election law by using religion in the campaign, advocating for an Islamic state, a claim which was totally false.

"So I started a new political party, the Union National Development Party (UNDP), in 2013 together with other Rohingya people who are full citizens. Some in the party also had been elected in 2010 and 1990, and some had lost. Still the registration of the new party has not been granted as of today. The government has said that we could compete as individuals, but not based on our political party. I then decided to run as an individual candidate from Buthidaung in 2015. For no reason, my candidacy was rejected by the Maungdaw district election commission. Buthidaung is now represented by an Arakan National Party [ANP] representative." I note to Abu Tahay that this is absurd given the fact that Buthidaung is so overwhelmingly Rohingya. "Other candidates were given reasons for their rejection, such as their parents were not citizens. I appealed to Rakhine State and the Union Election Commissions. The Rakhine State Commission upheld Maungdaw. The Union Election Commission hesitated to accept my application because they said they were only accepting petitions from ethnic candidates. But I argued I was an ethnic person by law and they finally accepted. Two months after the election, all commission members wrote to me saying they recognized that both me and my parents held national identity cards, but that they still would maintain the state commission ruling." Abu Tahay says that this clearly represents a "politicization" of the election process. His Burmese friends in a position to know told him that he is suspected by those in the government of being supported by the Organization of Islamic Cooperation (OIC), even though he actually has nothing to do with the OIC. When I ask him why the OIC is so feared, he says that they are suspected of supporting insurgent groups. (Clearly, this is Buddhist nationalist monk U Wirathu's position too.) But currently, in fact, there are no insurgency groups among the Rohingya, except for the possible group who attacked the border post in October 2016. I note that it is so unfortunate and quite ironic that the Buddhist nationalists and Tatmadaw are actually creating the conditions for the appearance of insurgency groups in the future. He nods in deep agreement with this assessment. "The Buddhist nationalist monks are actually their own worst enemies," he says.

In response to my question about the future of Buddhist nationalist monks, he makes a sweeping historical generalization that the Burmese have managed to establish themselves politically through militancy rather than through reconciliation, that they have expanded and consolidated their rule also through intermarriage. This is also why the Ma Ba Tha (the monastic organization that claims to protect Buddhist society and religion) doesn't want intermarriage. It understands this as a process of inclusion. Abu Tahay believes that if the NLD doesn't succeed within the next five years in finding a solution to the current problem with Myanmar minority peoples, then the forces that gave rise to the Ma Ba Tha will make a comeback. At the time of this meeting (mid-2017), the NLD government had managed to influence the Ma Ha Na, or the official national sangha governing body, to ban U Wirathu from giving public sermons for one year, and it also declared that the Ma Ba Tha cannot function in any public way in the future. Thus, the NLD was then trying to repress the nationalist monks, chiefly because it sees them as an impediment to establishing good relations between Buddhist and non-Buddhist people, and because Buddhism's reputation is suffering internationally as a result of Ma Ba Tha racist militancy.

Abu Tahay tells me, "The NLD won because of Aung San Suu Kyii, but the question of the hour is whether or not her government can really perform in the interests of the people. The government's National [Defense and] Security Council consists of six military, four NLD, and one neutral member. Moreover, how will the NLD parliament be able to overcome the Home Ministry, Ministry of Border Affairs, and the Ministry of Defense, all of which are controlled by the military under the current constitution?"

Abu Tahay was initially optimistic that Aung San Suu Kyii could recruit some of the military personnel in the parliament in a bid for "national reconciliation." The NLD would nominate one of its own for one of the vice presidential positions, either a member or former member of the military, as a Trojan horse type of move for the other vice presidential position. With this person, perhaps they could get the votes that would enable a change in the constitution. This had been his hope. But in January of 2017 that hope had vanished. Aung San Suu Kyii had underperformed in terms of establishing a progressive administration promoting an inclusive national unity. She clearly had veered into the Bamar (Burman)-centric path.

I ask Abu Tahay, given the grave disappointments in Aung San Suu Kyii, if he holds out any hope for the Kofi Annan Commission, which Aung San Suu Kyii had appointed in August of 2016. Abu Tahay says that he has met this group twice but that he has really lost hope because of Suu Kyii's recent statements regarding the citizenship process. "She has already released her perspective about citizenship before receiving the committee's advice. It is a hard-line stance based on enforcing the 1982 Citizenship Law promulgated by dictator Ne Win. So what's the point now? Suu Kyii couldn't even wait for the intermediate report due out in the next month or so. That's why we have lost hope. We are totally excluded from the process on all levels. So our only hope is an international force. But even here, Kofi Annan's recommendations, whatever they may be about citizenship, have already been excluded. The international pressure is not working. The exclusionary process is driving people to self-defense or armed struggle. The current government unfortunately has invited an insurgency. Now there is no hope until the process is changed. We have tried to get a response through diplomats at the state and union levels. That is why the Rohingya abroad are now resorting to supporting an insurgency. The situation is now even worse than in the past. Economically, educationally, internally displaced persons (IDPs) and refugees have no access politically whatsoever to the NLD, so the situation is now worse than it has ever been. Maybe the Rohingya radical groups will be inspired to launch other attacks. And perhaps the other ethnic groups [Kachin, Chin, and Arakanese Army] will come out of the jungle into the urban areas. The future does not bode well. Instability will get greater. The Rohingya groups will get active in other parts of Rakhine State [meaning Buthidaung]. It is now confined to Maungdaw, but militants may be headed away from a preoccupation with drug trafficking toward revolutionary militancy." While he paints a very grim picture, he still wants to struggle. He is not giving up.

I mention to him that downtown Yangon has been largely a model of inclusion. Why is this the exception rather than the rule in Myanmar? He responds, "Integration within Rakhine State has been much less possible than in Yangon or Mandalay. This is because of the powerful Arakanese Buddhist sentiments to retain their 'race.' The Rohingya also have this sense of preservation. Even though I have many close Rakhine Buddhist friends, we never meet publicly together as we do in Yangon. We cannot sit together in Rakhine. With regard to the so-called Burmese Muslims, they continue to claim their Burmese identity because of their assimilation. They have totally transcended ethnicity realities. There was a close associate of Aung San's by name of U Razak, whose father was an Indian Muslim and whose mother a Burmese Buddhist. So he represents a kind of archetype to Burmese Muslims. But, of course, most Muslims don't fit that archetype!"

Finally, I ask Abu Tahay about his thoughts on the recent election of Donald Trump as president of the United States and if it has any salience for the situation in Myanmar. He buries his head in his hands briefly and shakes his head negatively. I look at him intently and say, "To quote a political science colleague of mine back in Maine, 'We're all fucked right now.'"

July–August 2017. It is the monsoon season and is raining daily in Yangon. Abu Tahay is headed for Bangkok in a couple of days for medical treatment and isn't sure he is up to meeting me again. But in the end, he graciously agrees to meet me at the usual place. I am determined to get his views on the contemporary scene. But I begin, as a way of dislodging history this time, by asking why his approach is so historically oriented, and whether he thinks this approach is still strategically warranted. He replies, "Because the law is based on history, I've been historically oriented and have talked in terms of ancestors and their descendants." I respond to this by asking, "Why is so much respect given to the 1982 law when, not only is it so discriminatory; it was promulgated by a military dictator operating outside of a democratic process?" He agrees with me and then says, "But we have no access to participate in a discussion about changing this law." I say that it seems that "the lady" (Aung San Suu Kyii) is saying that this law will actually be the means by which the citizen problem will be settled.

Abu Tahay says, yes, that seems to be the case and that the situation is going to become something of a bureaucratic nightmare. "When birth certificates are issued, the birthplace is not mentioned." He shows me a birth certificate issued only one week earlier. "So this is going to create a big problem. Moreover, the majority of people in remote villages don't even have birth certificates despite the fact that since 1982, the government began attempts to provide them. And then in the 1990s, they collected the national registration cards, the village household lists, and birth certificates. These are needed for three generations to prove one is eligible to become or remain a citizen. In return, people were issued the temporary white cards that were supposed to be good for only six months." I shake my head.

I mention that I now routinely read that an insurgency with international backing is under way in Arakan and then refer to an article entitled "Talking about the Pot Calling the Kettle Black" in the most recent issue of the *Myanmar Insider*, a slickly produced magazine for expats, primarily businesspeople and possibly embassy workers. The article refers to Rohingya as "illegal Bengalis" and Rakhine Buddhists as having to defend against "aggressive aliens" in order to survive. I had been angry about this article when I read it, but I mention it to Abu Tahay to see if these views have become so regularized that they can be published without a thought that they might be challenged. He simply nods. This is nothing new to him. And I begin to think that maybe I've been a little naïve in reacting so strongly to what apparently has become so commonplace. So I shift the conversation to the question of the October 9, 2016, attacks on the border guard posts and who was responsible, since insurgents with international connections are now consistently blamed. Abu Tahay says that the first attack on the border guards was definitely the work of a drug group, which is what he had told me months earlier, in January. However, behind this initial group, the Myanmar security forces had made use of a second group of people (a group also used by members of parliament in Bangladesh) consisting of Rohingya from southern Maungdaw. This second group has been committing violence against local people and is also interested in sustaining the drug business and the extortion of money. Another band of so-called insurgents is yet a third group committed to self-protection and comes from the local Arakan community. Security forces claim to have found weapons belonging to this third self-defense group, and the weapons they claim to have found are the same guns that are used in Bangladesh. The photographs showing the seized weapons are actually taken with innocent women holding them, Abu Tahay says; the weapons are planted. He shows me one of these photos. Clearly, he says, the Myanmar security forces are trying to create an impression of instability. "The self-defense groups are definitely locally grown, but we don't know yet if they are linked up to Rohingya international groups outside. So far, there don't appear to be any links to Pakistani, ISIS, Philippine, et cetera, radical Muslim groups. However, it might just be a matter of time before they are. They sprung up following the brutal military reprisals in the aftermath of October 9 and they are rooted in Maungdaw. The self-defense people are already actually interested in getting funds for support from Rohingya outside of the country." He shows me a video of the questioning of a young teenage Rohingya in which the young man is interrogated at gunpoint. He shows me another video of ten- to twelve-year-old kids shooting pistols. The videos could be used by either the security forces to rationalize their presence or the self-defense group, which now may have an interest in raising money from Rohingya in Saudi Arabia. I ask him who he thinks was responsible for the killings of so-called collaborators then occurring in Maungdaw. He says that the killings are the work of the dacoits (the drug and human traffickers), the self-defense groups, and the Myanmar security forces. All of these groups are implicated in murders in the various videos he has seen.

I mention how a Thai army general and sixty others were convicted in a Thai court the previous week for their role in the human trafficking of Rohingya in southern Thailand, a case opened up by the spectacular investigative journalism conducted by Reuters in 2015. Abu Tahay's response is that this is just the "tip of the iceberg" and that it will be necessary to get a comprehensive look at many other cases as well, since these Thai might not have been the main traffickers. He says investigations eventually will need to take place in Myanmar as well "to find out this end of the link. Human trafficking is still going on. How and why are people leaving from Rakhine? They need to focus on the root cause. Arms supplies are also part of this trafficking. So how about the security forces of other countries and their involvement? Thailand and Malaysia alone are unable to stop the human trafficking and arms smuggling." He goes on to say that high-level security forces in Myanmar are also involved and that the Rohingya are victims in all of this. Though Rohingya are aware of the dynamics, they are still trying to leave because the situation in northern Arakan is getting desperate.

Abu Tahay then tilts the subject of conversation to the reasons why women are still trying to flee Arakan. He talks about the Hindu influence on Rohingya. I am very surprised at this comment and push him to elaborate. What he means is the manner in which the dowry system has been adopted by the Rohingya at virtually all levels of society. It used to be that only the elites engaged in this practice, but now it is widespread throughout Rohingya society. Many families, especially under these extreme circumstances, have no money to pay on behalf of their women, so women are leaving their parents behind, hoping that maybe they can get work and send money back to support them.

Abu Tahay is still working the case for full citizenship to give his people a legal basis to protect themselves in Myanmar. The United Nations supports this tack. "We are also seeking access to the political process with the goal of reinstating citizenship. We are trying to gain access at the grassroots level, to the peace process and to engagement with diverse ethnic peoples in the country. But we are still not getting access yet."

We then talk about the blocking of the proposed UN fact-finding committee, and the three persons appointed, including my old acquaintance from Sri Lanka with whom I worked when she was with the International Centre for Ethnic Studies, Radhika Coomeraswamy, who have been refused visas. Abu Tahay laments that the situation deteriorates further day by day for all ethnic peoples in this country. Even though Aung San Suu Kyii may not want to cross the military, she could at least begin to open up access to the ongoing process of a peace initiative. By bowing to the pressures of nationalism, she simply is not meeting her obligation for the government to take action on the citizenship issue. No changes have really occurred on the socioeconomic front either.

Moreover, now it is even almost impossible to renew passports. In his case, he had to pay 1 million kyats (750 US dollars) because even though he holds an NIC and is therefore a citizen, he is not from one of the 135 recognized ethnic groups according to the 1982 Ne Win–inspired law. "The Home Ministry is exacting bribes. Also, if they are aware that you are a member of another political party beyond the NLD, there could easily be a delay of months." What Abu Tahay explains reminds me of the problems faced by Jezima Akyabi out in Thandwe (2: "The Teacher"). And then I realize that Abu Tahay has just had to pay this bribe in order to get himself to Bangkok for medical help!

He goes on to talk about how the media is getting even more tightly controlled these days. It then becomes clear that he is not just referring to the domestic media, but that out of sensitivity to Aung San Suu Kyii's political situation, other important international media outlets may be shying away from some kinds of stories, especially those having to do with the Rohingya. "Now I am not even being contacted by VOA [Voice of America] or BBC. Reuters is still okay, though."

Finally, he offers a concluding historical observation that I find provocative. He says that "previous laws about citizenship, such as the 1948 law, did not depend in any way upon ethnic identity, and so people were not dependent on their identity and therefore did not assert it." I think about this for a moment and realize that something similar happened in Sri Lanka in the 1950s. Before ethnicity became politically significant, it was not really very present in national discourse or in raising boundaries between communities. But once it became an issue, legally, politically, or constitutionally, it raised the specter of difference, of competitive difference, and ignited a mind-set that discriminates against perceived rivals.

A torrential downpour with high winds and pounding rain assails us in the hotel garden. Abu Tahay quickly unfurls his umbrella and begins to dash to the front of the hotel, where there is a portico. I dart in the other direction, soaked by the time I find refuge in the coffee-shop area just off the lobby. I hope to see Abu Tahay once again in December.

December 2017. I do see Abu Tahay again at our usual rendezvous in late December 2017. He has been one of my most reliable conversation partners over the years. The few days before our meeting he had been preoccupied with his daughter's exams. All three of his children seem to have done extraordinarily well academically. His eldest son is now working as a doctor in the United Kingdom; his middle son is one of eight Rohingya recently admitted to the medical faculty at Yangon University. His daughter's prospects sound equally bright. He doesn't arrive with an agenda this time, but waits for me to orient our discussion after we exchange pleasantries.

My first question has to do with Pope Francis's recent visit, in November 2017, and his studious avoidance of the term "Rohingya" at the request of the Yangon cardinal. I want to know what Abu Tahay perceives as the rationale for warning off the pope in this way, even though the pope is a known sympathizer for the Rohingya's plight.

"Christian leaders are not friendly to us. That is the real reason why the pope was restrained. We are friendless at the political level, but not so much so at the local level."

I ask him, given what I've been hearing about how Burmese in Yangon are now distancing themselves from Rohingya acquaintances, "Is that now changing for you too?"

He interprets my question as being aimed at the local level in Arakan rather than in Yangon. He says, "Rakhines of Mongolian background are now against us, but Rakhines of Aryan descent remain friendly to us. If the government was willing to facilitate sitting down together, I think a common agenda for fruitful discussion could be arrived at. But the government has been unwilling to provide this kind of facility. A few Rohingya have already received citizenship, but they have had to assert a Bengali identity. Still, they are not free to move, to get a passport easily. They have to go to a special branch of immigration and pay something extra—100,000 to 500,000 kyats. The more money, the quicker you will receive—if you are not spending, you can't expect it anytime soon. This reflects the corruption of the government. This is even if you are a citizen!"

My second question is aimed at soliciting his reaction to the Kofi Annan Commission report, which was issued hours before the Arakan Rohingya Salvation Army (ARSA) launched its attack on August 25, 2017, against border posts. He replies, "They [the government] are not following the recommendations of the report so far because they are not in any way indicating that they will be granting citizenship. Instead, the government is still trying to issue verification cards. Issuing this card is not in accordance with either the current Resident Law or the 1982 Citizenship Law. So I don't think that they are going to honor Kofi Annan's report in this regard. They can and should offer the national identity card and then allow those with the NIC to apply for citizenship."

I ask him about the verification process and its plausibility as part of the repatriation process, in light of the massive refugee crisis now unfolding and the vague plans to begin the process during the last part of January 2018. By this time, somewhere on the order of 690,000 more Rohingya have fled northern Arakan, where the Tatmadaw has unleashed an unprecedented campaign of violence and terror. "The requirement to prove citizenship shows that they are not really serious about repatriation," he tells me. "How are these people expected to have documents when their documents were either confiscated back in 1994 or were recently burned up in their houses? As of today, people are still fleeing northern Arakan. Arbitrary detentions continue. Rakhine people are settling into Rohingya villages and lands. This pattern is being followed by the Rakhine politicians. The government is simply unwilling to do their duties in protecting the Rohingya's interests. The Rakhine politicians are asking that Maungdaw be divided into two: the northern part for Muslims and the southern for Rakhine. I have no idea if the government will agree to this or not. Initially the government announced the construction of four camps for repatriated Rohingya—two on the north side and two on the south. But construction has begun only on the northern side. Everything is upside down right now. There is no effort at all for provisions or planning to rehabilitate the individual houses that Rohingya have lost, while there is a concentrated effort being made for the construction of houses lost by the ethnic Rakhine, which are very few in number when compared to the massive losses of the Rohingya." I recall that more than 350 Rohingya villages have been burned, as confirmed by satellite imagery reported by the UN Operational Satellite Programme.[1] (As of October 2018 the repatriation process has yet to get under way, though the government had signed a memorandum of understanding with the United Nations to allow for access to northern Arakan to judge whether or not conditions were suitable for repatriation. This memorandum was staunchly opposed by the USDP and the ANP in public, so its chances of being effective were still not clear.)

My next question has to do with Aung San Suu Kyii; since the time we last met she had come under increasingly intense pressure and criticism from various international sources, including former fellow recipients of the Nobel Peace Prize. In response, Abu Tahay pulls no punches. "She is the one who is the main person responsible for the crisis. It's at her doorstep, according to her own protocols. Formally, she is the number two person in terms of having responsibility." He rejects the charitable view of her that I offer, a view that is often articulated by diplomats who say that putting her under pressure to undertake action on behalf of the Rohingya could jeopardize whatever progress toward democracy has been established in Myanmar. "But, in fact, she *is* a nationalist.

---

1. "A Visual That Shows Just How Many Rohingya Villages Have Been Burned," Reuters, January 1, 2018, https://www.reuters.com/article/us-myanmar-rohingya-rakhine/a-visual-that-shows-just-how-many-rohingya-villages-have-been-burned-idUSKBN1EQ0PO.

She says she is following the law, but we cannot find the articles she is basing her plan on."

Abu Tahay thinks that the burning of 350 villages resulted in at least ten thousand people being killed, since the army began its so-called clearance operations. "The government says that ARSA was responsible for initiating the current crisis, but so far no one who belongs to ARSA has been detained. Just ordinary people. There are about fifty thousand orphaned refugee children in Bangladesh according to the UN registration. What has happened to their parents? This means that if each comes from a family of five children [a very generous estimate], that means that at least twenty thousand parents are missing. We are still trying to get the data. In addition to this, some entire families were killed. In just one day in Rathedaung, about fifteen hundred people were killed. We are looking for eyewitnesses whenever we can. As of now, our verified figures indicate over ten thousand people killed. This is after two months of assessment, an assessment that is still not completed, as two more months have passed as well. These are supported figures based on reports from family members who are eyewitnesses. But some families were entirely wiped out, so we know our figures are incomplete." I add that Médicins Sans Frontières (Doctors Without Borders) reports that sixty-seven hundred Rohingya were killed in the month following August 25, 2017, alone. I am sure that the real final figure will greatly surpass the approximately ten thousand affirmed by Abu Tahay's sources to date.

Abu Tahay is in an expansive mood today and not tethered to the agenda of his formal presentations, which he has used as the bases for his discussions with me in the past. In view of this, I decide to let the conversation move in directions where he feels compelled to go.

He reports that his Facebook page has been hacked twice in recent months and that Facebook has asked him not to post any more materials having to do with Rakhine State. "There is a group of NLD youth who have reached a compromise with Facebook to monitor the postings," he says. This is clear manipulation of Facebook, I suggest, and he agrees. "While I am not allowed to post materials that are simply reports, Facebook is still publishing hate material against the Rohingya. We are not instigating hate messages ourselves.

"Initially, I thought we had only three main actors in the current Arakan scene. But now there are five. First, there are Rakhine Buddhists who want to establish an autonomous state and don't want to share it with Rohingya. From the Rohingya side, there are those of us who are looking only for equality. But the military and Rakhine say that the Rohingya all want an autonomous state. At the same time, our NLD government is trying to deny the very existence of Rohingya, going so far as to urge the avoidance of the term in public speech entirely. They have become the third actor with an objective. Then there is the military, with its negative view aimed at their illegal appropriations of northern Rakhine lands. The fifth actor is the international community, some from the humanitarian crisis side, some from the geopolitical side, and some from the perspective of global economic interests, or the multinational business interests.

All would have to come to the table to arrive at a common agenda." I say to myself, "Wow! Apparently, Abu Tahay still has hope if he's thinking about these parties coming into discussions."

"We are looking for equal rights and access. We need to address the discrepancy between ARSA and other Rohingya. We are not getting any access to the government though we have offered to function as a mediator with ARSA. Rakhines don't want to sit down with any of the parties. And we are totally friendless. Even my previous Rakhine and Burmese friends are moving away from me on the personal level. I was followed by the government's special service for three months." At that time, he began to worry about his personal safety and appealed to the American embassy to help him if he got into any trouble. They told him bluntly that there is no way for them to help in such an instance. As a result, he has recused himself recently from many opportunities to speak publicly. He hopes the situation will calm down sooner rather than later. "The authorities are trying to link local Rohingya [in Yangon] to the Rakhine violence" in Arakan. What he fears is that the government will see Rohingya as one undivided force, a view that would put all Rohingya at risk. He feels under great pressure. His community, of course, is suffering immensely in all manners, has no unifying leadership to assert a vision for the future, and has been excluded from any constructive processes. He says the situation has never been worse for his people and that he does not know where the future is headed.

Recently, he met with US senators and congressmen at the American ambassador's house. They were on a "fact-finding tour." Senator Richard Durbin from Illinois was ostensibly the leader. Abu Tahay mentions an issue that was raised by one of the liberal voices in the contingent; it is one that I have thought about often myself in recent months, as the Myanmar military began its seemingly unrestrained brutality against the Rohingya of northern Arakan. This is the issue of whether or not saving this so-called democracy of Myanmar is actually worth the terrible sacrifice of human rights or lives. That is, what is the worth of a government that has simply watched, publicly denied, and then abetted in ethnic cleansing or genocide of people within its borders, regardless of the citizenship controversy? How strongly should their accountability be weighed? I sense that perhaps Abu Tahay, in exasperation, has now come to the conclusion that this Aung San Suu Kyii government has proved itself inimical to the well-being of his people. Perhaps that is why he asked the contingent of American politicians, "'Are you aware that North Koreans are residing here in Myanmar, that our democratically elected government is allowing people here to do exploration needed to develop nuclear weapons?' One of the congressman who looked stunned said he would look into it."

I ask if specific sanctions by the American government against Myanmar were discussed in the conversation. Abu Tahay says, "Now General Maung Maung Soe has been targeted. But some of the responsible individuals are not under his command. There are subdivisions in the army that are responsible only to their specific commanders. For example, there is a Rangoon subdivision commander, a Mandalay subdivision commander, et cetera. We've asked them to target the subdivision commanders. We cannot get that information, but they can. These operations are cleared not just by the army, but by the police, nationalist politicians, and officials of the Border Guard Patrol in both Bangladesh and Myanmar. The involvement in the perpetration of atrocities is very widespread. Then there are paramilitary groups as well, which are Rakhine Buddhist. These are the so-called vigilante groups now operating." By discussing this, he hoped to paint a picture of responsibility that could not be so easily reduced to one target. He hoped that this contingent of American congressional officials understood this.

Because he was trying to explain aspects of the Rohingya crisis to American politicians, he went on to say that when he met with President Obama, Obama had promised that before his term expired he would try to do something constructive. But there was no result. He was the only Rohingya to meet with Obama during his first visit. David Cameron said this situation would be settled when Aung San Suu Kyii came into power. Everyone was deluded about her. "That's why I can say that there is not any bright future for anyone other than Burmese in Myanmar. Even the 88 Generation people are against our minority. This means we have no potential Burmese leaders who might sympathetically look out for minorities."

At this juncture, because I know this may be my last meeting with Abu Tahay, I float a very general thesis and ask him what he thinks. I speak about the fact that many Buddhists in Myanmar, Thailand, and Sri Lanka take a majoritarian perspective, insofar as they believe that these three countries are essentially Buddhist countries. Their understanding of religion and political history is so intertwined that they believe that the country (Myanmar, Thailand, or Sri Lanka) exists for the sake of the religion (Theravada Buddhism). Consequently, minorities who are of other religious traditions are regarded as foreigners or guests, beholden to the generosity of compassion of Buddhists for their continued welfare in each of these states. Under these circumstances, equality is virtually an impossible ideal. He replies very briefly that humanity in general, and not just the identity derived from particular religions, should come first in any consideration regarding belonging. "You should belong where you live."

I follow this up with a question asking if he would advocate constitutionally for a secular state. Yes, he says, and it should include protections for the ownership of land regardless of religion or race. Related to this, he says that the Chinese are paying their people to buy land around the city here in Yangon and also in Mandalay. He follows up this contention with the comment that "the Chinese have been adept in developing their business connections, particularly out in Rakhine." Here he is alluding to the development of a port at Kyaukphyu on Ramree Island and the building of the oil and gas lines from there all the way to China. I recall reading a recent post online that refers to a three-point plan announced by China in a bid to organize discussions between Bangladesh and Myanmar regarding the future of the Rohingya. The three-point plan was so simple that it seemed completely innocuous: (1) institute a cease-fire;

(2) solve the problem; and (3) develop Rakhine economically. It is particularly the third point that the Chinese would stress.

Hearing this, Abu Tahay says that the United Kingdom, America, Germany, and France are the only countries that appear sympathetic to the Rohingya problem. "Our own internal chief problem is that we have no leadership. We are not organized. We have activists but no overall leadership. If America wanted to take action, with whom can they discuss? The Palestinians, the Filipinos, et cetera, have leaders, but we don't. So, how are we going to address this problem? How can we control the destiny of our community? ARSA's attack gave the Myanmar army a ruse to do what they have now done to us. ARSA doesn't have a clear and comprehensive agenda. They have only a limited political objective. We would like to know who is financially supporting them. They pushed innocent people armed with only farm implements into an attack in which many of them were killed. It has been the innocent people who have gotten killed in the aftermath as well. Rohingya in Myanmar are not capable of providing this kind of support. Who is providing the modicum of support now in play? So, the major problem is that we don't have leadership to move forward. We cannot educate, we cannot communicate, we cannot give voice as one.

"This terrible situation has come about because of the mistake of the Rohingya international community. Their so-called leadership is coming from Rohingya expatriates in Saudi Arabia. There is no leadership from within Myanmar. Even though Malaysia has been supportive of Rohingya, why have they banned people like me from traveling there? Apart from ARSA, Saudi does not allow us there either, to study, or for whatever reason. Even Bangladesh is avoiding us. This gives us doubt about how to proceed. We have engagement with the United States, the United Kingdom, and some Europeans who are trying to help us politically, but so many others don't even allow us to travel to their countries. These are practical problems that are getting in the way of advancing any agenda. You can go on hajj to Mecca, but you cannot engage in any other purpose. We cannot gain access. Saudi Arabia seems to be the only source supporting the ARSA. We have found out that the ARSA organizers are Pakistani and Bangladeshi nationals. They are not really Rohingya connected to the grass roots on the ground."

Having entered a more geopolitical orientation of the Rohingya problem, Abu Tahay launches into what becomes a rather spectacular, if not bone-chilling, speculation. He begins by saying that "some Indians are sympathetic to our plight, but they are very cautious as well out of fear of Pakistani connections to ARSA that they have perceived. In September during the worst of the mayhem in northern Arakan, Prime Minister [Narendra] Modi [of India] came to Myanmar and expressed his solidarity with Aung San Suu Kyii and the Myanmar government." I mention that I found this a wholesale support for an anti-Muslim strategy, especially given Modi's own history as chief minister in Gujerat fifteen years earlier, when the Muslim minority was attacked without restraint by majority Hindus for several days. Abu Tahay points out, however, that Modi's government is sending support to the Rohingya refugee camps in India. And then I recall having read recently that India has offered to send prefabricated houses to northern Arakan, as they have done for reconstruction in the Tamil areas of northern Sri Lanka. Abu Tahay then says pointedly that "some Rohingya have had a strategy of cultivating Pakistan, and this is a problem for the Indians who fear a 'terrorist connection' with Pakistan. What further complicates the issue is India's competition with China for influence in the region. So, there are vying competitions. The final effect of this perception about Rohingya appealing to Pakistani interests is that the Rohingya in turn will suffer in the unfolding of India's anti-Pakistani strategy." He continues. "Only the very religious side and illiterate Rohingya people seem to support ARSA. Literate people would never come to face guns with farm implements. Literate people are challenging ARSA's methods and agenda. ARSA's official agenda is for equal rights, but their hidden agenda is autonomous rule. The Myanmar army knows this. And this is their ruse and what legitimates their actions in the eyes of the majority of Burmese. This is what had fed the anti-Rohingya strategies of the Ma Ba Tha, the Myanmar army, and the Rakhine Buddhist politicians. But the truth of the matter is that the army is not really addressing ARSA per se, but rather they are addressing only the normal innocent people. The ARSA people are *not local* [italics mine]. The government of Bangladesh is not supporting ARSA; neither is India. And of course, the NLD government of Myanmar is opposed. So how can ARSA function? The answer is that the Myanmar military is actually using ARSA; they are allowing them to operate, and ARSA has actually operated for the benefit of the Myanmar military." I find this a stunning accusation. Is he really saying that the Myanmar military is behind ARSA and its attacks on the border guard stations? He is! And he begins to explain why he has come to this conclusion.

"How can ARSA operate in areas where the Myanmar military is present? ARSA functions because the army allows them to. Why can't they [ARSA] be eliminated since they have such poor arms? Because the military is using ARSA as a reason for their genocide! On August 25, 2017, twenty-nine of the thirty ARSA attacks were on border guard stations, with only one attack on an army installation. And in these attacks, ARSA regulars were not in front of the attacks, but only the innocent farmer recruits with virtually no serious weapons took the barrages that came in response. The attacks, of course, occurred just after the announcement of the recommendations of the Kofi Annan Commission. Remember that the recommendations of the Kofi Annan Commission were welcomed by the Rohingya people in general, that Aung San Suu Kyii pledged to implement them, and that it was only the army generals who publicly rejected the findings of the Kofi Annan Commission on the grounds that the understanding of history was not accurate. And consider this: the day before the attacks occurred, there was lot of military activity in preparation for what eventually happened. Indeed, there seems to have been a plan in place at least ten days before the ARSA attack."

Maybe I had an incredulous look on my face when pondering that perhaps the Burmese military was somehow behind the botched ARSA attacks on August 25, 2017. I always have a problem trying to remain poker-faced. Perhaps my facial reaction unwittingly inspired him to continue in more detail and to provide more warrants for his speculations.

First, he backtracks a bit and says that "ammunition used in the earlier October 9 [2016] attack by Rohingya were bullets only available from the Myanmar military." Next, he asserts that "definitely there were some people who came from other countries who had been residing in northern Arakan for a year or more before the August 25 [2017] attack. Why were these people allowed to reside in the area? There's a lot of unanswered questions about how the security forces may have been using ARSA. And then ARSA killed a lot of Rohingya, and the military took no action against them. Some of these foreign people were tall, light-skinned people speaking Arabic fluently. They were also using Burmese phones. They appeared for prayers from the local imams before the attack. I can say definitely they are not Indians because they are racially different. Who were these agents? They were fluent in English and Arabic. Are they Pakistani or from Israel? More possibly from Pakistan intelligence?"

I ask, "What would be the Israeli interest in this?" He says that there really is no interest in the Rohingya per se. They would simply have been hired out because they have knowledge of Islamic people. Most of Myanmar's intelligence agents have been trained by Israel! On the other hand, there is considerable interest in the problem from Pakistan, and this is where he thinks the impetus is coming from—Pakistani intelligence. "Both groups [Israeli and Pakistani intelligence] have close connections with the Myanmar army. The ARSA leader is also Pakistani-born. Yet, the Pakistani government has not voiced concern over what has happened here; only in their parliament have a few voices been raised."

Abu Tahay continued. "I don't know who the so-called Rohingya in Saudi are, especially those who are supporting ARSA. Maybe they are Pakistani or Bangladeshi? We don't know what the future holds for ARSA in Arakan, if they will be eliminated or be allowed to grow in the service of the Myanmar army. It all depends on the Myanmar army and government. If China somehow intervenes, the situation will become ever more complicated. China is already in a secretive alliance with the Arakan Army as well as with the Kachin rebels. If ARSA links up with these groups, they can be linked as well with the Chinese. The more serious worry would be that ARSA links up with ISIS or al-Qaeda. It's possible. . . . This why I push for access in order to find out what is going on geopolitically behind the scenes here."

Abu Tahay is not finished with this line of thinking, revealing that he has considered various possible scenarios in some depth. What has occurred in post–August 25, 2017, Arakan indicates that the Yangon-based Rohingya leaders can no longer be regarded as leading the Rohingya community per se, that other forces have now become ascendant to fill the leadership vacuum in the community. Have Rohingya themselves been unknowingly coopted by the Burmese military in a manner that is leading to their own demise? One can certainly understand how young Rohingya could be drawn into ideas about revenge against the Burmese, given how the army used rape and murder as means of driving out seventy-five thousand Rohingya in northern Arakan following the October 9, 2016, border post attack. Abu Tahay is very suspicious that Rohingya young people were duped, set up, ultimately by the military, to set the stage for a counterattack that led dramatically to the exit from the country of more than two-thirds of the Rohingya population. Abu Tahay finds it significant that "no ARSA person in Myanmar has even been detained in the four months following the attack. And why is it that only one of the thirty venues designated for attacks by ARSA was an army installation and the other twenty-nine simply border posts? Consequently, there was not a single army casualty and by far the vast majority of those killed were young farmers armed only with makeshift implements. These ARSA recruits were simply no match for the firepower of even the border patrol posts. And why did these attacks correspond with a big-time drug deal on October 9 [2016] and with the release of Kofi Annan's report [on August 25, 2017]? Why were the foreigners who purportedly were the organizers of the August 25 attack able to reside in Maungdaw for a year before the attacks without any interference from the authorities? Their presence was certainly conspicuous enough to warrant suspicion. The actual physical appearance of some newborn children is genetic proof of the presence of these foreigners. The memorandum of understanding in the Myanmar-Bangladesh document of repatriation agreement has a statement that orphans without parents will require certification from Bangladesh. Why would Myanmar accept these children? Why? If even people who've lived for decades may not be accepted by the government, why are these children of unknown parentage to be accepted? Why does this problem explode just as the Chinese are beginning their projects in Arakan?" These are some of the tough questions that Abu Tahay is pondering that are not easily answered.

Abu Tahay has spent more than three hours with me doing his best to educate me about the dynamics that may be unfolding in Arakan. On this occasion, I see a fear and lament in his eyes that I did not recognize before. Also, for the first time, I begin to feel genuinely the hopelessness of the Rohingya plight. My feelings would only get exacerbated in the days and months ahead.

The Elder Statesman

July 2015. U Kyaw Min is also a prominent Rohingya political leader in Yangon and nominal head of the relatively recently formed Democracy and Human Rights Party, a thoroughly Rohingya political enterprise. He was released from prison in 2012 after serving seven years for a trumped-up charge by the Tatmadaw for sedition. His daughter, Wai Wai Nu, who also served a seven-year prison sentence along with other members of Kyaw Min's family, is a political activist as well, having founded her own NGO (Women's Peace Network Arakan) in Yangon. Both have been mentioned and profiled in articles written by Hannah Beech for the *New York Times* and *The New Yorker*. The two are clearly at the forefront in Yangon to establish the Rohingya as a legitimate presence in Myanmar society and politics.

The term "Rohingya," of course, is highly contested. My good friend Jacques Leider, the leading historian of Arakan, in very comprehensive reviews and analyses of the origins, etymology, and historical deployment of the term,[1] has pointed out that the political use of the term dates to no earlier than the 1950s and its popularity or widespread usage only surfaces in the early 1990s. But Leider has also presented evidence for the considerable presence of Muslims in the precolonial Buddhist kingdom of Arakan (fifteenth to eighteenth century CE), traced the expansion of Muslim growth during the time of the British, narrated the history of oppression experienced by the community at the hands of Burma's military juntas (1962–2011), and commented on how this treatment dashed political aspirations for ethnic recognition yet at the same time fostered a process of shared identity. Leider has also discussed the creation of a Rohingya diaspora community as a result of the exodus out of Myanmar to Bangladesh, India, Pakistan, Saudi Arabia, and Malaysia, noting how these people abroad have reimagined their understanding of history and political awareness. He has chronicled the rise and fall of various Rohingya nationalist movements that had only slight impact in Myanmar but managed to keep aspirations alive. He notes, "Although Rohingya nationalists failed to gain recognition among ethnic and religious groups in Burma, they have attracted increasing international acknowledgment. For postdictatorial Myanmar (after 2011), the unresolved Rohingya issue became a huge international liability in 2017, when hundreds of

1. For a full assessment of the issue and relevant scholarly literature, see Leider 2013, pp. 204–255.

thousands fled to Bangladesh following military operations widely interpreted as ethnic cleansing."[2]

This kind of analysis is much to the chagrin of U Kyaw Min, who, while regarding Jacques Leider as a "teacher and friend," believes that he is biased—"in the hip pocket of the Arakanese Buddhists." When Wai Wai Nu originally learned of my friendship with Leider, she immediately became somewhat skeptical of my intentions. In fact, Jacques Leider is a distinguished scholar from Luxembourg who now serves the École Française d'Extrême-Orient as its director in Bangkok and had previously served the school as a director for four years in Chiang Mai. He took up a six-month post as a research consultant for the United Nations in Yangon in January 2015 after he had been a diplomat for Luxembourg in Bangkok for two years, serving interests related to Thailand, Myanmar, and Malaysia. His articles and books about the social, political, and religious history of Arakan are regarded by many scholars as the gold standard in Euro-American academic circles. It is through my personal and professional friendship with Leider that I was able to meet U Kyaw Min. Within a month after Leider's UN appointment, he had been assailed in the public press in Yangon by both sides of the Rohingya–Buddhist nationalist divide. Nationalists decried his work as inaccurate, insofar as he has argued, quite convincingly, for a profound Muslim presence in Arakan dating back to the beginning of the Mrauk U era in the fifteenth century. This is an important argument that unmasks the extreme historical position now taken by many Arakanese and Burmese Buddhist nationalists, who argue that the Bengali Muslims are simply "illegal recent border jumpers" from Bangladesh (many of whom, it is alleged by some, including the leading nationalist monk U Wirathu, have bribed Burmese border patrols to gain their way into Arakan from Bangladesh); another more charitable but only partially correct view of Rohingya movements into Arakan is that they were simply brought to Arakan by the British as laborers in the nineteenth and twentieth centuries. While migration under the British was an important part of the picture, and seasonal labor migrations seemed to have been a general pattern for many decades and perhaps even centuries, the presence of people ancestral to Rohingya dates beyond 1823, the date unilaterally selected by the dictatorial Ne Win government back in 1982 to establish a timeline for determining whether or not an ethnic group could be considered as indigenous or not.

As I noted in the introduction, the Myanmar government has been so sensitive, and perhaps confused, about the term "Rohingya" that they initially refused to take part in a conference called by Thailand in the spring of 2015 to address the problem of Rohingya boat people fleeing Bangladesh and Arakan in attempts to reach Muslim Malaysia. Pirates and human traffickers had been using the dense southern Thai forests to establish camps from which they either extorted

---

2. Jacques Leider, "Rohingya: The History of a Muslim Identity in Myanmar," in *Oxford Research Encyclopedia of Asian History*, edited by David Ludden, May 2018, http://oxfordre.com/asianhistory/view/10.1093/acrefore/9780190277727.001.0001/acrefore-9780190277727-e-115.

ransoms or sold Rohingya to other traffickers. The discovery of graves in remote southern Thailand of more than a hundred Rohingya victims caused an international outbreak of concern that embarrassed the Thai government and prompted the convocation of a meeting of representatives of Thailand, Myanmar, Indonesia, and Malaysia, as well as American observers. Myanmar refused to participate initially because the term "Rohingya" was used in the conference's designation. The Burmese insist on using "Bengali" when referring to the Rohingya.

Leider's problems with the two sides of the political divide gave rise to a sober discussion when we met in London for a conference of the Theravada Civilizations Project in early July 2016. How history is invented or remembered, of course, is always a contested issue when its political significance is brought to bear on the present. Anachronistic interpretations abound as rival visions seek to claim historical legitimation. Moreover, Leider's problem, I think, signals another important theoretical issue that plagues academia. That is, what we have come to understand as relatively, likely, or absolutely true in our academic research often has little chance of being clearly articulated or understood in the general public domain, and thus has an even more remote possibility of informing the production of constructive public policies. In any case, while we certainly don't know enough yet about Arakan's social and political history, let alone accurate specifics regarding its contemporary demography, economy, and social fabric, we can know reasonably well that Muslim ancestors of those who now call themselves Rohingya have constituted a specific, identifiable community for centuries in the region now known as the northern Rakhine State of Myanmar. The issue for Leider has been that the term "Rohingya" has designated a political community only since the 1950s. He does not deny a Muslim presence, but only that Muslims in Arakan have not used the term "Rohingya" for collective political self-designation before the 1950s.

It was precisely this issue that U Kyaw Min wanted to take up with me when he generously agreed to meet with me for the first time in the offices of his political party in July of 2015. His main point, one that he made emphatically at the outset, was that while the manner in which "Rohingya" itself was now being politically deployed may have actually originated in the 1950s, his people's constitutive ethnic identity greatly antedated this politicized usage. That is, people who have come to be known politically more recently as "Rohingya" have a long social, cultural, linguistic, and therefore historical legacy in what is now known as Rakhine State. Whether or not they were known specifically as Rohingya is somewhat beside this historical fact. U Kyaw Min did not want this issue to be covered over by an argument about mere contemporary designation. In this way, he was in complete conformity with Abu Tahay's position.

U Kyaw Min's offices were quietly located on a side street in an emerging middle- and working-class neighborhood of downtown Yangon, on the fourth floor of a decaying building whose address was difficult to locate, owing to the fact that the street addresses were not listed on buildings in a numerically consecutive fashion. I was hosted in a suite of rooms, one of which was used as a conference room, replete with a long table to accommodate up to fifteen or twenty people; another was a side room with a desk and chairs that served as a reception space for the party political leader. U Kyaw Min, now a distinguished-looking, stern, and yet intermittently genial presence, was joined by two affable assistants, including the party's secretary, who patiently listened to our conversation, a conversation that eventually devolved into what I took to be the basis of U Kyaw Min's standard public lecture. I was fortunate to receive the two-hour version and not just the fifteen-minute stump speech. This would be the first of several meetings we would have over the course of the next three and half years. I met with him every time I passed through Yangon.

I found U Kyaw Min to be passionate, sincere, but, like most politicians, sometimes prone to excited exaggeration in order to have his desired effect, which, in the end, was to motivate me to contact my congressional representatives back in America to make them aware of the Rohingya's awful plight. (Indeed, I confess that by the time U Kyaw Min finished with me on that first occasion, I was even more sympathetic to the Rohingya's condition than when I had first arrived in Myanmar, which is to say that I was genuinely appalled at how these people were treated by the Myanmar government in the aftermath of the Sittwe riot in June 2012. This was before the late 2016 and 2017 Myanmar army assaults on Rohingya villages in which thousands of men went missing or were murdered, hundreds of women were raped, and many innocent children were murdered in response to raids on border posts on October 9, 2016, and August 25, 2017.) U Kyaw Min probably agreed to spend his afternoon with me because he now thinks that the future of his people does not lie within the domestic political dynamics of Myanmar, as much as an election that resulted in a dramatic power shift to Aung San Suu Kyii's National League for Democracy would perhaps begin an amelioration process. Buddhist nationalists concede or assert this, despite the circumspect manner in which Suu Kyii had danced around the Rohingya issue. Rather, U Kyaw Min believes that the fate of the Rohingya lies with the "international community." As an "international denizen" known for writing critically, or, better, analytically, about historical change within Buddhist cultural contexts, I was worth the time to provide some explanations regarding fundamental issues and forces now in play that affect the Rohingya. When I mention that the Rohingya have already gained the support of the General Assembly of the United Nations, which has passed a resolution urging the Burmese government to grant citizenship to Rohingya, U Kyaw Min reminds me about how Ban Ki-moon, then secretary-general of the UN, was first vilified in street protests when he visited Sittwe in 2014 and, subsequently, how the UN's representative, or special rapporteur, Yanghee Lee, was verbally abused by U Wirathu for being a "whore" to Muslim interests. (Later, Aung San Suu Kyii's government would refuse to cooperate with Yanghee Lee, and her term as special rapporteur came to an unexpected end in early 2018.) U Kyaw Min avers that the UN is virtually a powerless organization and that the only international forces that can effect a significant change in the Rohingya's situation are the European Union and the United States. U Kyaw Min and the

Rohingya lobby had been attempting to link the Rohingya cause under the wider umbrella of American diplomatic efforts to woo the newly minted yet still military-dominated Burmese political establishment into reforms that guarantee democratic enfranchisement on the one hand and encourage Burmese economic engagement with an international community that is not so dominated by the Chinese, who, since the establishment of military junta governments after Ne Win, had turned Myanmar into a practical client state. Indeed, the continuing presence and influence of the Chinese in Myanmar are major issues for U Kyaw Min.

When I visited Myanmar in 2010 twice for a couple of months, I heard a good deal of griping about how the Chinese had come to dominate the national economy in Myanmar. I heard stories about how military generals had sold vast amounts of teak from central and northern Myanmar forests that had gone into the flooring and furniture of new condominiums being built throughout the cities of eastern China. In earlier years of living in Southeast Asia, I had seen whole mountainsides in northern Laos denuded in that context: members of the Communist Party, the only political party in Laos, had managed to sell off huge forest resources to Chinese interests. Often, Chinese workers had come into Laos to do the work themselves on behalf of Chinese business interests. Back in 2010, not only had I heard about similar events occurring in Myanmar, but huge infrastructural projects were in the making in which gas and oil would be funneled through pipelines being built starting on the Rakhine coast, Ramree Island to be specific, and culminating across the northern border with China. Critically minded Burmese regularly referred to the north-south divided highway in Myanmar as a "conduit" or "vacuum" for the Chinese to expropriate Myanmar's natural resources, including its precious gems of rubies and jade. In Mandalay, the increased numbers of Chinese business entrepreneurs were an obvious presence. Local fears of Chinese domination were being expressed by people from virtually all segments of society. The popular vision being articulated had the military selling off the country's wealth for their personal aggrandizement.

U Kyaw Min is of the view that not only were the interests of the United States allied with those of most of Myanmar's people in relation to loosening China's economic noose on Myanmar, but the current troubles between Buddhists and Muslims were part of a larger strategy concocted by the government to deflect criticism away from the government's collusion with Chinese business interests. I heard U Kyaw Min's view of this motivation expressed by other activist voices in Yangon as well. Not only did this spectacular eruption of alienation provide camouflage on the national level, but it also deflected Arakanese Buddhist alienation from the Burmese-dominated national government. U Kyaw Min anticipates my following question as to why this strategy is so compelling by asserting that "most of the ministers in the upper echelons of the government are partly of Chinese origins." A good deal of the political unrest in Arakan before the breakdown between Buddhists and Muslims was Arakanese anti-Chinese sentiment. The government, he avers, is a master at playing one group off against another. In this instance, criticism in Rakhine State of a central Myanmar government dominated by China and ethnic Burmese was deflected with the emergent preoccupation of the "Muslim problem." U Kyaw Min also suggests that Arakanese Buddhist political leaders are now being bribed to keep quiet about the continuing presence of Chinese business interests in Rakhine, especially the seaport and pipelines that would ensure a steady stream of gas and oil into China. (In fact, in 2018, there has been considerable grousing by Arakanese Buddhist interests about how they are being excluded from the benefits of the Chinese projects being put into place on the Arakan coast. In Sittwe, there is also grumbling about how a new port project to increase trade with India has been put into place without any benefit to Arakanese.)

U Kyaw Min is keen to point out how historical fears of India were also an important factor in the psyche of the Arakanese Buddhists. I found this a fascinating discussion. On the one hand, one of the central foundation myths of the Arakanese concerns how the construction of the famous Mahamuni image, spirited away from Mrauk U to Mandalay (where it now resides as perhaps the most highly venerated of all Buddha images in Burmese religious culture), at the time of the Burmese disestablishment of the Arakan kingdom in the late eighteenth century, is itself regarded as a physical likeness to the historical Buddha, who allegedly visited Arakan during one of his *dhamma* (teaching) tours; insofar as the establishment of Buddhism is linked to the origins of the Arakanese Buddhists as a community, there are obviously very tight mythic or primordial connections with India. On the other hand, there are historically more recent reasons for why India, more precisely the presence of people of Indian origins (meaning Hindus *and* Muslims) causes apprehension. I ask U Kyaw Min if the general "dis-ease" historically about the presence of "Indians" has not been a "feeding factor" in how the Rohingya in particular, and Muslims in general, are now being regarded as such significant "others." He nods affirmatively.

That religion remains the most important factor in dividing people in the contemporary scene, according to U Kyaw Min, is seen rather dramatically in the fact that "Buddhist Rohingya," as he refers to the Magh[3] people in Sittwe, were not attacked in the waves of violence that swept through the region once the original trouble had broken out in 2012. U Kyaw Min is adamant in making this point regarding how centrally important religious identity is for the Burmese and Arakanese. When I mention this point in hope of corroborating it with the views of other scholars working in Yangon, it is pointed out to me that this argument is a bit strained, insofar as the community in question certainly does not understand itself as "Rohingya" at all. These are "Bengali Buddhists" who come from the Chittagong hill-track region in Bangladesh west of the Rakhine State–Myanmar border, which has for long been part and parcel of Arakanese Buddhist culture. They also speak a form of Bengali that separates them from both the Rohingya and the Arakanese. Some of them have been

3. Magh refers to Arakanese Buddhists who had previously migrated to the Chittagong hill tracts of Bangladesh. Some of these people eventually returned to Rakhine State.

resettled in northern Arakan at the behest of the Myanmar government to help deflect the increasing percentage of Rohingya living in the area.

As the hours of conversation unfold, U Kyaw Min dominates more and more of the flow so that the occasion becomes more of a lecture than a give-and-take resulting from question and answer. That is just fine with me. I am interested in trying to register U Kyaw Min's voice, a voice that becomes increasingly impassioned as he characterizes the current plight of the Rohingya in Arakan. He says his community had been abandoned by the British in the final negotiations for independence, this in spite of the fact that Rohingya had fought for the British during World War II, so that the problems for Muslims arose only in the wake of the country's political independence. This initial "abandonment" had contributed to the eventual difficulties the Rohingya encountered in claiming a space in the newly declared independent country. Following their total eclipse of official existence during the Ne Win–promulgated law determining 135 ethnic identities in 1982, almost all the traditional Rohingya roadside sellers of fruits and vegetables, of betel and coconut, et cetera, had been displaced. Unemployment among Rohingya now stands at a staggering 35 percent. Hundreds of mosques have also been abandoned. Compounding this dismal social and economic situation, the illiteracy rate among Rohingya stands at about 80 percent.

Having asserted these conditions, U Kyaw Min goes on to say how ridiculous the claims of Buddhist nationalists have become in asserting that Rohingya are part of an international jihadist conspiracy to seize control of Myanmar. "How can people who can't read or write, who work largely in a state of subsistence, be expected to entertain sophisticated religious and political philosophies?" In my own brief experiences of observing Rohingya within village contexts north of Sittwe and south of Mrauk U, I can only heartily agree with his assessment. These are abjectly poor people barely scratching out a living along the river however they may, hardly the stuff out of which madrasas nourish radical jihadists. The resistance that later emerged in Maungdaw and Buthidaung in October 2016 and August 2017 was born of a variety reasons having to do with abject oppression, and not of attraction to Muslim revolutionary jihadist ideologies, if, indeed, the resistance was not itself somehow orchestrated by the Myanmar Tatmadaw, a view advanced by U Kyaw Min in a later conversation, one shared, as I have noted, by Abu Tahay.

As U Kyaw Min launches into the conclusion of his presentation, he talks about the contemporary situation for the internally displaced people whose conditions have reified into permanence. I had asked almost everyone I encountered in Yangon about what the future held for the people in the camps, especially the camp just outside of Sittwe containing more than one hundred thousand people. I had been told that conditions were getting better, that the adjective "squalid" was now somewhat over-the-top, that enough aid from international NGOs was now reaching the camps so that the edge of desperation had now been somewhat blunted. I was also told by a militant monk in Yangon that so much aid was now reaching the Rohingya that some of it was winding up in local markets to be sold and then used for "jihadist activities."

What U Kyaw Min is interested in establishing is a comparison of the Rohingya plight to that of Palestinians on the West Bank, people who are walled off in their existence and in need of passes to get from one place to another beyond their designated camps. He talks about how a minor business had sprung up close to the camps in which passes had been sold like tickets or fees for people to get out. He also tells me that my best bet at gaining access to these camps, since I don't work for the UN or an NGO and since I'm not a journalist, is to pay a "fee" to the local Sittwe police, who could then escort me into the camp. Beyond this, however, he is interested, in conclusion, in quoting how the visiting Nobel Peace Prize laureate Rev. Desmond Tutu of South Africa had described the plight of the Rohingya as "apartheid," or how the Hungarian American financier George Soros had compared the Rohingya condition with his own youth in the Budapest ghetto of the early 1940s.

I came away from this session somewhat wistful about how this kind of suffering could be so publicly perpetrated, and yet so poorly understood not only domestically in Myanmar, but internationally as well. Yes, U Kyaw Min had a powerful message, but one that essentially was contingent on "uploading" local political situations into an international playing field. Yes, the Rohingya are hardly "jihadists," but the IDPs in Rakhine State are not enduring concentration-camp types of existences either. It struck me that perhaps Desmond Tutu's description of their condition as a type of apartheid was far more apt, insofar as Rohingya were now disenfranchised people politically and were being forced to live separately, without benefit of state security guarantees. In some ways, their situation could get worse if the more radical sections of the Buddhist nationalists have their way in deporting all of them. At the time, in 2015, I just couldn't imagine the events of post–August 25, 2017.

As I said, I came away sobered by my first meeting with U Kyaw Min. He gave me the names of several people to contact in Sittwe and even had his party colleagues place a call or two on my behalf. He then had our pictures taken, and I wondered if I would end up in the near future being shown as a sympathetic supporter on Facebook or some such organ of social media now becoming the chief means of passing information in Myanmar. Frankly, I didn't quite care, as I also felt somewhat honored to be in the presence of people who were so genuinely committed to a worthy cause in the face of such daunting and depressing political odds. I worried about their hopes—how dependent they had become on thinking that somehow the European Union and the United States would successfully champion their causes and thereby force the hand of a Myanmar government to recognize Rohingya as fully fledged citizens in a contemporary climate laced with fear, misconception, and ignorance. I didn't want to quote to him the well-worn adage "all politics are local," or tell him that my feeling that all of this "uploading" into the imagined constructions of the international geopolitical dynamic was part of the problem and not its solution.

I meet U Kyaw Min again six months later, on **December 31, 2015,** after the election in which Aung San Suu Kyii's National League for Democracy swept

80 percent of the seats in the parliament and was to begin sitting officially in March 2016. Aung San Suu Kyii had remained circumspect about the Rohingya problem and the extreme positions taken by the Buddhist nationalist monks and their government supporters. No Muslims, including U Kyaw Min and Abu Tahay, had been allowed to contest in the general elections. In many of those seats that Muslims would surely have won, the NLD ran its own candidates and easily defeated any candidates from the Union Solidarity and Development Party (USDP), the military's proxy party, the party that had dominated the first democratically elected parliament in 2010, an election that the NLD had boycotted owing to the rigged nature of the 2008 constitution. U Kyaw Min had been elected in 1990 from his own constituency in Buthidaung in an alliance with Aung San Suu Kyii. He had served, he surmised, seven years in prison because of his association with her. He remained quite guarded about hopes that the situation would now improve dramatically in light of the recent NLD election victory.

I begin by asking him about the immediate Sittwe situation, in which more than one hundred thousand Rohingya remained in IDP camps. He tells me that before the election he met with an adviser to President Thein Sein who was interested in developing interfaith dialogue. But interfaith dialogue does not mean that the situation for the Rohingya in detention camps will change. From the presidential adviser, U Kyaw Min learned that Thein Sein had no will, political or otherwise, to solve the Rohingya's problem and seemed content to keep the status quo. The idea of his government seems to have been to just let the Rohingya population dwindle and atrophy. This stance in other quarters was known as the "Arakanese action plan"—meaning basically no action. Moreover, there was no attempt to discourage the Rohingya from making dangerous attempts to escape from Myanmar by sea. Government officials said that Rakhine State was calm and tranquil and so it might be a mistake to introduce any change. U Kyaw Min responds to this by asking, "What about the education of children? What about the people's health care? How long can these internally displaced people live on help that comes from the outside? This current plight is little more than a prison for the people." The fundamental question, or the fundamental problem, he states, remains the assertion that the identity of the Rohingya is understood by the government and the Buddhist nationalist monks as simply "Bengali."

While the National League for Democracy won in a landslide nationally, the Arakan National Party won firmly in Rakhine State because of its strength in the northern region of the state. The southern part of Rakhine that includes Thandwe had voted for the NLD. It was being bandied about, but never realized, that the Arakan Army, a small militant armed group that had engaged in skirmishes with the Burmese military, could possibly be invited to participate in the so-called Panglong talks that Aung San Suu Kyii had proposed to end the civil wars, though continued skirmishes indicated that this remains far from certain. These skirmishes also indicated a partial divide between the aspirations of the NLD-led parliament and the Tatmadaw. The local ANP would continue to take a hard line against "the Bengalis" and keep them confined, says U Kyaw Min. "If these politicians can gain the chief minister position and can form the state government," which he thinks is quite likely, then they would persecute and continue to suppress the Rohingya as "illegal people." In fact, in the following months the NLD appointed its own chief minister, though this did not mitigate the vituperative Rakhine Buddhist rhetoric against the Rohingya. U Kyaw Min stresses that the Rohingya outside of Maungdaw and Buthidaung are thoroughly enculturated into Rakhine culture. They speak their own dialect, which is not exactly the Bengali of either Dhaka or Chittagong, but most also speak Arakanese.

Since the early 1990s, the Rohingya have not been allowed to move into other townships. These restrictions on movement were put into place in the post–Ne Win era by the State Law and Order Restoration Council (SLORC). The Rohingya's stateless stature, their so-called illegal status, was an invention of this particular government. The government fomented the perspective that the Rohingya were a threat to the country. So the beginning of the "siege mentality" among the Burmese in relation to the Rohingya dates to this particular time and represents a historic shift in perspective. And, as U Kyaw Min reiterates, it is in fantastic juxtaposition to the situation in the pre-Burmese Arakanese kingdom, where U Kyaw Min claims the Muslims dominated the court and military. "These Muslims had spoken Bengali and Persian. And these had been the official languages of the court. So during the time of the Rakhine kings, the relations between Buddhists and Muslims were harmonious." While the Rohingya situation began to get dire in the early 1990s, the first serious tensions arose as part of the general anti-Indian sentiments during the last days of the British in the 1940s. What was going on in Bamar regions, particularly urban Yangon and Mandalay, had then spread into Rakhine, and the Buddhist Rakhine politicians took up the cause in Arakan against the Rohingya. Meanwhile, Indians trying to flee the country couldn't pass through Arakan to escape, in part because of Arakanese Buddhist militancy but also because of the presence of the Burma Independence Army. This army, eventually led by General Aung San, in 1941–1942 killed thousands of Karen and Indians attempting to flee Myanmar, a little-known fact to history that besmirches Aung San's heroic stature as a culture hero or father to the country in contemporary Myanmar. The situation in Rakhine became calm again when the British returned. The problem now is the result of Rakhine Buddhist politicians who do not want to share power. The Ne Win government was responsible for putting policies (the 1982 law) into place. Prime Minister U Nu had established the Mayu Frontier Administration, which was essentially administered by the Defense Ministry from 1961 to 1965, when all administrators were military. This was a good period for the Rohingya. "But the creation of Bangladesh in 1971 had caused Ne Win to change his perspective," says U Kyaw Min. "The Arakanese feared that the Rohingya would come to power. It was at this time that local Arakanese Buddhist leaders began talking about revoking the citizenship of the Rohingya. First Ne Win introduced restrictions on movement and public employment, business restrictions, and denial of Rohingya identity was asserted. In 1978 there were indiscriminate offenses against Rohingya people, terrorizing them—burnings, extortions, even rapes of women."

It used to be that the Burmese army would protect the Muslims because they knew that the Rakhine Buddhists were very aggressive. But what has happened recently is a shift in the military's disposition. For two decades there has been a situation where government bureaucrats are taught that the Rohingya are a danger to society and must be removed from Rakhine State. "The main strategy now is simply to get rid of Rohingya from Rakhine state." According to Kyaw Min, before 1971 the Rohingya may have been a majority in northern Rakhine State. "In the 1973 census, the government did not count all of the Rohingya and they still numbered one-third. They showed only two hundred thousand when in fact there were four hundred thousand in Maungdaw and Buthidaung. The Rohingya could easily win twelve or thirteen seats from Maungdaw, Buthidaung, Sittwe, Mrauk U, and so forth, at least one third of the seats in the Arakan Parliament and in local government. The NLD would have taken the majority if Muslims had been allowed to vote, but the NLD feared the Rakhine. There are high-level associates of Aung San Suu Kyii who have made comments in which they refer to the Rohingya as 'Bengalis.' Aung San Suu Kyii appears to have changed her perspective out of fear of the Rakhines." U Kyaw Min's worry is that Rakhine State will be controlled by Buddhist extremists who will intimidate the NLD to maintain the 1982 law brought into being by Ne Win, who initiated it after he had accepted three hundred thousand Rohingya refugees from Bangladesh. From this time, the Rohingya have been degraded as a community.

As intriguing as this historical lecture has become, I want to shift the discussion to the contemporary situation before all of my time with U Kyaw Min has lapsed. I manage to interrupt him and say that in Sri Lanka, the militant and anti-Muslim Bodu Bala Sena has been largely quiet since the January 2015 elections, which swept Mahinda Rajapaksa and his chauvinist Buddhist allies out of power. I want to know whether the wind has similarly been taken out of the sails of the Ma Ba Tha since the NLD election victory. U Kyaw Min replies that "it's going to take ten to fifteen years for this Buddhist nationalism to abate, but the Ma Ba Tha cannot make serious trouble without government backing. Because the NLD is not firmly established yet, they have to be very careful in the steps that they take. It will take time to disestablish the four race and religion laws, as Aung San Suu Kyii has to move carefully so as not to aggravate the military."

It was still his hope that through the US and UN urging of the Burmese government some progress could be made in terms of the release of so many Rohingya from their confinement in IDP camps. "They can mitigate but can't solve the problem by simply 'urging.'"

For Kyaw Min, one of the fundamental problems of the then current situation was that the government bureaucrats were those who were raised up by the military, and they will give Aung San Suu Kyii a difficult time in processing any new policies or laws enacted by the now NLD-dominated parliament. "The senior bureaucrats are former military personnel. These people do not understand democracy. They only understand that they are ruling the country. They don't have a critical sense of how the military have ruined the economy and culture of the country over the past five decades."

U Kyaw Min genuinely fears for the future existence of Rohingya. The current NLD government, unfortunately, will make it very difficult for the Rohingya problem to be addressed, this despite the fervent hope that change would be ushered in by Suu Kyii. U Kyaw Min adds that because Suu Kyii did not look into what happened to him personally, and more or less brushed him off when he sought an audience with her after the two were released, he doesn't have a lot of optimism. He relates how a security adviser to President Obama told him that Aung San Suu Kyi "will handle" the situation. But Suu Kyii once said in 2012 while she was in India that Rohingya were from India or Bangladesh. She has said that the problem "will be handled by law." But now that means the 1982 discriminatory law promulgated by the dictator Ne Win! It is simply not acceptable because it ignores the claims of the Rohingya that they have a right to citizenship status. He goes on to say that Aung San Suu Kyii will try to evade the issue unless she is pressured by international forces in the coming years. She will press the Rohingya to accept Bengali identity. She says she is no longer a human rights activist these days but now a politician, which means that her integrity is at stake. U Kyaw Min points out how ironic this is, because Suu Kyii's grandfather on her mother's side was Indian. He then points out that the famous former UN secretary-general U Thant had Rohingya ancestors. In his book *The River of Lost Footsteps,* U Thant's grandson Thant Myint-U mentions that his ancestry is not from Pagan or Mandalay, but rather that one ancestor (the grandfather of his grandfather U Thant) came from the Sittwe Muslim community.

U Kyaw Min, like the venerable U Kyaw Hla Aung, who is the most articulate spokesperson for the Rohingya detained in the Sittwe IDP camp, worries about how the Rohingya now lack intellectual leaders because they've been largely denied university education for such a long time—decades. U Kyaw Min wants to have a grassroots movement to help foment conceptions of religion that are not fundamentalist—as most Rohingya are illiterate. Almost all Rohingya know nothing about al-Qaeda, ISIS, and the like. He sent one hundred books to Maungdaw, but very few Rohingya can read, and all these books had to be sent to his own home in Buthidaung, where they are now kept. He firmly believes, at that moment following the NLD's decisive election victory at the end of 2015, that Muslim fundamentalism will not take root in Myanmar.

The long afternoon is taking its toll on U Kyaw Min and he begins to wax nostalgic about his country, despite the crisis facing his community. He relates that he remains happy culturally in Myanmar and does not aspire to be living anyplace else. If there could be peace here, all the Rohingya who had left for abroad would return. He says that it is simply a matter of being treated equally. Almost all foreigners had to leave Myanmar since, that is, between

1948 and 1962. But seventy years after independence, it would be a real problem for Rohingya to have to leave. Where could they possibly go?

He begins to talk historically again. His grandfather's great-grandfather had been in Arakan fighting during the time of the British takeover in the 1820s.

As it is getting late, I vow to collect more of his personal story when I return in several months. For now, I try to channel his thoughts toward Sittwe, where I am headed. He tells me to see the beautiful mosque (the Central Mosque; see cover photo) adjacent to Rakhine State Museum in Sittwe, a museum that I was to find totally bereft of any references to a Muslim presence in the past. Indeed, the mosque was resplendent.

July 2016. On my next visit to Yangon, U Kyaw Min warmly welcomes me for a third time, this time to his new party headquarters. He begins by wanting to talk history again, very broadly, with his point basically being that Rohingya historically identified themselves as Muslims first, in the same way that all Muslims have done historically. He talks about how the original royal palace in Mrauk U was built of the same brick by the same construction workers who built the nearby mosque, and mentions that the courtiers of that time were largely Muslims who spoke Persian and Bengali and functioned as the interpreters and liaisons for the court, the link to the international community of the time. (I'm having a difficult time directing the meeting toward issues I had hoped to discuss—it's classroom time for history again . . . but that's okay.) The lecture's punch line is that Rohingya can call themselves Rohingya, a reference to the current controversy that involves the American embassy's recent assertion that minority peoples can refer to themselves however they wish. (We're interrupted by two young politicos who give Kyaw Min an invitation and in return receive a position paper of the Democracy and Human Rights Party, of which Kyaw Min, of course, is the chair.)

U Kyaw Min understands that now I have been to Sittwe twice. And he's impressed that I made my way into the large IDP camp where more than a hundred thousand Rohingya, mostly from Sittwe, are marooned. He talks about how bitter the Arakanese Buddhist nationalists are. I recount to him a corroborating note about my experience of listening to the rants of a very articulate English-speaking monk in Sittwe. He points out that many of the monks in the Ma Ba Tha are Arakanese and says that here in Yangon, about a third of the monks are Arakanese. Part of the reason is the economic condition in Rakhine and lack of alternatives, so even monks migrate out of the depressing socioeconomic scene in Sittwe. Indeed, the monk I had just referred to had decamped to Yangon by the next time I tried to find him.

I am determined to learn more about U Kyaw Min's past, to find the human behind the self-consumed politician. He understands and begins simply: "I was born in Buthidaung on March 19, Monday, in 1945. The propaganda of the Arakanese and Burmese governments in the last two decades has been so intense that many Westerners believe that Rohingya leaders come from Bangladesh. But the root of my family is in Mrauk U and goes back to the Burmese invasion. There was an insurrection against the Burmese due to many reasons but chiefly due to Arakanese refusal to accept Burmese hegemony. Most of the Muslims fled. Between 1785 and 1824 there were several insurrections against the Burmese. Perhaps more than two hundred thousand people fled to Bengal (both Muslims and Rakhine Buddhists). My ancestors did not go to Bengal but settled in the present Buthidaung area, which they found safer. The civil war that ensued was only in 'inner Arakan.' Seven generations past, my ancestors were in the Myanmar army. Most Rakhine collaborated with the British in the First Anglo-Burmese War, culminating in 1824, thinking that they would gain their country back. That was why the Burmese had to recruit Muslims from the Arakan side. My ancestor was one of those recruits. This gave me an intrinsic sense of belonging to Rakhine history. Many Muslims were skilled in martial arts at that time. Sittwe, along with Moulmein (now Mawlamyine), became the British 'headquarters.' Under the British, my fifth-generation great-grandfather became a village headman [a combination of collector and local administrative power]. This village headmanship (*thugyi*) has passed down through the generations to my eldest brother, after independence, when some form of popular consent was also added. That is why I think I have a natural taste for politics.

"My father died when I was very young, but my elder brother, by twenty years, taught me about the art of politics. He mentored me by always asking political questions. Often, he would correct me, especially during the time of U Nu and parliamentary politics [1948–1962]. We used to go hear the parliamentarians' speeches when they would campaign. While I cannot recall the substantive issues, I got a vision of political culture from these experiences. Minister Sultan Mahmud from Buthidaung became a role model for me. He was very charismatic as a speaker. Indeed, I took a law degree at the University of Rangoon in order to prepare for politics. I graduated at the time of Ne Win in 1968, during his full power. His power was absolute.

"I was very critical of Ne Win's socialistic scheme and the politics of discrimination that was gradually introduced. On paper, it seemed that socialism would be evenhanded. But because it was based on the welfare of the Bamar, it was discriminatory against everyone else. Ne Win crushed all intellectual life. He raised a lot of lowly, uneducated people to power. Those who came to power did not enjoy the respect of the masses. Many retired army people were given positions as governmental departmental heads and judicial authority. I could see what was happening and was quite dismayed, disgusted with the existing administrative and political culture of the country. I became cynical about law at that time and thought I had made a mistake by studying law. My knowledge was obsolete in that contemporary context.

"At that time, around 1970, the Burmese government began to fear Pakistan and perhaps their intentions to take part of Arakan [the Muslim-dominated part of Rakhine State by the border]. The Myanmar generals developed a good relation with the Pakistani generals so as not to spoil each other's political advantages in their respective states. Occasionally, Pakistani officials would express concern about the welfare of Muslims in Rakhine State. So discriminatory measures against Muslims in Arakan were not very harsh, though they did exist. The situation was tolerable. I was in Arakan at that time. Muslims were not recruited into the socialist program. From 1971, the discrimination was intensified, I think as a result of the fallout from the birth of Bangladesh. The Burmese thought that the Bangladeshi army was weak and so they began to act with more impunity. This really disturbed me and I wanted to take part in any kind of antisocialist activities that were afoot. I participated in the movement headed by U Nu for the reestablishment of parliamentary democracy. U Nu's headquarters was in Bangkok. After a few years, we had to give up the campaign because the direction was headed toward a bloody confrontation. U Nu didn't want bloodshed. Without the cooperation of the minority people in the borderlands [Shan, Karen, and Mon, et cetera], the movement, he realized, would not be successful. Because U Nu was Burmese, this was not about to happen. He wouldn't abide by the demands of the minority peoples, even though he needed them if he were to succeed.

"In 1988, the antisocialist movement arose. I was persuaded by the movement, though I did fear the reaction of the government. But I got involved anyway. Within a short period of time, I was discharged from my job as the principal of the high school in Buthidaung, a job I had held for four years. I had been a teacher and also the deputy township education officer, and twelve years as a senior school teacher of economics and English, and sometimes history. This encouraged me to become a full-time politician and to take part in the election. At that time, I remembered my old inspiration of Sultan Mahmud and was encouraged by my friends to pursue the political path. I became the cofounder the National Democratic Party for Human Rights and was nominated as a candidate for parliament. I won with 75 percent of the vote. Seven other candidates contested from several different parties. My family background, personal integrity, and my experience in education had led to my support.

"After the election I came to Rangoon. I took part in political activities involving NLD parliamentarians. We also had contact with UN groups and the International Labour Organization. But our electoral victories were never honored and a new government was never formed. After fifteen years of working with small shops selling medicines and also selling construction materials, I got arrested for associating with these labor groups. Finally, I joined CRPP (Committee Representing People's Parliament—an alternative in response to the military's refusal to recognize election results). At this time many harsh restrictions were placed on Rohingya, especially the personal movement from village to village. My presence as a Rohingya made me stand out as a target for SLORC. I was also attending a training course in English at the American Center (which also involved readings of political theory). This was an extra reason for being targeted. This happened in 2005. Within a short time, I was arrested and jailed for forty-seven plus eight years. (The eight years was imposed if I did not pay a fine of hundreds of thousands of kyats.) I tried not to pay the fine. They also intimidated my relatives and other people following my case. They confiscated my properties as payment for the fine. Within one month of my arrest, my family members (wife, son, and two daughters) were also arrested and sentenced to seventeen years. I had been in Rangoon and I was also charged with not observing documentation for movement from Arakan to Yangon.

"Life in prison was hell. For the first six months, I thought I would get out in a short period of time. But I was not allowed any visitors and I could not sleep at night from the mosquitoes. Only half an hour or so could I sleep in the mornings when the mosquitoes abated. The water you drink from the jail wells was not clean. The food was basically boiled beans and boiled vegetables and a fish paste. I ate to survive. After six months I was given a mosquito net and visitors were allowed. My relatives would bring me dried food that could last half a month. After a year, I got purified water and my health improved. I was in the Insein Prison for the first three years, so I was allowed to see my family members once a month. When I was transferred to Myingyan I had an iron chain attached to my legs for three months. But I also made some political friends and became familiar with the prison staff, including intelligence personnel (senior military officials). The food was a lot better and the situation made it more comfortable. Still, I developed a number of ailments, including a gall bladder infection. (After my release I had to go to Bangkok for two operations, one for gall bladder removal and the other for spinal cord compression.) Many people thought I would not be cured from these ailments, but I was. And I can do full-time politics.

"In 2012, January 12, we were all released. After my release, some of my colleagues and friends and pupils approached me to take part in politics again, to found the Democracy and Human Rights Party. After contemplation, I agreed and applied for the registration of this party. After one year, we got registration. (In retrospect, I am surprised and don't know why the government permitted us.) Even so, the Union Election Commission is not happy with us and gives us a lot of restrictions. We could not take part in the by-elections of 2012. In 2015, we applied to run for eighteen seats (fifteen in Rakhine and three in Yangon), but we were rejected in each case because we could not demonstrate that some of the parents of our candidates were Myanmar citizens. In my case, they gave no explanation—just 'according to election law, you are not eligible.' When I appealed, no reason was given when they upheld my denial."

January 2017. By now Kyaw Min greets me as if I am an old friend and makes a point of saying that it looks to him like I have been eating too much rice. He says he has the same problem and also is suffering from a hip problem that will require surgery. He is headed to Bangkok the next day for this procedure. I am really lucky to catch him this time as I am coming through Yangon. He is clearly physically uncomfortable.

I begin by asking, now that Aung San Suu Kyii has visited the White House during the waning weeks of Barack Obama's presidency and has succeeded in getting all of the remaining economic sanctions against Myanmar lifted, and Donald Trump has been elected, what are his thoughts? He grumbles about this, saying something to the effect that some of the Ma Ba Tha monks would have been pleased with Trump's victory. He is clearly depressed and tells me that the situation for the Rohingya is now so grim that he has given up all positive hope.

I ask him how long it has been since the Rohingya have been denied education. Is it just in Rakhine? He answers, "Since 1992–1993. Professional institutes [technical, agricultural, et cetera] are not allowed. Some have bribed their ways. In 1995, there were some exceptions [given] to highly qualified individuals who secured permissions from senior bureaucrats. From 2003, there was a quarrel between Buddhists and Muslims in Sittwe. From that time, ordinary students were restricted from Maungdaw and Buthidaung. It is from 2012 that not a single Rohingya has been allowed to attend Sittwe University, even if they are from Sittwe. The present problem is that our democracy icon has joined the military generals. She says we need time to solve the Rohingya problem. But the situation is desperate *now*. She has truly become 'a general's daughter.' She told John Kerry that the Rohingya issue should be kept in perspective. What is the meaning of 'perspective'? What she means is that she has many different aspects to consider and that she 'needs time and space,' which is what she told ASEAN representatives in Singapore a few months back too. The way they are dealing in time is actually giving time to allow the Arakanese Buddhists and military to eliminate the Rohingya in Arakan. But she is our last hope, so we can't criticize her in public." I mention that she is being criticized internationally increasingly, including by several former Noble Peace Prize laureates, the Dalai Lama and Desmond Tutu among them, to the UN Security Council. He says vehemently, "She shouldn't be simply criticized; she should be utterly condemned. Because the government bureaucracy is so entrenched in opposition to the Rohingya, she is simply acquiescing. Our problem is that our last hope, Aung San Suu Kyii, is not going to materialize. We had hoped, at least a little. She has said that this 'will be settled according to the law.' This means the 1982 law. If she doesn't try to solve our problem, she should be stripped of her Nobel Peace Prize."

I decide to ask about the significance of the October 9 border incident out in northern Arakan from his perspective. How is this going to change the equation in Rakhine? Kyaw Min says, "It's still not completely clear who did what to whom on October 9. But it seems to have resulted in the grass roots of Rohingya people in Maungdaw being terrorized and wanting to flee out of the country. That may have been, indeed, the objective of the October 9 drama. This was an area that was well defended by the Myanmar military and yet they were attacked by some fellows who had only machetes. About two hundred people are said to have participated in the attack. It's not easy for two hundred people to avoid the century towers of the border guard headquarters. The nine killed police personnel were never shown to the public. The head of the border guard police force headquarters was not present when the attack occurred. The police report and the president's report were also at variance. Lots of drugs cross at this border and the presidential press conference pointed to the drug mafia connection. Akmal Mujaheen are a group we had never heard of before. Zaw Htay, the government spokesman, said it was the work of a group called 'movement of Faith' [Harket-al Yaquin]. These are also new."

I ask if he is of the view that this clearance operation that led to seventy-five thousand Rohingya fleeing across the Bangladesh border in the face of unspeakable cruelties inflicted on them by the Myanmar Tatmadaw was a ruse to assert power in Maungdaw. Kyaw Min says, "The Rohingya diaspora is currently starting a movement and is thinking to do something, that is true—groups in Saudi Arabia, Pakistan, and Bangladesh." But he also thinks that the Harket-al Yaquin might have been invented by the Myanmar government. "Once the villagers are burned out, as people leave, the government has said that these people cannot come back to their villages unless they accept national verification cards [NVCs]. It is just a card that gives evidence that the person who holds it is living in Myanmar during a verification process or period. This is the strategy of the government: to give Rohingya this liminal status. All legal documents have already been taken from Rohingya, and this verification card really has no leverage. People have not cooperated with this scheme, except only those who have serious problems and need travel permits have agreed to take it. Actually, only about six thousand people in the entire state have agreed, out of 1 million. At this time Suu Kyii's government is trying to get people to accept this card. It is a big conspiracy. Twenty-five years ago [1992], all NRCs [national registration cards] were seized from the public and replaced by temporary registration cards. At the time, the head of the immigration office had promised that within six months to a year, permanent identity cards would be issued. It hasn't happened yet. The NVC is not even that. How have these people been living for at least seventy years in this area? Have they been given any residency documents? The problem is that most people don't have these kinds of documents. The government can't expel all the Rohingya at once, so they are taking their time via this NVC scheme. The government is planning to settle new groups of people in Maungdaw in place of Rohingya villagers. Some poor Burmese and prisoners are being mobilized. Cows, seeds for crops, and housing are provided to them. Many are Rakhine Buddhists from Bangladesh seeking to come back. Indonesia and Turkey have provided a lot of money for refugee resettlement that has been diverted for this purpose along the 'road for indigenous people,' a road that stretches eighty kilometers along the mountain range from Sittwe to the border. Around seventy thousand are now driven from their villages."

I ask him whether he can have any hope from the Kofi Annan Commission appointed by Suu Kyii in August to make recommendations about the situation in Arakan. Kyaw Min says, "I think he will try to bring a peaceful solution, but Aung San Suu Kyii will not implement it. She did this just to mollify the Westerners." Since then, the commission had issued its interim report, in which they recommended that the IDP camps be disbursed. However, the lingering problem is that approximately 120,000 Rohingya in these camps have no place to return to, an issue that has yet to be even admitted by the government. Kyaw Min says that he was invited to meet with the commission but he was not well at the time. But he had already presented what has happened and what the Rohingya aspiration is in five different written documents to the commission.

He continues to think that unless the international community gets directly involved, "our issue will have no solution."

U Kyaw Min then returns to the problem of October 9. He says that many Rohingya actually expected some kind of attack would occur soon because there had been decades of repression to contend with. But in the last analysis, this was not an attack led by any real Rohingya leaders. It was contrived by the military, at least the incredible response by the military to take advantage of the situation. Aung San Suu Kyii simply doesn't know this. "Unless the UN has direct involvement in the future, there is no solution. The power will remain in the hands of the military, who oppose the Rohingya entirely. In Maungdaw, it is openly being said that the Rohingya must be reduced to a minority because they are a threat to national security. The military has to be shown that this just can't be done. The UN has to comprehend the real cause of the problem, or all Rohingya will end up in Bangladesh!" At the time, the UN flash report based on 220 interviews with Rohingya refugees who had fled to Bangladesh following the October 9 attack (OHCHR 2017) had not yet been issued. I did not see Kyaw Min for about five months after this report was issued. He had not read the document, so I sent it to him at the end of July 2017, and I am quite sure he was as horrified as he was depressed when he read it.

"We need America's help," he tells me. But I raise the specter of Donald Trump to what sounds like a desperate reflexive plea. I hate to be negative, but I know that no help is going to come from an American administration led by Donald Trump. Indeed, the stereotypes about Muslims in America are having to be confronted in our courts to prevent Trump from banning Muslims from visiting or immigrating to America. I hate telling Kyaw Min that I am not optimistic that my country will be a source of help to the Rohingya. "It's a very desperate situation," he says. "Before the British, we're in sync; during the British times there is no problem of this nature; it's only after independence that the problem begins to arise. Before the problems arose, Rohingya were able to occupy positions in all government departments. But gradually 'the screw has been tightening.' At present, there isn't a single Rohingya government official. Still there are some schoolteachers in Buthidaung." When Kyaw Min was a schoolteacher in the 1970s and 1980s, 85 percent of the teachers were Muslims. Now only 5 percent are. "Since Rakhine Buddhists won't teach Rohingya teachers, education has been virtually paralyzed for Rohingya. Some Rohingya are taking tuition-based classes. The result is that all education is segregated. Hospitals also remain segregated. Rohingya cannot expect to come back alive from the hospital. Most of the pregnant women who are having difficulties with childbirth who enter a hospital in northern Arakan will probably die, as will their children. There is no doctor in or around the refugee camps, and the last resort is the government hospital. We need the INGOs [international nongovernmental organizations] to raise these issues with government."

I ask him his opinion regarding President Obama's lifting of the last sanctions. "Aung San Suu Kyii was very clever and did this to try to counteract the Chinese. But Obama ended up losing any leverage the Americans had left.

Wai Wai [Kyaw Min's daughter] met Obama along with many other young Muslims at the same dinner table. He promised to help make sure that Rohingya would be counted in the 2014 census. But the Americans never used their leverage to help us. Privately Obama seems like he understands and wants to help, but that did not translate into government action. The present situation is very difficult for us. We are experiencing an intentional raping."

It is time to leave and I have wearied this ailing man far too long. As always, I ask him whom I should try to meet in Sittwe, or especially Mrauk U, this time around. When I ask, he says that "the knowledgeable people from Mrauk U have shifted to Yangon and from Yangon to Malaysia. Now, the Muslims have been driven out of Sittwe town since 2012 and they'd be difficult if not impossible to meet. Try to go to a rural Muslim village and ask if someone can explain the situation." I don't have the heart to tell him that my own movements are restricted and I will not be allowed to visit a Muslim village, let alone gain any access to Buthidaung and Maungdaw. Instead, I will head in clandestine fashion to see U Kyaw Hla Aung (2: "The Spokesman") in the massive IDP camp outside of Sittwe.

July 2017. U Kyaw Min has remained gracious and patient with me during all of these meetings over the past two years. Whenever I meet him, I don't have to provide much of a cue for him to begin his desiderata. There seems to always be a lot on his mind. This time was no exception.

He begins: "We are really in a difficult position now because we don't have any sources to rely upon. We just can't depend on foreign help because they have all their own agendas that they are preoccupied with. Nobody is really ready to risk their own relations with Myanmar for our situation. And there's a lot of murky things that cannot be seen on the surface, which is the level that most foreigners operate with." He goes on to compare the situation with the Kachin in northern Myanmar, who are regarded as indigenous and have their own armed resistance group. "The Chinese on the other side of border are culturally and linguistically the same as the Kachin. What's different is that the British gave the people on this side of the border their name [Kachin]." In that sense, there is a similarity with the Rohingya and Bengali Muslims of Bangladesh, but the Rohingya are portrayed as foreigners in Myanmar. "And we don't have an armed group either" (like the Kachin).

U Kyaw Min notes that the then current US ambassador to the United Nations, Nikki Haley, had urged Myanmar to allow a three-person UN fact-finding commission permission to conduct their probe in Arakan. But, of course, he says, they will not be granted visas.

"I have written a thick memorandum to the Kofi Annan Commission that will also be sent to a number of other people and commissions. We are focused on contributing to his fact-finding mission. We also need to appeal to the International Criminal Court in Europe [to register a complaint against those in the government or army who have approved the army's atrocities following October 9]. The security adviser of the government has said that the Rohingya issue needs a new perspective. He has a ministerial-level position. A former information minister says the idea that the government should give Rohingya full citizenship needs full consideration. If not, the situation will become more complicated. So there are some good signs that our problem might get solved. But it depends on Aung San Suu Kyii's government. She is very cunning in her tactics and deceptive. She defends the Myanmar army's approach with its own fact-finding missions. Actually, Kofi Annan's committee has no power but can only make suggestions. The government can take it or not. But she is using this commission as a defense against the atrocities committed against the Rohingya. About the interim report of the Kofi Annan Commission, she said that they will implement the suggestions after getting the consent of the local people [the Rakhine Buddhists]. I think it will be doomsday before the Rakhine give the Rohingya equal status. So, she actually becomes part of the atrocity. She is not neutral. The UN has already passed the Responsibility to Protect agreement, to take action against a country that is not protecting its own civilian populations. This issue was taken up with two Rakhine leaders in an interview on the BBC on July 11. And they replied that protection has to be given for the Rakhine who lay claim to the land! The other people [meaning Rohingya] have to live according to law [the 1982 Citizenship Law]. That means that they cannot be equal to us as before. The Rohingya cannot be given the same status as the Rakhine.

"Previously, the Rohingya had access to all departments of the government." U Kyaw Min refers to the current situation as a kind of Jim Crow policy not to recruit Rohingya to any department. Until 2015, Rohingya enjoyed some kind of citizenship rights. But now there is nothing. He says that the discrimination began from the time of Ne Win's coming to power. I ask where the legitimacy for the 1982 law comes from, since it was promulgated by a military dictatorship, the same question I had put to Abu Tahay. He says that it has legitimacy because all the Burmese at the upper levels of government and the military can discriminate against the Rohingya! "A long time ago Aung San Suu Kyii said that the 1982 law would need to be replaced. So she is well aware of its discriminatory function. Most people do not question the legitimacy of this law. This law does not have a bad impact on the Burmese or the so-called indigenous people. It affects only nonindigenous people. Even about two hundred thousand Chinese near the border are recognized as one of the indigenous peoples, as 'Moong Wang Bamar' when in fact they are Chinese. Because most people are comfortable with the law, there is no urgency to change it. Gurkha, Nepali, and Chinese Muslims in eastern Shan State are also affected by this law. If the Chinese Muslims renounce their Muslim affiliation, then they can get the 'scrutiny card.' If they say they are Buddhists, they will be okay. There are Pashyu in southern Myanmar who are Malay-oriented people who are also regarded as aliens. There are also difficulties for people who are half Indian and half something else. It's very complicated for them. They are regarded as 'unregulated settlers.' Rohingya are not hybrid. During this government's time, they are trying to disenfranchise the entire Rohingya community. After seventy years since independence, they are doing this to us. The effort is psychological, legal, and political."

I ask him about the language issue, about which I have always had some problem with clarity. Rakhine Buddhists say the Rohingya speak the same language as Bengalis from Chittagong. Rohingya dispute this. U Kyaw Min says that "pure Chittagonian Bengali cannot be understood well by Rohingya, and pure Rohingya cannot be understood by Chittagonians. Adjustments are needed, in the same way that Shan talk with Thai and the same way that Rakhine speak with the Bamar. The same relation exists between the Kachin and the Chinese on the other side of the border. In 1973, the Barua [Buddhists in Bangladesh whose forefathers came from Arakan] were regarded as foreigners, but under the 1982 law they became indigenous. The list of 135 was formulated two years later in a party conference in Mandalay. This didn't go to the parliament actually until the 2014 census final count. In fact, over six hundred identities were determined in the 2014 census. So, citizenship is based on blood. The 1982 law was articulated by Dr. Maung Maung [one of the government's theoreticians]. Everyone born before British occupation (1823) who lived in present Myanmar territory is regarded an indigenous person. Maung Maung's explanation has been taken as valid. Rohingya suffer because of the interpretation of the law. The 1982 law contained Article 5 that said that if you are a citizen at that time (1982), then you are a citizen. If you falsely claim citizenship, you'll get ten years' imprisonment. All those holding a green card earlier were regarded as citizens at the time of independence. Rohingya enjoyed citizen rights from independence until 2010. The military is now saying that the Rohingya were brought to Myanmar by the British, so the British should take care of them now! All those Muslims who came during the British times were eventually given citizenship, pensions, regular Myanmar passports (for pilgrimage to Mecca). There was no question until the military made these recent declarations.

"There are some desperate people who are now trying to gain a foothold who are not ISIS or Taliban but who are now militants trying to fight against the government. They are not well equipped; at least until now they haven't been aided internationally for equipment or modern arms. There now may be some ideological training taking place. Harket-al Yaquin, which means 'conviction,' or firm determination, is not a religious movement. It is not a matter of faith. In English it is now known as the Arakan Rohingya Salvation Army [ARSA]. These people are not our focus now. Our concern is to bring a fact-finding mission to Arakan. Failing that, we'll have to bring the military to the International Criminal Court [ICC]."

I mention how the army has used rape and murder to drive the Rohingya out, according to the UN flash report of February 2017 (OHCHR 2017). I'm surprised that U Kyaw Min has not read this report and so I promise to send him a copy as soon as I get back to my hotel. U Kyaw Min says that taking the army to the ICC "is the only way to bring these leaders to book. If this is not possible, there should be a boycott of Myanmar." I don't have the heart to tell him how

Sri Lanka has gotten away with impunity since 1983. Even if the UN demands an accounting, these countries can just refuse to cooperate. Or, in the case of Sri Lanka, they can say they agree to cooperate but then never really follow through on their promises.

U Kyaw Min seems to be getting restless and frustrated. I don't blame him. He says, "If no one is going to help us, we'll just have to help ourselves. If the military has persecuted us and Aung San Suu Kyii cannot rescue us, I still have some hope in the international community. But failing that, we'll have no choice but to fight the military. We have formulated a final set of suggestions to the Myanmar government. If they do not respond, things will turn another way." I find this an ominous statement, the first time I have heard a Rohingya leader in Myanmar come to this dreadful conclusion. He says, "The other night I had a dream that dogs were biting me." I say, "That's not an auspicious sign."

U Kyaw Min is really worried. The cultivation season out in Maungdaw and Buthidaung is being missed this year because the people are afraid to farm. The military has created an atmosphere of terror. The situation is about to turn even worse than previously imagined.

December 2017. I'm back in Myanmar again during the final weeks of 2017 and the first week of January 2018. Kyaw Min had written in response to my e-mail that I am "always welcome" to see him. He is usually rather brusque and not overly personable, so I am heartened by this genial response. But a couple of days later I receive a note from his daughter, Wai Wai, that he is in Bangkok recovering at a hospital and unlikely to return while I am in Yangon. I am resigned to missing him until he sends me an e-mail just a few days before I am leaving town. On Christmas Day, the day before I leave Yangon, we meet at his office in the afternoon for almost four hours. A couple of weeks earlier, he had been the subject of a *New York Times* article written by Hannah Beech in which he was profiled as an inveterate campaigner for Rohingya rights within a hostile environment. I ask him if he is happy with the article, as it was quite sympathetic to his cause. He response is curt: "Not bad." I don't want to follow this up, but I have a hard time imagining that he could not feel positive about the article, insofar as it clearly was very supportive of his efforts and profiled him in a heroic way.

I decide to open up our discussion by referring to the monk Sitagu's recent sermon given to members of the Tatmadaw in which he had retold the saga of Dutthagamini, the ancient king of Sri Lanka who had united all peoples under one umbrella to defeat the Tamil king Elara and his forces. The tale is epic in many ways, and it is controversial insofar as Dutthagamini is portrayed as going into battle with a Buddha relic on his spear. His remorse at slaying so many people is met by eight *arahants* (arhats, Buddhists who have reached the stage of enlightenment), who tell him that the karma from his killing in battle is equal to the deaths of only one and half persons, with the inference that the Tamils who were killed are somehow less than human or deserved to be killed. Much has been written about how Tamils are consistently viewed as *yakkha*s (demons) in the *Mahavamsa* text. The indirect teaching here by Sitagu is that

Myanmar's military need not worry so much about the gravity of moral recompense involved with having killed so many people, because the Rohingya, analogously, are somehow less than human. Kyaw Min was not aware of the sermon and the controversy it stoked. He is rather irritated by the end of my retelling of the story and says, "All the rubbish about religion in this country is coming from him [Sitagu]. His model is Iran. He wants to bring the army and sangha together. He wants to be like the ayatollah."

I then dare to ask him his current view of Aung San Suu Kyii, since he has spoken a lot about her in the past. This time I find him to be more forthright on every topic we discuss. What happened after August 25 definitely caused a sea change in the hearts and minds of many people. I am not surprised that Kyaw Min is one of them.

"She's a racist. She told the minorities that they can't always be asking, but that sometimes they have to give. But the minorities have nothing left to give to Myanmar. Her next meeting of the Panglong conference [for peace and national reconciliation in Myanmar] will involve one thousand people over three days. This is not the way to accomplish consensus on such an important matter [the peace of the country]—there should be limited representatives of each group. The public is being kept in the dark. The idea is to woo the leaders and then let them inform their constituents of the outcome, rather than striving for a bottom-up solution in which the will of the people is ratified in parliament. Whenever we complain to her about our situation, she says, 'You are not alone, the Rakhine people are also suffering.' Now she seems to advocate that foreign aid only be directed to the Rakhine people right now.

"They [the Rakhine Buddhists] have created the fake news of ARSA killing Hindus and other minority people. So the government is going to resettle them [Rakhine Buddhists] on Rohingya property. Those who were murdered, whose corpses have been discovered, were not really Hindus, but they were actually Muslims. How do you discriminate between Hindu and Muslim bodies? If ARSA killed these Hindus, then other Hindus would have run to the police and military. But they didn't; instead, they fled to Bangladesh. And they ran away with the Rohingya. The military is playing this out. There will be no public examination of the bodies to prove who got killed and how.

"The villages that were mixed Hindu and Muslim—the military has forced the Hindus to say that they can no longer live with the Muslims. The idea is to support the Rakhine contention that they cannot live in an integrated fashion with the Bengalis." Kyaw Min has put his finger on a major issue, because now it seems as if the plan going forward with regard to Rakhine Buddhists and Rohingya in Arakan is to have them live completely separately. There is no longer any talk about integration.

I decide to ask him about the significance of the pope's visit, especially his decision, at the behest of the Yangon cardinal, not to use the term "Rohingya" publicly. Kyaw Min responds, "Though he did not speak the word in Myanmar, he said it in Bangladesh. That is sufficient. I don't think he took any sides. He used general terms." I suggest that his language was formulaic, generic, and abstract. Kyaw Min nods and says, "His subordinates have to worry. This cardinal has actually spoken out in support of Rohingya rights in the past. Perhaps Aung San Suu Kyii requested that the pope not use the term while in Myanmar. Anyway, the world understands why he did not use the term here. For emphasis in Bangladesh, he said that it is God who is present among the Rohingya."

He then asked me what people in America are thinking these days. He says that a senator recently said to him that the situation here reminds him of Germany in the 1930s. "It's worse than apartheid. It's like Hitler's camps." I say that Americans are trying to understand what is going on here, but many are perplexed at how Buddhists, whose image is quite pacific in general, can be violently attacking Muslims, who unfortunately are seen as prone to violence by many Americans. The situation at first appears upside down to them. But because that is the case, there seems to be a greater attempt to understand the dynamics in play than there might be otherwise. Almost everyone is aware that the leader of the country won the Nobel Peace Prize, and that further confuses everyone.

I ask Kyaw Min if he could spell out the Asian geopolitical dynamics of the current crisis. He responds, "Rohingya can do nothing on their own and Bangladesh is under pressure from India and China. India just wants negotiations directly with Myanmar to sort this out as far as the refugees staying in India are concerned. China will support Myanmar whether it's right or wrong, no matter what. China wants a naval base in Kyaukphyu and also wants to construct a big dam with 85 to 90 percent of the electricity going to China. And China has offered 3 billion dollars to erect a barrier between Bangladesh and Myanmar."

I say, "It's the same idea as Trump has had with Mexico."

"But actually," Kyaw Min says, "Bengalis really don't really want to come into Myanmar. This is a fiction that the Rakhines have mounted. There actually have been many stations preventing illegal immigrants all along. Rakhine is actually poorer than Bangladesh on a per capita basis. On average, their per capita income is higher. Formerly, people in Maungdaw used to go to work in Bangladesh for four to five months and then return home." I tell him of U Thar Pwint's (2: "The Senior Citizen") portrayal of the situation, that circumstances in Bangladesh are so bad that the Bengalis are trying every which way to gain entrance into Myanmar so at least they can eat.

"Each and every Rakhine will tell the same story about illegal immigration. If their accounts were true, then where are all the people who would have been detained?" he says.

"Locally, there have been a lot of threats to people not to talk about what has happened out in Maungdaw and Buthidaung. The government is on full alert to counter the pressure and narrative from the international community."

I ask, "What about the domestic committee formed to oversee the economic development of Rakhine State?"

"Right now, that committee is headed by Aung San Suu Kyii and they are aiding only non-Rohingya. They have received money to help the Rohingya but they are not using it for that. They got 27 million dollars from India. India wants to behave fairly in order to avoid the condemnation of other Muslim countries. It is India who gave regular information about Muslim extremists infiltrating the country before August 25. We had never heard of ARSA before now."

Kyaw Min veers onto the topic of ARSA. "We don't have confidence in their movement. How can you fight against the army with just sticks? How can you call these people terrorists? We need real strong stakeholders. Though there is rhetoric from the American government, there is no action beyond the rhetorical from them to help us. That is why I say we'll have to take matters into our own hands with a well-trained terrorist group of our own. Otherwise, the Rohingya will have to flee. Most of the ARSA are Rohingya—some born in refugee camps in Pakistan. The leader's parents shifted to Pakistan when he was young, along with three hundred thousand to four hundred thousand Rohingya. Atta Ullah is his name. But we need real, active, effective terrorists. Unless the crisis is solved by an international intervention, there will be a terrorist response. We'll have to solve the problem ourselves. Some will come from Saudi, Pakistan, and refugee camps in Bangladesh. There are desperate young people who will do whatever they are asked to do, especially if told they will get some money."

Then Kyaw Min makes the stunning claim that I first heard from Abu Tahay a few days' earlier that "ARSA is fabricated by the army. Thirty places were attacked at the same time and yet there were no casualties on the army side! The 'attacks' were strategically located to give the Myanmar army an excuse to try to drive the people away. They had tried something similar in 2014. The ultimate objective was to expel people, and they would do anything to achieve this purpose."

I mention that many people in Yangon seem to be in denial as to what is happening out in Arakan, that they believe the military's and government's accounts that the "search-and-clear operations" have been clean.

"The general public here is silent and doesn't show any sensitivity," he says. "Only the USDP are vocal. The NLD people do not have courage to solve the problem because they are expedient in relation to the nationalist majority. Since Aung San Suu Kyii is silent, her party members don't speak out and they continue to condemn the Rohingya to appease the military. Aung San Suu Kyii has had to capitulate to military demands including her silence on the Rohingya. There will be no peace in the country as long as the military is left unrestrained to do its own bidding. The Christians have been encouraged to express their sentiments this Christmas to demonstrate that there is no discrimination. There may even be some government funding of this. Appeasing the Christians strengthens their hand. But Christians know what in fact is happening. And yet there is an active movement in Kachin to convert people to Buddhism in association with economic development. Their position is not like the Rohingya. They can enjoy all the basic rights."

I ask him if he thinks that the repatriation of refugees is actually going to begin in late January as the government has announced. He says, "My understanding is that the refugees are not going to come back unless there are some guarantees. Initially there was some hope because the Bangladeshi prime minister asserted five points that had to be met. The most important was that a safe zone would be established for the Rohingya. People were happy to hear this, as they might have some hope for peace on their return, as 80 percent of them are women and children. But in the current bilateral agreement, no one really knows what has been agreed to. If they process only 150 a day, as I have heard, it's going to take a long time! We are suffering also because Bangladesh does not show concern for our suffering. So Myanmar becomes emboldened due to Bangladesh's weak stance toward the Rohingya. Only when the fight is taken to the Myanmar army, not just at the Bangladesh border, will the situation change. No one will come to rescue the Rohingya here. They will only express sympathy and condemn publicly. Obama simply did not want to take risks. As far as our hope in Aung San Suu Kyii, she has made it clear that democracy is for the Burmese only. The democracy movement was her only chance to take power. We supported her. When she came to power, she didn't allow me to see her. The government and the country are not going to advance politically and economically because of the racist nature of the Burmese. The other minorities don't speak out on our behalf because of the burden of their own plights. They are expedient and don't want to jeopardize their own interests. They will lose whatever little leverage that they have. The only public support we have received is from the Progressive Voice, in addition to the Karen Women's Organization, who have both spoken out in our support."

I mention the recent Myanmar government decision to stop cooperating with Yanghee Lee, the UN rapporteur who has issued periodic reports on the repression of the Rohingya and other ethnic minorities. Kyaw Min says that "stymieing the UN (including the proposed fact-finding mission) is a ploy to buy time to hide the evidence. The chief of army says that there is still some unfinished business." I say that such a statement is really ominous, and Kyaw Min continues by saying, "The UN secretary-general does understand and will seek the attention of the international community. We need a safe zone under UN surveillance so that people can feel secure. The Bangladesh prime minister has now withdrawn this idea. If we had the previous prime minister we'd have the problem solved. We also need Kofi Annan to clear up the ambiguity of what he means by giving citizenship to the Rohingya. It's not clear." He remains skeptical of the advisory commission overseeing the implementation of the Kofi Annan Commission's recommendations. "Nothing will really get done, as Aung San Suu Kyi will stonewall."

Kyaw Min seems to be getting increasingly anxious and even angry as the afternoon hours start to blend into evening. I don't see any signs yet that he is tiring in giving his assessments. But I'm starting to weary at the task of typing up his words verbatim while simultaneously thinking about the next question or topic. So I decide to ask the tough question, the elephant-in-the-room type of question: "Do you have any hope left?"

"I don't expect much from this Myanmar government. I'm just looking for the international community to come in in any possible way. Maybe the deployment of a UN force will provide us some space. But that doesn't seem very practical, as in remote villages, even with a peacekeeping force, there will be a continuation of looting and killing. We have to have international help to become free and secure. There is no restitution in the lawless Rakhine area right now. There is no rule of law. At present the big business in Maungdaw and Buthidaung is extortion. They threaten people by identifying them with ARSA. Some have to give millions of kyats to be cleared of links with ARSA. If you are accused, you have to pay or you'll be tortured and sent to jail.

"If Aung San Suu Kyii is sincere in heart, to make peace in Rakhine State, she should know all of these things: people cannot go to hospital, cannot go to school, and cannot get any legal assistance. The military is still in the villages to catch people for their extortion purposes. Some villagers have shifted to other villages where they have relatives. But they are not allowed to build new houses. How can we say Aung San Suu Kyii is a fair lady? Unless there is some action taken against the police, army, and government officials who have it in for the Rohingya, the trouble will continue. That is why we need urgent action against these culprits.

"Perhaps there's no solution except to fight—people coming from all over the world. I expect some people will come to this conclusion and begin the struggle. Try to convince your government about how serious this issue is. If America does not lead a movement to salvage the Rohingya, the Rohingya will face more devastation consequentially. If the international community comes and fights for us, it will be a big burden to the Myanmar forces."

Still Kyaw Min retains the faint hope of international intervention. And if that is not in the offing, then he thinks that one has to expect that desperate Rohingya youth will begin to take up arms in a very serious fashion. I shudder at these closing thoughts as I make my way down the side street where his office is located to hail a cab to get back to my hotel. As at the conclusion of my time with Abu Tahay, I feel deeply the increasing desperation of the moment. I can see how the Burmese have made all the moves necessary for a self-fulfilling prophecy. The same kind of army tactics used in earlier years against other minority groups in remote areas of the country were undertaken against the Rohingya on an unprecedented scale. And so the difference this time is that the number of refugees leaving the country and living to tell of their terrible experiences is so vast that the reality of these crimes against humanity cannot be hidden. They are so extensive and undeniable in their scope and variety. I ponder: how long can the majority of Burmese live within their fictions that the Western media is simply reporting what Muslims tell them, that international NGOs have been abetting a Muslim "terrorist insurgency," and that the army is nothing short of genuine national heroes for suppressing the so-called insurgency? I was to get something of an answer to that last question as I headed north to Mandalay for meetings with two progressive monastic friends, conversations reported in part 3.

The Gadfly

Wai Wai Nu is a passionate and resilient thirty-something feminist activist who spent seven years (2005–2012) in prison during the military junta led by General Than Shwe. Her father is U Kyaw Min, who, as we have just seen, is a prominent Rohingya political leader who founded the Democracy and Human Rights Party. The fact that she is his daughter was the primary reason that she was imprisoned. But she is now much more than just her father's daughter, though he continues to see her as his political protégée or successor. She has developed an international reputation of her own. When she was released from prison in 2012 at the age of twenty-four, she immediately set out to complete her degree in law at Yangon University and to become proficient in English. She has gained a high degree of fluency, but at times she still struggles a bit to find the exact term she needs for precision. She has become familiar with and uses phrases and adjectives one often hears in the NGO community or among progressively and politically inclined academics. I met her several times, the last at her new office in January 2017, sportingly dubbed the Yangon Youth Center and located rather innocuously on the second floor of a building not far from Kandawgyi Lake in a middle-class neighborhood of Yangon. From here, she and her staff planned and executed various seminars aimed at raising the political awareness of Yangon women.

Wai Wai has drawn the very favorable attention of diplomatic authorities at the American embassy in Yangon, as she has traveled to the United States on at least two occasions that were sponsored by the American government. First, she was a resident guest at former president George W. Bush's ranch in Crawford, Texas, for a seminar aimed at cultivating young political leaders of "emerging market" nations. She spoke very favorably of Mr. Bush, noting in particular his congeniality and encouragement. On a second trip, she attended a seminar in the spring of 2015 at the Carter Center in Georgia. While in America, she also gave some lectures at various colleges and universities about the current political situation in Myanmar, especially the condition affecting Rohingya in Arakan. Independently (that is, not sponsored by the US government), she also attended a six-week seminar at Stanford University in the summer of 2016 and returned for summer programs at the University of California, Berkeley in 2017 and 2018, where I was a visiting professor in the spring of 2018 and met some of her well-wishers. During her 2015 trip to the Carter Center, she even joined other young activists from around the world for a dinner and evening with President Barack Obama at the White House. Later that year, she was also brought to Oslo for a controversial conference sponsored by the Nobel Institute and the Parliament of World Religions that focused on the genocide of the Rohingya in Myanmar, about which I had learned not only from Norwegian colleagues but also from two prominent and progressive Buddhist monks who were also invited. She is clearly a rising star and knows it. Indeed, hers is a remarkable story. She told me that a French journalist had approached her about writing her biography. I encouraged her to write her own story as it evolves. If Myanmar continues to liberalize, especially if it decides to allow Muslims to run for political office in the future, she will clearly be a force to reckon with. She is a very determined young woman. While she describes herself as "resilient," I would say she is a rather irrepressible presence who is not easily intimidated.

I had originally met her in **January 2015**, on one of my earliest forays into the post-2012 religiopolitical world of Myanmar. I was introduced to her through my journalist friend Wai Moe's networking. Our meeting in a Yangon coffee shop was brief, perhaps only an hour or so, as an official from the American embassy was also waiting to meet her. She seemed a little skeptical about my motives. Yet, she briefed me on the activities of her own NGO (Women's Peace Network Arakan) and expressed her desire to work on women's adult education regarding civic responsibility. She was clearly interested in the task of empowering women.

I met her again a year later, in **January 2016**, after she had visited the United States for her stint at the Carter Center and her dinner with Barack Obama and after her visit to Oslo. She gave me more than three hours of her time. I found her keen to engage and to inform me about the current situation in Myanmar regarding the Rohingya. I had tried to see her several months earlier, in the summer of 2015, but she was already very booked up, often sought after by journalists eager to record her remarkable story. Moreover, I failed to connect with her in the summers of 2016 and 2017 while she was in America, though my spouse, Sree Padma, did meet her in the San Francisco Bay Area in 2016 while she was studying at Stanford.

I did, by chance, also meet her very briefly while on a plane that had landed in Sittwe in **August 2015**. She was visiting Arakan then (specifically, she and her father were headed out to Buthidaung from Sittwe, I believe, for political rallies before it was clear that Muslims would be largely sidelined in the November 2015 elections), and it was my impression that this was her first visit in a very long time, perhaps for both, but more certainly for her. She had left Arakan for Yangon when she was nine years old in the late 1990s, old enough to have substantial memories of life as it had been in the 1990s. What she saw now shocked her. The situation in Buthidaung had deteriorated dramatically since the time she had lived there. She said that segregation and discrimination (her terms) had become ubiquitous (mine). Rohingya people were being treated "inhumanely." "Divide [separate the indigenous people and Buddhists from the *kalar*,[1] Muslims, or illegal immigrants] and rule, or

1. For an extensive discussion of *kalar*, which essentially means a foreigner from the West, see 2: "The Senior Citizen" and "The Neglected."

'*taindar* rule' political conceptuality, has gotten completely institutionalized. Schools, roads, all public contexts had become segregated. One hundred and fifty *taindar* villages had been settled for Buddhists to inhabit. And these were all Burmese, rather than Arakanese Buddhists, who formerly were inmates in Yangon prisons." When she was in prison for seven years, between the ages of seventeen and twenty-four, about every three months authorities would come around offering the "indigenous peoples' development program" (*nathalar*), wherein prisoners could be released if they agreed to resettle in the western border area of Arakan. The program also operates in Shan, Kachin, and Chin States. It is clearly a program for Burmanization. Now in northern Rakhine State (Arakan), roads have been built that are for villages of Burmese Buddhists only. In contrast, no water, transportation, electricity, or facilities have been given to Rohingya. The resettled people from the prisons are far better looked after than even the Arakanese Buddhists. The military is everywhere. "If you want to travel, you need permission, and if you want to get permission, you need money to give to the military or police." None of this was the case when she was young. Only the Rohingya Muslims and Rakhine Buddhist were living together back then. There were no Burmese. But now security is everywhere and the many resettled Burmese are also a conspicuous presence. Wai Wai Nu recalled wistfully that when she was a child, there were no Burmese people around and therefore no Burmese language being spoken. No public servants are Rohingya any longer. Only a very few Rohingya teachers are left in the schools. "Now there are no longer any doctors, lawyers, policeman, or professionals who are Rohingya. They are all gone. Impunity on the part of the Buddhists, especially Burmese, is so high in general." For example, she spoke about how Buddhist women do not have to pay boat owners to travel on the waterways, but Muslims are required to pay. She emphasized that this discrimination and impunity exist at every social level: from very small matters to great matters of justice. I said, "It sounds like apartheid." She replied, "Of course. It is totally apartheid."

Beyond her account of how life had changed in Buthidaung, we talked about her NGO work and her views of the contemporary evolving political situation. She had started her Women's Peace Network Arakan with women as a focus so as not to be controversial or draw the attention of authorities. She had consciously avoided the terms "Rohingya" and "Muslim" for the sake of not being so conspicuous. Though her NGO is ostensibly focused on the women in Arakan, she was working extensively with women, and not just Rohingya women, in Yangon. I asked her if her NGO had been institutionalized in Arakan and she replied, "Only through individual people."

Through her NGO, she teaches seminars (usually a week long) on "civics"—political theories, liberal democracy, pluralism, leadership, and so forth—to about fifteen women at a time. Typically, she would organize groups (ethnic, religious, youth, human rights, etc.) to discuss how to end discrimination. She brings the group together in the end to forward recommendations to the government. She inaugurates each seminar with a general public event inviting government and embassy representatives along with participants to signal the presence of the project to the Yangon civic-minded community. The final session is always aimed at forwarding constructive recommendations. Her primary aim in these seminars is to assist women in becoming more politically aware.

More specifically, Wai Wai Nu also wants to organize minority forums to emphasize the importance of minority rights to be enshrined within a revised constitution. I think her primary mission is to foster efforts aimed at establishing public sentiment for a new constitution. The 2008 constitution was written entirely by the military for its own interests in a new semidemocratic framework that it could ultimately control. The plebiscite was hardy held in a freely democratic context insofar as public discussion was not forthcoming and the constitution was passed with a near unanimous vote, a sure sign that the entire process was not open or fair.

Wai emphasizes that it will take deep commitment and hard work to achieve any level of prosperity and peace in contemporary Myanmar. She says that "the Burmese don't understand democracy yet—they're only looking out for their own interests. For democracy to work, you must understand what equality really means. People who know about it have a responsibility to share that knowledge with the community. You'll never get peace when your neighbor does not enjoy it. All of our communities have to share in fostering these ideals." This was her response to my question about developing discourses about civil society that transcend ethnic expediency. Her focus is directly in line with concerns about democracy and human rights.

At the time of one of our conversations, efforts were being made to accommodate some Rohingya refugees in Malaysia and Indonesia who had successfully navigated the perilous journey. (The perils of attempting to escape Arakan by boat and the consequent problem of human trafficking involving various parties—pirates, corrupt Myanmar and Thai military officials, and so forth—had been exposed by the Reuters investigative report of December 4, 2013, which I discuss in the introduction.) Wai Wai pointed out that Indonesians and Malaysians are not very sympathetic to Rohingya refugees because they don't want any more outsiders to take care of. They rightfully aver that they are not responsible for the problems the Rohingya face—it's the Burmese government and people who are the problem. Indeed, this was the consensus reached at an international conference convened by Myanmar, Thailand, Malaysia, and Indonesia, that until the Myanmar government addressed the root problems in Arakan, the refugee problem would persist in one form or another. However, because escaping by boat became so dangerous, and so many Rohingya failed to successfully reach their destinations, the numbers fleeing by boat dwindled dramatically. Throughout this discussion, Wai Wai's fundamental argument was that "people should have a right to live in the country in which they are born."

I ask, "Why do you think that the Burmese Buddhists are trying to push the Rohingya out and consciously exclude them at this point in time?"

She replies, "It's not just hatred or Islamophobia, but a political agenda to further their popular position with the Arakanese people and their continued control over the land. Since 2012, more Burmese and Rakhine people have become more and more racist. The Rohingya became a scapegoat for the problem that erupted out in Arakan. The racism has been seeded now and could erupt again violently at any time." Indeed, the army's post–October 9, 2016, and post–August 25, 2017, "search-and-clear" operations would seem to be clearly indicative of that. "The political agenda is to control Rakhine State: if you can pit the Rohingya against the Rakhine, then you can deflect the Rakhine/Burmese conflict and the Rakhine desire for independence. Instead of protests being organized against the Burmese government, now the protests are against the OIC [Organization of Islamic Cooperation], UN, NGOs, et cetera. They are also able to sell land [in the Kyaukphyu area, for instance] to the Chinese. So their approach has a territorial agenda and is aimed at increasing political support for the central government. This process actually began in the 1970s under Ne Win and was intensified by SLORC [the State Law and Order Restoration Council] in the 1990s. The separation of the communities through alienation made this approach possible and easy to create conflict."

The whitewashing of the Rohingya presence in any government circles is illustrated by the career of her own grandfather, a man who spent forty years in the Burma military. In recalling his experience, she notes that he referred to an official order by Ne Win back in 1969 that anyone who was Muslim should get out of the military. The order was refined to refer to just higher ranks at the beginning but then was extended to every rank. So her grandfather was never promoted. This discriminatory policy was implemented to a lesser extent in relation to Christians. The next generation of military officers reified this practice. And then the army and its Union Solidarity and Development Party (USDP) political voices actively put it into practice for society at large after 2012, in the name of majoritarian "democracy."

After making this point, she goes on to say, "The problem among the Buddhist nationalists is one of entitlement. They have to see that the minority populations are full citizens too. They are seeing the minorities as 'other.' Everywhere the Buddhists are given priority because of this sense of entitlement." I assert that this is probably because the country is understood by so many Buddhists as essentially a Buddhist country. She then reviews how it is that the Burmese, after the formation of the union, forgot that the "borderlands" had been included as well. She says, "Don't forget that this is not a country only of Burmese. They [the Burmese] forget about that. They think the entire country belongs to them. But now they are trying to define the future of marginal people by excluding them. They have come to occupy and are colonizing our states. Now everyone is required to speak Burmese to be citizens. Back in the day, there were no Burmese in Arakan to speak their language. They have forgotten that they are outsiders in Rakhine State."

Like most Rohingya, Wai Wai is no longer hopeful about the new NLD government. "They may not actively persecute us, but they are going to retain the Burmese attitude. Some of the NLD leaders are now echoing the nationalist rhetoric."

She sees one of her own responsibilities as being a gadfly to Aung San Suu Kyii, to goad her into action on what it means to be the leader of a multiethnic state. I forwarded to her some of the rhetoric being used by the current Sri Lankan prime minister, Ranil Wickremesinghe, about pluralism and the multiculturalism of Sri Lanka's heritage, though I hastened to explain to her that this was essentially rhetoric, and that little of this rhetoric had yet to be processed in terms of unfolding public policy. (Nine years after the civil war ended in Sri Lanka, no formal or serious talks have occurred between the government and Tamil leaders, for instance.)

I ask Wai Wai what she said to President Barack Obama when in 2015 she was invited to dinner at the White House along with other young activists. When it was her turn to address him, she spoke out about the genocide of the Rohingya people in Arakan and about how the United States needs to take a stand on the basis of human rights and not let the Burmese government get away with its program. She said Obama was a bit defensive in response and said that she should be patient and wait for an election that might yield positive results, but that he would also try to work on the problem whenever he had a chance. The election came, but the Rohingya were denied the right to run for office or even to vote. She sees that the Obama White House is sensitive and sympathetic but that other members of the cabinet are not. Business interests do not want to upset the climate for American investment. Secretary of State John Kerry was understood to be a more business-oriented secretary of state than Hillary Clinton, who was more human rights oriented. Wai Wai sees US policies for Southeast Asia as dominated also by the China card, wanting to woo Myanmar away from the China orbit, which means providing carrots to those who are in power and not driving them further in the direction of the Chinese. She has since had conversations with Ben Rhodes, who was a deputy security adviser and speechwriter for Obama and continues to press for American responses to the human rights conditions in Myanmar. In that way, Wai Wai is following her father's lead in trying to gain international support for the Rohingya's plight.

Wai Wai is sometimes very blunt, but this is what is refreshing about her company. She articulates an unvarnished perspective forcefully. "Almost all of the Rakhine Buddhist politicians are super racists. Before there was a kind of equality between the Rakhine and Rohingya, but now the Arakanese want to expel the Rohingya. There were always some anti-Rohingya, but now it has become normative across the board. Ethnic cleansing is occurring."

I ask, "How do you try to transform this situation?"

She says, "Only when you set up a new set of laws to be imposed and enforced. [This brings her interests back to the constitutional again.] Peace education is needed in the community too. Structural change and institutional change have to take place. Discriminatory laws need to be abolished. People who are privileged do not want to lose their privilege, so you need to mandate the change."

In retrospect, Wai Wai's comments about how there would be attempts to expel the Rohingya, about how "ethnic cleansing is occurring," turned out to prescient. Nobody I had spoken to at that point in time had been as direct and accurate about what was happening then, and what would further occur over the course of the next year.

The Stringer

Wai Moe is a savvy veteran journalist who was primarily a stringer for the *New York Times* but also worked for other publications on occasion. Many of the stories on Myanmar that appear in the domestic and international editions of the *New York Times* are written based on the information he provides. Before working for the *Times,* he worked for several years as a reporter for *The Irrawaddy* magazine, probably the best-known and one of the most reliable news outlets for political coverage of Myanmar. For about twenty years, *The Irrawaddy*'s offices were located in Chiang Mai, Thailand, where Wai Moe lived for several years himself. But *The Irrawaddy* shifted its offices to Myanmar in 2012. Wai Moe also now works for *Foreign Policy* magazine and splits his time between Myanmar and Chiang Mai. I was first referred to Wai Moe by Min Zin, his friend and a fellow Burmese political activist. Min Zin was a politically progressive PhD student in political science at the University of California, Berkeley, when I met him.

Wai Moe was always difficult for me to track down. He often disappeared for days at a time while on assignment. But when he was able to meet with me, he proved to be the most well-informed and incisive Burmese observer of contemporary political forces in play in Myanmar I met. I learned immensely from him each time we talked. Moreover, he was extremely generous in giving me contact information for, or introductions to, a plethora of people, including five of the people featured in the conversations comprising the main part of this book. I came to respect him enormously and remain very grateful to him for facilitating so much.

Wai Moe was part of the so-called 88 Generation of student activists, as was Min Zin. This is the group of students, many of them from Yangon University, who, on August 8, 1988 (hence the 8888 Uprising), led the first serious challenge to military control of the country and precipitated the eventual downfall of the dictatorial Tatmadaw army general Ne Win. Moreover, the six-week movement actually was the catalyst that gave birth to the National League for Democracy and the rise of Aung San Suu Kyii as a symbol of new political hope. The 88 Generation activists and the NLD fell out somewhat leading up to the 2015 elections, when the NLD did not support the candidacies of many 88 Generation activists.

When he was but fourteen years old, Wai Moe was arrested for producing a student magazine that contained activist ideas. He was interrogated and detained for a short while. But four years later, he was given a sentence of five years, some of which were spent in the notorious Insein Prison, which held hundreds, if not thousands, of political prisoners and dissidents during the military junta era. He was also sent to another prison, tortured there, and spent three years in solitary confinement. Wai Moe was arrested a second time and jailed for another significant stretch of time by the Tatmadaw. Of all the contacts I enjoyed in Myanmar, he was understandably the most critical of the Tatmadaw's presence in causing strife throughout the country. He had his own good reasons for this. He knew personally what kinds of violent methods and psychological warfare that members of the Tatmadaw were capable of perpetrating.

When I returned to Yangon from my first visit to Arakan in **December 2014 and January 2015** and expressed to Wai Moe my astonishment at some of the outlandish things I had been told by Rakhine Buddhists about Rohingya and Americans, he explained that the Tatmadaw had a very sophisticated psychological warfare department, expert at formulating and spreading disinformation to its decided strategic advantage. A lot of this disinformation was passed on through monastic networks and most especially social media, in addition to the government's newspaper, *New Light of Myanmar.* He told me the Tatmadaw was probably responsible for fomenting much of the contemporary trouble out in Arakan, because it was in the army's firm interest to cause problems between the Rakhine Buddhists and Rohingya Muslims: (1) to reinforce its own claims to constitute a continuing and necessary powerful force in the region, that is, to act like defenders of the Rakhine in particular and Myanmar in general by means of posturing as a valiant defense against a Muslim insurgency; and (2) to deflect attention away from the rising hostilities among virtually all segments of the population against growing Chinese business and political interests that were being facilitated by the Tatmadaw generals, many of whom were of part Chinese descent. The first rationale actually coincides with the perspective put forth by the insurgent Arakan Army, now an inveterate enemy of the Tatmadaw. The second rationale was important for several other related reasons beyond the drive for the generals' personal profiteering. Maintaining these interests with the Chinese was lucrative for those running the government, particularly those interests out in Arakan where an important oil and gas port was being located on Ramree Island. From there, by a pipeline conduit through almost the entire north-south length of the country through to China, Myanmar was facilitating part of the energy engine fueling the exploding Chinese economy. In addition, for years, China had been carefully turning Myanmar into a client state of sorts, Wai Moe said. In Mandalay, for instance, one could see over the years the increasing presence of Chinese retail business interests taking root. Teak, gems, and religious statues were traditionally exported to China from Mandalay, but Chinese retail products, including the ubiquitous inexpensive motorbikes, the new favorite means of public transportation, now flooded the streets and were one of the more conspicuous expressions of the larger unfolding pattern. New shopping malls were built, filled with goods produced in China. I saw clear evidence of this in both Yangon and especially Mandalay. In any case, Wai Moe taught me to watch for the Tatmadaw's hand at almost every turn in the developing tragedy of Buddhist-Muslim relations.

I realized the verity of Wai Moe's lessons increasingly as my conversations with many stakeholders took place. Virtually every Muslim voice I heard eventually referred to the manner in which Muslims had been systematically excluded from the ranks of the military, first by General Ne Win's ban on Muslims being promoted to senior positions in the late 1960s, then by a gradual refusal to allow any Muslims at all into the army's ranks. This discrimination within the military was a forerunner of the more systematic public exclusion and disenfranchisement of Muslims in general and Rohingya in particular. Stoking Buddhist nationalism eventually became the Tatamadaw's strategy to legitimate its discrimination and even its pursuit of ethnic cleansing, so evident in the post–October 9, 2016, and post–August 25, 2017, violent rampages through and arson of the villages of Maungdaw and Buthidaung in northern Rakhine State.

Despite the fact that I had spent a week in Mrauk U and Sittwe in December 2014 and January 2015, it was Wai Moe who first alerted me to the extreme conditions that Rohingya actually faced in northern Arakan. He pointed out to me how members of the Arakan National Party (ANP) could continue their heinous rhetoric against the Rohingya precisely because it was so easy to generate both Rakhine public support in Arakan and the simultaneous blessing of the Tatmadaw. Indeed, Wai Moe argued that much of the ANP rhetoric against the Rohingya had been supplied by the Tatmadaw. What I first learned directly in conversations from Wai Moe and later confirmed with my Rohingya interlocutors was that no Rohingya were allowed to go to university or to travel outside their camps without special permission, which was often very difficult to secure, often only through bribes; that virtually every township in northern Rakhine now had a camp for Rohingya internally displaced persons (IDP); that the Sittwe IDP camp situation was the worst of all the camps by virtue of its overcrowding; and that the other IDP camps were getting somewhat better in their conditions after a very difficult first two years, especially in terms of nutrition, sanitation, and medical programs.

Whenever I was able to meet Wai Moe, it was usually in a well-known Yangon coffee shop. He preferred to sit in the back and always faced the entrance, his eyes frequently scanning the horizon. I don't know for sure what was going on in his mind, but I suspected that he was conditioned to case his surroundings. On a couple of occasions, before the NLD's November 2015 election victory, he complained about his cell phone being tapped by the Tatmadaw. It was in these coffee shop settings that Wai Mai tutored me about aspects of the contemporary political scene, advising me of the significance of the machinations surrounding the removal of Shwe Mann (a Tatmadaw general who had become the speaker of parliament) from the USDP political ranks, why the death of Aung Thaung (a powerful USDP politician) might herald new changes for USDP–Ma Ba Tha relations, and so forth. I was a neophyte when I first came to Myanmar to begin this project. Wai Moe exercised great patience in bringing me up to some kind of speed and pointing me in profitable directions.

When I meet him in **January of 2016** following the NLD's decisive victory, I have many questions to put to him. I begin by saying that in Sri Lanka, the militant anti-Muslim Bodu Bala Sena movement had been largely quieted (until some resurfacing in mid-2017 and spring 2018) since the January 2015 elections, largely because the tacit support they had enjoyed from the nationalist Mahinda Rajapaksa government had evaporated with the new government led by Maithripala Sirisena, whose stance on ethnic relations was based on the assumption that Sri Lanka was a multicultural and pluralist society. My questions to Wai Moe are: "Has the wind now been taken out of the sails of the chauvinistic monastic Ma Ba Tha since the NLD election victory? Did the election prove that the Ma Ba Tha is not as powerful as many had thought?"

Wai Moe first responds, "What the election proved was that most people had more of an abiding disgust for the military than a fear of being overrun by Muslims." Two months before the election, Wai Moe says, he could see that the Ma Ba Tha was losing steam. He had interviewed rural monks in the Irrawaddy River delta area who saw that the Ma Ba Tha was really a tool of the government and the USDP, and so they ultimately supported Aung San Suu Kyii in the general election. They had refused to distribute the flyers about Aung San Suu Kyii being associated with "the Muslim movement." (As I think back on this, I wonder if perhaps this attempt to portray Suu Kyii in such a fashion hasn't added to her reticence to come out in any way in sympathy with the Rohingya's plight since her landslide electoral victory; in other words, she has been at pains to deny her associations with the Muslim community, perhaps precisely because it had been so overtly and intensively asserted by her enemies.) At the time, Wai Moe had interviewed a high-profile former Tatmadaw general who said that the Ma Ba Tha was basically a campaign strategy for the USDP and the Tatmadaw. The heart of the Ma Ba Tha monkish membership, Wai Moe asserts, was rooted primarily in the teaching monasteries of Mandalay and Yangon. This explains, in part, the popularity of U Wirathu, insofar as he fashions himself as essentially a leading monk/teacher from Mandalay. Indeed, that is how he spends most of his time at his monastery in Mandalay, which has almost three thousand monastic *samaneras* (novitiates).

I then ask Wai Moe if there are any signs yet that Aung San Suu Kyii might directly address the Arakan situation on behalf of the Rohingya. He begins by pointing out that the Arakan National Party won twenty-three seats in the upper parliament, second only to what the Shan people elected outside the NLD. This number was a good indication of how powerful the ANP had become. I interrupt him to mention that I noticed there was a skirmish the other day between the newly emergent Arakan Army and the government forces. I want to know if the Arakan Army would become part of the civil war cease-fire or the reenergized Panglong peace and reconciliation talks. Wai Moe doesn't think they will and goes on to say that all of this (the apparent widespread support of the ANP and the appearance of the Arakan Army) would seem to bode ill for the Rohingya, because Aung San Suu Kyii would not be eager to anger the Rakhines. The chief minister of the new Rakhine State government would soon be appointed by Aung San Suu Kyii, and Wai Moe indicates that an NLD member is being tipped for this position, but that he will face a very delicate situation in the Arakan parliament because of the strong ANP presence. The ANP is particularly powerful in northern Arakan, while the NLD dominates in the southern regions, especially Thandwe. I point out that one of the reasons that the ANP showed so well in northern Arakan and gained so many seats was that the Rohingya were not only not allowed to contest any office, neither federal nor state, but also not allowed even to vote. Indeed, this seemed to reflect a strategy first brokered by the military that benefited both Burmese and Rakhine political strategies in Arakan.

Wai Moe, a progressive thinker, points out that the 1982 law remains in play, though it is thoroughly "out of date and unfair." It is his hope that perhaps Aung San Suu Kyii will work to remove the factors of race and religion from the national ID card and thus pave the way for another means of verifying citizenship. I admit that I have a difficult time understanding why the 1982 Citizenship Law remains such a force and why its amendment or removal is not one of the first items to be taken up by the new NLD-dominated parliament. After all, it was virtually a decree that came from the military dictatorship of Ne Win. Moreover, it essentially requires a community to prove its ancestry back to 1823, the year before the British established their first seats of power in Mawlamyine (formerly Moulmein) and Sittwe (formerly Akyab). The political implication of the law is that the British were responsible for bringing in so many *kalars* (in this case South Asians) to Myanmar that they distorted the country's demography. And, of course, as I noted earlier, when the British finally disestablished King Thibaw in Mandalay in 1885, they proceeded to govern Burma as a part of the British Raj. The assumption of the 1982 law is basically to ignore the last two hundred years of history and to condemn any community that has since settled in the county to statelessness. Rather, this law is based upon a primordial vision of what ethnicities belong in Myanmar. I sarcastically mention that if the date were moved back another thousand years, then the Burmese, Arakanese, and Muslims could all be excluded from citizenship as well! My point is that such anachronistic rendering of what constitutes "authentic" citizenship is historically quite arbitrary. It seems draconian that people would need to trace out community histories of almost two hundred years to prove their authenticity in relation to claims of current national belonging. This is actually what Rohingya political leaders like Abu Tahay and Kyaw Min have tried to do in their own research.

Wai Moe was the most well-informed source I had on how things are going for the new NLD government. He knew that expectations would be really high in a situation fraught with danger, given the Tatmadaw's historic xenophobia and the continuing government administration by employees who have only known the ways of autocracy. In the immediate months following the NLD victory, Wai Moe had insightful comments to make about what to expect and why certain directions were being taken. First, he noted that international investment, at least investment beyond the 70 percent or so of international investment that comes from China, had been disappointingly weak since the NLD came to power, and that in this context, the Ma Ba Tha had been seen as a liability, insofar as the notoriety it has generated has been bad for the country's emergent brand. The NLD's hard line taken against the Ma Ba Tha, first in the summer of 2016 and then the following spring in publicly silencing Wirathu and essentially requiring the Ma Ba Tha to reconstitute itself under another name, also represents something of a response to Euro-American pressure. I would think it is not just US pressure, but also the result of a total international embarrassment about what is happening to Buddhism in Myanmar. While that may be so, it is also a bit inconsistent with Aung San Suu Kyii's refusal to acknowledge publicly what the Tatmadaw has done out in northern Arakan. Wai Moe says that the Tatmadaw now wants to show that it is not behind the Ma Ba Tha. It is happy to see the previous government take the blame for this shameful display of Buddhist nationalism, though in fact the Tatmadaw is quite responsible for its emergence in the first place.

Aung San Suu Kyii, though she had earlier called for the practice of "engaged Buddhism," is simply not very clear about the role of religion in Myanmar's future. Wai Moe says that she has a kind of patron-client relation with some specific senior monks, including some who have been active in the Ma Ba Tha. Nonetheless, Wai Moe expects the four race and religion laws to be amended during the first year of the NLD's domination of parliament. That did not happen, perhaps because it might have set off a firestorm in response from the Ma Ba Tha and its supporters. Instead, the NLD preferred to work through the established monastic Ma Ha Na to disestablish the Ma Ba Tha directly. The laws are quite arcane anyway, and so their actual implementation can easily be deferred so that collectively and practically their existence becomes a nonissue.

Wai Moe says that the Tatmadaw needs Aung San Suu Kyii in order to temper the United States and its pressure. He says that the army benefits more from dealing with Aung San Suu Kyii than Aung San Suu Kyii seems to be benefitting from them. She can't touch the military budget or security issues. As such, the country's democratic future depends on the liberalization of the military. Wai Moe thinks that there are some officers high up in the military who appear to be open to this, who see a stage-managed development coming to fruition in the future. I find this fascinating insofar as it echoes my Rohingya friend Abu Tahay's earlier hopes that the way forward involved cultivating some possible progressive-thinking military minds. It was also in concert with what Ashin Kumara (3: "The Rector"), the rector at Sitagu's academy in Sagaing, hoped in terms of the future education of those who would be part of the army. But while Abu Tahay had eventually given up on this possibility, especially after October 9, 2016, Wai Moe remained ever hopeful. What was currently dragging the NLD down, in Wai Moe's view, was that many of the leaders in Aung San Suu Kyii's cabinet are not reformists. Even Wai Moe seems a bit disappointed in how some of these surrounding figures are conservative Burmese Buddhists whose perspectives are of the Buddhist nationalist sort, and who are not alive to the multicultural realities of a peaceful unified Myanmar existing under an umbrella of true federalism. For them, Myanmar remains essentially a Buddhist country.

January 2017. If Wai Moe had a criticism of Suu Kyii, it is that she was trying to micromanage so many of the decisions that must be taken in a context of great complexity. Without due delegation of power or decision making, the government moves slowly, waiting for her to carefully calibrate how to move forward without upsetting various constituencies, especially the Tatmadaw. Also, she is not prone to giving the leaders of identity politics what they want. She seems to be resisting their aspirations for more autonomy without providing them with the kinds of necessary incentives to accommodate themselves to the union. Has there been a statement about the past practices of "Burmanization"? Even Rakhines in northern Rakhine are aware of the many villages that have been established with the aid of the government for the sake of resettling poor Burmese. Thus, in these specific instances of Burmanization, there has been no letup in the centripetalizing process.

Wai Moe is always interested in whom I was able to approach successfully and what I had learned from my various contacts. I had encouraged him to contact a couple of the people I had been successful with, people he did not know personally whose stories might be interesting to him. When I told him that I had interviewed U Kumara, the rector of the Sitagu International Academy in Sagaing, he was very curious to know what kind of perspective I encountered. On Sitagu, he said, "He seems to say we should become like Iran to be a real religious country! The Ma Ba Tha movement is not enough. Pro-democracy forces are not sympathetic to him. He donated a lot of money to the NLD because he knew they were going to win. He's a complicated person—straddles the line."

Wai Moe tells me that some members of his family are getting a little worried about his safety these days. I remark that working for the *New York Times* certainly provides him with a measure of protection, because the Myanmar government is very unlikely to want to take on the kind of burden that would ensue from a dispute with that paper. At this time the two Burmese Reuters reporters had not been arrested yet and the post–August 25, 2017, pressures on Burmese public perspectives had yet to take on force. At the time, Wai Moe agreed with me but then said he's not worried so much about the government these days. He's more worried about "the mafia" instead. A few months earlier, Wai Moe had contributed to an investigative article in which drug money was found being laundered through the construction of a number of high-rises now being built in Yangon. I could only imagine how that article might have been received by the principal parties involved. Speaking truth to power is sometimes risky, no matter what the political or cultural context. But Wai Moe is committed to that.

A week after I last spoke to Wai Moe, in January 2017, Ko Ni, the prominent Muslim lawyer and adviser to the NLD who was reputedly working on constitutional reforms aimed at clipping some of the army's power, was shot dead at Yangon International Airport while holding his grandson. Two people were arrested—one a former prisoner convicted for the illegal trading of Buddhist artifacts. A second was arrested out in Kayin State, but it is clear that these thugs were not the masterminds who reportedly were offered big money or a car for pulling off the hit. In January 2019, the defense of two additional alleged "masterminds" was being adjudicated in a Yangon court. Sometimes the lines blur between the various power brokers in Myanmar.

In the fall of 2018, Wai Moe finished conducting an extremely risky investigation of how the Tatmadaw for years had developed an extensive system of disinformation by creating fake Facebook platforms (*New York Times,* October 15, 2018). The finished article not only found fault with lax Facebook supervision, a problem continuously plaguing that particular social media business, but also asserted that the multiyear campaign was very significant in legitimating and distorting the Tatmadaw's genocidal attacks following August 25, 2017. When I saw this article, I wrote to Wai Moe to offer my congratulations, and he immediately warmly responded that we needed to meet again when I came to Yangon or Chiang Mai. Privately, I worry for his safety and look forward to the day I can place a copy of this book in his hands.

I tried to see Wai Moe on every visit to Myanmar, even though he sometimes proved to be elusive. Meeting him early on in my quest proved to be a highly auspicious moment for what was to follow over the years.

The Commentator

On previous visits to Yangon, I had twice met, through and with Wai Moe, a well-spoken information officer who worked for another country's embassy in Yangon. On the occasions when we met, I found that he was very well attuned to contemporary political dynamics and articulated a healthy critical perspective. After reading many news dispatches that included perspectives from informed Yangon sources, I discovered that my conversation partner was a well-known political analyst frequently appearing as a consultant on television news programs and internet podcasts. In January 2017, while I was staying in Yangon and Wai Moe was out of the country in Chiang Mai, I decided to seek him out for a private conversation on the latest religiopolitical developments just before I headed out to Arakan for ten days. This time in Yangon, I had been talking almost exclusively with Rohingya leaders, and I wanted to gain a somewhat different point of view before heading out to Rakhine State. My conversation with him occurred after the first "clearance operation" conducted by the Tatmadaw late in 2016, which resulted in about seventy-five thousand Rohingya fleeing northern Arakan for Bangladesh, and eight months before the second massive military onslaught that led to the flight of almost 698,000 additional Rohingya refugees. I had a second long conversation with him again in the final days of December 2017, after the massive Rohingya exodus. I had just seen him interviewed on an *Irrawaddy* broadcast about a month earlier, and I was struck by how general his answers were to specific questions. Though articulate, he could also be evasive for reasons of political expedience.

Unfortunately, I am not free to use his name or refer to the embassy that employs him because of the sensitive nature of his position. And I cannot discuss, as he was reticent to do, any issues now alive between Myanmar and the country he represents. But I can report that he has held his current position for ten years, he is well educated (he has earned his PhD), and he is a seasoned Burmese observer of Myanmar politics and culture. Given his personal background and vocation, he is at once urban and urbane. In **January 2017** he asked me to meet him on a Friday night in the back room of a Black Canyon restaurant out in the new imposing and resplendent Myanmar Plaza, a huge new five-story complex of shops, restaurants, and a massive atrium that was reportedly funded by Vietnamese money and built in conjunction with the business interests of a Tatmadaw general. It was another side of Yangon that I had never seen before: designer clothing shops, European restaurants, that unmistakable upscale suburban mall experience of the "globalized" world where one could spend a lot of money on Louis Vuitton, Gucci, Armani, and Christian Dior luxury products. This looked like the beginning of a Bangkok-style retail invasion to me, as the merchandise wasn't simply stuff from China; only I had to wonder if there were that many well-heeled people in Yangon these days after the military government had decamped to Naypitaw. (There must be, because an even grander shopping complex, Junction City, opened in June 2017 just opposite Scott's Market on Bogyoke Aung San in the heart of downtown Yangon.) Because of a fiercer-than-normal traffic jam getting out of downtown Yangon, I arrived twenty minutes late. Fortunately, my would-be conversation partner had been patient. We were seated in a tucked-away spot so that it would be very difficult for anyone to observe us directly, except for a few other obviously upper-middle-class patrons of the restaurant. Our conversation would be private. My conversation partner obviously wanted it that way. We spent the next two and half hours in an intense exchange.

I open the conversation by asking him what he thinks of the new verification process that basically requires Rohingya to give up their very term for self-designation in favor of "Bengali Muslim" as part of the process involved in qualifying for an associate citizenship status. The government has insisted on this rubric and Aung San Suu Kyii and Shwe Mann (at the time the speaker of the lower house of parliament) had lectured the newly arrived American ambassador several months earlier about not using the term "Rohingya" in public. Pope Francis had also been advised as much by the Yangon cardinal in advance of his November 2017 visit. My colleague replies by saying that "Myanmar really needs a classification system. The government is working on it. The first tier or group in the scheme would have a pink card, which is basically full citizenship. Immigration rules seem to be very loose or elastic, and a good deal of bribery has occurred in the past, which is going to make determining who is really whom very difficult. At the same time, Muslims who hold permanent IDs [less than full citizenship] are very worried about their status being revoked in this new system, along with their children's statuses as well. They are reticent about engaging a new system, thinking they might lose what they already have. They will all have to be recognized as 'Bengali.' Meanwhile, it is clear that the government authorities are manipulating the rules of immigration to make it difficult for Muslims to register as citizens."

I first mention that it seems rather ridiculous that "Burmese Muslims, fully acculturated Burmese citizens, should have to register as 'Bengalis' when it is obvious that ethnically and racially they are clearly not such." I then say that I think it will be doubly difficult for poor Rohingya of Arakan, given their lack of documentation, either through sheer negligence on their part or through the haphazard culture of registration that exists in the very underdeveloped parts of the country. Moreover, many Sittwe Muslims lost their papers in the fires of 2012 and have had no opportunity to recoup official documents. (Now in the post–August 25, 2017, world of hundreds of thousands of Rohingya refugees, having proper documentation would be extremely unrealistic when many people fled with absolutely nothing but what they wore on their backs.) He nods, though I don't think he has considered this practical side of the problem before. He goes on to say that "it is also clear that to be fair the parliament needs to review the 1982 law, but I don't think that they will. The whole process hasn't really started yet in earnest. In answer to your question, I really don't know if this verification scheme is going to work or not." In my own mind, I doubt that it ever will because it requires Rohingya to basically give up on their self-designating identity as "Rohingya." By referring to themselves as "Bengalis," they would be forfeiting their claim to belonging to Myanmar. Aung San Suu Kyii has tried to maneuver around this issue by referring to the Rohingya as "Muslims of Rakhine State." But that designation has not gained widespread currency, though perhaps it is most responsible to the historical reality. Nationalists, both Rakhine and Burmese, insist on "Bengali," and Rohingya insist on "Rohingya." Even among moderate Buddhists, I find the default designation is "Bengali." I am reminded of U Kyaw Hla Aung's (2: "The Spokesman") wistful observation in the IDP camp outside of Sittwe that his family comes from many generations of living in the Sittwe region, how he worked for twenty-four years in the law courts for the government, and now he's been stuck into a camp that he cannot escape from and is labeled as a "Bengali"!

With regard to the current difficulties being encountered by the Rohingya community and the nature of the contemporary controversies playing out, my friend says that "the military is using Aung San Suu Kyii to utilize their plans in every field that they can. The international community needs to provide Aung San Suu Kyii with hard evidence for the atrocities that we have heard about from questionable sources. It is the EU, UK, and US who need to effectively engage her with this evidence, not just NGOs who have been informed by Bengalis." In hindsight, I can see how much trust this man had placed in Aung San Suu Kyii and how much he doubted the sources reporting on the atrocities committed by the Myanmar army. In a conversation with him a year later, he continued to express doubts about the veracity of international media and UN reports regarding the Tatmadaw's crimes against the Rohingya of northern Arakan. Even a person like him, who is very sophisticated and critical-minded, had been somewhat conditioned by the government propaganda campaign to delegitimize the reports of atrocities appearing in the Western media and reported out by the UN as well.

About a month after our conversation, the UN Office of the High Commissioner for Human Rights released its scathing forty-three-page flash report (OHCHR 2017) based on more than two hundred interviews with Rohingya, mostly women, who had escaped to Bangladesh in the wake of almost unspeakable atrocities visited on their villages by the Myanmar military, police, border patrol, and Rakhine vigilantes after the October 9, 2016, attack on government border posts. It now appears that perhaps as many as a thousand people may have been killed, including many women and children, and scores, if not hundreds, of women were savagely raped by soldiers. The report indicates that Burmese soldiers, referred to by the Rohingya as "the Buddhist Army," mocked and taunted Muslims about the powerlessness of Allah to save them while engaging in their atrocities against defenseless and innocent people. Moreover, the report suggests that the Tatmadaw has used a calculus of terror to instigate the wholesale evacuation of scores of villages, many of which were burned to the ground. Many Rohingya captives were ensnared by the fires. Even if only a fraction of the interviews conducted under the auspices of UN interviewers and interpreters are credible, veritable crimes against humanity have clearly taken place. But still, presented with this kind of overwhelming evidence, supported by forensic physical evidence obtained by medical doctors and nurses, the only response by Suu Kyii's Ministry of Foreign Affairs (she is formally the country's foreign minister) in the week following the release of the UN report had been that they would like the UN to supply more information and then they would look into the matter internally. It has been reported that Suu Kyii had been directly informed of the contents of the report by the UN high commissioner in two separate phone calls. In previous responses to the report and supported by a domestic commission earlier appointed by Suu Kyii and headed by a former army general, the Myanmar government denied the claims made by Rohingya survivors and had gone so far as to suggest—fantastically—that Rohingya had set fire to their own villages in order to make the Myanmar army look culpable in the eyes of the international community. Predictably, a chorus of criticism from a variety of sources in the international community descended on Suu Kyii, including condemnation by former Nobel Peace Prize laureates who had written an appeal to the UN Security Council to take this urgent matter up at the earliest possible moment. No doubt the report from the UN OHCHR will reinforce this request. The US embassy in Yangon, even during these times of political transition, stated that it was "deeply concerned" by the UN report.

The post–October 9, 2016, "search-and-clear" operations conducted by the Myanmar military exacerbated an already torturous set of relations obtaining between the Rohingya and the Arakanese Buddhist majority in Rakhine State. That scene makes even more improbable my embassy interlocutor's suggestion that what needs to occur now are exercises of "trust building between the two communities. And both need to refrain from creating fake news. Most of the Muslim intellectuals are 'Burmese Muslims' and not Rohingya. Most of them are also very close to the Burmese Buddhist community, the educated Burmese. And most of them have moderate ideas. The trust building should begin between these Burmese Muslims and the Buddhist intellectuals and then extend to the other Muslim communities."

Two things struck me as significant in his comment. The first is that the Myanmar government has tried very hard to discredit all reports that the Rohingya have generated regarding their maltreatment. Several times, Burmese acquaintances told me about a fake photo of an obvious Cambodian context in which a young boy was being badly abused. That example had been passed off by Rohingya sources as evidence. The government has been almost relentless in its denials and its own characterization of the attackers on their border post as terrorists and Muslim extremists. The campaign has been so effective that even progressive and moderate Burmese assume that most of what gets reported to the West about the Rohingya situation is bogus information. There is such a long history of propaganda emanating from government sources in Myanmar that it is not surprising that so many Burmese would place some modicum of credibility in the government reports, especially since they have been so buoyed by Aung San Suu Kyii's sweeping election victory. It is clear, however, that many in the NLD government are hardly progressive or critical in their perspectives and harbor deep-seated prejudices against Muslim people, especially the Rohingya. So I am not taken aback by the posture of my confidant, even though he is an information officer for an important embassy in Yangon. That Rohingya produce fake news is a staple in virtually all conversations that refer to government violence or discriminatory policies. Social media, especially Facebook, has been complicit in enabling the spread of blatantly untrue propaganda from government sources. At the same time, there have been many reports that Rohingya Facebook and YouTube accounts have been disabled in Myanmar. This is not to accuse Facebook and other social media of being biased or in support of the Myanmar government, but to point out that they are not prepared for or capable of adjudicating a complex situation about which they are likely quite innocent in terms of religio-cultural-political awareness. That social fact only underscores the verity of my interlocutor's suggestion that trust building is the order of the day. But for that to happen, the culture of the government is going to have to change. It cannot simply turn its eyes away from such wanton military criminality. A generation of Rohingya will not soon forget what the Myanmar military and government have done to their community. Burmese and Arakanese Buddhist fears of a Muslim insurgency, aided and abetted by external forces, may very well become something of a self-fulfilling prophesy, given the despicable manner in which Rohingya have been treated by the Myanmar government and military. It is often said in Myanmar these days that "only one side of the story is being reported by the international media." I have had occasion to ask, in return, "What is the other side to the story of a well-armed military with a history of brutality (just ask the Shan, Karen, and Kachin) descending on villages of farmers with a violent cruelty that produces almost four-fifths of a million refugees within ten months' time?"

I mention to my interlocutor how downtown Yangon and downtown Mandalay with their complementary presence of Buddhist, Christian, Hindu, and Muslim communities could function as a model for the nation as a whole. He simply nods, and it seems that he is used to hearing this kind of thing. He says that the fact of the matter is that inner-city Yangon and Mandalay are stark exceptions to the predominant mode of perception that dominates Burmese consciousness. This is depressing for me to hear. He goes on to say that "the determination for trust building right now seems to be less than robust. The army has managed to marginalize not only the Muslims, but also Christians who live throughout the country." Here he is referring to the Chin, Kachin, and Kayin States, where Christians form a very significant percentage of the population and find themselves largely excluded from the benefits of any realized or potential development. Government support for education in these regions is also barely negligible. He continues. "So this army has become a national military of Buddhists. In the near future, I'm afraid that the army will become even more ultranationalist. It would like to influence or curry favor with the sangha." Here I recall Juliane Schober's assessment in her *Modern Buddhist Conjunctures* (Schober 2011) that the sangha is virtually the only other organization on a national scale besides the military that exists throughout Myanmar. It makes sense that the army would want to coopt it. This seems, very much, to have been its plan. The cultivation of U Wirathu by the USDP, especially his connection to the late Burmese Buddhist militant nationalist Aung Thaung, seems to reflect this aspiration. But my friend adds, "Very few in the sangha would like to see this happen, though there are a few leading monks who would like to see a rapprochement between the military and the sangha." With this, I am reminded of recent sermon given by Sitagu about the desirability of the military, sangha, and laity becoming united in purpose. And then there is Sitagu's other recent sermon to soldiers about Dutthagamini's lack of culpability in slaying so many Tamils, a parallel to their onslaught on the "less-than-human" Rohingya. The thought frightens me and I understand why some of Sitagu's critics, like Wai Moe, see him as holding out for a country that is similar in profile to Iran, where the clerics and those who possess weapons collude in power.

My friend is of the view that "both sides [the Ma Ba Tha and the Rohingya] appeal to the media in extreme fashion. "The Rohingya overemphasize their suffering while the Ma Ba Tha is always assailing us with unbelievable statistics" supporting their claim about how the Muslims will soon overrun the country. I say I am a bit troubled by this attempt to arrive at a "balanced assessment" because I don't think that the Rohingya and the Ma Ba Tha are exactly comparable social entities. The former is simply a religio-ethnic community, while the latter is a hypermilitant religiopolitical movement actually striving to eliminate the former from a future presence in Myanmar. And what is comparable about trying to report on genuine suffering on a massive scale on the one hand and the promulgation of lies and hate-mongering on the other? One of my enduring concerns in Myanmar has been how little most Burmese actually know about the plight of Rohingya in northern Arakan. Not only have extremely few of them ever been to Rakhine State, especially since 2012, but they really are not aware of the genuine state of suffering visited on hundreds of thousands of people, many of them interred within IDP camps that function as massive stalls. I am worried that even intelligent and critical minds like my friend's are impossibly conditioned by the influence of normative Burmese political discourse in its present state of development.

Given the recent UN report based on interviews with Rohingya refugees in Bangladesh, my friend's next statement, in retrospect, is especially precious. He says, "Aung San Suu Kyii should consider more of a potential role for the UN in the verification and trust-building processes. A third-party mediation is much needed." I ask, "What would the Rakhine Buddhists say to that?" His answer: "They would just have to accept it at some point." Unfortunately, I can't imagine that Rakhine would ever accept this possibility. Their state parliament even voted to boycott the work of Kofi Annan's Commission, which was charged with making recommendations to the union government. I express some skepticism, but he continues in a constructive fashion.

"We need a psychological rehabilitation of both communities. The government should initiate it! Progressive Buddhist monks could be a part of this. Further, Aung San Suu Kyii and the government should engage Muslim intellectuals such as former ambassadors, former parliamentarians, et cetera in order to discuss practical problems like health and education for Muslims and also to begin to establish trust building. She needs to engage more high-profile Muslims. The majority of Muslims are moderate." This is precisely why I have enjoyed talking with my acquaintance in the past. Despite the seemingly intractable problems facing Myanmar, he remains hopeful and makes suggestions that could plausibly improve the future track. I wonder now how he reacted to the brazen murder at Yangon International Airport of the prominent Muslim lawyer and NLD adviser Ko Ni during the last week of January 2017. Ko Ni had been an advocate for changing the 2008 constitution to scale back the sweeping powers of the military still in place.

After all, my friend is not optimistic about the military and what their presence will mean for the country in the future. He says, "There has been no tangible sign of reform from the army since the time that the US sanctions were lifted [by Barack Obama during Aung San Suu Kyii's visit to America in September 2016]. With regard to the constitution and civil war problems, there haven't been any steps toward constitutional reform or coming to terms with the Shan and Kachin. In fact, now the Shan and Kachin are being labeled terrorists, as they were referred to in the 2017 New Year's message delivered by the head of the military. There has been no sign of the army engaged in any form of trust building. It seems that the military needs to fight to maintain its dominant status. 'The lady' and the international community need to figure out how to minimize the military's dominance. The army and ex-army people [USDP] are very united in their aims and objectives. Most of the NLD politicians think that there are divisions (such as between Shwe Mann and Thein Sein) to exploit, but actually they are a closely knit community. The appearance of divisiveness could even be part of their strategy. Add to this their cultivation and support by the Ma Ba Tha. They remain formidable. Since 1962, the army has promoted xenophobia, and this is what has inhibited any progressive mind-set among the Burmese, especially the countryside Burmese, that transcends any single religious community [Buddhism]. So, foreigners are seen, especially in rural areas, not as friends. *Kalar*, or foreigner, signifies the invader. The army postures as the 'protector,' as does the Ma Ba Tha. What we need to do is to encourage these people to open up their minds. We're still in a closed society, with the vast majority of people not knowing what is happening beyond our borders."

Knowing that I am headed out to Rakhine State on a flight to Sittwe the next morning, my friend begins to engage in stereotypes about the Rakhines in a playful way. Charitably, I compare his comments to what one can hear from

Japanese people in Kyoto talking about people in Osaka, although there is more of an edge to what he is saying. What he has to say echoes what my eighty-year-old Bengali friend William in Yangon (2: "Real Bengalis") had told me four months earlier about the Rakhine, so I realize that my friend is not articulating a private prejudice only. He says, "Rakhine people are not hardworking, while the Muslims do most of the heavy lifting. Rakhine will tell you that themselves. Most Rakhine would prefer a Muslim trishaw driver. Rakhine will try to charge you more and complain about the price, while the Muslims are humble and hardworking and take what you give." I didn't get a chance to find out if this piece of information was true or not, because now all of the bicycle rickshaw drivers in Sittwe are Rakhine. The Sittwe Muslims are all in the IDP camp several miles north of town, where they have been held since the riot in mid-2012.

I meet my friend over lunch a year later, in **January 2018**, this time in a quiet restaurant of my choice in downtown Yangon, as I don't want to negotiate the choking traffic again. He is as articulate and yet as cautious as I remember, and still well intentioned. He asks me about the progress of my book, and I tell him that I thought I had the manuscript almost completed before the post–August 25, 2017, mayhem occurred. He shakes his head in an understanding way and reminds me that I am not to use his name. I mention to him that I had recently seen a broadcast in which he was interviewed by *The Irrawaddy* and he smiles.

My first question to him has to do with the pope's recent visit and what he makes of the fact that the pope was advised by the Yangon cardinal not to use the word "Rohingya." He says that the Christians worry that any provocation of the Buddhists will lead to a lessening of trust between the communities. The Christians simply did not want the pope to be seen as interfering in Myanmar's affairs because it would discredit their community. While he agrees that there is some anti-Muslim sentiment in the Christian community, he points out that the Rohingya do have a modicum of sympathy from other ethnic minorities who have previously suffered at the hands of the Myanmar military. I am aware of a statement made in the past month by the Karen Women's Organization expressing solidarity with the Rohingya community, but I say I haven't seen any other public statements. My friend says that it is also well known that many Burmese activists are also sympathetic.

I had just come from an extraordinary interview with Abu Tahay, who had speculated about who was behind the so-called terrorist ARSA (Arakan Rohingya Salvation Army) attacks of August 25 that precipitated the current crisis. So, I asked my friend directly, "Who was responsible for August 25? And exactly who is ARSA?" My questions produced a long, indirect response.

"ARSA has a relation to Rakhine. Some of them are staying in Bangladesh now. Back in U Nu's time [intermittently from 1948 to 1962], there were radio broadcasts in the Rohingya language two times a week. Rohingya terminology in the Burmese encyclopedia [*Birminica*] was used. There was also use of that terminology before the 1990 elections in the name of political parties. Though most Burmese people don't want to use that name, there is some evidence of its use [historically]. Use of the terminology also began to spread in peripheral border areas near Bangladesh in the 1990s. Some Rakhine scholars don't accept the name. They think that it has been appropriated by the Muslims, as it refers to indigenous people of Rakhine. U Nu got the support of the Muslims in Rakhine; that's why he agreed to accept the term. He opened the space for broadcasts. This was self-serving politically. Even Aung San had difficulties with the Rakhine. U Nu was cultivating support in this region by appealing to the Rohingya."

When he visited Maungdaw following October 9, 2016, my friend says that he could see that "some of the younger village people were connected to Bangladesh, moving freely across the border. So maybe they were getting some financial help from Bangladeshis. These young people seemed influential in the village and could speak English. For many villagers, there is not even an issue about whether they are Rohingya or Bengali. Many have purely a local awareness. During the military time [military dictatorship, 1962–2011], the local people simply obeyed and followed the rules and maybe occasionally had to provide bribes but generally were living peacefully. In 2004, military intelligence was dismantled and so security became quite lax. Before this, good relations were maintained between the military and the religious leaders. After this, a broader identity among the Muslims seems to have surfaced. In 2011, the joint border force [police, immigration, and military] was also dismantled. The joint force had a lot of complaints against it and did not have good relations with the local people. Maybe it was complicit in the drug trade. Rule of law in the region was very weak. Law enforcement was not up to the task—it was lackluster. It failed to set up good communications/intelligence with the Muslim community. However, Muslims were the people who did the actual physical labor for the law enforcement, so law enforcement had to remain on decent terms with them. Sort of like what the Sittwe Buddhist people had to do when they had problems with, say, the sewer.

"In any case, now we have to consider the possibility of separation and not integration."

At this I say, "Do you mean separate but equal?" I'm quite sure that he did not understand the implication of that phrase for an American. But that is what he was arguing for.

"We need a transparent and systematic verification process. The former chief of immigration for the government says that his department had compiled a list of all Muslims in northern Arakan. I asked in 2013 the chief minister if they still had such a compiled list. He said yes. I asked why not use that list for the process of verification? The chief immigration minister had already submitted this list to the union government and was waiting for a response on what to do. So they could have sped up the verification process if they had used that list. I don't know why they were reluctant to use the list for the verification process. By using this list, at least they could verify how long a family has lived locally. It was the decision of the union government not to use the list. We cannot say whether they [the government] were truly interested or not. In the relocation process, integration is now not practical. The Buddhists are afraid of the Muslims." He proceeds to tell me about how Buddhists in Kyaukphyu were in a state of fear before 2012 because the population there was fifty-fifty Buddhist and Muslim. Following the incarceration of the Muslims, they have become comfortable and do not want to revert back to a condition in which they have to fear. "Now the Muslims have been removed and so the Buddhists prefer to maintain the status quo." I reflect on how the same situation obtains in Sittwe.

I ask him directly why there is such a wave of denial on the part of so many Burmese to admit what the army has done out in Arakan. I know that this is a question that in his eyes is rigged, or one-sided. He winces a bit and says without much confidence that "we simply don't know exactly what has happened out there." I see that he is back to equivocating like he did in our meeting the year before. He's on the verge of referring to the need for a "balanced" perspective again. So I press him harder than I would like on this and say firmly that "there is now incontrovertible evidence that the army has committed crimes against humanity out in Arakan. The whole world, except for people in this country, seems to be aware of this." He senses that I am not about to settle for the "on balance" response and says, "The psychological trauma of fifty years of repression affects how people view this problem. More than 70 percent live under poverty and are uneducated, with very limited knowledge. The military actually prefers this. The Rakhine don't even trust the Bamar and see the Burmese as intruders." He doesn't want to go any further than this and changes the direction of the conversation.

I let it go at that. However, rather than "psychological trauma," I would refer to the conditioned perspective of the Burmese masses as a matter of socialization. By that I mean that the sangha and the state have set themselves up as unquestioned authorities in Myanmar and people have been socialized to accept their authority and their versions of reality. There is simply no other credible alternative that has emerged yet. The independent media has a tiny audience, and since it has begun reporting, however sparingly, about the troubles in Arakan, it has come under siege from the police and the army. About a dozen reporters were arrested in 2017, the best known being the Reuters reporters who may have secured damning evidence against the military and government regarding the murders of ten Rohingya villagers in northern Arakan, specifically information about a mass grave site.

In any case, my friend wants to move on and so observes, "Sanctions might push Myanmar back to Russia and China. They are ready to welcome Myanmar. The good thing is that only [Tatmadaw general] Maung Maung Soe was targeted by the Americans. We should not close the door in dealing with Western nations. We need good relations with India, Japan, and South Korea as well in order to neutralize Chinese dominance. Why hasn't the Chinese president visited Myanmar? Not since 2001 has a Chinese president visited. Has Myanmar been dealing with China equally? China has the upper hand. Obama visited twice! But this is one of three countries, Thailand and Brunei being the other two, that the Chinese president has not visited." He seems offended by what he perceives as China being eager to exploit Myanmar but being somewhat aloof diplomatically. I don't see this myself, as the Chinese have consistently protected Myanmar diplomatically whenever germane issues have arisen for discussion at the UN. His perspective seems to be a hangover from the anti-Chinese sentiment I heard so strongly expressed back in 2010.

I shift the conversation back to the impending repatriation process that purportedly is to begin in a few weeks' time, in late January, according to an agreement reached between Myanmar and Bangladesh. He says, "They will not send the people back to the same places; at least half will be relocated in newly built villages." Privately, I worry that this will mean more camps and that these camps turn into permanent apartheid-like conditions. He says that he has heard that the government will begin to work through the mullahs and seek their leadership in getting the rank and file to cooperate. But it seems that they (the government) are delaying the issue of citizenship for the Rohingya as long as possible. In fact, as of early 2019, no repatriations have occurred.

Finally, I broach the topic of Aung San Suu Kyii and how she is being criticized internationally for a lack of leadership during this crisis. He says, "She needs to engage and have a dialogue with the army leaders. She needs to point out to them what are the benefits of a cease-fire. She should mobilize the support of the people as she engages the army. We (Myanmar) are sailing without a compass at sea. The question in the present now is 'How can we improve the civilian-military relation in the country?' Aung San Suu Kyii could neutralize the military's presence in politics. She has wasted a lot of time in not doing this. Is she entrapped? She must negotiate the rewriting of the constitution. Until now, there hasn't been a single step toward this. We can't build a democratic union without a new constitution." Indeed, that much is very clear.

Real Bengalis

In July and August of 2016, I made the acquaintance of three late-middle-aged Bengali brothers who operate a well-established medicinal supply shop in busy downtown Yangon just a few blocks away from the Sule Pagoda. All three were born in Mandalay during the 1950s, before the situation for ethnic South Asians had taken a more dramatic turn for the worse in Burma. Tensions had first arisen during the economic downturn of the 1930s and many South Asians had left at the time of independence in 1947 when their positions as middlemen between the British and the Burmese and other ethnic groups evaporated with the demise of the colonial political and economic framework. But still many other Indians had remained behind, families who had lived for generations in Burma and regarded it as their home. Such was the situation of the family of these three brothers. Their father had been born in Yangon in 1912 and their mother had come from Calcutta well before World War I. Their paternal grandfather had come to Burma from Calcutta around 1900 and had worked on the railways for the British as an executive administrator living in and working all over the country. Burma was part of the British Raj at that time and so the movement from Bengal to Burma was not understood as radical. The three brothers proudly claim Myanmar as their homeland and still take an optimistic view of the country's political and economic future. Our main conversation, aside from earlier introductory moments, including one several months earlier on a previous visit to Yangon, was held in the back of their bustling shop in the late afternoon and evening on a sultry early August day. They were eager to help me once they learned of my background more fully. The warmth of their demeanor made me feel as if I were among friends of the family. In a sense, I was.

I ask the brothers straightaway what caste their grandfather belonged to, but they answer that caste had not remained a very important a factor through the three generations of the family's time in Myanmar. While I think that this may have been an evasive answer, the fact that all the brothers regarded themselves as *both* Hindu and Buddhist simultaneously may have had to do with the lack of interest in maintaining a specific caste identity, since caste is not a factor at all in most Buddhist societies, Sri Lanka's being the exception. Indeed, as many Indians in Burma reportedly "intermarried" with other castes due to the limitations of finding suitable matches within their own subcommunities, this may have been the rule with these brothers as well. In any case, I can only describe these three brothers as Bengalis, yes, but staunch, now patriotic citizens of the new Myanmar. As far as they were concerned, Burma is and has always been their home. One of them in particular seems extremely well integrated or invested insofar as he has served as an accountant or treasurer for one of the leading Burmese Buddhist monks of Myanmar and accompanies the monk's entourage whenever he travels abroad. He has even been to the United States with the monk, in charge of paying bills and keeping track of all expenses. It is his way of helping to promote the *dhamma* and earning merit at the same time.

While the brothers are quite friendly and open with me, owing ultimately to the fact that one of their cousins had migrated to America and her son had been my student about twenty years earlier, they ask me not to use their names in whatever I write. I take this as a sign that despite what some, including my friend Ashin Kumara at Sitagu's international academy (3: "The Rector"), may have said about how freedom of speech had opened up so dramatically with the NLD's November 2015 landslide victory, and some have even felt free enough to openly criticize the government in the aftermath, others remain quite circumspect about speaking up publicly, especially regarding political matters. This reticence may be, to some extent, a hangover from the military dictatorship days, when public political discourse or criticism (except for hilarious lampoons lobbed by the famous comedy group the Moustache Brothers in Mandalay) was pretty much forbidden. Or it may be because the contemporary political and security scene in Myanmar is not quite as free or safe as one might hope. Indeed, freedom for the media is now a matter of circumspection. This is precisely what Yanghee Lee, the UN special rapporteur for Burma, had said on a number of occasions at the conclusion of her fact-finding stints in Myanmar. People are generally not quite relaxed enough yet, or secure enough, to be completely open about their political thoughts or feelings. Fear still hovers in the background. The three brothers were open with me, but they also did not want their names published where future government officials could identify them and perhaps cause them some trouble. The political situation in Myanmar is confused now, despite the NLD's sweeping victory. Former military hard-liners have mixed into the new government, and the military's obvious control of the border, home, and defense ministries means that even if the NLD was consistently progressive, which it clearly is not, real control of order by the police and the army is not vested in a civilian government. It is this explanation that has become the charitable view regarding the deafening silence, until now, afforded by Aung San Suu Kyii in relation to the Rohingya crisis, especially in the aftermaths of October 9, 2016, and August 25, 2017. Indeed, the continued posture of denial by her foreign ministry office regarding the increasing evidence of crimes against humanity betrays a willful posture on the part of the NLD to appease the Tatmadaw. After years of repression by the Tatmadaw, most sensible people remain wary. Moreover, there is also some growing evidence of mob or mafia influence or control in urban Yangon operating extrajudicially. But all of these considerations didn't stop my friends from expressing some of their candid views about recent political events.

In their youth, all three boys had attended a Roman Catholic school from grade one to grade twelve in Mandalay. The medium of instruction, of course, was English. The school was nationalized when they were in fifth, third, and first standards, respectively. All missionaries had left by 1965, and the schools, including theirs, were eventually switched to the *swabasha* Burmese medium. This, they agree, was a pivotal moment that had led to the decline in the quality of education throughout the country and the introduction of more parochial modes of thought. (Their understanding of the significance of *swabasha* [education in their parents' language] was exactly what is often heard in Sri Lanka regarding the language-of-instruction shift that occurred there in the 1960s.) But as a result of the timing of their educations at the Catholic school in Mandalay, they are completely fluent in three languages: Burmese, English, and Bengali. As such, they have something of a rare skill in Myanmar these days: the ability to converse in more than one language. And, consequently, they can think conceptually beyond the horizons of their own subcommunity. In other ways, the three brothers and their cosmopolitan perspectives epitomize what downtown Yangon has continued to symbolize with its robust and intermingling Hindu, Muslim, Christian, and Buddhist populations. During my visits, I often observed major South Indian Hindu processions in the streets, the Muslim calls to prayer heeded in and around downtown's many mosques, the sermon and fund-raising campaigns of Burmese Buddhist temples in the streets, and the chiming of bells announcing daily mass at the impressive Roman Catholic cathedral that celebrates five hundred years of Christian presence in Southeast Asia, dating to the first appearance of the Portuguese, not to mention the classic Anglican cathedral just west of Scott's Market. The presence of many other religious communities is evident in the streets too: including Sikhs, the Arya Samaj, thriving Chinese temples, a Telugu Christian congregation, and Karen Baptist and Burmese Lutheran Protestant congregations, in addition to Methodists and Anglicans. My Bengali friends were but a subset of the South Asian presence, one that was fostered by the colonial aspirations of the British from the end of the nineteenth century until independence in 1947. In downtown Yangon, they were one of many different communities that had continued to persevere through the troubled years of military dictatorship and growing Buddhist nationalism throughout the twentieth and twenty-first centuries.

When prompted about the legacy of military rule, the eldest brother begins to reminisce: "When Ne Win came to power, he announced that no Indians could work for the government anymore and so many of our people left for Singapore and Malaysia. He also nationalized all of our properties, leaving us without any accumulated personal wealth that had been invested. On March 19, 1964, all shops were nationalized in the name of socialism, thereby completely eliminating the private sector. He had started nationalizing the mining and banking sectors in 1962 and 1963 shortly after his coup removed Prime Minister U Nu. But the big takeover occurred in 1964. Not only did Ne Win eliminate all 50- and 100-kyat currency notes, but kyats could no longer be traded for other currencies. It was truly a revolutionary time. At once, we felt isolated from the rest of the world and we had also lost control of our private means for making a living. Our properties (house, car, apartments, et cetera) were nationalized."

The second brother then picks up the thread: "From 1964 until 1988, we were selling our wares on the black market or 'on the street.' It was very difficult to survive! This shop did not get established officially as a private enterprise until 1994, and since then it has thrived. We are doing well because we have continued to work hard and honestly. We have a lot of loyal customers as a result."

I ask, "Why then did you stay when you saw so many others leave?" The eldest responds immediately: "We stayed because we love Myanmar. Burmese people are very polite and hospitable. We were raised as both Hindu and Buddhist and so have been practicing Buddhism and patronizing both types of temples all our lives. This is Myanmar and it is our home." I am not surprised to hear this. Most Burmese also suffered from the same repressive policies of Ne Win, and I surmised that something of a kinship had developed among all those affected, regardless of religion or ethnicity. These three Bengali brothers evidently felt a sense of kinship with Yangon's general population. They had shared a common grouse with the Tatmadaw.

The middle brother is especially vocal about recent political developments. When I ask about the fairness of the 1982 law formulated during Ne Win's time that established the "legitimacy" of indigenous communities on the basis of whether their communal presence in the country before 1823 was provable, he responds by saying, "The 1982 law is bullshit! This 'guest nationality' rubric is now the main problem at hand. If a father is not born here, then the children, even though they are born here, are regarded only as 'guests.' In 1948, anyone born here who wanted Burmese nationality could receive it. Our father was given the UCC [Union Certificate of Citizenship] status after swearing allegiance in the court." The 1982 law, in retrospect, seems as if it was formulated directly with the South Asian community in mind, because the Hindus, Muslims, and Christians of South Asian descent who were brought to Myanmar by the British would all be flagged as ineligible for citizenship under this rubric. It is precisely this law that calls the status of almost all Rohingya Muslims into question. It is the enforcement of this law that makes one worry about Aung San Suu Kyii's statement that the current problems "must be settled according to the rule of law." With this law in the background, it also makes comments made to me even by progressive monks like Jotika and Kumara in Mandalay (3: "The Anti-Nationalists" and "The Rector," respectively), who say that "the Bengalis must respect our laws," problematic, morally so, given the obvious discriminatory intent of Ne Win's promulgation and his history of excluding people of South Asian descent.

The second brother begins to feel his oats more and senses that I not only understand him but am entirely sympathetic. "Back in the day, there was religious harmony, especially in Mandalay. You can even see it today. Our last kings brought in people from many parts of Asia, especially India. We didn't see any tensions whatsoever in the country between religions until 2012. The Burmese military were worried about Aung San Suu Kyii coming to power and so used the religion card to divide people." He goes on to express confidence in the religious leaders of the country by saying that the religious problems will now be solved soon given the recent stance made clear by sangha leaders. By this, he is referring to how the Ma Ba Tha had been recently sidelined by the Ma Ha Na, the formal governmental administration of the sangha.

I counter a bit because I think he has overreached with his comment about no problems between religions until 2012. Maybe he is actually accurate in asserting this, given his own personal experiences, but I want to see if he and his brothers will agree that the anti-Muslim sentiment among the Burmese today might have its roots in the British period, when the Burmese resented what was perceived as Indian collusion with the British, as a result of their middleman functions. Yes, indeed, they heartily agree. Ne Win's actions had been motivated precisely because of the anti-Indian sentiments that had first arisen in the 1930s. I also note in passing how the last of the Burmese kings had been referred to as "our kings" and given credit for Mandalay's multicultural character. The comment not only reflects an interesting ownership of Burmese kingship by a "Bengali citizen" but also attributes greater impact to royal policies than could be merited historically, owing to how the British administration under the Raj was no doubt much more of an influence in drawing more people from the Indian subcontinent to Burma's cities.

The conversation then takes a different turn. The middle brother again assumes command: "Ninety percent of the big powerful Buddhist monks do not like to see a woman as the country's political leader. This isn't just because she [Aung San Suu Kyii] married a Britisher and has British sons. Traditional monks want men as the political leaders in the tradition of their kings. Even during the days of Queen Shin So Bo [who built the Shwedagon Pagoda], there were monks who opposed her reign." While his comment, if true, is a powerful indicator of the misogynist character of many Burmese Buddhist monks, it also underscores how remarkably powerful the legacy of General Aung San continues to be for many. Aung San Suu Kyii, as the daughter of the general, is the link to the origins of a free Burma in the minds of so many, and that fact alone seems more powerful than the gendered conception of political power that seems embedded in most. Nevertheless, I have also been struck by how gender is so hierarchically expressed in the Buddhist religious culture of Myanmar, to a much greater extent, I felt, than in either Sri Lanka or Laos ritual contexts, and probably in Thai and Khmer as well, though I am on less firm ground in those two latter contexts. The most conspicuous example of this gendered hierarchical consciousness in relation to power that I had seen is how women are prevented from getting close to worshiping the Mahamuni Buddha image in Mandalay. As a consequence, women are not allowed to press their gold leaf offerings onto the body of the Buddha and must find a surrogate to do so. Even as a foreigner, and therefore presumably a pollution-carrying persona, as a male I was allowed on the topmost dais directly in front of the image. A second example springs to mind as I quickly weigh this comment. While there is such a thriving *thila shin* (unordained Buddhist nun) population in Burmese Myanmar (very few in Arakan), the issue of full ordination has not surfaced in a very powerful way, in stark contrast to the manner in which it has been pursued in

Thailand, but especially in Sri Lanka. Women, in general, do not seem as if they are overtly challenging the social reality of gendered social hierarchy in Myanmar, at least not yet—or at least not in the same degree as in Sri Lanka. If Aung San Suu Kyii realizes her great potential as a leader, perhaps this will create a more widespread momentum for the women's movement in Myanmar, I muse: her support among women throughout the country has been as deep as it is ubiquitous.

The middle brother continues his line: "The power of the 'big monk' is so persuasive that so many of the Burmese have followed the anti-Muslim sentiment coming from the powerful Ma Ba Tha. This had been the USDP [Union Solidarity and Development Party] strategy that seemed to be working so successfully until the election results were made clear. Fortunately, the move to disestablish the Ma Ba Tha came from within the sangha itself. This showed that the Ma Ba Tha emphasis on preserving the religion really has little to do with the cultivation of *sila* [morality], *samadhi* [concentration], and *panna* [wisdom]." I find his statement profoundly insightful. He goes on to say that he thinks that the four race and religion laws passed by the USDP-dominated parliament before the November 2015 elections will all be undone in a matter of course. All of the brothers believe that Aung San Suu Kyii will try to separate religion and politics. I wonder to myself if that particular aspiration would ever gain any traction in Myanmar, at least not until Buddhism as it is articulated publicly is displaced from its hegemonic influence among the Burmese. This would take many generations, if it happens at all. At least that is how I reflected at that time.

While these three brothers are "Hindu Bengalis" who speak the Calcutta dialect within their family and are therefore regarded differently by those educated people who care to discriminate beyond the broad South Asian national or ethnic brush, they remain deeply sympathetic for what is happening to Rohingya. They do not use the term "Bengali Muslims" in their references to the Rohingya. They recognize that the Rohingya language is not simply the Bengali Chittagong dialect but has elements of language (especially vocabulary) quite separate from their Calcutta-based Bengali and the Chittagong dialect as well. This was a very important confirmatory bit of information for me, as many of my Burmese and Rakhine conversationalists, as I have mentioned earlier, had clearly stated that the Rohingya speak the "Chittagonian dialect" and left it at that. When I asked Rohingya in the camp outside of Sittwe about their language (see especially 2: "The Spokesman"), they were adamant in saying that it was different from the Bengali spoken around Chittagong. I had yet to confirm this with many others. As I mentioned in my conversations with Abu Tahay (1: "The Historian"), there are some Rohingya who want to claim that their language has affinities with Vesali, the indigenous language spoken in ancient times in what is now northern Arakan. We need a definitive linguistic analysis, in the same way we need fundamental anthropological studies in northern Arakan.

As the hours wore on, I learned about a brother-in-law also living in downtown Yangon who was married to the three brothers' eldest sister. One of the brothers suggested that I meet him, since he fancied himself as something of a historian of the Bengali community in Yangon. Was I interested in meeting him too? A phone call later and I was whisked off in a car to another neighborhood not far away. I was guided to a ramshackle apartment house and I climbed the stairs to a third-floor apartment on a busy downtown street. Stairwells in Yangon are notoriously poorly lit and maintained. I was a bit spooked before a friendly face appeared behind a slowly opening door and I was warmly invited inside. My host was a genial but not-so-spry eighty-year-old man living with his son and daughter-in-law, both fairly successful people working for an international shipping line. In the living room, the first thing I noticed was two different collections of religious images kept in separate spaces on mantels, one Hindu and the other Buddhist. On the left were Hindu images of Laksmi and Visnu and on the right several Buddha images in different postures. I learned that the family regularly worships at both venues but never combines their pujas.

After I briefly explain the reason for my visits to Myanmar, at my behest William (an alias) proceeds to talk about his life story. He begins by recalling what it was like in Burma during World War II, his childhood years. I gather that he was born in 1936. His older brother had served as an interpreter for the Japanese occupiers. Before then, his brother was teaching Japanese in Santiniketan, in Bengal. After the war, his brother studied medicine, became a doctor, and left for India. His other elder brother also was a doctor but didn't leave for India until 1967, after Ne Win had made it so difficult for Indians in Burma. William had stayed behind here in Rangoon attending the Bengali academy that was formally affiliated with Calcutta University before graduating from Rangoon University in commerce and law. When all of the businesses in Burma were nationalized by Ne Win in the early 1960s, there suddenly was no future in the field of commerce! So he became an accountant for a private factory that was subsequently nationalized in 1967, which meant that he then became a government servant for the Ministry of Industry. More specifically, he was always employed in the manufacture of foodstuffs—sugar, alcohol, biscuits, and so forth. He was brought to work in the head office and audited food-manufacturing plants from 1967 until 1993. He was employed in this way until he finally landed in a sugar factory, where he worked for his final years before retirement in 1997. Given the sugarcane shortage of the 1990s, these sugar factories were transferred to the Ministry of Agriculture, for which he worked for his final four years before retirement.

He does not sound very enthusiastic while giving me this brief account of his career. I ask him, "Why did you stay after Ne Win took over?" He begins by saying that his father was a landlord and his lands had been expropriated in 1947 at independence, the first time that Indians were more or less forced to leave. "The tiller became the owner. We lost everything and came to Rangoon under an uncle's care. A year later I was taken to Bassein, where there were tensions between Burmese and Karen. But somehow, we managed as a family and this is where I lived until I attended the academy before university. After 1967, many Indians were taken by ship to India. My mother wanted us all to go back then.

Lands were being given around Calcutta for refugees from Burma. Practically my whole family left, including my father, who had been very keen to stay. But he had lost his land and was without citizenship. Before my father left for India, he had tried his hand at groceries, but there was so little money to be made in such an underground activity. So both my father and mother left, and both older brothers and sister left too. My uncle had obtained citizenship and I had gotten citizenship myself when I was eighteen [in 1954] by applying for a Union Citizenship Certificate, which at the time was issued if you were born in Burma. The main reason I stayed behind was because I had been married in 1963 and my in-laws were very supportive.

"We all struggled mightily during Ne Win's time. I got by with a paltry salary. But the good thing was that Ne Win provided everyone with rice for just 3 kyats per kilo, and petrol was also very cheap. This kept the cost of transport down very inexpensively and we had the basic food to eat. And there was always trade in the black market, of course. Ne Win kept us all in the dark about what was happening internationally by controlling the press and radio outlets. Also, there were no books available for us to read. We were kept busy scrambling for the basic necessities of life. Very few people were allowed to travel internationally, so I didn't have a chance to see my family for thirty years. Only high-level government people or big businesspeople with connections to the military were allowed to go outside. It was not so strict early on, and many, especially engineers, left for Singapore. But government servants on the whole were not allowed to exit the country. Remaining Hindus had to unite and further overcome their regional, linguistic, and caste differences in order to survive. The Jain population really declined. But the Hindus have remained and managed to sustain by a kind of eclectic worship. This is a cosmopolitan community here. Goenka's son is now the chair of the Bengali Hindu community in Yangon." Goenka was probably the most well-known teacher of *vipassana* meditation in the world. A prize student of the even more esteemed meditation teacher U Ba Chin, Goenka organized retreats in India and throughout the world for several decades and, perhaps more than any other individual, was responsible for the worldwide spread of *vipassana* meditation centers. I was impressed to hear that his son was now the nominal leader of the Bengali community in Yangon.

I ask William about the term *kalar,* and he explains that it originally meant an outsider from the West but came to designate South Asian in general during Ne Win's time. It has since morphed into a more precise designation of Muslims. This became a segue into a more general description of the nature of the Indian community as it had evolved in Yangon. It was fascinating and provided a perspective rarely heard—at least I hadn't known some of these facts before. First, he refers to the Kurangi (from the name of a village in Andhra) people, who were brought by the British to do the street sweeping in Yangon. "Even after independence, these latrine cleaners were allowed to stay and were kept here with special privilege. They never married. Indians generally never married outside of the Indian community. All the sweepers were Indians and I think that their status was just so low that no one ever considered the possibility of marrying their daughters into their lot. In any case, these sweepers were allowed to remit 100 kyats per month through the post office, again another exception. Different types of people were brought from different provinces in India to work for different purposes in Yangon. For instance, the refined work required for the making of public sculpture required bringing expert craftsmen from Orissa. Chettiars were brought from Madras to assist in the banking and accounting worlds. In fact, the Chettiars were called Madrasis (as were some Tamils and Andhras). Of course, the Chettiars were the infamous collectors to the Burmese and are always cited as heartless and greedy mercenaries interested only in usurping land from the Burmese or exacting outrageous terms for extending lines of credit or debt. Rarely do the Burmese talk about the Kurangis or others. Bengalis were often fishermen, and many South Indian Tamils and Andhras were also fishermen. Indians were often the middlemen in terms of providing transport, especially Muslims. Gurkhas came to be part of the army and were assigned to the hilly places in Myanmar. Most of the people who came here from India were poor and looking for a break, an opportunity of some kind. Agricultural people from Uttar Pradesh and Biharis were brought in to farm sugar for the sugar factories."

William is proud of the Indian diversity that had melded together into a community in Yangon. He is also concerned specifically about the future of the sub-Bengali community. For all the recent controversy referencing the Rohingya identity being a fraudulent front for "Bengali" interlopers, difficulties had been created consequentially for these Bengali Hindus, or "real Bengalis," as William had put it, absurd as that might sound. "We could not hold our 125-year celebration of our temple's foundation because of the Bengali association. People are not always well educated here, and so we are now getting classified in some quarters with the 'Bengalis' who are Rohingya. Even some ignorant government bureaucrats sometimes confuse us with the Rohingya. Of course, this has happened because the Burmese and others have insisted on using the term 'Bengali.' Many Burmese officials and Burmese in general have always had a difficult time distinguishing between Muslims and Hindus and Christians. These days it is easier because the Muslims are wearing distinctive clothes. For some, we are all *kalar.* But as I said, increasingly the term is saved for the Rohingya." The turn of the discussion enables me to ask William for his take on the current difficulties between Buddhists and Muslims. He is eager to share his perspective.

William immediately betrays his cynicism about the Myanmar military when he opens up this thread of discussion: "Our army wants to keep insurgency problems alive in order to thrive. The army is not eager for peace with all the ethnic groups, as they would lose their importance without live conflicts and thereby being seen as protectors of the Burman nation. Than Shwe is still pulling the strings." I had heard this perspective articulated by a number of well-educated people in both in Yangon and Sittwe. The distrust of the military remains palpable among many. Hatred of the military remains deep and widespread. Than Shwe was the last of the military dictators, and William's comment about him still being in control signals his own broader skepticism about the NLD's real power.

William also speaks about the connection between China and many of the elite generals in the army. Indeed, he claims that many of the generals in the Burmese army have a lot of Chinese in their family backgrounds. "Burmese are suspicious of the Chinese because of the fact that the Chinese constitution makes all those who have any Chinese blood as citizens. So, here in Myanmar, special actions have to be taken to ensure the loyalty of such people to the state."

It is no secret that many of the generals' major business deals have been made with the Chinese. The one now drawing the most attention is the oil and gas pipeline that begins on Ramree Island in northern Arakan and continues the length of Myanmar, all the way to Kunming in Yunnan. There is also a lot of talk about how the Chinese have bought up teak and jade at concessionary prices from the military. The double-lane highway leading north and south in the country is sometimes referred to derisively as "China's vacuum," which is sucking the wealth out of Myanmar. William explains, "Anti-Chinese sentiment first built during Ne Win's time. Mao's group was propagandizing and university students protested against this. The Chinese were also behind building up an anti-Indian feeling, including the Muslims, in order to divert attention away from them." I had heard this accusation leveled by a number of others as well.

William is both sympathetic toward and critical of the Rohingya. On the one hand, he says that "old books and encyclopedias do mention the Rohingya as an ethnic group in Myanmar. So they have been in this country for a long time." He then talks about how all Muslims, not just the Rohingya, have suffered during the recent "senseless violence" and how across the border in Bangladesh even Bengali Buddhists have suffered as well. He goes on to assert that "the Thein Sein government, of course, invented the 'guest citizenship' scheme to prevent having to give full citizenship to the Rohingya. There really is no legal basis for doing this, but it was only a scheme to keep *kalars* from gaining the foothold they need." Moreover, "border officials receive bribes, making it difficult to determine who is legitimate in Myanmar and who isn't. It's a big mess to sort out now."

William is also somewhat critical of the Arakanese Buddhists, who "are not very well educated, nor really hardworking people. Most of the heavy-lifting work in Arakan is done by Muslims, often women. It seems that almost all of the laborious works out there are done by *kalar*." I ask William if he thinks this division of labor reflects a class consciousness of sorts among the Arakanese, and he nods positively. But then he adds immediately that there are many very poor Arakanese Buddhists as well, and that is why there is a group of insurgents [the Arakanese Army] skirmishing with the government troops around Kyauktauw.

William feels that "the mistake of the Rohingya is that they want part of Arakan for themselves." He then makes a sweeping generalization that nearly bowls me over: "Muslim people can betray you anytime. Look at how there is violence even now in Pakistan between Shia and Sunni." This is one of those kinds of statements I often heard in Myanmar, uttered without the slightest sense of how prejudicial and utterly essentialist it might sound. I wince inwardly, regretting what I just heard, for most of what William had been telling me had made a good deal of sense to me. I didn't want to believe that I had just heard this claim.

But our conversation, which lasts very late into the night, ends on a different and positive note. William notes that a "democratic voice of Burma announced yesterday [July 28, 2016] that a council of interfaith dialogue would soon be established" and that "there is a movement to bring this current constitution in line with a true democratic federalism. Aung San Suu Kyii is involved in direct negotiations with each of the ethnic groups. She knows that no proper investment will be attracted in the ethnic areas until a peaceful negotiation is established."

As I just mentioned, it was dead late at night, past midnight, and I know that I had taxed William by my curiosity and persistence. He had reminisced about his life and offered his considered views about the current unfolding political scene. Except for his one sweeping generalization about trusting Muslims, which had taken me aback and surprised me, I felt I had been fortunate to gather these perspectives from people who understood themselves to be both ethnically Bengali and politically Burmese. William's memory spans more than seventy years, and he still harbors great hope for the well-being of the country. Clearly, he feels that democratic forces are ascendant and a return to the dark days of repression dictated by the military is now unthinkable.

I walked back to my hotel for about thirty-five minutes in the deep-dark and deserted streets of downtown Yangon, thankful for my flashlight and the Japanese initiative that had repaired many of the sidewalks along the main thoroughfares of the city. That night, I felt as if I had touched a bit of history.

A year and half later, just before Christmas in **December 2017**, I walk unannounced into the three brothers' shop in downtown Yangon on a mid-Tuesday afternoon. (I had sent an e-mail weeks earlier that had not been acknowledged.) Two of the brothers, the eldest and youngest, are in the back of the shop being held captive by another South Asian businessman, who continues his animated chat with them for about ten minutes before finally leaving. The eldest brother motions for me to sit down, so I wait patiently for my turn to greet them. As I wait and gaze about the shop I can see clearly that their business has continued to thrive. Medicinal stocks on the shelves are full and business seems brisk. Customers come and go in the front of the shop while several phones ring and are answered, some by the two brothers. I know as I wait, judging from the muted reception I just received, that my chances for a sustained conversation are slim or next to none. I gaze at prominently displayed photos of Sitagu, clearly a local object of the brothers' devotion, and a photo of the eldest brother holding some kind of document and joining hands with a smiling Aung San Suu Kyii. To myself, I marvel at how the profiles of these two previously lionized figures have been altered so dramatically in the eyes of Western observers. Here in Myanmar, they remain heroes almost bigger than life. I have a feeling that the obvious differences in perception about these two icons between the Bengali brothers and me might preclude any more thoughtful exchanges like we had enjoyed a year and half back. The middle brother, who had been so forthright in our extended conversation, is nowhere to be seen. Finally, the businessman who had preoccupied the brothers' attention finishes his monologue and I have a chance for the brothers' undivided attention.

"Can you remember me?" I open the conversation. The eldest brother begins to mime typing at a keyboard in reference to my manic obsession at recording their words. I say, "Yes, I thought I would be finished with my book by now, but the developments of the past several months made me determined to speak to my conversation partners again." A look of concern seems to well up in his eyes as he glances at the open door in the front of the shop. Even though I had written an effusive e-mail of thanks following my days with the brothers a year and half ago, I quickly continue the conversation, hoping to reestablish some friendly ground. "I want to thank you for introducing me to the Venerable Kumara [3: "The Rector"], with whom I have met several times and hope to see again next week."

"U Kumara and I are very close devotees [of Sitagu]. He can talk with you."

Sensing he was trying to end our conversation abruptly, I inquire about William, his elderly brother-in-law, since William had appeared quite frail and hobbled back in mid-2016. "Oh, William is just fine. Right now, he is in America with our [middle] brother visiting with his sick sister. So, you can't see either of them now. . . . It is past three o'clock and I need to get to another bazaar where I have rented space for the rest of the afternoon. I'm too busy to talk."

I ask if he would be free the next day or two and he replies curtly that he will be too busy. By now I have gotten the message quite clearly, so I decide to ask, "Given the current situation, are you too uncomfortable to talk with me?" He nods affirmatively. I then ask, "Are you *afraid* to talk with me?" Again, he nods, and this time I can see some mounting concern in his eyes. But I press forward anyway. I ask him if someone has advised him not to talk with foreigners. He replies, "I'd rather not say." At this I turn to the younger brother, who has been quietly observing our exchange. Two years ago, he had been alone in the shop when I first came. The other two brothers had been away at the time. At that time, he had quietly explained to me how he had felt that the Rohingya were being discriminated against and had asked me to return the next day. When I did, he had given me a privately published magazine entitled *Treasures of the Rohingya.* He had made his perspective quite clear. I turn to him now and ask, "Would you be able to speak with me for a few moments?" Before he can answer, the elder brother intervenes and says, "He doesn't speak English." Obviously, he doesn't realize that I had engaged his younger brother in conversational English on previous occasions while he was abroad. The younger brother looks sheepishly at me. I decide it is time to leave. As I get up from my chair, the elder brother says, "Maybe when you come next time . . ." I reply quietly as I turn to go, "I don't think there will be a next time." I don't mean to be rude. I am just stating that I believe that this will be my last visit to Myanmar.

This exchange was a sobering experience because these Bengali brothers had received me so warmly a year and a half back. Clearly, the atmosphere in Yangon had changed and the elder brother feared that my mere noticeable presence in his shop might put them at risk. And maybe this apprehension was felt for good reason, as these brothers had witnessed decades of repression in their own personal histories and were no doubt keen to steer a course away from any potential new dangers. Within the past month, I had learned that I would not be able to see U Kyaw Hla Aung in Sittwe (2: "The Spokesman") because the Rakhine State legislature had made visits by anyone not officially working for an NGO or a diplomatic post illegal and he had advised me that it would be too dangerous to attempt a visit using the clandestine routing I had pursued on two previous occasions. Also, I had been curtly informed in an email by the retired Kaman Muslim schoolteacher (2: "The Teacher") that she did not want to meet me anymore either. On the same day as my visit to see the Bengali brothers, I learned from Wai Moe that his mother did not want him to work in Myanmar right now because the two Reuters journalists had been detained the previous week and remained incommunicado in the custody of the police, who are controlled by the Home Ministry under the auspices of the Myanmar military. Maybe I could see Wai Moe in Chiang Mai. Finally, Kyaw Min and Wai Wai Nu were in Bangkok indefinitely, where Kyaw Min was being treated for health issues. The numbers of people with whom I had enjoyed cordial relations and had developed sustained conversations over the past three and half years would be drastically reduced this last time around. I considered myself fortunate to have been able to engage so many people previously, before the horizons of free speech had again been darkened in Myanmar's increasingly cloudy public sky. I repaired back to my hotel on foot and awaited instructions from Khin Zaw Win (1: "The Activist") on how to meet. At least I would encounter a new voice on this visit, likely my last, to Yangon.

The Activist

December 2017–January 2018. Khin Zaw Win is a friendly, poised, energetic, and affable late-middle-aged man who lives in a quiet neighborhood of north Yangon along with his wife and three grown children and their families. He is currently in high demand in Myanmar and abroad as a public speaker and participant in seminars dealing with ethnic and religious conflict in Myanmar. He recently founded the Tampadipa Institute, which, though now still in its seminal virtual state, may affiliate with Mandalay University in the near future and become a venue for the free exchange and debate of ideas regarding national identities within the social and political realities of contemporary Myanmar. More specifically, the central objective of the institute will be addressing the problem of Buddhist intolerance of Muslims in this country. The discussions will involve not only locals, but also visitors from abroad, with the idea to cultivate a broader, more cosmopolitan perspective. This will also mark a significant development for Myanmar's universities insofar as they remain under state patronage and only now are beginning to open up to the rest of the world. Khin is spending a lot of time these days getting his institute organized and raising the necessary funds for its endowment. He says that "the clock is running" on his efforts, as he hopes to pass on a legacy of his work to younger people concerned about Myanmar's political future. He is a very busy man, indeed, with an ambitious agenda, to say the least, but is gracious enough to meet with me at relatively short notice on two occasions in December 2017.

Khin Zaw Win had been highly recommended to me by my colleague and friend Iselin Frydenlund, a very active Norwegian scholar of religion who has been studying the nature of religious conflict within Sri Lanka and Myanmar for the past fifteen years. I think Frydenlund made this recommendation because of a conversation we'd had in November 2017, in which I had spoken about how I found that it was very difficult to locate, even among progressive voices in Myanmar, articulate people who could engage in analytical discourses about ethnic and religious conflict beyond self-interested political or religious perspectives. I was referring especially to how a Buddhist conceptual canopy often hovers over even the best of the well-intentioned intellectuals in the country and how inspiring it might be to find others who had managed to transcend that canopy. Iselin was surely right about recommending Khin Zaw Win to me, because one of first assertions he made in our first conversation was that he hoped that when a new constitution was framed for Myanmar, it would be thoroughly secular in orientation. His main objective now involves trying to promote rational discourse regarding the idea of a pluralistic state for Myanmar's multiethnic society while arguing for secularism in a new constitution. "Since the state is already supporting Buddhism, I'd like to see a state that supports all religions. A US-styled secularism wouldn't work here. We need discussions about secularism and national identity. There is no direct translation of 'secularism' into Burmese, and it takes some explaining." I mention that there may not be a word for "democracy," or "communism" either. The conversation then morphs into a discussion about how the term "Theravada" is one that has only recently gained widespread currency as well.

During our first conversation, I think I spent far too much time talking, especially about the term "Theravada," but he waves away my apology for this by saying that we need to get to know each other's views. Yet I worry about putting words into his mouth, since I am so eager to join him in a constructive conversation. Early on, I say that I feel that a fundamental problem at hand now in Myanmar is the basic lack of a conceptuality in play to field the complexities and conflicts now facing a fledgling democracy. I also say that I am chagrined that, like in Sri Lanka during the days when the Bodu Bala Sena was running amuck by publicly assailing Muslims and their businesses and mosques with impunity, the voices of responsible and moral Buddhist monks and laymen have been muted. With these assertions Khin Zaw Win seems to agree wholeheartedly. "Exactly the same situation here," he affirms. We would return to these points later in our discussions.

Like many other of my conversation partners, Khin Zaw Win has spent considerable time as a prisoner of the military junta—eleven years to be precise, from 1994 until 2005. The first three years were endured in the notorious Insein Prison in Yangon, while the last eight were spent in far north Mykthina in Kachin State. Khin Zaw Win retrospectively sees his transfer there as a blessing in disguise because the prison in the north was much more relaxed in its discipline than Insein and afforded him the opportunity to work on his studies, the practice of Buddhism (reading about Zen and Tibetan fighting monks, etc.), and studies on human rights and to read widely in a number of different subjects while listening to updates about the contemporary political situation in Myanmar on a smuggled-in radio. He also did a lot of writing. "Having so much time sharpens the mind. I also read about genetic anthropology." He lightheartedly referred to prison as "the longest continuously held seminar still operating in Myanmar." Indeed, he mentions that he also did a lot of teaching while in prison and that one of his surprising findings was that so many young political activists put into prison actually hailed originally from military families. "In Mykthina, the air is clear; it was quiet and quite congenial to reflection, like a religious retreat can be." He says that were it not for the Red Cross providing funding for transportation, he would not have been able to stay in close contact with his family. "In 2004, there was a big purge in the secret police, and eight months later I was released with a group of 240 others. There is a now a 'former prisoners' society' that has been organized and I attend these meetings whenever

I can. These are knowledge-sharing events. Some money given by expatriates and the National Endowment for Democracy supports the group. They've called on the NLD for help, but there has been no response. They are looking for more sources of funding to sustain the meetings. When I got released, I got involved in human and political development causes. Soon I found that I'm in high demand because I can speak, and when I do, I speak forthrightly.

"When I got out of prison, I got a sum of money from an Australian diplomat, not just for me but for others who were also released. So I distributed a lot of money." Médecins Sans Frontières gave him a project assessing the problem of HIV/AIDS in Myanmar for about a year, going all over the country determining how people coped, worked, got access to drugs, and so forth. The Swedish International Development [Cooperation] Agency (SIDA) invited him to steer a project on capacity building for democracy for a year and half. He put on about twelve activities or events, mostly in Yangon, that were concerned with nurturing democratic political culture. He made about 60,000 dollars at that time, "which gave me a first taste of running a development project. After that, SIDA merged with a UK agency that funded capacity building for parliamentarians. I invited people from abroad to give talks to them in Naypitaw. I then did some work with Oxfam involving capacity building for local development. It was very difficult to get department officials from the government to attend." During these years, he was on the ground, or doing grassroots work trying to fertilize a newly born political culture. "Now I realize that I have to do this again. I was unfortunate earlier that I did not have a good staff. In 2015, I made fifteen trips abroad. Now there is a Norwegian agency interested in supporting me, but they want to examine my financial situation. The problem is that my financial situation doesn't exist!" We talk about the bureaucracy of managing and accounting for funds.

But to back up a bit, Khin Zaw Win also recounts to me that his father was in the Burma foreign service and that he is eldest sibling in the family. "Everything I am doing now is due to my upbringing when I could learn foreign languages. We learned Burmese at home while we lived in Sri Lanka. I was there for three years, age eight through eleven (1958–1961). English had become my first reading and written language. I was taught written Bamar along with my two brothers by Burmese monks, who also made us study a fair share of Buddhist literature as well. Colombo was far more cosmopolitan and modern than Yangon at that time. We were first posted to Delhi and Madras in the mid-fifties. And we came back to Burma in 1961. We stayed here after that as my father worked at the foreign ministry in the Americas section for some time. My grandfather was a member of parliament at the time of U Nu's government, and I can remember him running up the stairs one day to tell us excitedly that the military had taken over [in 1962]. My high school years were spent in Yangon and I attended an English-speaking Methodist high school with a principal from Scotland. All schools had been nationalized by 1965. I got through just before the nationalization. It's been all downhill for the schools since then. The schools were not expensive then, unlike now, where exorbitant prices are charged if you want anything like a decent education.

"I was brought up as a Theravadin, but now I follow the Vajrayana—specifically the Tibetan Nyingma tradition. Burmese Buddhists here don't recognize Vajrayana. I now look at Theravada dispassionately and can see its strengths and weaknesses." I ask him if he can elaborate on its strengths and weaknesses, and he says, "One of its strengths is that it is a simple religion. It also has a view of itself as being nonrevisionist and the original form of the religion. Early on it spread from India to Sri Lanka and from there to Myanmar. The disciplinary Vinaya tradition survives, especially in the Shan State. In the Bamar regions, the Vinaya is in decline. There's a lot of commercialism and prestige seeking within the sangha these days. It's a state religion in all but name and so has great cachet among the people. While it was strong during colonial times in terms of inspiring the people, it doesn't unify the people anymore. It has always had a positive influence on education in the rural regions of the country. As for its weaknesses, it has a kind of fundamentalist approach in relation to the Tripitaka; it has become intolerant as well, as evidenced in its attitude toward other religions, which is now so problematic." I ask if he thinks this has always been the case. He says, "It has simmered for a long time. Now monks in Mahlaing are agitating for a monastic political party to be formed, similar to how the monks in Sri Lanka have organized."

At this I begin to wax too expansively about how during the days of the Kandyan kingdom in Sri Lanka (late sixteenth through early nineteenth centuries), there seemed to be a place for people of each of the religious traditions: Buddhists, Hindus, Muslims, and Christians. I mention a public talk given a couple of years earlier by Sri Lanka's famous anthropologist, Gananath Obeyesekere, entitled "What We Can Learn from the Kandyan Kingdom," a talk in which the concepts of pluralism and multiculturalism in precolonial Sri Lanka were illustrated. To exemplify, I mention how the last four kings of Sinhala Buddhist demographically dominated Kandy were Nayakkars, originally descended from a line of Dravidian or Telugu speakers in Tamil Nadu and Andhra; that Muslims functioned efficiently as the kings' traders with the outside world, thereby earning the disdain of the colonial Dutch, who controlled the coastal littoral regions; and that on occasion these Kandyan kings provided refuge to Sinhalese Roman Catholic Christians seeking relief from the abuses of Protestant Dutch Reformed colonials, instances in which a non–Sinhala Buddhist king intervened to protect one set of Christians from another. Khin Zaw Win seems impressed by this portrait of late medieval Sri Lanka, so I suggest that perhaps the intolerance he now sees in Myanmar is partially a by-product of the more recent nationalism that arose in Burma in reaction to British colonialism. He nods vigorously in agreement and returns to his narrative. But I am still worried about talking too much and framing the conversation in a way to capture his agreement. My sense is that he is such a polite man that he would not want to contest my perspective and thereby betray his obligation to be a benign host to a foreigner. I inwardly vow to be more passive in the exchange and to let his voice emerge without so much direct prompting.

"When Ne Win took over in the early sixties, a kind of fossilization in the country began to set in. Many Indians and Chinese were driven out of the country.

Smuggling arose in part as a result of losing these channels of trade, and the economy spiraled downhill, culminating eventually in the dissatisfaction that fueled the 8888 revolution." He then refers to a new political party that has emerged composed of people of the 88 Generation who have been relatively disenfranchised by the National League for Democracy—basically ignored by the NLD in the 2015 national election. "During these years of stagnation and decline, I attended dental school at the university and then served in the health service for six and half years following my graduation. I was at dental school in the university from 1965 to 1971, then held a one-year internship before I entered government service in late '73. When you entered public service, you had to undergo four months of basic training, which included military training and ideological indoctrination of the one-party state. During the time of my government service, I was in Shan State and the government hospital here in Yangon. My work was hospital based. But I also studied and sat for exams during this time in order to go abroad to the UK, which, unfortunately, though I was accepted into a graduate program, didn't materialize in the end. At that time, we could not go abroad unless we were sponsored by the government. We could not get access to writings about Buddhism either. The country was closed off in oh so many ways. Passports finally started to be issued again in the late 1970s. I resigned from my government position in '79, got a passport, and went to Malaysia (Borneo) in April 1980, working as a dental surgeon. I did this until 1983 (fulfilling two-year contracts) in this far-flung location. I then had the freedom to travel, and I took advantage of this by going to India, Australia, and Europe. While in the UK, I also attended a course of study at Sheffield, but this was the time of Margaret Thatcher and opportunities were quickly drying up as her retrenchment policies took hold. My visit to India was actually a pilgrimage of sorts, as I went to the major sites associated with the life of the Buddha (especially Sarnath and Bodh Gaya) for three months. When I came back to Burma in 1985, my kids were entering their teenage years. I found the country in so much further decline, and I did some translation work for Western embassies to draw a salary and put food on the table. This was a dark time and reform was in great need, but it wasn't forthcoming. That's why the situation exploded. I knew there had to be reform, but it just didn't happen. In fact, in 1988, Burma was classified as among the 'least developed' nations, so it qualified for concessionary aid. In a few months, the 88 revolution had begun. I witnessed the fiery student speeches and so I knew that something big was in the offing. There had been so much extramural killing going on that I became involved in human rights and contacted Amnesty International to see if they would enlist my services. I never heard back. I was not directly involved with resistant political parties, but I worked for the local UNICEF [United Nations Children's Fund] office as a consultant on two one-year contracts during these years [1991–1992], concerned with a variety of projects having to do with literacy, children's health, et cetera. I then applied as a private, nongovernment-sponsored individual to a master's degree program in public policy in Singapore and got accepted. However, I could not complete the program. I got about two-thirds of the way through, but then I got arrested while on a visit back home just as I was trying to depart at the airport. The secret police were very efficient in those days, though very blinkered in their perspective. I got fifteen years, simply because I was involved in human rights work. So, it was then that I was sent to Insein for three years and then the Kachin State prison, which, as I mentioned before, turned out to be a blessing in disguise because it was small, out of the way, and a prison mostly populated by army deserters and junkies. It was laid-back comparatively.

"When I came to Yangon later in life, once I was finally released from prison, I was told things about Muslims by Buddhist monks that were so prejudicial. Monks used to even stone Muslims during the time that they offered their prayers in public. There was talk among them about Muslims marrying Buddhist women, killing animals for sacrifice," and so on.

He shows me a book in Burmese about some of the Muslim people who have been involved in establishing the democratic process. He points out that Aung San Suu Kyii has turned her back on them. Khin Zaw Win knows Kyaw Min and Wai Wai Nu. I think of them specifically in this connection but do not mention that Kyaw Min has lamented how at one time he was relatively close to Aung San Suu Kyii in the early 1990s and then paid the price for his association, only later to be rebuffed or ignored by her when he was released from prison and sought an appointment with her. In any case, Khin Zaw Win is showing me other instances of this same pattern.

"Aung San Suu Kyii is now at the center of a cult. She has sucked up a heroine's adulation and become a micromanager." I add that she seems like an inexperienced politician who is learning on the job. He agrees with this observation and adds, "Not much has happened with her government because the adulation has lifted her above the crowd. In addition, relations are actually quite strained between the NLD and the military side of the government right now. There is virtually little coordination between them. And now it seems like there is a vendetta being launched against the media, not unlike what has happened in other Asian countries. Her government is now mired in the generation of misinformation and disinformation." He agrees when I suggest that many in the country are in a state of denial about what has happened out in Arakan to the Rohingya. He adds, "Often it's like running into a brick wall when the Rohingya issue is brought up here.

"Aung San Suu Kyii is not handling the Rohingya crisis well. Naypitaw was built to be isolated. That isolation has now been institutionalized by the NLD and Aung San Suu Kyii, who are merely going with the flow. Most of the ethnic leaders are now disillusioned, but no new ideas come out of them either. The larger peace project is now stalled. And so, day by day our country is slipping."

He mentions that Muslims are having problems getting passports now. "There is a separate line for people of mixed parentage. If you have Bengali in your background, it takes a lot longer." He then talks about how he tried to persuade his Muslims friends to run for office back in 2015, but then they were not allowed to run. "Those in the NLD were expressly forbidden by Aung San Suu Kyii.

The NLD won by a landslide, but the party is run in a very top-down manner. And because Aung San Suu Kyii is silent on the Rohingya crisis, no one else dares to come out to speak about it either. Some in the NLD have pressed for an anti–hate speech bill, but it's not clear whether or not it will get the needed support. Society needs to be brought along because while some liberal laws might be passed, they will mean nothing unless they reflect the will of the people. In this regard, it will also mean having to talk to the monastic hard-liners to bring them along as well."

As far as the situation is concerned at the moment, he was at a meeting a month earlier at a luxury hotel in Yangon where young Muslims told him that discrimination under the NLD government is getting worse than it was under the USDP (2012–2016). He plans to visit the Bangladesh Rohingya refugee camps in February 2018, to ascertain the situation firsthand. His tour is being sponsored by the United States Agency for International Development. He says that he is now one of the few locals using the word "Rohingya." He's been focused on the problems of the Rohingya for a long time, long before the mayhem that broke out in August 2017. Unfortunately, he says, "what the government has been doing is not much to ameliorate the situation. This condition is an everyday problem. Moreover, almost all of the Muslim cosmopolitan presence is no longer part of the scene. They have withdrawn." I say to myself that now, with the government's announcement of its refusal to work with the UN's special rapporteur, Yanghee Lee, and its continuing refusal to allow the UN to send a fact-finding mission to Rakhine, this is not only a matter of not doing much, but a matter of intentional obfuscation and obstruction of justice. I tell myself to ask him in our next meeting if he feels that Aung San Suu Kyii and General Hlaing are actually complicit in the ethnic cleansing and genocide of the Rohingya, as the UN's human rights chief has recently suggested.

We had spent four hours that had passed very quickly in animated conversations. I ask to meet him again before I leave Yangon and he readily agrees. That gives me a few days to consolidate all that I had learned from him and to return with a fresh set of questions that lent more specificity. My main question had to do with why Burmese people seemed to be in a state of denial about what had happened in northern Arakan during the past four months. He responds only briefly: "Many people hope that this issue will just go away. A friend of mine in the US complains that this is what all the Americans want to talk about." I mention a counterdemonstration led by a large Burmese Buddhist temple in Los Angeles that just took place in November (2017), a public statement by Burmese in America standing up to support Aung San Suu Kyii. Khin then says rather poignantly, "This is the kind of attitude that the NLD and military are counting on."

Following up on my thoughts at the end of our first meeting, I ask, "So, what do you think about the UN's human rights chief's suggestions that Aung San Suu Kyii and General Hlaing are complicit in the ethnic cleansing and genocide of the Rohingya?" He replies, "The UN human rights chief is a Jordanian prince and I have looked at his history. He also has a record of criticizing Islamic militants.

He's highly educated and wouldn't make comments like this lightly. He did say carefully that it's a matter for judges to decide. In this Burmese context, these comments might be regarded as inflammatory. However, the military has engaged in behavior that just cannot be condoned or ignored. When the US delegation came to Yangon led by Senator Richard Durbin with a number of congressmen and women, I told them that this matter had to be handled firmly. About the UN human rights chief, certain processes have been put into motion now. A single high-ranking person cannot make this happen and now a backlash is in play. I think he's pretty exasperated."

I ask him about the pope's decision not to use the word "Rohingya" at the request of the Yangon cardinal. He sees wisdom in that decision because the pope did not give the Burmese military an excuse to assail Christians any more than they already have. I suggest that this is a good diplomatic explanation but that there may be another explanation in play as well: that the Christian community here, like other minority groups, is not at all sanguine about the Rohingya. Indeed, it is not at all rare to hear their anti-Muslim statements as well. That is, there are a lot of Roman Catholics who do not like the Rohingya too! He agrees. I say that the dislike of the local Catholics for the Muslims was not the reason per se that Pope Francis refrained from using the term "Rohingya." He accepted the ostensible rationale to protect his Christian flock. But the request from the cardinal was absolutely expedient and also responsive to the anti-Muslim sentiments one finds within the Catholic (and for that matter the Burmese American Baptist) community as well.

At this, Khin Zaw Win mentions how the Kachin resent that too much foreign aid is going to the Rohingya rather than to them, and they are a larger community that has been seriously ravaged as well by the military over the past several decades. As a matter of fact, at the time of our conversations, the military had just launched new offensives against both Kachin and Shan resistance forces. I acknowledge understanding this point and also how it is that the Rakhines resent how much aid has flowed to the Rohingya despite the fact that it is now dwindling, owing to the withdrawal of many NGOs responding to local Rakhine harassment and state government pressures. I continue by mentioning how there are local groups, like the Wan Lark Foundation (2: "The Social Worker"), that concentrate on giving aid to the Rakhine and other smaller ethnic minorities who have been affected by the fallout from conflicts between the Arakan Army and the military. I suggest that even some Chin may not like the Rohingya because of the spillover of disruption to life that has occurred in Chin regions bordering northern Arakan. Khin Zaw Win is interested in knowing more about the Wan Lark Foundation and I promise to provide him with information.

I ask him what he thinks about the sermon that Sitagu, perhaps the most well-known and powerful monk in the country, recently gave to army troops in which he invoked the *Mahavamsa*'s saga of Dutthagamini (see "Setting the Recent Context" in the introduction). I explain how this story occupies an inordinate amount of space in the *Mahavamsa* and became exceedingly popular in Sri Lanka during the 1983–2009 civil war because of its stress upon how

Dutthagamini united disparate forces among the Sinhalas in an effort to defeat the Tamils in an epic battle. In the end, Dutthagamini himself defeats the righteous Tamil king Elara in a duel and proceeds to honor him during death rites. Following the victory, Dutthagamini is crestfallen because his victory over the Tamils has come at such a human cost. He worries about the karma that awaits him. The king is consoled by eight *arahants* (arhats; perfected Buddhist practitioners) who advise him that the sum total of his negative karma will be the equivalent of having killed just one and half human beings. The *Mahavamsa* consistently refers to the enemies of the Sinhalas, usually the Tamils, as *yakkhas* (subhuman "demons"). The implication of the story, as I've mentioned earlier, is that because those who were killed in battle were not Buddhists, and because they were killed in defense of the country whose national mission is to protect the Buddha's *dhamma*, they are less than human. The gist of Sitagu's purpose in invoking this epic story in his sermon to military personnel in this contemporary context can hardly be missed: the Rohingya are less than human, so don't worry about the negative karma effects that might arise. Khin Zaw Win is appalled by the elaboration of my account and says he is really very disappointed because of the manner in which this eminent monk is so well respected throughout the country. I tell him that the saga became very controversial in Sri Lanka during the civil war and that it resonated much with articulations of chauvinistic nationalists. Obviously, this instance only further illustrates the degree to which Buddhists feel justified in the persecution of the Rohingya minority in Arakan.

As if to emphasize that perhaps the Burmese are not even the most nationalistic of the lot, Khin Zaw Win offers that "Rakhine nationalism is even stronger than among the Bamar, even stronger than among the Karen, Shan, and Mon. And the Rakhine monks have been a big part of this assertion. Rakhine was the first area of Burma that was colonized by the British. The Rakhine were so much more expressly exposed to the suppression of colonialism as a result. They are such a poor people to this very day. Many Rakhine, as a result of the lack of economic opportunities in their home state, are migrating to Yangon in large numbers. The Rakhine are the second largest minority in Yangon these days. Because of this, there is a Rakhine national in the local Yangon government." He goes on to talk about Rakhine resentment regarding the lack of development in the state, their eclipse in development plans drawn up with the Chinese and Indians, and how aid from the outside now goes only to the Rohingya. I point out that the new advisory board that will supposedly oversee the committee appointed to implement the Kofi Annan Commission recommendations does not include a Rakhine; nor, of course, does it include any Rohingya. It makes me recall how activists in Sittwe on both sides of the divide have stressed the importance of on-the-ground observations from local people in the formulation of recommendations to implement change.

While there is certainly a need for close-up grassroots-based understandings, Khin Zaw Win says that many in the country have suffered from narrow-minded and naïve perceptions. Of course, he understands that because he has had the opportunity to live abroad, especially during his formative years, he has benefited from comparative insights drawn from his experiences with and exposures to other cultures. In general, he believes that by comparison, Myanmar is much worse off in terms of exposure to other cultures than Sri Lanka or Thailand. He also faults the university system, which, since reopening, "has become more and more of a diploma mill" rather than an educational site cultivating independent and critical thought. Because few passports were issued during the Ne Win regime (and it is not easy to get one even now unless you are ethnically Bamar), few people were allowed abroad, except for a few monks who went to Sri Lanka for advanced degrees. Still, monks are going to Sri Lanka for this purpose and he hopes that this experience will have a broadening impact on them. To this I mention a brief survey I had undertaken for me by a trusted academic colleague in Kandy. It surveyed fourteen Burmese monks studying for advanced degrees at a new monastic university in Kandy funded by the Thai Dhammakaya Foundation. In this survey, conducted in the early months of 2015, thirteen of the fourteen monks surveyed supported the ideology of the Ma Ba Tha Movement. I hate to dampen Khin Zaw Win's enthusiasm for how Sri Lanka could broaden the horizons of Burmese monks, but this brief survey indicates otherwise. In any case, he goes on to aver that "people in government need broader exposure. This is really critically necessary for the military people who are especially blinkered. After '88, only one army officer each year was sent to Fort Leavenworth in Kansas for officer training. But even that has now stopped. The mind-set of the officer corps is in need of so much reform."

My second interview with Khin Zaw Win concludes with two rather interesting observations or speculations on his part. The first is that "during U Nu's time, he passed a law about Buddhism as a state religion, though it did not get sustained by Ne Win. So there was a law to that effect on the books for a while. Paradoxically, during Ne Win's time, there were virtually no ethnic or religious disturbances during the time of the one-party state. Only after 1988 did we get these animosities expressed." I mention that I have heard it said that the trouble in 2012 between Rohingya and Rakhines occurred because tensions between the two had been suppressed for so long. When there was finally an opportunity for release, there was an eruption, much like a bottle of soda shaken up and then opened.

Finally, he makes a rather chilling observation having to do with drugs. Earlier I had mentioned the drug factor out in northern Rakhine State and how three of my Rohingya conversation partners (U Kyaw Min [1: "The Elder Statesman"], Abu Tahay [1: "The Historian"], and U Kyaw Hla Aung [2: "The Spokesman"]) had mentioned the scenario of drug deals gone bad as perhaps one of the reasons for the October 9, 2016, attack on border posts. Khin Zaw Win waits until the end of our discussion to refer to his understanding of a lingering legacy of the nineteenth-century Opium War conducted by the British, how they had planted opium and sent it to China to try to get the Chinese elite addicted. He then says: "Some people think that the army and its associates are using drugs in the same way, especially leaders in the USDP as well as Rakhine politicians who are implicated in the drug trade. Disseminating drugs among the Rohingya or Bengalis has become a method of debilitating them. Perhaps the worst-case scenario in this regard is occurring up in Kachin State, where addiction levels have spiked dramatically. This is a way of debilitating the enemy. But this is the tip of the iceberg." I am blown away by this assertion.

PART TWO

Arakan

U Kyaw Hla Aung with John Holt, "The Spokesman"

Classrooms built by Save the Children in the IDP camp, Sittwe

Rohingya children in the IDP camp, Sittwe

I visited Sittwe four times for at least a week or so, and Mrauk U twice for four or five days each time from **December 2014 until January 2017.** Each time was an adventure of sorts. Sittwe is the capital of Rakhine State (formerly Arakan), once a bustling grand port known as Akyab and the British point of entrée into Burma beginning in 1824. Along with Moulmein (now Mawlamyine) to the southeast in Mon State, Sittwe was the hub of British colonial efforts for a generation before they established themselves in Rangoon (now officially Yangon). Apart from some neglected old military buildings on the outskirts of town, there not much of a sign in Sittwe of its grand colonial days.

Rakhine State is the second least economically developed in Myanmar, making northern Rakhine, the traditional heart of Arakan, including Sittwe, Mrauk U, Kyaukphyu, Maungdaw, and Buthidaung, possibly the poorest region of the country. Southern Rakhine State is healthier in terms of its economy, owing to its more developed agricultural and fishing sectors, its closer proximity to the economic transformations occurring in Yangon, and the recent intensive growth of tourism around Thandwe at Ngapali Beach. The lack of development in northern Arakan is especially evident in terms of its very limited infrastructure, its dusty roads, its mostly ramshackle buildings, and its virtually nonexistent sewage and garbage collection systems (I found it difficult to stay healthy while in Sittwe). Bicycle rickshaws and motorcycle-driven tuk-tuks still dominate traffic. There is a complete lack of modern retail shopping facilities, and so on. The old traditional city market, with its warrens of specialty stalls, still thrives as the center of commerce, while the main street, with several banks and a few hotels, is comprised mostly of modest, family-owned, single-product-oriented, struggling businesses, except for the surprising myriad number of gold shops plying their trade. While there are a few SUVs powering about to kick up dust, the numbers of privately owned sedans and hatchbacks are very limited indeed. In other ways, arriving in Sittwe each time reminded me a bit of being in India decades ago, probably owing to the British colonial style of fencing, road construction, and buildings that can be found similarly in India and in Sri Lanka. The vegetation, especially north of Sittwe, is also decidedly more like Bengal than the Irrawaddy delta. The sense of isolation is palpable here, and the effects of fifty years of imposed isolation from the outside world is much more obvious than in Yangon and Mandalay, where change since 2010 has been borderline phenomenal, certainly giving rise to great generational changes. This is not at all the case here in Sittwe. For an American like me, even one with extensive living experience in South, Southeast, and East Asia, entering Sittwe is a bit like entering into the other side of contemporary otherness, a world that feels left behind. Perhaps that feeling of being left behind is one of the reasons for the undisguised feelings of discontent that are easily prompted in conversation.

I was uncomfortable in Sittwe. When staff at the hotel where I stayed figured out that I was in contact with Rohingya (I had to place phone calls at the front desk), I felt as if I had become persona non grata, because I was either ignored when I asked questions or disapprovingly stared at whenever I passed through the lobby while coming and going. Twice I was denied when requesting the aid of the hotel taxi to get to interviews in other parts of Sittwe. After the second such episode, I did a lot of walking throughout that dusty and hot town.

The Neglected

The manner in which the intercommunal troubles in Myanmar have been reported internationally usually focuses on the Buddhist-Muslim religious nature of the conflict. As I mention in the introduction, in addition to social, economic, and political factors, reflexive relations between Burmese, Arakanese, and Rohingya have to be sorted out and recognized in order to more completely understand the nature of the dynamics in play. Of the three communities, the Arakanese and their problems are the least known to and understood by the outside world. They were also the most difficult for me to gain access to, owing to the prevailing conditions of tension in northern Arakan. Maungdaw and Buthidaung were strictly off-limits. I tried very hard to find Buddhist monks with at least a modicum of English whom I could speak to directly about the current situation in Arakan, or those who would want to speak with me through a translator. I did speak with a few monks, but I was not very successful in establishing a sustained relationship with any, though I did learn from my limited encounters that many Arakanese monks can be extremely nationalist in their perspectives, often feel somewhat alienated from their Burmese brethren, and maintain strongly that the outside world just does not understand their predicament. I did manage, however, to develop conversations with four remarkable people, two Buddhist laymen and two Muslims (one Rohingya and one Kaman), amid a number of passing conversations in both Sittwe and Mrauk U.

In Mrauk U, I met a thoroughly unorthodox monk who was formerly a politician before he joined the sangha back in 1990. I got the impression that he had become a monk just as the political situation was a getting a bit too hot for him. He lived alone in a small temple whose entrance was flanked by statues of Subhas Chandra Bose and U Ottama. Those two figures, a fiery nationalist and a progressive nationalist monk from the 1920s, respectively, seemed to capture the orientations of his perspective and those of many others I was to meet. But he didn't want to discuss politics per se. Instead, we ended up talking about Abhidhamma as the continuing experience of "subject/object, subject/object, subject/object." One of his best friends, however, whom I was fortunate to meet and to interview, was a leader in the Arakanese National Party and had been released from twenty years in prison only in 2012. He regaled me with his perspective on the Rohingya and the Burmese long enough for me to become initially aware of how the Arakanese see themselves as sandwiched between two adversaries. He spoke, like most, about the impending doom his people face in light of what he characterized as an overwhelming Rohingya historical surge in population. But he also laced his comments with appreciation for how hard Rohingya can work, especially on his own farm, where he employs many. His harshest terms were aimed at the Burmese Tatmadaw, quite understandable given his long incarceration on what he deemed trumped-up charges. His hope was that eventually the Arakanese could establish their own autonomous country, for he believed that as long as Arakan was part of the Myanmar union, his people would be beleaguered as neglected and subordinated second-class citizens. As he spoke of recovering Arakan's autonomy, though I didn't raise the issue, I thought it was clear that he was a staunch supporter of the Arakan Army, the militant and armed militia that shares his ultimate political aim and trains its cadres up in Kachin State.

A few days later, during my first visit to Sittwe, I met a vociferous monk who many years earlier had started a museum dedicated mostly to the collection of old (nineteenth- and early-twentieth-century) Buddha images, as well as Burma currency dating back to the early twentieth century. He was the most nationalist-oriented monk I met in Myanmar, with the possible exception of Ashin Wirathu, ranting stridently as he did about the foreign interventions or intrusions of NGOs, the favoritism of the United Nations and the United States for the "Rohingya menace," and the admirable steadfastness of the Arakanese Buddhist people in bravely defending their land against all of these challenges. Were it not for these international intrusions, "the Rohingya would have been driven from the land of Arakan by now," he exclaimed. He bragged loudly about the marches he had participated in and had helped to organize against then UN secretary-general Ban Ki-moon and other UN representatives when they visited Sittwe in 2013 following the 2012 riots. Like Wirathu, he saved his worst vilification for UN rapporteur Yanghee Lee. (I had seen photos of these demonstrations in international news sources.) When he discovered that I was an American, he insisted that I promise to take a message back to Barack Obama asking him to stop funding the purchase of weapons by Muslim radicals who were perched along the Bangladesh border ready to invade. I demurred and just quietly shook my head. And just when I thought I might have never met such a racist, narrow-minded, and misinformed Buddhist monk, I learned that he had supported about thirty orphaned children whom he had saved from the grinding poverty of surrounding village areas and had provided them all with educations in a safe environment. He was by no means a seething nonhumanitarian. Just terribly misguided, I thought. I tried to track this monk down again in January 2017 (two years later) but discovered that he had decamped for Yangon the year before, leaving his museum/orphanage/monastery to a new charge. I had especially wanted to speak with him again not only because he so clearly represented one of the perspectives that needs to be reckoned with within the controversial context of northern Arakan and the Buddhist contribution to that controversy, but also because he had a reasonable command of the English language, a rare ability found among the Buddhist monks of Arakan. I had twice tried very hard to find monks with a command of English through U Thar Pwint (2: "The Senior Citizen"), but he had said that he could not think of any he knew personally. The current elderly monastic incumbent of the museum/orphanage/monastery was a friendly sort but spoke no English at all, so he called upon one of the university students staying at the orphanage to help us. Together we managed to piece together a conversation during which I learned of the former monk's new whereabouts and explained my own purpose in seeking him out. When I used the word "Rohingya," the university student sternly corrected me, saying that in Arakan that word is not used. "Bengali" is the term to use. I listened stoically to his insistence. Finally, the elderly monk suggested that, if I wanted to know how Rakhine Buddhists genuinely felt about the current "Bengali" situation in Arakan, I should find a new book just written by Khin Maung Saw that might be available in local bookshops. Following our good-byes, I visited two Sittwe bookstores that late afternoon, but to no avail. During the following morning's search, however, I found Khin Maung Saw's *Arakan: A Neglected Land and Her Voiceless People* at a bookstore out by the university. It had been published for a second time in Yangon privately in late 2016. Reading the book during the next couple of days, I could see that some of the author's reflections, which did not disappoint me in terms of his radically nationalist sentiment, were very recent, dating to the final months of 2016. And they corresponded very well to the perspectives I had thought I would have encountered with the vociferous monk who had left for Yangon.

During my first visit to Arakan, in **January 2015**, I had been accompanied by my spouse, Sree Padma, herself a well-published scholar and student of South Asian cultural history. On more than one occasion, astonished by some of the nationalist, if not racist, perspectives we heard being articulated, she had asked about sources for the claims being made. (She did this so often that I almost asked her to stop because the vague answers prompted were always somewhat embarrassing and sometimes stunted the further progress of the conversation.) I thought of her persistence in raising this issue as I began reading through Khin Maung Saw's collection of "research" essays. Indeed, now there was a source in print to cite some of the alarming claims one hears from Rakhine Buddhists about Rohingya. There was something else that made me feel that Khin Maung Saw's contribution was valuable. Earlier I had reasoned that Rakhine Buddhists were capable of unequivocal racist rhetoric because maybe they simply had not been educated or socialized about the impropriety and stark offensive nature of the language they often use in public discourse about the Rohingya. I had thought that many of the prejudicial statements that they make were likely a by-product of their isolation. But Khin Maung Saw points out in the opening pages of his book that he is a former lecturer at Humboldt University of Berlin and a former scholar-in-residence at Ohio University. In the notations regarding the printing history of his book, he puts "(U.S.A.)" beside his name, indicating that he is now a permanent resident of the United States. So isolation cannot be the sole excuse for his slanted and sometimes hateful point of view. (Of course, America is not a land free from bigoted and racist discourse either.) In any case, there is now a published source to cite some of the more uncharitably dishonest accounts that Rakhine Buddhists have formulated regarding Rohingya. Having had to characterize Khin Maung Saw's book as such, something I have not relished doing, I need to give a brief account of some of its representative contents as a way of filling in elements of a Rakhine Buddhist point of view that, unfortunately, holds some considerable sway in the northern regions of the state. While it purports to finally give voice to a "voiceless people," it may also be said to complement U Thar Pwint's views (2: "The Senior Citizen"). Khin Maung Saw's views are considerably to the right of U Thar Pwint's perspective.

Khaing Aung Kyaw, who says he is an author and a poet and puts "(New York)" next to his name, indicating that he, too, now lives in America, supplies a foreword to the book, in which he asserts that "the Rakhines or the Arakanese were and are the majority natives or *Bhummi Puttras* [*sic;* literally 'sons of the soil' or 'indigenous'] . . . and the Bengali Muslims [whom he later identifies more specifically as 'Chittagong Bengalis'] . . . came to settle in Arakan when it became a British Colony" (Saw 2016, p. 9). Primordial claims are thus established at the very outset. He goes on to describe how through false history, fake photos, and the backing of the Organization of Islamic Cooperation (OIC), which "has a strong voice in the UN," the Bengalis' "first aim would be the Islamization of Arakan and slowly by slowly the Islamization of the whole of Myanmar. Past history has proven that the Buddhist nations of Afghanistan, Indonesia, [and] Bengal were engulfed by Islam. It is the duty of historians to protect the rights of the natives by pointing out these true historical facts" (p. 10). This perspective is frequently heard not only in Rakhine State, but from many Buddhist monks in other parts of Burma. Khin Maung Saw's book is thereby framed as a duty-bound effort to help save Rakhine Buddhists from the onslaught of insurgent Islam. The foreword concludes with this statement: "If one doubts on the statements in this book, I would like to suggest that person to go to our native land, Arakan, and check the situations personally" (p. 10). I certainly agreed with the sentiments of his invitation and can say that, indeed, I learned a great deal about "the situations personally" during my four trips to Arakan, enough to generate a motivation to make known the views that Khin Maung Saw's book contains, especially since it is touted as being so representative of a "voiceless people."

Khin Maung Saw (hereafter KMS) then provides his own "prologue" to the "research papers" that comprise his book, which he begins by debunking faked photos that he says have duped the United Nations, the United States, and Western journalists into supporting "the claims of the Rohingya without knowing the facts and history properly . . . that the real sufferers are the Arakanese . . . [who] have no big donors for propaganda" (p. 12). Later in the prologue he paints a picture of how wealthy Muslims "with the financial support of oil-rich Muslim countries" take "poor women from Burmese and other ethnic minorities," (p. 14), thereby grounding the beginning of his narrative regarding the 2012 violence in Sittwe, a narrative when told by Rakhines or Burmese Buddhists that always includes initially a reference to the rape of a Buddhist woman by three Muslim men. This establishes a moral high ground to legitimate the violence that followed as a righteous response to moral transgression. It cannot be an accident that a beautiful and shyly demurring Arakanese woman in the presence of a Buddha image adorns both the front and back covers of KMS's book. To round out his "prologue," KMS tells "an Arakanese/Burmese proverb" about a kindhearted farmer who takes in a starving mother monkey and her offspring, only to have the monkeys eventually bring around so many of their kind as to drive away the generous farmer from his own land. So, "All ungrateful monkeys attacked him from all directions and he had to run away for his life" (p. 15). While the Rohingya are thereby analogically compared to ungrateful monkeys, he also shares this when introducing the Burmese: "The majority Bamas or Burmese usually want to play 'the Role of the Big Brother' [*sic*] and sniffling [*sic*] their nose [*sic*] everywhere in the places of the minorities . . . [to] interfere too much in the minorities' affairs" (p. 13). The reader is thereby invited to understand that the Arakanese Buddhists are an aggrieved party, owing to machinations emanating from two different directions.

The first substantive distinction that KMS draws between Rohingya and Arakanese is based on a translation he has made of a statement allegedly given by an Arakanese Buddhist monk to a member of the royalty in the eighteenth-century Mrauk U kingdom, which reads, "Your Majesty, we the *Mramars* [Arakanese] and they, the *Kalas* ['Bengali Muslims'] are same only in one fact that both races are human beings but we are very different in mentality. We, *Mramars* traditionally believe in 'the three gems,' namely Buddha, Dhamma and Sangha, but they don't have this kind of faith. They said: It was written in their scriptures that if one worshiped the statues and relics, his or her hand should be cut off. It were the wish of their god" (p. 34). This first move of delineation indicates how religion is identified as the chief signifier that separates the Arakanese from the *kalas*. Later, KMS makes it clear that the Arakanese should be regarded as the natives of Arakan since they believe that they are the actual descendants of the Sakyans (the Buddha's own clan; see pp. 47 and 66) who accompanied the Buddha to Arakan when the Mahamuni image was first fashioned as the likeness of the Buddha. He says that it is this "fact" that is responsible for why some Arakanese are of "Aryan" descent while others are Mongoloid (p. 55). He then cites a myth in which the founder of the primordial Dhanyawaddy kingdom of Arakan, the progenitor Marayu, was the offspring of an "Indo-Aryan" Sakyan prince named Arjuna and his queen, Indra Mayu, who was "Indo-Mongoloid of Tibeto-Burmese stock." This myth of origins thereby is made to explain why the Arakanese "race" can lay primordial claims to the region dating back to either the second century CE (p. 55) or to the time of the Buddha himself (the sixth century BCE)! (It is not completely clear which.) In terms of his account of the Rakhine language, KMS avers "that the language of ancient Arakan was Magadha or Pali" and that "modern Arakanese is a dialect of that language which came to be spoken during the time of the Pagan dynasty" (p. 61). He argues that modern Burmese is also derived from that language spoken in Pagan and thus infers that Arakanese, evolving from Pali, may be the real trunk of the Arakanese/Burmese language tree. While all of these fanciful presentations are fascinating to note, including his subsequent chapter on how "the British brought tens of thousands of Chittagongian Bengali Muslims into Arakan" (p. 107) and thereby need to shoulder "great blame" for their colonial intervention, it is KMS's discussion about *kala,* or *kalar,* that I would like to focus upon before then taking note of the discussion of what KMS refers to as the "'R' word."

KMS is intent on dismissing any significance attached to Francis Buchanan's 1799 reference to "Rooinga" people when he was visiting Amarapura. Within the context of this discussion, KMS says, "'Kala,' regardless of their faith [as] either Hindus or Muslims, are lesser assimilated into the Burmese and Buddhist community. Despite that fact, they want to name themselves as 'Bama' or 'Mon' or 'Shan' or 'Karen' . . . rather than their own ethnic identity 'Kala'! It happens most probably because of the term 'Kala' which means black or dark in Indic languages. . . . Although the word Kala has a harmless meaning, the people from the subcontinent do not like to be called 'Kala.' They feel insulted because . . . the word 'kala' means 'coloured' or 'blackie'" (pp. 147–148). So KMS surmises that since people whose ethnic origins may have been South Asian may have not liked the appellation of "kala Rakhaing," they told Francis Buchanan that they were really something else, in this case "Rooinga." While this is "just-so" reasoning, what I want to underline is how KMS regards "kala," though he recognizes that it means "dark" or "blackie" and people of South Asian descent take offense at it, as simply "harmless." He displays the same remarkable innocence (or ignorance) when he specifies the term "Rohingya" as the "'R' word" in no less than two of his chapter headings. In these chapters, he endeavors to debunk any legitimacy to the use of this now self-referential term. What is remarkable to me is that KMS does not seem to understand that his use of the phrase would be recognized by any American (in whose country he is now living) as an unfortunate appropriation of the phrase "'N' word." What KMS has done is to infer that the term "Rohingya" is analogous to the old and now universally condemned use of the pejorative term "nigger."

Many other questionable assertions and biases lace the remaining contents of this publication. But I need summarize only the little bit that I have elucidated here. For a Rakhine Buddhist with a view commensurate with KMS, the Rohingya are Chittangong Bengali Muslim interlopers who may be compared to monkey-like "blackies" or "niggers" threatening the native sons of the soil who trace their ancestry back to the Buddha's own clan. It is this quality of conceptuality in play that one might encounter when coming to Sittwe, Mrauk U, or other Rakhine-dominated cities in northern Arakan to see "the situations personally" for oneself.

The Senior Citizen

January 2016. U Thar Pwint is a genial "senior citizen," or town elder, in Sittwe. For U Thar Pwint, however, "senior citizen" does not mean what we Americans usually refer to by the term. Here, it refers to someone who voluntarily assists the town's governmental administration. U Thar Pwint has done so since the time of the 2012 crisis, when the fiery riot between Rakhine Buddhists and Rohingya Muslims left hundreds dead and displaced more than one hundred thousand people, including those Rohingya now removed to the IDP camp just north of Sittwe that I visited when meeting U Kyaw Hla Aung (2: "The Spokesman"). I first met U Thar Pwint in January of 2016 and had a congenial second follow-up session at his home in January of 2017. We got along quite well over about six or seven hours of talk. Of course, he is a pious lay and learned Buddhist, so I think he respects my knowledge of Pali, Theravada history, and Sri Lanka.

A Buddha image of the new Mahamuni type is at the center of a mantel in his living room, and his wife lit incense and worshiped both mornings when I visited his home. He is a lawyer by training and was dismissed by the government from practicing law in 2003 because he was accused of misconduct in relation to the chief justice in Rakhine State. He had simply reported that a lower judge had not followed de rigueur the proper legal protocol in a case he was representing. The court said that U Thar Pwint had no right to report that a judge had not acted according to the proper protocol. Later, he was informed that he could make a petition to ask for clemency after he was dismissed—since the legal authorities actually recognized that he was correct (just insubordinate)—but as a matter of principle he refused to subject himself to any further possible judgment. And so he lost his license to practice law for good. (He said parenthetically that the American Bar Association says that it is the right and duty of a lawyer to report judicial misconduct. He was simply doing that.) For the rest of his career, for about a dozen years or so, he has supervised or coached his junior colleagues in cases. Indeed, during the second time we met, a junior colleague appeared who needed his advice on a brief she was filing. In Myanmar, there are no separate forms of law practice. It's all rolled into one. He preferred civil cases. Indeed, that is the perspective he brings to the current problems plaguing Rakhine State. He sees himself as an advocate for the interests of Rakhine Buddhists, caught between the historical hegemony imposed on Arakan by the Burmese and the contemporary threat posed by what he perceives as the ever-surging tide of the Bengali Muslim community.

He refuses to use the word "Rohingya," winced whenever I did, but did not scold me as others had done.

U Thar Pwint deems himself to be a real *bhumi putra* (indigenous person). He was born in Sik Pokh Shaung village, located about sixty miles from Sittwe, a very remote location, in 1950. Still there is no road to his native village, only waterways. His father was a contractor who built dams for rice fields. One of the insurgent groups of the time wanted his father to stop building these dams. So his family heeded the militants' warning and came to Sittwe in 1956. Here, U Thar Pwint attended grammar and high school and ultimately made his way to university studies—including two years at Rangoon Arts and Science University, the precursor to Yangon University. First he earned an agricultural certificate and then took what was known as the "high grade" course in law, rather than the "advocate course."

When I ask him big questions in **January 2016** about whether the recent election in November 2015 that resulted in the National League for Democracy (NLD) landslide will make a difference for Rakhine State, he begins by simply saying that "the election was fair." In my own mind—and I'm not altogether sure about this—I took him to mean that the exclusion of the Rohingya from voting and fielding candidates had been acceptable to him. It turned out, from the later reasoning he would articulate, that this was very much the case. However, he immediately goes on to say that the new NLD government will need the support of the army because, in fact, "it is the army that controls the power, just as they have for the past fifty-plus years. In terms of the local government, although the Arakanese National Party has the majority of representatives in the state parliament, the president of Myanmar nominates the chief minister and the party has no right to form a government." He surmises correctly that Aung San Suu Kyii would appoint a Rakhine Buddhist who is a member of the National League for Democracy as the chief minister, rather than a supporter of the oppositional Arakanese National Party. Moreover, his opening comment about how the military would still retain power proved very accurate indeed.

At the outset of my first visit with him in January of 2016, I mention that I have just read a BBC article about how Aung San Suu Kyii had declared that she wanted to solve the basic problem with the country's ethnic minorities, that this would be her government's initial priority. This had given Rohingya friends some hope. U Thar Pwint responds by saying that she had yet to formulate a specific policy and that "these are just words." Indeed, U Thar Pwint is very skeptical about whether the new NLD government would be able to effect significant change in the political status quo of the country, at least in terms of successfully addressing the many fronts of conflict that the army had generated with various ethnic communities during the past fifty years. He includes the Arakanese among these alienated ethnic communities. His negativity then, back in early 2016, turned out not to be misplaced, especially in light of the spectacular post–October 9, 2016, and post–August 25, 2017, "search-and-clear" army operations in northern Arakan that sent approximately 775,000

Rohingya fleeing to Bangladesh as traumatized refugees, and the continuing small-scale violent attacks on the military mounted periodically by the increasingly emergent revolutionary Arakanese Army.

In our original meeting, I tread lightly before I finally broach the issue of the Rohingya. I make the reference very generally to allow U Thar Pwint to frame his own approach to the post-2012 problem. He begins by saying that Western countries do not understand Arakanese feelings about the current situation, which he referred to as a "crisis." He says that "some Bengalis have lived here for a long time and we want to give them citizenship rights." The sense of ownership in this statement is palpable insofar as it clearly reveals that citizenship is something that the Arakanese could *give* to the Bengalis, not something that the Rohingya are somehow naturally entitled to. He continues: "But we can't differentiate between those who are newcomers and those who have stayed for a long time. They want to mix newcomers with the old people. While we cannot differentiate among them, the Bengalis want to mix them all together and call themselves collectively as Rohingya. They want *every* Bengali to become a citizen under the name of the Rohingya. If we accept this name, then all future Bengali newcomers will want to be Rohingya citizens. If they are honest, they must classify who are the old and those who are the new." This much sounds reasonable to me, but the classification system that seems to be complementary to the current verification process has proven very controversial, since it requires Rohingya to register as "Bengalis," therefore forfeiting any claims they may have to being an indigenous people according to the 1982 law enshrined in the Ne Win period. As I have mentioned, this law says that people who can establish their communities as living in Myanmar before 1823, a year before the British arrived, are entitled to state citizenship.

January 2017. When I meet U Thar Pwint again a year later, perhaps I feel a little more secure or safe with him, and I sense he with me, so I press some issues a little bit further, trying to get more at the rationale for his perspective. I ask him: "When you were growing up in Sittwe, how did you refer to the Rohingya, as 'Bengalis'? And when did you first begin to hear the term 'Rohingya'?" He says, "We called them *kalar. Kalar* means 'from the West.' The word *korthaw,* which we also sometimes used, means 'how much.' When they [Rohingya] would come to the market during British times, they would go from one vendor to another asking 'What's the price?' while rarely buying. These terms did not make them angry and sometimes they actually used the terms to refer to themselves. We referred to Europeans as 'white *kalar*' [*phu kalar*], and we called the Koreans and Japanese something different. This nomenclature is from old times. There are about sixty different uses of *kalar*—all of these different peoples who came from a different country, but primarily those who have come from the West."

U Thar Pwint has absolutely no awareness that his anecdote about the origins of *korthaw* might be understood as offensive or demeaning. (Several times I had this kind of experience in Arakan listening to Rakhines talk about

Rohingya. It reminded me about how some Sinhalese in Sri Lanka behave in relation to the indigenous Vaddas, as if they are simpletons who have yet to be introduced to higher culture.) But rather than take this up with U Thar Pwint, I ask if he has any sense that the term *kalar* might be understood as a derivative of Sanskrit or Pali *kala,* meaning "time," or "dark." I tell him about the Hindu goddess Kali, who is very famous in Bengal, and relate that the term is often used in conjunction with *yugas*[1] to refer to the present increasingly degenerate age, the last of the four *yuga*s of this *kalpa* in which we live, according to the traditional worldview of the Sanskrit *purana*s. I am surprised to learn that this perspective is entirely new to him. I wonder out loud to him if there isn't a degree of awareness of this possible meaning among these "Bengalis." That is, that the term *kalar* might be understood by them as a reference to their generally darker features and other associations linked to blackness and thereby construed by them as offensive. As I noted earlier (2: "The Neglected"), although Khin Maung Saw is aware of how the term is quite offensive to South Asian sensibilities, he sees "no harm" in the unintentional "misinterpretation." U Thar Pwint isn't even aware that the term might have these connotations. As for the second question I asked, U Thar Pwint says that he can't remember the term "Rohingya" being used until the early 1990s. If it wasn't being used much at that time, it would square with Jacques Leider's contention that the political significance of "Rohingya" is a rather recent phenomenon.

I decide to ask about antipathy for Indians in general in Myanmar historically. He thinks for a minute and then replies, "The Bamars didn't hate all Indians. Ne Win just used them as a pretext for his advantage. He made the Indian a bogeyman, and especially raised the specter of moneylenders. Basically, Myanmar people did not like to differentiate by race. The Burmese, Karen, Arakanese, are all Buddhists. Our religion has taught us to sympathize with all people. But Muslims won't eat with us. In my childhood, I remember my father teaching me not to be cruel to people of other traditions." In the next breath, he adds, "There are three kinds of Bengali: Buddhist, Hindu, and Muslim. The problem is only with the Muslims. It all depends on the religion. Religion makes all the difference. If we don't check these Bengali Muslims, they will overwhelm us and our race; the Rakhine Buddhists will vanish. There are many Chinese in Myanmar, but they never involve [themselves] in political affairs. But Bengalis want to be involved.

"In our view, they are not loyal to the state. In our constitution we have eight indigenous people. If Chinese people come to upper Burma, they cannot demand a separate state. They can become a citizen, but not demand a separate state. If we accept Rohingya, then we must admit they are one of the indigenous people and therefore they would have a right to a separate state. So this is what

---

1. There are four *yugas* (eons) in each *kalpa,* the first *yuga* commensurate with the upholding of dharma (cosmic and social order based on adherence to duty) with increasing disintegration occurring in the next three so that the Kali *yuga* is regarded as chaotic and existentially problematic. *Kalpas* comprising these *yugas* endlessly follow one another.

Arakanese people basically fear. In 1984, the Bengali population was four hundred thousand. Now it is over 1 million. At that time, the Arakanese population was 2 million. It is now basically the same. We've had two or three children per family, and many of our children have gone to foreign countries and other parts of Burma, while their families have had fourteen or fifteen! [And of course, they are not allowed to move into other parts of Myanmar, so they are all here.] They are expanding their population. In 2012, there were ninety thousand. Now there are 130,000 in Sittwe in the past four years. Forty thousand people have come. Every day and every night they come in from Bangladesh. It's very difficult to patrol the ocean when there is only one or two navy vessels. They come by sea. In five or six hours they can come by fishing boat. Every day, the authorities catch some of the newcomers. Some of them are carrying narcotics."

Now that U Thar Pwint has mentioned narcotics, I say that one theory about who attacked the border posts on October 9, 2016, an attack that resulted in a massive army response, is that it was a narcotics gang seeking revenge on border guards who had earlier confiscated some of their drugs and weapons. I ask him what he believes happened. He says that "the attackers only hit the border authorities and not the army or Rakhine people per se. There are many people who could have done this." He recalls that innocent people get hurt in times of war. He does not think that this violence against the Rohingya that occurred after the attack on the border station has been a policy of the NLD government. He says that this shows that the NLD cannot control the army. "If Aung San Suu Kyii requested that a regional commander abide by her wishes, he would obey his general and not her. The problem would be the same within the American military," he says. I nod. He leaves it at that and I get the sense that even if he knows more about what happened, he doesn't necessarily want to reveal it to me. The significance of October 9 was a game changer in northern Arakan, as the army then reasserted its brutal, menacing power. U Thar Pwint is quite aware of this and is divided in his comments about the military. "Maybe after two or three more elections there may be some more devolution of power from the army. We, on the one hand, do not trust the army, yet we depend upon them for our security. Up until the 1970s, the army was the army. But afterwards they penetrated into all of the government departments. This happened in the business sector as well. Retired military people become the managers of mills. There is so much bribery and corruption [the giving over of business concessions]. They probably control half of the national economy. The military never accepts any suggestions made by scholars. They simply rule by force."

I ask, "Are the military exercising divide and rule in Arakan? I ask this because others who are activists in Yangon see how the manipulative methodology of the military is in play in contexts like this; that is, how, by pitching one group against another, both remain weakened and unable to mount any kind of challenge to their hegemony."

U Thar Pwint replies, "Maybe, but it is not the sole answer to the problem here. Without the military, the problem would still be here. The military is not the origin of the problem."

From the beginning of our first encounter, I could see that U Thar Pwint is traditionally very religious. As I mentioned, he pays me some respect because I know some Pali and asks me how I first got interested in Buddhism. I tell him that while I find many Buddhist concepts, particularly *anicca* (impermanence), *paticcasammupada* (conditioned origination), and *dukkha* (unsatisfactoriness), to be profoundly true, I am not a card-carrying member of any religious tradition, though I can be empathetic to them all. I think he takes this as a cue to begin expounding his philosophy of religion. "My view is that just as Buddhism unites the various peoples of Myanmar [the Bamar, Arakanese, Shan, Mon, and Karen], Islam unites its own various peoples. If there is a fight between Bangladesh and Myanmar, the Muslims will definitely side with Bangladesh." He says that he sees this kind of religious loyalty in play whenever there is a soccer match between Malaysia and Myanmar. I nod and comment that I noticed something of the same kind in Kandy, Sri Lanka, with local Muslims who supported Pakistan over Sri Lanka in a test cricket test match I attended years earlier.

U Thar Pwint says that Rakhine are usually very hospitable to Bengalis, but in his experience this has not been personally reciprocated. "All religions teach, like Buddhism, not to kill, but Muslims teach to kill nonbelievers. I cannot follow every point of Buddhist teaching. I am far from being an *arahant* [arhat; perfected practitioner]. It is my personal fault. But their religion teaches to kill nonbelievers. I cannot be sympathetic to that kind of 'ism.' I cannot accept this as a true religion. Western countries attacked communism. One day, they will attack Islam because it is only an 'ism.' Other religions, Hindu, Buddhist, Christian, do not teach to kill others from other religions. We Rakhine Buddhists are accused of being aggressors. The Westerners cannot see the problem of the expansion of Bengalis. Why don't the Westerners see the danger of the Muslims? Is it because the theological root of all these religions is the same—that God is eternity? Everybody except God will die. Other religions, though, also say that even God will die. This is a major difference—contingency. Christians see that Islam is the same, depending as it is on Allah. Muslims, though, are even divided between Shia and Sunni." He goes on to say that "the current problem between Saudi Arabia and Iran is about power, and not religion. Iran wants to become the leader of Islam. Saudi's dynasty is about retaining power. This conflict between them is not about religion." I wonder whether the contradiction in this statement might have to do with how U Thar Pwint understands the nature of religion. Perhaps wanting to become the leader of Islam is not a religious issue to him.

"But is the problem here one of religion, specifically because Islam teaches to kill?" I ask.

"This is but one of the problems. Westerners accuse us of discriminating against Bengalis. But we don't discriminate. It is the Bengalis who discriminate. They will only eat by themselves, for example. Bengali children come around here in our town every morning. We don't trouble them. And yet we are not allowed to come to their villages. They are secluded communities and do not mix with other societies. There's a Hindu quarter here in Sittwe and they are comfortable. I've had many Bengali friends during my life but I have never been invited by one of them to their places. If I invite them to my place they cannot eat our food. Separation by religion is one of the causes of discrimination. Religion is not the sole cause. The main cause is the expansion that pushes us aside."

I swallow hard. Reports about Rakhine Buddhist villagers joining the army and police in invading—better, devastating—Rohingya villages in the post–October 9, 2016, mayhem are fresh in my mind from the conversations I recently had with Rohingya political leaders in Yangon. A few weeks later, during the first week in February, an especially chilling report of the UN's Office of the High Commissioner for Human Rights would lay bare and thereby confirm the sorry details of systematic murder, rape, and disappearance of hundreds of Rohingya in a post–October 9 scourge undertaken by the Burmese military.[2] The report understood the military's violence as a "purposeful policy designed by one ethnic or religious group to remove by violent and terror-inspiring means the civilian population of another ethnic or religious group from certain geographic areas" (OHCHR 2017, p. 43). How could religion, then, not be a factor? It was the chief means by which people were being discriminated against. The OHCHR would even report that as members of the Burmese military were pillaging, raping, and murdering, "many victims mentioned that soldiers and officers taunted them by saying that Islam is not the religion of Myanmar; that Rohingyas are Muslim Bengalis; and that Rohingyas would be eliminated from Myanmar. They were mocking their religion while beating and arresting them, saying things such as 'call your Allah to come and save you,' 'What can your Allah do for you? See what we can do?' This raises serious concerns that these acts amount to persecution against a particular ethnic and religious group" (p. 42).

I decide to push U Thar Pwint's perspective a bit further and ask why people who come from Bangladesh would want to come Arakan in the first place. I ask this pointed question because the fact of the matter since 2012 is that hundreds of thousands of Rohingya have attempted to flee Myanmar, not enter it. They are not coming into the country in any dramatic way when compared to those who are trying to leave. U Thar Pwint is ready with an answer: "Many Bengalis don't even have a spoon full of rice. Bangladesh is poorer than us. There are 170 million people in an area where in Rakhine there are only 3 million. If they come here, at least they can eat rice. This is the issue that most foreigners do not understand. The situation is so bad in Bangladesh. At least the Bengalis can eat here. They are starving there. And once they start eating here, the Bengalis here in Arakan are connecting with their relations back in Bangladesh and bringing them here. Most of the people want to go to Malaysia. The situation is like in Sri Lanka where the Tiger leader married a woman from Tamil Nadu. The Bengalis here will marry girls from Bangladesh and bring them here. If my son is in

2. See OHCHR 2017. This includes details of a report garnered by interviews with more than two hundred Rohingya, of whom most were women and children of the seventy-five thousand who fled from Myanmar to Bangladesh. Refused access by the Myanmar government, the UN conducted these interviews in mid-January 2017, precisely the time during which I was in Sittwe.

Rangoon, he continues to connect with me here in Sittwe. The same it is with the Bengalis who continue to connect with their people back home. If they want to make harmony with the native Rakhines, they can establish a classification differentiating between those who have been here and those who are new."

He continues in a historical vein: "In Buthidaung in 1900, there were only seven Bengali houses. And now? It is 85 to 90 percent Bengali. In Sittwe, before 2012 there were about 35 to 40 percent Bengalis, but now it is 60 percent. If the army and police were not here, the Bengalis would attack us. In 2012, a Bengali leader said that 'if the army and the police withdraw, we could occupy the entire city in three days.' Western people don't understand because they take the entire population of Myanmar and see that the Bengalis are a very small minority. But not here in northern Arakan. The problem is similar in Sri Lanka where the Sinhalas see themselves as a minority." What he is saying is that the Arakanese, who are a majority in Rakhine State, suffer from a minority complex. I want to ask him if the 60 percent "Bengali" population includes the one hundred thousand Rohingya penned up in the IDP camp just north of Sittwe, but I refrain from being so provocative. Indeed, very few Rohingya can be seen these days plying the streets of Sittwe. The main quarter of town that they used to occupy is now almost entirely emptied of their presence and is being repopulated by poor Rakhines.

I had been told by Rohingya in Yangon about government efforts to settle Burmese convicts out in the Maungdaw and Buthidaung village areas. So I decide to ask U Thar Pwint, "What about Burmese expansion into Arakan?"

He replies in this way: "In the 2008 constitution, Section 9C: a state can change its name if it wants to. . . . This is a Burmese plot. By this section, if the Bengalis become a majority, they can change the name and nature of the state." As for the pressure from the Burmese, he says that "in villages near Maungdaw, criminals are given two acres and two cows to settle. But these beggars leave the areas frequently and return to the Burmese areas after having sold the cows! Now the military wants to settle the area by force." When I look back at this last statement with the benefit of hindsight, after what transpired in the fall of 2017, I can see just how clearly U Thar Pwint understood the dynamics in play in northern Arakan at that time.

"We Rakhine Buddhists are between the horns of Bangladesh on the west and Burma on the east. There is no 'union spirit' here now. Every indigenous people in Myanmar wants to separate." I interrupt and ask if this includes Arakan, and he nods yes. "The matter of a union is actually a matter of military empire."

It seemed to me that U Thar Pwint was being completely consistent in his appraisal of the northern Rakhine situation. In both of my conversations with him, in January of 2016 and 2017, he emphasized that the reins of power belonged to the military. By saying that the military seemed to want "to settle the area by force," he was identifying what was, de facto, the Myanmar government's posture and real methodology. Now arguing that they faced an insurgency with international connections, the military felt justified in the brutality of their response. In fact, if an insurgency had not been inspired yet by the manner in which the Rohingya had been treated since 2012, then the recent scourge in northern Arakan might go a long way in materializing a self-fulfilling prophecy.

In my second conversation with U Thar Pwint, in **January 2017**, I try to turn the conversation away from the Rohingya to get him to articulate his grievances with the Burmese.

"One of the policies of the Burmese government is consciously to isolate us. We are so physically isolated from the rest of the country because we don't have bridges like there are across the Irrawaddy. I told this to the vice president of the country, who said there were no funds in the budget for bridges. Although there are many Arakanese serving in the government, all of the decisions are made by Burmese. In every department this is true. There are many Arakanese in the army, but the commanders are all Burmese. Even during the U Nu period, when the president was Shan, the real power was Burmese. Aung San Suu Kyii says our problems will be solved by rule of law. But there is no established rule of law yet in this country!

"We Rakhine feel that the central authorities have not created equal rights. We have no arms; therefore the Burmese bully us. As a result, some Rakhine have organized to form the Arakan Army. From independence, we never got equal rights. The central government sells gas from our area and does not share much, if anything, with us. There is only one bridge in Kyauktauw compared to all the other bridges that have been built to link the country. It takes five hours to get to Myebon. We did not get infrastructure. In my opinion, money from the gas is ours. But this money we are able to take only when they give [it to] us. There is currently a big project to develop an Indian port here in Sittwe, but there is no plan for giving us any share of the port income. We were told that we would not get any share of it. All power is in the hands of the central government, and practically that means the army."

I ask if the situation hasn't improved some under the NLD and specifically mention the legal culture because that is what he knows the most about. "The legal culture is not any better under the NLD. I have many friends from the NLD and they say they don't have full power because of the army. I ask them, 'If you get full power, will the government be clean?' We Rakhines and other races never have trusted the Burmese government during these sixty years because we have not been treated fairly. We now have democracy but the situation for us has not changed. Every *putthujahana* [person] is selfish, but the Burmese race is collectively selfish! There are three hundred immigration people serving in Rakhine. They are all Rakhine, but they are controlled by just one Burmese."

At that comment, I ask, "Why are there immigration procedures for entering Rakhine State [as at the airports in Thandwe and Sittwe]?"

He says, "We are another country! They never really control our borders and allow the Bengalis to pass with bribes. But they treat us as having to enter a different country here in our own place. The government always makes a good speech but never really acts. There are many Rakhine in the Myanmar army. But all the top people in the army are Bamar. One of the brigadier generals here in Sittwe is Rakhine, but he reports to another general who is Burmese. The vice chairman of the parliament is Rakhine but really doesn't have a voice—it's only for show.

"I have no trust in the government. They won't give any more power at the state level. This NLD government is even more strict than the past government."

I ask him, "Why?"

"Because they are insecure! Colloquially, the Burmese people call Aung San Suu Kyii 'mother,' and they all always look to her for what to do. So the NLD power is so centralized in her. Everyone looks to her being worried about blame for acting individually and not looking for what is to be done according to what arises in each situation. The current prime minister of Rakhine State parliament, and NLD representative, has no management experience in his life. He is an honest person, I think, but no experience to govern. So government cannot really control the local state officers either. The last government's chief minister was a puppet, but this government is even more a puppet."

He mentions that George Soros is now in the country talking with Aung San Suu Kyii, a development that I actually found to be an encouraging sign because Soros is on the public record expressing his concern for the disenfranchised Rohingya and has referred comparatively to his own experience of growing up in the Jewish ghetto of Budapest during World War II. But U Thar Pwint says he has no idea what they were talking about, that "there has yet to be any transparency with this NLD government. If the president of our country tours the country, if he says something somewhere, it is never broadcast elsewhere. It is only referred to indirectly. We never hear the actual speeches of the president. We still have institutionalized censorship! The NLD has continued the custom."

I ask him directly about the criticisms now being leveled at Aung San Suu Kyii and refer to the letter written by Nobel laureates submitted to the UN Security Council.

He opines, "The problem is very difficult. If she sides with the Bengalis, there is going to be a big problem. If she sides with the Rakhines, a big protest will also occur. But the government does have sovereignty and it should use it one way or another to solve this problem. This is true not just of the current problem here in northern Arakan, but all problems. Our municipality is even afraid of solving our local problems. There is no practical authority at the local level. The township officer kicks it up to the minister, the minister to the central minister, and the central minister looks above him. It all disappears into a vortex."

I ask him what happens after Aung San Suu Kyii.

"I don't know! If Aung San Suu Kyii died tomorrow, the NLD would disintegrate and the army would regain absolute total control. There is no organization other than them."

While I am interested in further exploring how the Rakhine are in tension with the Burmese, U Thar Pwint is more interested in making his case against what he perceives are the Rohingya's aspirations. I can't seem to keep him away from addressing the case. It's as if he sees it as his duty to argue his case with me, one of those Westerners who is in need of knowing the Arakanese perspectives.

"Our fear is the sustainability for our race. If the current conditions pertain for the next twenty years, the result will be two to one and three to one. We face the extinction of our state. On the one hand is Bangladesh and on the other is the Burma government. There are 4 million Myanmar people in Thailand; are they entitled to a new state in Thailand? Do the Hispanic people in America who claim Indian blood try to occupy the white people's land or torch their houses, and if they did, what would be the result? We need to respect 'verification,' and the notion of Rohingya cannot be 'verified' because the term is not accurate. You cannot change the name of your race. I cannot accept this invention of the 'Rohingya.'

"Now we are quarreling with everyone including the UN community. If there is a thief and a householder, how can you stand in the middle [as the UN postures]? I have explained this to the UN personnel. We don't want to kill anybody. This situation depends wholly on the central government. I went to Singapore last year and was asked if because of the multiculturalism I observed there that I now looked at the situation here differently. I can see that historically there is harmony in Singapore, but in fact there is discrimination in favor of the Chinese against the Malays. And this has gotten solidified on the basis of quotas. We have no adequate law here with regard to proper classification of people. No foreigners can own land, but there are many Bengalis in Maungdaw and Buthidaung who own land. What's needed is a system of classification. It is their [Bengali] policy to foment conflict. For instance, in America, you cannot become president unless you were born in America." He says he mentioned this to Joseph Young, who at the time was the undersecretary of state for Southeast Asia and who had pointed out that while he was not born in America, he was completely accepted.

"The Rohingya want to become citizens as a whole community, rather than being individually vetted, under a new name of their race, as one of the indigenous people of Myanmar. If they are eligible, we can agree to their citizenship. But if we accepted all of them, we'd become a Rohingya country and every newcomer would come and be granted citizenship. Some Rohingya have gone to Saudi and Kuwait and call themselves Rohingya. If all the expatriates of Rohingya are counted, they would be more than us. If they are granted citizenship en masse, we'll be overwhelmed by returning Rohingya and they'll try to create their own state."

U Thar Pwint is a frequent consultant for fact-finding visitors to Sittwe, probably because he is fluent in English and quite articulate. He does try to be a spokesperson for the Rakhine Buddhist community. I ask him if he addressed Kofi Annan's commission when they visited. He says that he wanted to speak with them, but the Rakhine parliament had voted to boycott the commission because it smacked of outside interference.

I ask what will happen to the one hundred thousand people now in the IDP camp just north of Sittwe. I mention that all of these people are from Sittwe and are not interlopers from Bangladesh.

He says that "their fate will depend on the verification process. Every country verifies its citizens. But our government has not done this yet." I ask him if he thinks that the current verification process is fair and if it can actually work. I mention the difficulties of poor people who often simply have not been provided with proper identification papers, including birth certificates. And there have been times when, if they did have any papers, they had been asked to surrender them. But U Thar Pwint doesn't seem especially troubled by these issues. Like the good lawyer he is, he thinks that there are ways in which people can be legitimately sorted out as being longtime residents or recent newcomers. In this connection, I mention his old friend U Kyaw Hla Aung, and he breaks out into a smile. "Yes, of course, he is an old friend and we would welcome him back into the community."

With that, U Thar Pwint begins to wax philosophical. He says, "All of us, except for *arahants,* are dominated by self-interest." He gives the example of a child crying along the side of the road whom you go to help, but in the meantime a child related to you is on the other side crying. Which do you attend to first? He wants to make the right decisions based on the conditions.

I say I understand his point but go on to say that in Buddhism, you try to transcend self-interest. He remembers my point a year later and says he values our conversations. I say I value them too.

I have a question for him about the sangha. I tell him about the earlier encounter with the especially nationalist monk at his museum-cum-orphanage and wonder how typical this might be.

He responds by shaking his head affirmatively and says that "the sangha is not free but under the control of the government. There is a seniority system and they function in the same way as the government by looking up." It doesn't surprise him to hear that monks are such nationalists. "Theravada is a step-by-step hierarchy. The older monks have more authority and control. If these older monks are conservative nationalists, then many of the monks in general will toe that line, especially if it is in conformity with the government."

I recall the recent talk by Sitagu in which he says that Myanmar's problems will be significantly lessened if the army, the sangha, and the people are united. I kind of shivered when I first heard that, but I think U Thar Pwint is trying to say to me that that's just the way it is now. I ask him if there is there any segmentation of the sangha according to race.

"No! We pay homage to the universal sangha. We pay homage to the collective and not just one person."

As time is passing and he has generously spent all of his morning—from eight thirty until almost noon—discussing these matters with me quite frankly, I ask him in general if things are better with the return of democracy. He says they are in some ways, but that one of the flaws of democracy has to do with the dissemination of bad information. Part of the problem nowadays is a result of social media. I tell him I couldn't agree more, but of course we differ about what constitutes "bad information."

Finally, he wants to say something unprompted by me, sort of like a final thought he wants to impart. He says that "what's changed these days is that we cannot criticize the youth. Before, there was respect for age, a deference. That seems to be going away. The whole world is changing. Asian civilization is based on Buddhist ideas. But now there is some mixing with the culture from the West. If good result comes, that would be great. If not, it's a problem." He then tells a yarn about how a beautiful American actress had once proposed to George Bernard Shaw. She had thought that beautiful and smart children would be born as a result. But it could be that they would be ugly and dull! I say yes, that is "perhaps the chance you take when *paticcasammupada* is globalized." We both laugh and vow to meet again.

The Social Worker

January 2017. I had heard from my friend the journalist Wai Moe in Yangon that Khine Kaung Zan was a moderate Rakhine Buddhist and that it would be a good idea to talk with him to balance out the views that I was sure to get from U Thar Pwint. It certainly was a welcome alternative voice to the one articulated by Khin Maung Saw. Khine Kaung Zan was very difficult to reach, an extremely busy man who was consumed with his work at the NGO he had established back in 2010, the Wan Lark Rural Development Foundation, located in an unpretentious middle-class house outside of the downtown Sittwe area, not far from the jetties serving the harbor. I found the place without much difficulty, a couple of dusty blocks off the main road. I had tried on two previous visits to Sittwe to contact him, but he was out of town on both of those occasions. He was out of town this time too when I reached him by phone up in Mrauk U, but I was around in Sittwe long enough for him to return and grant me an interview several days later. On the agreed-upon day, he arrived around forty-five minutes late, having told his secretary that his appointment with me was at ten a.m., rather than the nine a.m. time we had agreed to on the phone days back. Waiting for him gave me a feel for the people working at his foundation, as four or five came into work and chatted me up as I waited on the first floor, a converted garage area. They were a friendly, congenial group. When Khine did arrive, it became clear that we would need a translator, as Khine was less confident about his English than he might have been. Perhaps the problem was more with understanding me, though I tried to speak in a slow, measured fashion. His own English was not that bad, but he would often quit in the middle of a sentence and defer to his assistant to finish his thought. I thought that the two worked extremely well in tandem.

In response to my opening general questions about the work of his foundation, he responds by saying that they are working for peace, justice, and equality, primarily by trying to fill the gap between what the government can get done and what disadvantaged communities need. That is, "The gap consists mainly in trying to do what the government cannot. If there is armed conflict and the government can't reach the troubled spot, then we do our best to be of assistance. There is now a conflict between the Arakan Army and government military forces, so there are a lot of Rakhine and other indigenous refugees in northern Arakan who need our help. We try to provide the basics for them. There are about four thousand refugees now. There are villages affected by the conflict right now in Kyauktauw, Mrauk U, and Buthidaung townships. Our work is not confined to simply Rakhine Buddhists but also among the many indigenous people living in Arakan as well." I notice that he has left out the Rohingya in his account.

Khine's foundation regularly assists three or four schools in Sittwe by supplying learning materials for students and teacher training for making use of the learning materials effectively. They are trying to move education beyond simple rote learning to teaching students how to think and make decisions. I was impressed with this focus because almost everywhere I walked in Sittwe, or when I was walking about in Thandwe as well, I could hear the choruses of rote learning taking place in both monasteries and regular school venues. There are many in Myanmar who are pinning their long-term hopes on increased education throughout the country, but the very nature of education is going to have to change for the desired results of responsible citizenship to be obtained.

Khine's foundation also provides relief from natural disasters when it can. It has concentrated on building up reserves for these unexpected occurrences. But right now it is focused on the fallout from the conflict between the Arakan Army and the Tatmadaw. Khine points out that for the past several months (in 2016), the Arakan Army has been aggressively attacking the Tatmadaw in various areas throughout northern Arakan, and so the villagers are fleeing from these areas. Khine thinks that this problem is only going to get worse in the near future, as the Arakan Army seems to be growing and gaining confidence. "They have inflicted a lot of damage on the Burma army, with about forty dead this January alone. But the problem is that refugees have lost their livelihoods and have become entirely dependent."

Khine then changes the subject, as if to seize the opportunity to give me a broader picture of his foundation's work. "We give human rights training, leadership training, and women's participation training. Two years ago, we provided microfinance assistance in thirty-nine villages in two townships. During the summer vacation we give English training for middle and high school students. We also provide food and clothes to refugees and shelter kits [bamboo poles and a plastic roof] and also seeds for paddy planting if their land is still available."

I ask about funding. "We get our funding from international NGOs and from individual donors, from expatriates as well as from locals. If there is an emergency, we collect money from going around the city [Sittwe] and online, and also from Thailand, Malaysia, and other national communities. Some of the refugees need long-term support. We try to provide that."

Having learned specifically about the worthy work of the foundation and impressed by the sincerity of the effort, I shift the conversation toward the problem between the Rakhine Buddhists and the Rohingya. I ask in an open-ended fashion, "What's going to happen here now?"

"The main problem is how to solve this problem practically and not just theoretically. It will depend on whether or not the government and the other stakeholders take into account what is actually happening on the ground right now. The international NGOs, including the UN, should maintain the good work that they are doing. But sometimes the NGOs end up inadvertently making the problem bigger. Now the situation is very quiet. Unfortunately, by quickly responding to the Bengalis' problems, sometimes the international NGOs make the Rakhines feel as if the treatment is not fair. When the Rakhine people see all the toilets in the IDP camps, and they don't have any toilets themselves and still have to just go out and shit in the forest, or the kinds of food that the Muslims have distributed to them in the camps, they get jealous and cry out that this is unfair."

This was a theme I had heard repeatedly in Arakan: what about the poor Rakhines who have also suffered? Why is there so much attention given to the "Bengalis"? In trying to surmise and answer, one often hears that the reason lies in the international Islamic response, or even a conspiracy, to support the Rohingya to the exclusion of the Rakhines. I sometimes have pointed out that perhaps the Rohingya have received attention because they have been rounded up and put into camps, are not allowed to leave them, are prevented from furthering their education in public institutions (there have been no Muslim students at Sittwe University since 2012), have been stripped of legal representation, and have been prevented from contesting elections. I have listened, sometimes incredulously, to people say that being placed into the camps is seen as an advantage for the Rohingya.

Khine feels, in any case, that when the government implements any of its policies, they should be much more transparent. With regard to the Rohingya situation, he said (echoing U Thar Pwint), "We need to devise a way to know who is who to determine those who are refugees and those who are migrants."

I ask if the current verification process is working in a functionally efficacious way. "I have chatted with an immigration department officer recently and I found out that they don't really have any transparency. We have to monitor the verification process carefully. The immigration department has had a problem with corruption from the time of independence until now. Because of this, there are a lot of individual problems that are going to need to be sorted out. Sometimes it was the case that if you did not give money for the card, you couldn't get a card." In other words, not only do the very poor often lack proper documents, but the means by which they could be secured is problematic.

The integrity of immigration officials in Myanmar is a theme that often came up in my discussions, as these officials are notorious for demanding bribes. In their own cultural world, perhaps they simply see what we regard as bribes as an entitlement that goes with their position. That's how it was explained to me in Thandwe when my Kaman Muslim interlocutor confronted some of her ex-students working in immigration (2: "The Teacher").

Having raised the issue of immigration officials, I ask, perhaps far too bluntly rather than deftly, if the events that occurred on October 9, 2016—the attack on border guards that left nine dead—hadn't fundamentally changed the situation by providing the Tatmadaw with more leverage to repress the Rohingya.

In retrospect, I castigated myself for asking and then answering my own question! But Khine and his assistant nod in agreement with me before adding, "The international community should also say to the Bengalis that they need to follow the laws of the country. And that is the 1982 law. The government cannot control the overpopulation of the Muslims in Rakhine. This is a fundamental problem. The international NGOs provide material support for the Rohingya, but not educational help. Among the Rakhines, a lot only reach the fourth grade or perhaps an eighth-grade education at best. But the Muslims don't ever seem to go beyond the seventh grade and get very little education. The grip of the Muslim clerics is very strong on them. Education is such a big problem here, for both communities. In asking for a specific separate state, the Rohingya are exacerbating the situation. Education is acceptable, et cetera, but not the demand for a separate state."

Khine goes on to say, "Because people are not educated, they have a difficult time separating fact from opinion. They see a post on Facebook and they think it's true. Rumors are spread, such as about the rape of Arakanese Buddhist women by Muslims, that get understood as fact. For the Muslim people, they are also badly educated. Their religious leaders define for them what is true. The lobbyists for Rohingya are effective at spreading propaganda to news agencies like Al Jazeera. The Muslims are getting lazy as a result of the assistance they are getting from international NGOs." This last comment seems to have been inspired by the Ma Ba Tha's own propaganda machine, which had provided "proof" that much of the aid intended for Rohingya ended up being sold by them on the black market for profit. From U Kyaw Hla Aung on the Rohingya side (2: "The Spokesman"), I heard a few days later that some of the aid intended for Rohingya had been hijacked in Yangon by wealthy non-Rohingya Muslim businessmen. Recently, a large tranche of aid from Turkey had been diverted from Sittwe to Yangon, and the fate of its cargo of rice remained unknown. Another ship's cargo from Malaysia intended for the Rohingya was also directed through Yangon because the government asserted that it alone would be responsible for the distribution of aid originating from foreign sources.

I ask Khine about hopes for the Kofi Annan Commission appointed by Aung San Suu Kyii. He begins by saying that "most people don't understand how policy might get formulated. Many Rakhine Buddhists think that the Muslim problem is the only problem being addressed and don't see the international or regional nature of the problem localized here. We gave a suggestion to Kofi Annan's commission that they work and talk not just in Yangon. There should be an office of the commission in Sittwe, Maungdaw, and Buthidaung to do research on the problem. The recommendations would have more legitimacy. In Yangon, there is just talk. The government has been trying to 'balance' the populations in Maungdaw and Buthidaung. The government also needs to create the ability to simply walk about. Now the people living in those areas [Rakhine] do not have paddy fields, so they cannot live there, and many of them come back to Sittwe. Maungdaw is 97 percent Muslim and Buthidaung is 94 percent. The Muslims control the land. The situation cannot be understood from afar, especially since the entire commission is made up of outsiders to the areas where the problem is most acute [Maungdaw and Buthidaung]."

Khine then points out that there is also a government commission that is supposed to be looking into the Rakhine problem. He says that ultimately there is the possibility that the government may not implement any recommendations from either Kofi Annan's or the government's commission. "Our only hope is that the problems on the ground can be taken into account, and not ignored as they have been so far." He goes on to say that the NLD has ideas about the rights of the ethnic people but cannot implement them because of the Tatmadaw.

And so again a conversation ends with a familiar point, that the Tatmadaw still holds the cards in the country's realpolitik. The intentions of the NLD government remain circumspect because of a consideration of what the Tatmadaw might intend itself. The army remains thoroughly Burmese Buddhist in its orientation, and historically now a central source of discrimination against Muslims. As such, it is not trusted entirely by many Rakhines, who point out that the army's senior leadership includes none other than the Burmese. As for the Rohingya, it's been many years (decades) since any have been allowed to join the army. So when one sees the sprawling military complex outside of Sittwe, between the city and the massive IDP camp for Rohingya, one cannot but think of its current raison d'être as an occupying force that keeps the current order, much as it did before the startling events of June 2012 that ushered in a new divided social and political reality for both the Rohingya and the Rakhines.

I couldn't get back to Sittwe in January 2018 to follow up with Khine and to ascertain what his Wan Lark Foundation was then focusing its work upon. I am quite sure he would have been appalled at what the army had perpetrated upon the Rohingya after August 25, 2017, and would fear the future consequences of those atrocities. His was the most measured Rakhine voice I heard in Sittwe. He had firsthand knowledge and deep awareness of the struggles encountered by the poor, whether Rakhine or Rohingya, who were victimized by the larger political forces playing out. He knew intimately of the local dynamics in play and believed that unless these were recognized, national or international pressures would dictate unworkable solutions for the nature of local problems. That is, he worried deeply about how locals were not being represented on the much-vaunted national commissions and advisory boards. He had no faith that Burmese initiatives could solve Rakhine Buddhist and Rohingya Muslim problems, nor the problems causing the conflicts between them.

The Spokesman

Coming to Sittwe from Yangon reminds one about how Myanmar was before 2010, when the country first began to open up. It is not all that different from Mrauk U either, which is still thoroughly a big village of more than two hundred thousand people. Sittwe may be a bit larger; it has an airport that links it to Yangon and about three or four hotels that serve the traffic that comes in and out of northern Arakan. It is definitely the gateway to the rest of the northern state. And it is now bereft of more than one hundred thousand of its former residents, Rohingya who were removed to internally displaced persons (IDP) camps following the riot of June 2012. They are still there—languishing, supported by perhaps a dozen various international NGOs but making no palpable progress in improving their collective situation. There is no virtually no livelihood in the IDP camps, save the few jobs scared up by NGO workers who need local assistance, or the hoarding of supplies that might be sold off.

I had come to Sittwe chiefly to see U Kyaw Hla Aung. I had visited him exactly one year earlier, in **January of 2016**, when he had given me a "soft copy" of his biography. It had been compiled and written by his son, who had recently finished a master's degree at Mahidol University in Bangkok. It is not easy to unravel, but it begins by noting that U Kyaw Hla Aung was a clerk and stenographer in the Sittwe District Court from 1961 until 1983. In 1984, he began a career as a lawyer and in 1986 sought to represent Muslim farmers whose lands had been confiscated. Somehow, the fact that he was representing these farmers led to his arrest and imprisonment in the Sittwe Prison, where, for a time, he shared a cell with a recalcitrant Buddhist monk. The monk appealed to other Rakhine prisoners to make sure that U Kyaw Hla Aung's needs were cared for. The 1988 uprising impacted the prison in that a rebellion within had led the authorities to release many of the prisoners, including U Kyaw Hla Aung. In 1989, he helped to establish the National Democratic Party for Human Rights and stood for parliament representing the first electorate in Sittwe. But during the campaign, he was arrested again in relation to the old charges of sedition, and yet additional charges were also brought against him. He was sentenced to fourteen more years in prison. Meanwhile, he threw his political support behind a Kaman Muslim lawyer whose candidacy was successful, but like all others in the 1990 election, the Kaman candidate was not allowed to claim his seat, as the military refused to recognize the results of the election. U Kyaw Hla Aung spent the next seven years in prison, before being released in 1997. While in prison, he assisted other prisoners in helping to draft appeals.

After his release from prison, he served as the local administrator for Médecins Sans Frontières (Doctors Without Borders) from 1998 until June 2012, when he intended to retire. On June 10, "Rakhine extremists posted a rumor on the website Freedom News Group. It was said that the police got two boxes of weapons at his house . . . and he was arrested," according to his biography. U Kyaw Hla Aung was arrested again, this despite the fact that he had been a stalwart critic of religious extremism within the Muslim community and had preached nondiscrimination against all non-Muslims. He was in prison for more than two months before international diplomatic pressure mounted by Médecins Sans Frontières led to a presidential pardon by Thein Sein in August 2012. But U Kyaw Hla Aung's legal troubles continued. Case after case was leveled against him beginning in 2013. From what I could ascertain, the charges had to do with sedition and were probably mounted as a result of U Kyaw Hla Aung's consultations with many Western diplomatic observers, including the US ambassador Derek Mitchell. Altogether, U Kyaw Hla Aung had to serve an additional year and a half and he was not finally released, again due to an amnesty, until October 2014.

Ultimately, U Kyaw Hla Aung's efforts to provide education and to speak articulately on behalf of the IDP camp were recognized internationally. In June 2018 he was awarded the Aurora Prize for Awakening Humanity, "a global humanitarian award given to an individual for the exceptional impact their actions have had on preserving human life and advancing humanitarian causes. . . . The Aurora Humanitarian Initiative was founded in memory of the survivors of Armenian genocide and in honor of their saviors by the descendants of survivors."[1]

January 2016. I was surprised at how eagerly and enthusiastically U Kyaw Hla Aung welcomed me during my first visit. We talked at length about the political situation for the Rohingya now that the NLD had defeated the USDP. He was cautiously optimistic, though also a bit anxious because no Muslims had been allowed to run for office in the election, and he had seen no signs from NLD leaders that the on-the-ground situation for his community might change significantly. He noted that the USDP's attempts to characterize Aung San Suu Kyii as sympathetic to the Muslims were really baseless, though he wished there actually had been some substance to the USDP fears! So the prospects for the future were really cloudy. U Kyaw Hla Aung described to me the current plight in the camps, how various NGOs were attempting to provide basic food and sanitary requirements, and his own considerable efforts aimed at educating young children. He had personally secured teaching materials and supervised the training of teachers in short order. The NGO Save the Children had built classrooms for younger children. It was clear to me that he enjoyed the confidence not only of American diplomats, but of the Turkish ambassador and

1. "About the Aurora Humanitarian Initiative," Aurora Prize for Awakening Humanity, https://auroraprize.com.

others in the international diplomatic community as well. He had become a spokesperson of sorts for the camp.

At that time, in January 2016, following our first conversation at his newly built modest house on the fringe of the IDP camp and adjacent to a traditional Rohingya village, I had toured the IDP camp in a clandestine fashion with one of his assistants and then returned to Sittwe very sobered by what I had seen, especially from my casual encounters with many young children in the camp whose futures could only be charitably regarded as bleak.

I had thought long and hard about the dehumanization process that the interred had experienced during these past three or four years, condemned as they were to crowded, impersonal, deteriorating, and vulnerable conditions, from which they were refused any escape. And I had been chagrined by the "official" process I had refused to engage in, in order to gain access to the camp: several days of bureaucratic waiting around in Sittwe only to pay a hefty "fee." Not only were these Sittwe Rohingya interred, but their official administrating captors enjoyed the privilege of charging expensive "fees" to gain very limited, short-term access to them. So I had chosen the informal route to make contact, the details of which, while at moments a bit harrowing and dramatic, I cannot reveal for the sake of my enablers. I will only report that I was warned by my host that the camp has its fair share of spies for the government.

I think my visit the first time did not go completely unnoticed. A few months before, I had applied for a Fulbright Global Flex Award and had been congratulated in writing just two weeks before my visit to Sittwe that my application and research proposal had been recommended by two academic review committees (composed of scholars in the fields of religion and Southeast Asian studies). Having received Fulbright fellowships before and having served four times myself on earlier incarnations of the national academic panels that had just approved and recommended my application, I knew, as I was informed in my congratulatory letter, that my application still needed to be cleared by the embassies of the countries (Myanmar, Sri Lanka, and Thailand) within which I had intended to work. The letter said it could be "several months" before I received the final official approval of my fellowship. As part of the application process, I had received sterling supporting letters of recommendation from universities (Peradeniya and Mahidol, in Sri Lanka and Thailand, respectively) indicating that I would enjoy a welcome affiliation with them. I had been told that no letter from a Myanmar institution was necessary, that the embassy in Yangon would handle any affiliation issues if I were to be given the award. So my only slight doubts about receiving this award were concerned with the US embassy in Yangon. Just five days after I visited the Sittwe IDP camp, I received an e-mail (not a letter) informing me without explanation that my application for the fellowship had been rejected. Despite persistent efforts to find out specifically how and why my application had been rejected, I was never able to summon anything other than generic responses about how "there were far more applicants than available fellowships." I found this development just a bit more than coincidental with my informal visit to the IDP camp.

January 2017. When I visit with U Kyaw Hla Aung for a second time a year later, he has just returned, the day before I meet him, from a visit to Sri Lanka, where he was hosted in an effort by an NGO to build interreligious understanding. He was accompanied by two Burmese Buddhist monks from Bago and seems genuinely moved by the intercommunal spirit of the occasion. U Kyaw Hla Aung told constituents of the Sri Lankan NGO the Center for Peace Building and Reconciliation to come to Myanmar to see how the government is supporting Buddhism exclusively while depressing other religions. He is excited about how the Sri Lankan military is now helping Muslims on the Jaffna Peninsula to rebuild their houses and mosques after some twenty-five years of exile. He says, "We don't know whether their real land has been returned or not. Since we were like tourists, we could not ask people directly about their situations." There seem to have been some restraints placed on his group in terms of interactions with war-affected Sri Lankans, though I'm not sure where that restraint was emanating from. In any case, I explain to him how I was actually living in Sri Lanka in 1990 when the Tamil Tigers gave the Muslims of Jaffna—approximately one hundred thousand of them—just two hours to flee the city. I say that this was the clearest example during the civil war in Sri Lanka of ethnic cleansing, apart from the 1983 riot in the southern Sinhala regions of the island (see "Comparative Contexts of Conflict: Sri Lanka, Myanmar, and Thailand" in the introduction). I point out on his map of Sri Lanka the locations of Jaffna and then Puttalam, the site of the camp that existed for about twenty-five years before some Muslims, perhaps some of those he had observed on his recent trip, were allowed to return and to reclaim what they could. I mention that, when visiting my daughter, Sarah, in Doha, Qatar, I met two Sri Lankan Muslims now working in Qatar as drivers whose families had evacuated Jaffna and had eventually domiciled around Puttalam. They told me that very few were able to return to Jaffna after all these years. I express fears about how "temporary" camps had a way of becoming permanent, and Kyaw Hla Aung nods soberly in agreement: it goes without saying.

I then talk a bit about how the situation has changed in Sri Lanka because of the change of government following the elections of 2015 that swept aside the nationalist government of Mahinda Rajapaksa, which had tacitly supported the Buddhist militancy espoused by the Bodu Bala Sena. I want to use that as a segue into talking about the hope that the situation in Myanmar could have changed following the electoral victory of Aung San Suu Kyii and the National League for Democracy ten months after the Sri Lankan election. In my initial view, it seemed to me that the Ma Ba Tha monks had lost a lot of their leverage in the Myanmar election's aftermath, or that their decision to align with the Union Solidarity and Development Party (USDP), the party that is basically constituted by retired military officers and promotes the military's interests, had now cast them as espousing a political perspective of militant nationalism that had been seemingly resoundingly rejected by the people. Moreover, during the past year, the central sangha's authority, the Ma Ha Na, had declared that the Ma Ba Tha actually had no institutional standing, a move that had undercut its apparent strength and influence. But U Kyaw Hla Aung is adamant, as are his two attending associates, in asserting that the general situation in Myanmar has deteriorated significantly during the past year since the NLD's victory and since we talked before, in January 2016, especially for the local Rohingya community. Now Sri Lanka seems like a model Buddhist-dominated country to him, one that he hopes might inspire the future of Myanmar's political aspirations. Having seen so much political darkness over the years in Sri Lanka, having lived so closely with people in Sri Lanka over so many years of despair, I privately marvel about how perceptions of polity can be so radically pliant. Before 2015, I couldn't imagine Sri Lanka ever being idealized by other Southeast Asian countries as a beacon of hope. I still doubt that Sri Lanka will be able to resist the domination of the Buddhist nationalist persuasion. So recently, Myanmar had seemed like the genuine ray of light in the region, before Aung San Suu Kyii and the NLD had disappointed the great expectations.

I ask U Kyaw Hla Aung if he met with Kofi Annan, and he shows me a formal letter in which he asked Kofi Annan's commission to investigate specifically the destruction of mosques in Maungdaw and other sites of carnage that have been wrecked by the Tatmadaw since the October 9, 2016, border incidents. He says he is skeptical about the integrity of the commission because there are members on the commission who will likely obstruct and obfuscate, specifically U Aye Lwin (of the Islamic Centre of Myanmar) and U Khin Maung Lay, who are both so-called Burmese Muslims. In other discussions, I had learned that "Burmese Muslims" had been Muslims deemed acceptable to the Burmese community because they had fully enculturated: Burmese is their native tongue, their women dress like Burmese women, and they are fully integrated into the urban business communities. They were regarded as genuine patriots before the verification process was established and even now many of them had been forced to register as "Bengalis" if they wanted to retain citizenship. "We can believe Kofi Annan," says U Kyaw Hla Aung, "but we don't know what his report will be like because of the others on the committee." He goes on to say that the commission should spend less time convening sessions in Yangon and actually get out to Maungdaw and Buthidaung to see what has happened since October 9. This is the same thing I heard at the Wan Lark Foundation a day earlier from Khine Kaung Zan, who said that the commission should have offices set up in the two Muslim towns and in Sittwe, so that the on-the-ground situation can be better understood.

What is very depressing to hear from U Kyaw Hla Aung is this: "I have no hope for the current situation. Even if Kofi Annan makes helpful recommendations, I have little confidence that these will be put into effect." Indeed, the Kofi Annan Commission was advisory, with no guarantee of leverage, even if it made substantial recommendations on behalf of the well-being of the Rohingya people, itself a questionable outcome. "What is clear in all of this is that the

Tatmadaw has used the events of October 9 as an excuse to strike out at the Rohingya, to play its xenophobia card that strengthens its position among the majority Burmese that it is the defender of the nation." It certainly would have bolstered its position among the Rakhine Buddhists, who have often regarded the army as their protectors against what they regard as an ever-increasing Muslim tide emanating from Bangladesh, but also part of a worldwide coordinated effort backed by wealthy Muslim countries to Islamicize the entire country. This understanding puts the Rakhine Buddhists on the "front line." Indeed, in August of 2017, after several bodies of indigenous people were found at the foot of the Mayu mountains, the Arakan National Party asked the Union Parliament [now called the Assembly of the Union] for more security for their villages out in rural Maungdaw. Several hundred Rakhine had temporarily fled the town in fear of "insurgents." The parliament and the Tatmadaw responded by sending two planes full of heavily armed soldiers, who landed at Sittwe on their way to Maungdaw in defense of their Rakhine compatriots. It is extremely likely that these newly arrived and specially trained soldiers were deeply involved in the mayhem that subsequently unfolded in northern Arakan, where heinous crimes against humanity were committed, where textbook instances of ethnic cleansing took place. The Tatmadaw has a long history of engaging in the murder and rape of civilians as part of its waging war against other ethnic minorities in Myanmar. But what appears to have occurred in northern Arakan following August 25, 2017, raised the Tatmadaw's own bar in terms of the level and degree of atrocities committed. As of this writing, while there has been a continuous stream of denials from both military and government sources about what the army has perpetrated in its "search-and-clear operations," an investigative news effort by Reuters uncovered military complicity with Rakhine Buddhist villagers in the murder of ten Rohingya men. If any weight is given to the descriptions provided by Rohingya among the seventy-five thousand who fled following October 9, 2016, and the 698,000 who fled after August 25, 2017, the exposure of this murder scene is by no means an isolated event. (The two Burmese reporters working for Reuters on this specific murder case were arrested on trumped-up charges in December 2017, were convicted in September 2018, and remain incarcerated as of January 2019, as I finished revising this manuscript.) Their most recent appeal has been denied.

U Kyaw Hla Aung remains in good communication with Rohingya people in Maungdaw and Buthidaung and so has a good sense of what actually happened there on October 9, 2016, and since then. He says that he believes the attack was organized by big-time drug dealers attempting to retrieve drugs that had been confiscated earlier. This attack was also aimed at regaining some of their arms. The drug group was made up of both Rakhine and Rohingya individuals. Drug groups for many years have been suspected of being in collusion with border security personnel. Even Rakhines can be heard to complain about how the border guards have been bribed to allow in illegal Bengalis. It is often part of their standard narrative. So what happened on October 9 was probably the consequence of corrupt cooperation having gone bad, one side becoming disgruntled with what has happened recently in the cross-border drug trade. The three Rohingya political leaders I spoke to—U Kyaw Hla Aung, U Kyaw Min (1: "The Elder Statesman"), and Abu Tahay (1: "The Historian")—all of whom are well connected to the situation on the ground in northern Arakan, essentially agreed on that narrative, and yet both the domestic and international media tended to accept and restate the Myanmar government's position that this was an attack by Rohingya political insurgents. In any case, the army's terrible response, which led initially to perhaps as many as a hundred Rohingya people killed, several hundred "missing," the reportedly widespread rape of women, and consequently seventy-five thousand refugees fleeing across the Myanmar border into Bangladesh thoroughly terrorized Rohingya villagers. "You know, until now we have no real arms," says U Kyaw Hla Aung. And yet Aung San Suu Kyii says that it was the RSO (Rohingya Solidarity Organization) that was responsible for the initial attack on the border posts. "The problem with that hypothesis is that the RSO was destroyed a long time ago; either that or they've gone completely silent over many years. Now [as time as has passed], we have to live carefully not to communicate openly with some of the people in Maungdaw because it will put us in peril here." He shows me the latest Amnesty International letter to Aung San Suu Kyii asking that 485 Rohingya people who have been detained by the army for investigation be released. One heartening aspect to this is that at least this specific matter has been brought to Aung San Suu Kyii's attention. Earlier, she had repeated reports from the army itself denying any culpability, claiming that the army was innocent of any of the atrocities that have been reported by local sources in Maungdaw to the international media. And even though she was later provided with a copy of the of the United Nations Office of the High Commissioner for Human Rights report, based on more than two hundred interviews with Rohingya refugees who had fled to Bangladesh (OHCHR 2017), she still refused to acknowledge in public the atrocities against the Rohingya people that have been perpetrated by the Tatmadaw. Moreover, as I have mentioned earlier, she went so far as to deny visas to the distinguished three-person fact-finding commission that had been appointed by the UN to find out exactly what happened following October 9 in northern Arakan.

Unfortunately, the aftermath of October 9 brought increased pressure on the IDP camp. It became even more difficult for visitors to enter the camp. Those who go through the process of securing official permission to enter often have to spend several days negotiating the bureaucratic process in Sittwe. It is typical to have to return several times to the appropriate office to finally secure the needed letter of permission, and the cost is often 150 dollars or more. As I mentioned earlier, it struck me as insidious that people in the government were making money off the Rohingya in this way—charging what is locally a very handsome sum to visit people living in such destitution. Moreover, I was told by U Kyaw Hla Aung that not only are there multiple checkpoints that eat up the visitor's limited time (only daytime visits are permitted) and at which one has to declare to whom one will be speaking, but the process puts those Rohingya being interviewed in a later compromising situation of having to answer questions from the police or army about the conversations they have engaged in with visitors. For that reason, I was not surprised to learn that everyone agreed that "informally" visiting Rohingya in the IDP camp was the best policy for everyone concerned. Under the Thein Sein government, apparently the situation was not nearly as difficult. It didn't feel that way the year before when I had visited U Kyaw Hla Aung in the IDP camp the first time. This second time, my passage was rather nerve-wracking, as the car ferrying me to U Kyaw Hla Aung's little house weaved through the warren of narrow lanes of the old Rohingya village, completely avoiding the main road to the IDP camp once it cleared a large open field. On my way back out, I had to duck down in the back seat, covered by an overcoat, to avoid being seen by a passing vehicle. My Rohingya guides were visibly worried about detection. A year earlier, I was taken by the main road and also allowed to walk through a portion of the IDP camp. No such visit was possible this time. One of U Kyaw Hla Aung's associates said, "The government has its own spies among some of the older Rohingya people and the Muslim clerics. They do this for a little bit of money and favors. So we had to be especially careful today." I heaved a sigh of relief when I cleared the army checkpoint on my way back to Sittwe.

But these are relatively minor tangible concerns reflecting a greater problematic. "The torturing of Rohingya is starting to cause a radical response among some of the youth. The NLD government is helping to create IS [ISIS] here!" U Kyaw Hla Aung told me. I had to agree with him that the government's actions, ostensibly motivated by a fear of insurgency, may very well lead to a self-fulfilling prophecy. When people see no hope for the future, they resort to ever more desperate measures. U Kyaw Hla Aung says that now that the boat passage to Malaysia has been closed off, referring to the previous seasons of Rohingya trying to reach that Muslim country by boat, the alternatives for what to do are narrowing.

U Kyaw Hla Aung reports that the dominant mood in the IDP camp is increasingly one of depression, because there is no hope of leaving. Still there is no hope of students attending school or university. "How can this country improve if our Muslim students are not allowed in the university? While the other minorities might have arms to resist, we don't have any. We don't want any. We are trying to get peace without having arms." I point out rather wistfully that it was the lack of opportunity for Tamil youth in Sri Lanka during the 1960s, including the quota system that factored many deserving students out of university educations, that led to the upsurge in Tamil militancy. I wince at myself for adding only a further depressing note to the conversation.

I ask what has been the general situation in the camp since I last visited a year earlier. The answer is that "the situation has actually gotten much worse under the NLD government. The IDP is barely surviving right now." The previous year, U Kyaw Hla Aung had told me about his efforts to organize education for the children of the IDP camp. I had seen a couple of classrooms constructed by the Save the Children NGO, an NGO that since has left Myanmar and set up its efforts in the deep south of Thailand and Cox's Bazaar in Bangladesh, and had spoken to two teachers who had been hastily trained to help U Kyaw Hla Aung in his mission. He now shows me stacks of simple reading and math exercise texts that he has stored on the second-floor verandah of his home. He has had to stop "all the education efforts that had been going on," because "after October 9, the army and the police are suspecting we are organizing against them."

As for the general physical condition of the camp, the actual structures within which people are living were specified "for six months' duration of use. They are now four and half years old. Some have been renovated, but some are now destroyed."

One of U Kyaw Hla Aung's associates reiterates that people can't leave the camp, at least without paying about 50,000 kyats in order to go to Sittwe for an important reason, such as a medical emergency, and even then they might be denied help. It is never guaranteed. People who come out and who get permission are stopped at many checkpoints, and those to whom they speak will later be questioned by the police. I wryly point out that U Kyaw Hla Aung was just allowed to travel to Sri Lanka for a week but isn't allowed to go to downtown Sittwe. Nervous light laughter follows. Abu Tahay (1: "The Historian") had spoken to me weeks earlier about how he had been allowed to travel to Norway but not to other parts of Myanmar.

This inability to travel even into Sittwe makes me realize again how isolated these people have become. So I ask U Kyaw Hla Aung, "Are there any Buddhist leaders in Sittwe that you can still talk to?"

He replies emphatically, "No!" We then talk a little about U Thar Pwint, since I know that they are old friends from their days in court. But he says that he simply is not able to talk to any Rakhine Buddhists in Sittwe anymore, despite the fact that he had many such good friends.

He talks about how financially destitute everyone in the camp has become and how his little house is the result of the charity of some of his Rohingya friends in Yangon. "We don't even have any bank accounts. We are completely confiscated." He says that there are some Rohingya people in Rakhine who are due pensions, but they have not been able to gain access to them since the mayhem of the 2012 Sittwe riot.

"From where do you get any sense of hope?" I ask. He mentions that a Turkish ship came to donate rice here in Sittwe, but the government deferred the ship to Yangon, seized all the cargo, and put it in warehouses. The government said that if any relief comes from abroad, it would take charge of its distribution. "The Turks are trying to help, but the government is not allowing us to accept. I'm writing to the Turkish ambassador not to send any more help if it can't be distributed. The aid is in vain. There are some brokers who are trying to take advantage of the situation, such as commandeering aid that comes here. Very rich Muslims in Yangon are benefiting. While we starve! I constructed this house with the help of colleagues. I built it in order to be able to host my guests, and I had to do it secretly. The government people would not allow it if they were aware."

I ask him what his views are regarding the verification process that the Rohingya have been encouraged to engage in by Aung San Suu Kyii. "It's not for us," he says. "It's for those coming from other countries. When we applied in the 1990s and used the word Rohingya as our 'race,' they would not accept our application for a citizenship card. How can people who don't have cards now get them when no birth certificates have been issued for the past thirty years? How can people come into our area and be called illegal when it is impossible for us to move about in this region?

"I told the American ambassador's political officers that you are encouraging her [Aung San Suu Kyii] to be democratic, though right now she cannot be. The Americans should review her activities, because she is certainly not implementing democracy. What she says and what she can do is limited by the army. I told all the ambassadors that after being regarded as citizens at the time of independence in 1947, how can after forty or fifty years we then be denied citizenship? Is there any country in the world that has done this? They just kept quiet."

We begin to talk a bit about language and dialects. For some reason the American dialect seems easier to understand, he says. I ask about the Rohingya language, specifically if it is the same as the Chittagong dialect of Bengali, as others like U Thar Pwint have described to me. A day or two earlier in Sittwe, a university student had sharply remonstrated me for using the term "Rohingya" rather than "Bengali," and I had replied by saying that "Rohingya" was also a language and not just the name of these people. But I was told emphatically that "Bengalis speak Bengali." Now U Kyaw Hla Aung and his friends mention how Rohingya and Bengalis can clearly differentiate the two languages from each other and that the Rohingya language is influenced by many languages and isn't simply the Chittagonian dialect of Bengali, as Urdu, English, and Rakhine are all mixed in.

This talk about language makes U Kyaw Hla Aung very animated and perhaps even bitter as he talks about the absurdity of the current situation. "When I was arrested in 2012, it was alleged that I was organizing to burn houses—and it was my house that was getting burnt! We lost everything! I was put in jail for two months and five days before Thein Sein intervened to release me. And then after another year-and-a-half stint in prison for various trumped-up charges, I was sent here. My family was brought out to the IDP camp to be with me. But before that, I could not get any information about them, nor could they get information about me. I was in court six times. I was suffering from gout and arthritis. It is difficult to be suspected of being a terrorist." I think ruefully about what it must be like for a man in his seventy-eighth year, with a wife and four children to support, to lose everything he has and be placed in such a position of destitution. "I served the government in their courts for twenty-four years, only to find myself arrested, then placed in a camp and called a foreigner, a 'Bengali'!" He laughs at the absurdity of his own situation.

"Why hasn't Aung San Suu Kyii visited Rakhine State? If I am the elder of the house, if something happens in the kitchen, I have to see what has happened there! If Kofi Annan came here, why can't Aung San Suu Kyii?"

At this stage of our conversation, U Kyaw Hla Aung and his assistants are nervous and keep looking out the windows as if they suspect we are being watched. Maybe we are. I'm getting nervous too.

"She's absolutely afraid of the army. If the army gets a chance, they'll put her under arrest again. The Turkish ambassador met Aung San Suu Kyii and she asked who he had met in Sittwe. He mentioned me especially but so far no one has followed up, even though he gave my cell phone number."

U Kyaw Hla Aung says that there are some progressive Buddhists in Sittwe who would like to organize peacefully, but they just can't because of the trenchant opposition. He again talks about the two monks from Bago who accompanied him to Sri Lanka who want to genuinely seek peace in the country as well. I tell him a bit about Jotika (3: "The Anti-Nationalists") up in Mandalay and say I hope that U Kyaw Hla Aung will contact him.

I sense some rivalry when he says, "No one from Yangon can do what I am doing these days. I am the spokesperson for the people here, and for that very reason they [people in Yangon] want to shut up my mouth. I am talking faithfully and sincerely working for my community. I am doing this for these human beings who are suffering. I used to be a lawyer, but now I call myself a human rights activist. When I worked for Médecins Sans Frontières for many years, I had no discrimination in terms of religion and dealt with everyone on an equal basis. I love the poor and want to work for their welfare."

I am grasping to find some little bit of hope in what he has to say. Though the Rohingya political leaders in Yangon—U Kyaw Min, Wai Wai Nu (1: "The Gadfly"), and Abu Tahay—have been very clear about how the situation for the Rohingya has not improved, but rather has perhaps become even worse since Aung San Suu Kyii came to power, I go ahead and ask if the legal culture isn't better since Thein Sein and the USDP ceded power. He responds, "The legal culture has not changed since the NLD came to power. The NLD is a huge disappointment. Everybody is disappointed. America cannot help Aung San Suu Kyii either. This is the army that is controlling the administration of the country. It doesn't help to lobby Aung San Suu Kyii because it is the army who is in charge. The Mon got citizenship under Thein Sein. Why didn't they accept us too? Because of our faith in Islam? We are facing, therefore, fundamentally a religious problem. And this problem is inviting the IS [ISIS]." He laughs at his suggestion, but unfortunately it may be true. The other Rohingya leaders are wringing their hands over this possibility for the future as well.

It is becoming midafternoon and it is clear that I need to be getting on my way back to Sittwe soon. I wish I could stay longer. I wish that I could somehow help these people materially to alleviate their difficult conditions. My emotions are stretched thin by the absurdity of their comprehensively hapless condition. This is not karma. These people certainly have not deserved this fate. Some of my academic colleagues, like my good friend Jacques Leider, have written about how the "victimhood" card is being played by the Rohingya and that it does not help to clarify the reality of the current tragic situation, but I can't think of any other way to characterize the plight of these people in the IDP camps. If they are not being victimized, what then is the nature of the process in play? I am reminded about how so often I have been told by Burmese and Arakanese that "there is another side to the story," apart from what the Muslims are telling the international media. But, I wonder, what could be the other side of the story to murder, rape, and the senseless incarceration of an entire community of people, the vast majority of whom are women and children?

My plan was to meet U Kyaw Hla Aung again in January 2018. But in the weeks leading up to my visit, I realized that another visit was not going to happen. I had read that the Rakhine State legislature had recently passed a law forbidding any foreigners, apart from diplomats and NGO workers, from visiting IDP camps in Arakan. Then U Kyaw Hla Aung wrote that it might be possible to try the clandestine method again, but he personally thought it was too dangerous a plan now. He then made a plea that I help to raise funds to support his renewed educational efforts within the camp. I have remained in touch with him periodically, and rejoiced when I heard that he had received the Aurora Prize for Awakening Humanity in June 2018. That development *was* karmic indeed!

The Teacher

July 2015–July 2017. Jezima Akyabi (a pseudonym) is a recently retired English teacher in Thandwe (also called Sandoway), the "third city" of Arakan (after Mrauk U and Sittwe), located just inland on the midcoast of Rakhine State. Thandwe has a population of about thirty thousand now, but it is an old city that was known to many early European travelers. It probably dates back more than a millennium. Muslims, including possibly Arab traders, have lived in this coastal vicinity for a very long time. But it is the Kaman Muslim community, not the Rohingya, who have had a foothold here for probably more than two centuries following the fall of the Arakan kingdom to the Burmese in the late eighteenth century. The Kaman Muslims are a community of about forty-five thousand who are recognized as one of the 135 indigenous communities according to the 1982 Citizenship Law. But many of them in Arakan have been treated as if they are Bengalis by various government officials. In 2017, the government released fifty-five Kaman families from an IDP camp in northern Arakan and resettled them in Yangon. This move was contested by nationalists in parliament, where one MP urged his colleagues to help "prevent the spread of cancer" involved in allowing the relocations of Muslims to Yangon. The effort to prevent the move gathered the support of about 40 percent of the voting members of parliament.

There are some nineteen Kaman Muslim villages around Thandwe, so this is the area in Myanmar where most of the Kaman Muslim people are living. Jezima says, "There is something of a class difference between the Muslims living in Thandwe and the Rakhine Buddhists, many of whom are poor fisherfolk. About 15 to 20 percent of the population in Thandwe town are Muslim. And almost all of these are Kaman. During the British time, some East Pakistanis were also brought in, and they intermarried with both Kaman and Buddhists. In fact, so many Buddhist women have intermarried with Muslim men over the years. It was an upgrade economically for them. Some of the Buddhist women did not really convert, as they came to practice no religion in fact." Later, in further conversation, Jezima revealed that her two grandmothers were Rakhine Buddhists who had married her Muslim grandfathers. Perhaps she was also referring to her grandmothers and herself by noting that some Muslim women are not very religious at all. She confided to me that she is not that observant.

Thandwe was the site of terrible violence in 2013. Five Muslim people were killed, but the property damage in Thandwe town and in surrounding villages was quite extensive. Then president Thein Sein visited Thandwe following the violence, and the famous Buddhist monk Sitagu and a well-known Muslim cleric also visited in the aftermath in bids to calm the situation. Jezima says that the violence sent "shock waves" through the community and life has not been the same in its aftermath.

Jezima believes that some of her ancestors migrated to Thandwe from Mrauk U following its fall to the Burmese in the late eighteenth century. As long as she has any sense of history, as far back as she can imagine, she believes her people have been living in Myanmar. She grew up regarding Myanmar as her native country, to which she proudly belonged, but has gradually felt an increased sense of alienation, and then, as a result of the 2013 violence perpetrated by Rakhine Buddhists against Kaman Muslims in Thandwe and its environs, she experienced great fear. Even before the outbreak of violence, however, she admits that at times she has deeply resented, even hated, the systematic discrimination and exclusion that she and her extended family have experienced at the hands of Arakanese and Burmese Buddhists.

To make a living during her retirement, Jezima is a freelancer, teaching "tuition" classes to help high school students to prepare for the national qualifying exam in English. "It's mostly lecturing," she says. "When we were young, critical thinking was emphasized. But now it's just a matter of memorization. If I used the 'international method,' then no one would sign up for my teaching."

Of all the people I had spoken to in Myanmar during the past four years, Jezima's command of English was the most proficient, in terms of her conceptuality, vocabulary, pronunciation, and ability to understand my American dialect, a fact that allowed me to converse with her in a sophisticated and sometimes colloquial and often nuanced fashion. In our extended conversations, we reached a considerable degree of mutual understanding. She knew what I was trying to ascertain about the unfolding situation in Myanmar. Initially, she was quite curious about why, as an academic committed to the study of Buddhism, I would be so interested in her own community's problems. I explained to her that conflict between Buddhists and Muslims in Myanmar inverted dominant stereotypes about the two religions that were current in Europe and America, and that people in the West needed to know that these stereotypes often confounded or masked reality. I also told her that the Buddhist-Muslim conflicts in Sri Lanka and Thailand compare in various ways to that in Myanmar and that I was seeking to understand what was unique about its unfolding in Myanmar. Eventually, we came to regard each other as genuine friends. Early on, she seemed to build trust in me and thanked me for hearing her out, as if there were few others on whom she could unload her fears. At times, she sent me e-mails almost on a daily, if not weekly, basis. We seemed politically compatible. We visited frequently on the five different occasions when I traveled to Thandwe for a number of days at a time. The last two times, we met for several long afternoon hours in her home in Thandwe, as we reviewed her earlier comments in conversations and entries from her diary. She had also produced a draft translation of U Wirathu's private biography for me. While wonderfully fluent in English, of course she spoke Arakanese and Burmese too. She was thoroughly trilingual.

While I have written at length about the substance of our conversations on the following pages, some of what follows has been drawn from her private diary, which she unselfishly shared with me. Jezima's diary is written in such a way that it is primarily addressed to a former university roommate who is a Rakhine Buddhist woman now married to a senior government bureaucrat. Throughout the diary, she questions her friend as to why she is now being treated in such a discriminatory fashion. To begin with, however, I draw on Jezima's own story as she reconstructed it for me over a number of meetings.

"Both my grandparents from my mother's side were born in Thandwe and moved to Myebon, a very small coastal town near Kyaukphyu, when my mother was twenty. My grandfather used to be a lawyer under the British regime. My father's parents were born in Yanbyae, also a small Kaman town near Kyaukphyu. They, too, moved to Myebon to make their living, as my grandfather became a building contractor. My father and mother got married in Myebon and settled down there. My father was intelligent and hardworking and he had become a successful businessman by the time I was born in 1952.

"Yes, my mother's family didn't agree on a marriage for me. The reason at that time was that they didn't want their children to settle down in Myebon, as they thought Myebon was not going to be a very good place to live in the future for Kaman people. In Myebon, about 90 percent of the population was Rakhine Buddhist and the rest of us were Christians and Muslims. The place was like a big village and quite behind times in almost every way. People were largely uneducated and there was not one person in the town who had graduated from a university at that time. My older brother was the very first person who did. The Buddhist people were very superstitious and believed in ghosts, spirits, and witchcraft. They thought people of other religions were evil. Most people were not like my family, and we were regarded differently from the other Muslims as well.

"In Myebon, there were no Kaman Muslims at all except for our family. My father's parents were born in Yanbyae, a Kaman village. As I mentioned, my grandpa was a contractor and first came to Myebon to build a hospital. [Muslims continue to be a significant force in the construction industry in Myanmar.] Later the entire family moved to Myebon as he took on more construction jobs. All my teachers in Myebon while I was growing up were Buddhists, apart from my aunt and my uncle, who were teachers at the school we attended.

"The transportation of the town was really bad, even in summer. You could come and go just by boat. The passenger boat between Kyaukphyu and Sittwe came but once a week. And my mother used to be a teacher at the primary school before she got married. To tell the truth, we were the top students at school. So we didn't need to feel integrated or alienated. We were educated.

"The standard of living of the Myebon Muslim community was very low. These people spoke their own language that we didn't understand. We spoke Bamar [Burmese] at home; we spoke the Rakhine [Arakanese] language at school. There are many variations of Arakanese; there was a written Rakhine language, but it is quite rare to find people who can read it these days; every year there is a magazine published in Sittwe of short articles in written Rakhine, but little is written in that language now. Some Muslim families lived inside the town, and they could speak the Rakhine language and were friendly with Rakhine people. But they were only a few, just ten or fifteen families. Other Muslims lived outside of town on a hill. They didn't understand the Rakhine dialect. These were people who came from East Pakistan. They were very poor and just ate rice and salt or chilies. They were very isolated. They grew vegetables but they didn't eat them; rather, they sold them at the Myebon bazaar. Their women didn't go out. But as they didn't speak the Rakhine language, it was a little bit difficult for them to communicate with other people. The other Muslims who had been living in Myebon for years had a very old mosque from the eighteenth century and spoke a language that was different from the Rohingya [those from what had become East Pakistan], and it was not Rakhine or Bamar either. Most people in the town were fishermen. They didn't send their children to school. They were very ignorant and not very strict in religion like Muslim people from Maungdaw.

"When I was young in the 1950s [during U Nu's time], many people from East Pakistan came to work during the rainy season to help grow rice. When we were young, we didn't have deep wells, so we just used surface water. These people did a lot of hard work in transporting water. They'd stay for a year or two, save money, and would go back. So at that time the government seems to have allowed this movement of people. Myanmar then was much richer than East Pakistan. But since Ne Win's time [1962–1988], our country became more and more impoverished. Now the people in Bangladesh aspire to go work in the Middle East rather than here. People used to just come and go across the border freely."

Jezima's account of the Muslims and Buddhists in the small and isolated town of Myebon gives us some insight into the variegated nature of the Muslim community, even within a small town on the Arakan coast. Her family comprised the only Kaman Muslims in town. It is clear that the reference to Muslims originally from East Pakistan living apart on the hill outside of town growing and selling vegetables and not able to mix with people in town because of language barriers were Bengali Muslims, or people who might now call themselves Rohingya. The other Muslims in the town, who were integrated and spoke Arakanese and another different language, formed yet a third group. These were not the so-called Burmese Muslims. While I pressed her on the possible identity of this group with an eighteenth-century mosque to worship at, she was at a loss to identify them or their language. I suggested Urdu, but she could not confirm this.

"In Myebon, just like in the Muslim community, there were different types of Buddhist people. One group lived in the southern part of town, where the school, the hospital, the police station, and government offices were situated. Natives in this part [who were Buddhists] were poor and uneducated, but nevertheless their general situation was better than the ones who were living in the northern part of town [the difference was a matter of class]. As I said, there were very few educated people and the entire town's standard of living was pretty low. Fishing was the main strength of the economy. Others were shopkeepers and government employees. When I was young, there were no problems between Buddhists and Muslims. Some monks, friends of my parents, sometimes came to our house, and my parents offered them whatever they needed or wanted. From the time of Ne Win, there had been some changes gradually in how people were getting along, which I had heard about, but these changes in relations were not in my own experience.

"There have been lots of changes in Thandwe since the time Ne Win seized power. Before I tell you about this, I guess I should tell you about a boy I met when I was a teenager. He was from Maungdaw and had moved to Thandwe. This was my very first and last experience to stay together in the same house with people from Maungdaw whose [Rohingya] customs and culture were very different from ours. The boy's brother-in-law was a health officer and he had been transferred to Thandwe. That was in 1971. That means that a Rohingya could become a government employee at that time. The family lived in our house. I'm still not sure if he was my boyfriend or not. We were very different in many ways. He didn't like my Buddhist friends and he didn't like many things I did, but he still said he liked me. For me, because our lifestyles were very different, I didn't know exactly whether I liked him or not. After two years, I decided he was not the right person for me, to be even a friend.

"My father was highly respected by the Muslim community because of his education and knowledge. He was arrested in the 1980s during the Ne Win government and put in prison for seven years and was released during the 1988 turmoil. He was never tried or convicted."

At this point in Jezima's narrative, I ask, "Why was he arrested?"

She answers, "Nobody really knows, but the family thinks it was because my father tried to prove that all Muslims are not illegal immigrants. He was looking for witnesses to prove this when he was arrested. He was taken to Sittwe for prison and we were unable to see him. He said he was treated well in prison. At the time, there was no tension between Arakanese Buddhists and Muslims in Thandwe. My father had done a lot of charity work on his own. He was a self-made person, as his parents were quite poor. He was a very intelligent man. He had a rice mill so that he was rich enough to help poor people. Every year my parents donated five hundred or so bags of rice to whoever needed. He was well liked by the local people because of his generosity. The second woman he married was a Buddhist. At that time, Buddhist monks (the good kind, not like the politicized monks of today) also began to frequent his house. He had a lot of admiration for these monks. While my father was not especially religious, his second wife became a devout Muslim, though she was never encouraged to become so. She was very poor and uneducated and somewhat naïve and gullible. That is probably why she became devout. Women who have converted to Islam are usually not well educated."

I interject and say, "Sounds like something Wirathu would say!"

"On the other hand, I have five or six first cousins who have converted to Buddhism. They are living in Yangon now. Also, my niece by my youngest brother has recently married a Buddhist man. Religion is not a boundary for my family. What kind of person you are is more important than the religious label. My grandmother on my father's side was actually a Buddhist.

"In fact, I know much more about Thandwe communities than about the ones around Myebon. My parents wanted us to stay close to the relatives in Thandwe, so every year we visited our relatives in Thandwe for three months. My parents sent the children to Thandwe after finishing our middle school to attend high school. For me, I came to Thandwe to attend school when I was thirteen, and as far as I remember, I just visited Myebon once more when I was twenty-five for a short time. At that time, my parents had split up and my mother was living in Yangon with my brother. I was working as a teacher at a school in Thandwe and lived with my two aunts, who were unmarried like me.

"In 1986, I was transferred to a small town called Kawa in the Bago Division as a senior teacher. There were no Muslims at all in this town. But everything was fine for me. People were very friendly, helpful, and good to me. I enjoyed staying there for three years. Unfortunately, I caught malaria, but my friends and students looked after me with great care. That was in 1989. Because of my health, and the country's political situation, I had to be transferred back to Thandwe again. The schools were closed at that time for three years. So you can see, until that time, there had been no serious problems between different religions in the whole country. When I was back in Thandwe, people of the three religions remained the same as before: friendly, united, and frightened under military rule. Curfew was still in effect.

"The Muslim people in Thandwe, in general, are better off both economically and educationally than most of the Rakhine Buddhists. In my opinion, this is not the main reason for the hatred and riots between the people from the two religions. Until 1994, I'm sure, there had been no racial or religious discrimination at all in our town. People from the three religions were very good friends and even people from the other two religions used to take part in the religious events of the others. And marriage between people from different religions was very common.

"As you know, there was a big unrest all over Myanmar when the famous '88 revolution occurred in Myanmar on August 8, 1988. That was a period of anarchy! There was no rule of law! On the eighteenth of September a military junta seized state power and curfew was on for the entire country. People dared not go outside their houses in the daytime for months, as streets were full of Burmese soldiers who appeared ready to shoot anyone. One of my cousins was shot in Thandwe during that period. Schools were closed for over two years. I have no idea why curfew was on for so long. In 1994, the immigration department took back our national registration cards from everyone in the country and gave us new ones. On the old cards, there was no religion mentioned, but on the new ones (and we are still holding these cards), there is our religion cited. All Muslims in Arakan got the cards with 'Rakhine Islam.' But everything looked fine with Muslim people at that time. Even some Rohingya in Sittwe were given this designation. I don't know about the Muslims in Maungdaw and Buthidaung.

"Around 1996, I think it started that the government stopped employing Muslims in its various departments. At that time, in Thandwe, Muslim and Buddhist communities were still very friendly and stayed very close. There were no problems between us. As I said before, marriages of people from different religions were common and so you can imagine the situation here at that time. But in the defense service or military, no Muslims were employed anymore and all Muslim staff who had already been in the military were dismissed gradually for no apparent reason. One of my mother's younger brothers used to be an officer in the navy. He died in action. The government supported his family a lot after his death. That was in the early 1960s. In Thandwe, all Muslims on the staff of the Telecommunication Department were fired in the 1980s. Although the military junta tried to divide people by religion, people still remained the same. Until 1994, a Muslim could get his NRC (national registration card) with Rakhine nationality noted. I still remember that when I got my new NRC in 1994, the immigration officer suggested for me to get one with 'Rakhine Buddhist' nationality, as two of my great-grandmothers were Rakhine Buddhists and one was a Kaman Buddhist, but I got the card signifying that I am Kaman Muslim.

"When I was young and a student at Yangon University, one of my Muslim friends from Maungdaw said it was very difficult for her to come to the university. I was very surprised at this. When we became teachers, and I began teaching here in Thandwe, my same friend wanted to visit me here but was not allowed to travel. So the travel inhibitions have been going on now for forty years. I went to the university between 1969 and 1974.

"The 'Dragon Strategy' under Ne Win in the early 1970s after the establishment of Bangladesh was to try to expel the Bengalis of Maungdaw and Buthidaung, which led to an argument between Burma and Bangladesh. A general from Burma went to Bangladesh and a Bangladeshi general came to Burma, with the result being that the people who had been expelled were called back into the country. This also led to a substantial border security presence between the two countries being mutually upheld. Meanwhile, some Rakhine Buddhists cooperated with the military to conduct substantial smuggling operations of wood and drugs that proved to be very profitable. There remains a big market for narcotics in the town of Taung Gote [see the map of Arakan]. There are five banks in Thandwe, which seems like a lot for a town with so little commerce. One of the banks seems normal, with a lot of business, while the other four barely have any business. They are probably set up to handle 'black money.'

"In the 1950s, U Nu had tried to make Burma a Buddhist nation. He didn't succeed. In my point of view, Buddhism in Myanmar is deteriorating. Buddhists may think that they are ascending or that their religion is superior to other religions. But in my view, though the origin of their religion is very respectful (I like Buddhism—it's very peaceful), the political policy is to use the religion as a weapon. On the other hand, many people are ignorant. As for the current example of this, this strategy didn't work in the recent election that the NLD won recently.

Young Buddhist progressive people feel sad because Buddhism is losing its image in the world due to the Ma Ba Tha and their militant ways. This is due to the fact that global communication is speeding up. These young progressive people are more sensible. Some young Buddhist monks are arguing that religion and politics should be kept separate. Yet, still the radically conservative Buddhist monks have a lot of influence."

Jezima's diary is filled with incidents over the years that have saddened and depressed her. For instance, in 2004 she writes how the government regarded the Kaman Muslims of Thandwe in the same way that they regard the Rohingya of Maungdaw. While fifty schoolchildren from each school in Thandwe were selected to greet the army's divisional commander, all the Muslim students were excluded from the group so as not to offend the commander, and this despite the fact that the Muslims were often the best students in school. On another occasion when the school was celebrating the opening of its multimedia lab and hosting government officials, all Muslim teachers were kept in room with all the doors and windows closed until the officials had left the school.

She also writes about how her niece has not been able to return to Thandwe since she began her university and professional studies in Yangon and then abroad. "Muslims have not been allowed to travel outside the town without a visa, for which they often need to wait weeks, fill out detailed forms, provide recommendations from four or five relevant people along with statements guaranteeing return, and pay bribes totaling between 50,000 and 100,000 kyats (about 75 dollars). Sometimes the permission never comes. The only valid reason that is often accepted, it seems, is for medical treatment. Even then, one can travel for only ten days at a time. Moreover, when traveling, Muslims are often stopped at checkpoints and have to pay further bribes. It is really embarrassing to have to get down from the bus and be looked upon by everyone as if I were a potential criminal. It is not as severe when flying. In Yangon, one has to report to the immigration office on arrival and then the day before leaving to show proof of intention to return [a bus ticket]." One time her sister's daughter returned from Turkey in 2006 after she had become a doctor there. She had left through the paying of a bribe to airport staff, military officials, and the like, to get herself to Yangon years earlier. Some of the officials were previously high school students of Jezima's who said that while they didn't want to take her niece's money, it was their custom and they needed to share what they could from bribes. In other parts of the country beyond Rakhine State before 2012, Muslims did not need a visa to travel. Now, however, it depends. But when her niece "reached the Thandwe airport to leave for Yangon and then from the country, the immigration officials demanded a 100,000-kyat bribe. Without an NRC, it is impossible even to apply for travel. Traveling without permission is illegal. A Muslim lawyer in town who was diagnosed with lung cancer waited three months for a visa before he died, hoping to go to Yangon for treatment not available here."

Another of Jezima's nieces stood first in the state, with distinctions in every subject, but was not allowed to travel to Sittwe to receive her prize, nor was the prize ever forwarded to her.

"In 2004, a young Muslim who was my next-door neighbor (a Buddhist woman married to a Muslim) got distinction in five subjects but was not allowed to traveled to Yangon. After two years, he got inside a wooden box and went to Yangon as cargo. Ultimately, he managed to go to university in Norway.

"In 2012 or 2013, a university was opened in Taung Gote [where ten Muslim men were martyred after the alleged initial rape of a Buddhist woman that started the Sittwe riot in 2012]. Before that, the only Arakan university was in Sittwe. People in Thandwe wanted the university in Kyaukphyu, where a previous university had been located back many years ago. For Muslim people, this situation has been very difficult to accept. Because these towns like Taung Gote were really radicalized, all the Muslims were out of the town twenty years ago. This was during General Than Shwe's time. This is a university for day students only. Where would Muslim students be able to stay? So some seven Muslim students from Thandwe applied to study in Yangon instead and were turned down. Since 2012, Muslims students have not been allowed to study at Sittwe University either. In 2014, faculty from Sittwe University came and taught for a month or two and the students sat for the first- and second-year exams. The teachers seemed happy with the experience. But at this time, Ma Ba Tha monks from Yangon came and intimidated the teachers from Sittwe, some of whom are originally from Yangon. So the teachers said they would not return for the next year. Almost all the students failed because one or two months is not enough preparation time. For this year, no one knows what will happen. The seven students whose parents have NRCs with Rakhine nationality previously, and now probably Kaman nationality, will simply wait. The children haven't been given NRCs. They've been given 'white cards' instead. Now, just before the elections, the white card was taken and they don't have anything right now. Muslims in Rakhine State right now are being regarded as 'Bengalis.' Just yesterday, a 'green card' was being offered for the first time. A green card is the first step toward getting the 'pink card' (NRC). The person who holds this card needs to be examined or investigated. The immigration officer says he's not sure that even this card will guarantee travel or allow students to study at the university. The immigration people here will often write 'Muslim' for 'nationality' on the NRC. The nationality is 'Muslim' and the religion is 'Islam'! Both 'nationality' and 'religion' are put on the national registration card. But now the nationality is 'Bengali' for many!" Jezima is allowed to put Kaman for "nationality," one of the 135 indigenous groups. Yet, many in government are now erroneously regarding Kaman as "Bengali."

"The situation now is that most Muslims, whether Rohingya or Kaman, now would like to leave Arakan, even Myanmar if possible. Even I, born and raised here, would leave if I had the opportunity. And my situation in Thandwe is no trouble at all compared to what the Rohingya are experiencing in northern Arakan. The Muslim community here in Thandwe was relatively well positioned economically. Unlike the Rohingya, who are so much a part of northern Rakhine, the Muslims in Thandwe were fairly well off as merchants and professionals. They have suffered economically since 2012 due to the 969 boycott [against Muslim businesses] instigated by U Wirathu and the Buddhist nationalist monks. Many Muslims in other parts of Rakhine have tried to leave for Yangon, to get out however possible. Even those who left for Yangon have had a hard time there finding work and a place to live. Here it was not so bad and the situation economically is now improving for the Muslims, although there are still some Buddhist people who are trying to create trouble. The government has been indirectly encouraging the monks and nationalists to create trouble for the Muslims, especially by propagating the view that Muslims are encouraging their own to kill people."

I had just heard that exact claim from U Thar Pwint in Sittwe a few days earlier, in January 2016 (2: "The Senior Citizen").

"The local 969 people are trying to prevent me from getting an NRC for my niece's ten-year-old child in Yangon. The local head of immigration was instructed by the Rakhine government to give NRCs to local Muslims and was then threatened with a public demonstration against him if he continued the policy. So he acquiesced. As a result, he was transferred to another office out by the Bangladesh border. I'm trying to get a card right now for my niece's son, and I face a delay and more delay tactics by the immigration authorities. The 969 is saying that if cards are to be given to Muslims, they should be designated as 'Bengalis' and not Kaman."

Her roommate from university days, now a teacher, believes that Muslims are trying to take over Rakhine State. Jezima is very tearful in relating this story—how someone she had been so close to, "like a sister," could be so ridiculous. I ask why her roommate would say something like this. She replies that she is really a simple person whose husband is a minister of the state parliament in Arakan and is just repeating what she has heard. Her husband once came and visited Jezima in Thandwe. They had also been close during university days. While he listened to her problems quietly and said that she should call him anytime, she knew that he really hated Muslims and that she was only an exception for him. As I mentioned, Jezima's diary is pretty much directed at her Rakhine Buddhist university roommate, trying to explain to her what has happened to Muslims in Thandwe. She provides a detailed description of how, in 2013, Rakhine Buddhist mobs made their way to Muslim villages about fifteen to twenty miles from Thandwe and burned down the villages entirely, in the process killing a ninety-four-year-old Kaman woman who was too infirm to flee. Two of these Buddhist terrorists were killed in the process, and sixteen Muslims were arrested in connection with their murders, three of whom received sentences of thirty years, but no Buddhists were ever prosecuted for the crimes they perpetrated. Indeed, the police simply observed the destruction of Muslim property and did nothing to protect the Muslims. Under international pressure, President Thein Sein came to Thandwe in the aftermath to at least register that the conflagration had caught the attention of the government.

Jezima notes, "Just the day before yesterday (January 8, 2016) some Muslim villagers had their paddy burned. So the local hostilities continue. It is difficult to know how the police [and army] would respond to any outbreak of violence on a significant scale now. At the moment, they seem to be delaying as much as possible the transfer of power to the NLD.

"In the seventeen townships of Rakhine State, the NLD won four, USDP won two, the ANP [Arakan National Party] won eleven or twelve seats. The southern part of Rakhine State, including Thandwe, went for the NLD. No one expected this local landslide. The USDP [Union Solidarity and Development Party, the proxy party for the military and the party endorsed by the monastic Buddhist nationalist Ma Ba Tha] thought they could at least win 26 percent of the vote that, along with the 25 percent of seats guaranteed to the military in the 2008 constitution, would provide them a majority in parliament. Thandwe went for the NLD with a big margin. Village people voted ANP, but inside the town almost everyone voted NLD. They didn't like the USDP candidate. The people in Lin Tar Oo village on Ngapali Beach wanted the government to fall. Even in Mon and Karen States, the sentiment was the same. The worst resistance to the government is in northern Rakhine. Of the fourteen states and divisions, Rakhine is fourteenth based on the percentage of people who have passed the equivalent of the high school exam even with the notorious levels of cheating that occur. In terms of economy, Rakhine is second to last. It is a severely depressed area and the people there usually blame the government for their depressed conditions."

The local Thandwe Muslim community in southern Rakhine had "great hope" in the aftermath of the NLD's victory. "Because she had never really spent a lot of time around Myanmar people, Aung San Suu Kyii was not aware of the degrees of ignorance and racism among the Buddhist nationalists. After the death of the ten Muslims purportedly in response to the rape of the Buddhist woman, she met Muslim leaders, trying to comfort them. There was a photo of her trying to comfort them. The next day online, there was an avalanche of protest against her, calling her 'Amina Suu Kyii.' From that time, whatever she said was seen as a matter of support for Muslims including help from Muslim countries. The Kachin people protested that she won the Nobel Prize because she neglected them. Before she came to Thandwe during the election campaign, people here were skeptical about Aung San Suu Kyii, but her talk was persuasive and an inspiration. She hasn't done anything for Muslim people so far [as of August 2016]. But what can she do right now? She and her party during the past five years had to be extremely careful in what they say. She has been waiting for the right time, the suitable circumstance. That is why Muslim people hope that she will try to help us. In my opinion, this will take some time."

In our conversation during the **summer of 2016**, I ask if it isn't the case that Aung San Suu Kyii doesn't have much time to accomplish reforms in the country, owing to the fact that she is seventy years old. Jezima readily agrees. "That is why the current situation is so pressing and fraught with uncertainty. She has a lot of things to get done in Myanmar. It was amazing how much she traveled throughout the country before the election. For me, I really admired her and thought of her like my own mother in terms of trust. I don't understand the political situation now. She must have a reason for why she isn't doing anything for us. I like her and admire her and always see her good side. Because I like her and believe her, I'm not sure what to think about the current situation. [Again, at that time, it was still summer 2016, months before the Myanmar army's assaults on the Rohingya in Maungdaw and Buthidaung.] I believe that she will never do anything unfair and will think about the welfare of the entire country and the world. I don't have a deep knowledge of politics, but I just believe her. Almost all Muslims here, who voted for her, have now given up hope."

"Most people in Rakhine State still want a separate nation. Last week in Sittwe there was a big memorial ceremony at the end of **December [2016]**, when the fall of the Arakan kingdom is remembered. Online, people noted that they still want their own country. They are not Bamar. This is true in northern Rakhine, where they feel as if they are but a colony of the Myanmar government. The theft of the Mahamuni image is always cited in this regard."

Jezima says that she thinks ISIS is really disgusting in causing suffering to others. It also puts other Muslims into difficult positions. I mention that I have often heard Buddhists in Myanmar cite ISIS and al-Qaeda as significant threats. They fear a radicalization of the Myanmar Muslim community. Jezima winces at this but then goes on to say that things are better now (**January 2017**) with her Buddhist former students and friends. It was only during the trouble back in 2013 that they became cold and indifferent. She adds, "Still, every morning now at four thirty the Buddhists use loudspeakers for their chants, but also sometimes wedding songs, and sometimes a sermon, in order to disrupt the five a.m. Muslim call to prayer. It used to be the case, before 2012, that anyone who wanted to use a loudspeaker system in public needed to get permission from the town officials, a town council. Muslim people do not dare to speak up against this current harassment." I tell Jezima about the 1915 riots in Sri Lanka that began over an argument regarding the noise generated by a *perahara* procession in front of a mosque during the time of Friday prayers. I also tell her about one Christmas morning I spent in the largely Christian mountain enclave of Nuwara Eliya, Sri Lanka, in 1990 when sunrise was greeted by the blaring sounds of Buddhist *paritta* chanting over loudspeaker systems. Noise is often a weapon.

"Local imams of the Kaman Muslims in Thandwe are not well educated and hardly have a cosmopolitan view. The community is quite insular and outside influences are not readily accepted, so any argument about local Muslims being impacted by Middle East religious fashions would not be so true here. Rohingya of northern Rakhine State are more 'superstitious.'" By this Jezima means that they observe customs such as purdah and wear burkas. "So, Kaman are much more enculturated to the local scene. They are very local." This was her major point in stressing to me how it is the "village level" that is the most important factor in how the world is perceived for local people. She related a story about how a local boy was struck down on the road by a tuk-tuk whose driver came from another village. The local people wanted to harm the driver, and the local policeman tried to extort him before even tending to the young injured boy who lay in the road. Finally, Jezima summoned some transportation to get the injured boy to the hospital. Her point was that the local people can get worked up emotionally very easily when they feel that they are being threatened from the outside. "They close ranks very quickly and react collectively, even violently, to outside perceived threats. They are not well educated and don't think very critically. Rather they react emotionally." She believes also that they very easily follow the leadership of their religious leaders and that is why the posture of the monks is so important. She is aware of progressive monks, but she is also aware of how the vast majority of Buddhist monks seem to have become critical of Muslims without benefit of understanding. She also pointed out how in almost every instance, the flashpoint for violence—things are pretty "normal" here in Thandwe right now—has been the purported rape of a Buddhist woman by a Muslim man. "The 'original rape' occurred in Taung Gote, about three hours from here, before the ten Muslims were then murdered in reprisal. However, the violence here has resulted in a rupture of trust in that now people are very careful about what they say and to whom. The original societal multicultural fabric has been frayed.

"The original trouble that set off the problem in 2012 occurred in Kyaung Ni Maw, located two-thirds toward Thandwe from Sittwe. Five days later, in Taung Gote, ten Muslim men were pulled off a bus and killed by a mob. They were hacked to death. Six of these Muslims were from Mandalay and Yangon, and four were from Thandwe, so none of them were Rohingya from northern Arakan. There were no problems that occurred in Thandwe when the funerals were held for these four Muslims. But two to three days later, it was rumored that in Maungdaw, clerics in mosques preached revenge and so the violence started with Buddhists minorities in that region being attacked. After this, a series of attacks were systematically orchestrated against Rohingya in their villages and neighborhoods, culminating in the major conflagration in and around Sittwe that resulted in the mass dislocations. All of these attacks were simply watched passively by government forces, both local police and military. Some believe that these attacks were somewhat organized by clandestine forces within the government."

In July 2013, the leading modernist, progressive, and wealthiest Muslim in Thandwe, who had contributed charitably to hospitals and Buddhist temples, had his house burned down, apparently at the urging of Ma Ba Tha monks. According to Jezima, the Ma Ba Tha's local plan was to eradicate Thandwe of progressive Muslim forces.

"There is a monk and two or three allied henchman who daily check buses for Muslims who want to travel to Yangon. The immigration police check hotels on a daily basis to see who is staying where and for how long. When the OIC [Organization of Islamic Cooperation] came to Thandwe on a fact-finding mission, the ANP offered people 5,000 kyats to demonstrate against their presence. They shouted slogans that 'We don't need Bengali!' 'We don't need OIC!' (Some shouted, 'We don't need IOC,' and others shouted, 'We don't need Ovaltine!,' which shows that they didn't even know exactly what they were protesting against!)"

Jezima agrees that the current anti-Muslim sentiment could be housed within the more general anti-Indian sentiment earlier experienced during the late colonial period and up to Ne Win's decision to confiscate all property of foreigners, a move particularly designed to expropriate the remaining Indians. It is part of the outsider fear.

Thandwe's Muslims have, by and large, tried to simply absorb and carry on in the face of discrimination. But Jezima feels wounded. Some Muslims, because of the acute problem since 2012, have converted to Buddhism. How ironic, I say, given the recent conversion law seeking to prevent Buddhists from converting to Islam! "But the practicality of the situation is that employment by the government for Muslims is now impossible. If Muslims and Buddhists are involved in a court case, the Buddhist will definitely win the case. That is one of the reasons why Muslims might convert.

"I'm not afraid to die, as I'm now over sixty, but not the way in which some people are being murdered. I don't want to see or hear about the people from both sides being killed, or properties being destroyed. What I'm concerned about is jihad, the personal struggle that I have to wage and then the war for the sake of religion. Almost all Muslims in Myanmar, including women, have been pushed so far that they are now ready for a fight. For me, we should just wait and see how the NLD government handles this. I hope everything will be all right, but I have this sense of having to defend my identity." She says that she needs to be as positive as possible in her perspective in order to cope with depression, to maintain her health. "Previously, I listened to BBC, VOA [Voice of America], and followed the national news, but it was contributing to my depression. I have had to just reduce the level of my concern about my community's plight."

I ask her what she thinks of the election of Donald Trump as president of the United States. Her answer is simple: "He is a madman." She recognizes that someone like Trump only feeds the anti-Muslim sentiment of the Buddhist nationalists.

Historically, Jezima sees Prime Minister U Nu in the 1950s as the one who started all the talk about Burma being essentially a Buddhist nation. She says that he used Buddhist rhetoric to his political advantage and thereby raised consciousness of how Buddhism is related to political power.

I ask Jezima to respond to the claim made by many Buddhists (and here the articulate U Thar Pwint and Ven. Jotika are examples from opposite sides of the Buddhist political spectrum) regarding the Muslim disposition toward killing, since Buddhists often delineate between their religion and Islam precisely by referring to this aspect. Jezima says that while cows may be sacrifice, it's a great sin to kill people. "I'm not saying that killing animals is right either, as they also have life. Actually, our religion does not encourage killing. If I have food to eat and my neighbors don't have food, if I don't share my food with them, it is a sin. Our 'rule' [zakat] is to pay 2.5 percent to needy people. The first priority is to give to relatives, the second is to neighbors, and then to others. I'm just an average Muslim who is not really that religious, but I regard killing people as a serious sin. In my life I never have told anyone that I like killing. Maybe I just don't understand my religion and I need to study more about why animals are killed. I know the history of the reason for why animals can be killed." She then tells the story of Abraham's sacrifice. "Besides, when animals are sacrificed, they are purchased just days before the sacrifice. But it does not carry the weight of a human death!"

I nod. It is getting toward late afternoon. I get ready to go and she says, "May God be with you."

I say, "And with you." It is **January 2017**.

I reached out to Jezima again before my **January 2018** visit to Myanmar, hoping to see her one last time. I quickly received a curt reply that said, "I don't want to have anything more to do with you." I was stunned by this response. I thought it over for a few days and wondered if a British friend who had originally introduced us, an unusual and politically odd Westerner in that she had consistently voiced her support for the USDP and the military machinations of the Tatmadaw, hadn't somehow frightened her about sustaining her friendship with me in the current circumstances. In the months following August 25, 2017, when the military unleashed its wrath on the Rohingya of northern Arakan, there had been, as I've noted, a very concerted public campaign backed in no small part by Aung San Suu Kyii's government to discredit the reporting of Western media sources about what actually had been happening in northern Arakan as a result of the Tatmadaw's brutal response to the August 25, 2017, attack on the border guards. Indeed, I would confront a very different set of conditions when I actually arrived in Myanmar a few weeks later. Maybe Jezima was also caught up in this anti-Western sentiment that had become so intense and widespread. I wrote to her again a few days later and expressed my surprise and disappointment in her message. She immediately wrote back and told me "not to take her message personally—it's just me and my fault." I am still a bit perplexed at this, but I suspect that she had come under pressure from various quarters about the time she had been spending with me, and what she might have been revealing to me. Maybe she had become worried, or had been made to worry, about her translation of U Wirathu's autobiography for me. I don't know. But I had to respect her decision to cut me off, and it brought more sensitivity to me about the risks that remain for those in Myanmar who want to cooperate with foreigners by telling their stories. Now, more than ever, I wanted to know her disposition about Aung San Suu Kyii and the NLD government. But that was not to be.

PART THREE

Mandalay

U Wirathu, "The Nationalist"

University of Global Peace, Mandalay, under construction

U Jotika (Zawtika), "The Anti-Nationalist"

U Kumara, "The Rector," with John Holt

Like those in Yangon, the changes in Mandalay since 2011 are visibly substantial. Cranes on top of the metal skeletons of new buildings can be seen in many directions, marking the construction of new high-rises. A brand-new shopping complex in the southern part of the city could be mistaken for a suburban Southern California setting, were it not for the fact that virtually all the goods in the stores are exclusively from China. A number of other new shopping centers have been built in other parts of the city as well, in addition to so many new condominiums that one has to wonder who will be living in all of these new apartments. Is the economy doing that well to generate so much upper-middle-class living style?

I had not been to Mandalay before 2010, so I'm not altogether sure that it had changed so very much from the 1990s until then. In 2010, the main conveyance around town was bicycle rickshaw. While the city is not flooded by cars to the same extent as Yangon, there now are many, but motorbikes have taken over the city's streets as the chief means of conveyance. Mandalay is largely built on a flat river plain, and its streets, while confusingly numbered, are laid out to form oblong rectangular blocks from north to south. Life here isn't plagued by the traffic jams that one now encounters in Yangon, and the old palace breaks up the monotony of the grid layout. Mandalay Hill to the north and the mountains to the east and west provide pleasing vistas beyond the canopy of trees lining the streets.

Mandalay, unlike Yangon, was never a colonial center, though the British did immediately transform the old royal palace inside its impressive square moat (two kilometers on each side) into a prison, much like they did in the sacred area in Anuradhapura in Sri Lanka. The city remains a veritable bastion for Buddhist monasticism, in part because Mandalay was the capital center for the last line of Burmese kings, the last being Thibaw, who was deposed by the British and carted off to India in 1885 after a brief, seven-year reign. His predecessor, Mindon, left a legacy still discernible in the center of town—not just the palace and the number of monasteries he supported during his thirty-plus years of reign, nor the impressive Tripitaka cast in stone at the base of Mandalay Hill, but a multicultural or multireligious presence as well. Like Yangon, Mandalay has an impressive population of Hindus and Muslims, despite the migrations out of Burma that began in the 1940s and that continued into the 1960s. Muslim mosques, Christian churches, and Hindu temples are plentiful, particularly in the downtown area, amid the welter of Buddhist monasteries located largely in the southern and western sections of town.

Across the Irrawaddy River to the southwest lies Sagaing, a hilly tract that is home to many more Buddhist temples, many of them dedicated to meditation practice not only for monks, but for *thila shin* (nuns) as well. The approach to Sagaing on the bridge crossing the Irrawaddy yields a spectacular scene of manifold stupas dotting the hillsides. The pace of life there is decidedly pacific.

I came to look forward to my visits to Mandalay, especially because of the cordial relations I developed with two of the three Buddhist monks I had come to see, and the relief it provided from the oppressions of Sittwe, on the one hand, and the urban intensity of Yangon, on the other. Mandalay would shut down by around nine p.m. Strolling the moat in the evenings provided a measure of relief among the hundreds of others seeking respite from the day.

The Nationalist

January 2015. Outside of an unimposing building within a sprawling monastic campus on the southeast side of Mandalay city, in a teaching monastery with a staggering enrollment of more than three thousand monks, stands a two-times-life-size action photo of Ashin U Wirathu, signifying the presence of one of the most recognizable Buddhist monks in modern Myanmar. Internationally, perhaps, Wirathu is *the* most recognizable Burmese Buddhist monk, having rocketed to infamy as a consequence of his photo adorning the cover of the international edition of *Time* magazine in July 2013, little more than a year after being released from eight years in prison for inciting hatred against Muslim people. At least a score of enlarged photos and two paintings of Wirathu (some in the company of the famous and internationally renowned monk Sitagu) are prominently displayed inside a modest reception hall replete with peeling linoleum over an aged and well-worn wooden floor. While Wirathu is locally regarded within his monastery as a kind of rock-star celebrity, his private quarters are modest. He is tended to, or handled by, a small coterie of trusted monks who guard his privacy, run his errands, and administrate his time and presence on the internet. It is reported that Wirathu, before he was publicly silenced in the spring of 2017 by the state monastic supervisory organization, Ma Ha Na, commanded huge fees for public speaking engagements and that these fees were used to help fund the monastic and nationalist Ma Ba Tha. I am not sure that this last statement is true, especially now that Wirathu is not giving public sermons and has resigned as of May 2017 from Ma Ba Tha as a result of its acquiescence to a Ma Ha Na directive to cease its use of public signage throughout Myanmar. In any case, his movements continue to be documented far and wide, including his tours in the spring and fall of 2017 of Maungdaw and Buthidaung, the heart of Rohingya country, where Wirathu reportedly distributed rice to the minority Rahkine Buddhists of the grief-stricken area, a symbolic act of support for people he regards as especially beleaguered, on the front lines of what he regards as a Muslim tidal wave. Wirathu continues to attract and address large crowds as of this final writing in January 2019, having recently whipped up a crowd at Yangon's Mahabandoola Park to protest against moves in the United Nations aimed at bringing the Tatmadaw's leading generals to book for genocide.

Unfortunately, that cover on *Time* magazine was captioned "The Buddhist Face of Terror," and the article went on to refer to him sensationally as kind of "Buddhist Bin Laden." This was regarded as so obnoxious to some South and

Southeast Asian religious sensibilities that the magazine issue was banned from circulation in Sri Lanka and certainly fueled further mistrust of the mainstream Western media in Myanmar. Subsequent combative interviews followed with the BBC, and in 2017, a film profiling Wirathu appeared at the Cannes Film Festival that was dubbed the third installment of a trilogy focused on the history of evil. It is true that many of the things that Wirathu has said, particularly about UN special rapporteur Yanghee Lee, are shocking and disturbing, and that there is little doubt that his sermons and postings on social media have contributed to the poisonous perspectives that many militant Burmese and Arakanese Buddhists have cultivated in relation to the Muslim minority, especially the Rohingya people.

At least a portion of the manner in which Wirathu has been portrayed is a consequence of how Buddhism has been given such a naïve free pass in terms of its presentation in the West. For at least a century and more, Westerners have fielded what they admire about the Buddha's *dhamma* (teaching) and practice and ignored what they have chosen to relegate to the dustbins of superstition and precivilized behavior. In the process, Euro-Americans have cultivated their own forms of Buddhist culture focused predominantly on the individual or personal practice of meditation while eschewing its intimate historical enculturation by the societies in South, Southeast, and East Asia. Western practitioners are usually quite unaware of the manner in which Buddhism and politics have intertwined historically, especially in the last hundred years, when various forms of nationalism have emerged in juxtaposition to the European hegemonic colonial presence in countries like Sri Lanka, Myanmar, Laos, Cambodia, and Thailand, where the Theravada forms of the religion have evolved over millennia and centuries. The articulations of the Buddhasasana (Buddhist tradition) in South and Southeast Asia have probably never approximated the popular pristine image of peace, nonviolence, vegetarianism, and the single-minded and seemingly detached otherworldly pursuit of nirvana. So an account of aggressive expressions of Buddhist nationalism in contemporary times sets off waves of cognitive dissonance among the tradition of Western admirers.

Recently, like every major religious tradition in the world, radicalized right-wing politically inspired movements have mounted what they regard as a defense of their religion in the face of perceived contemporary threats. Many of these movements have formulated narratives of siege. The phenomenon of Ashin Wirathu can be understood within this general sort of reactionary defensive posture. To his followers, Wirathu is a brave leader helping to stem the tide of external threats to the tradition. To his detractors, he is something of a heretic, distorting the teachings of the compassionate Buddha. To be clear, it is not only Westerners who share an antipathy for Wirathu's cause. Many Buddhists in Burma have also been alarmed by his message and antics. But the scope and intensity of his activities do not belong in the same category as a Hitler or an Osama bin Laden. Wirathu may be an uncompromising reactionary, but he is certainly not a revolutionary terrorist or armed with a systematic plan to kill off an entire race of people.

Wirathu has an unassuming personal presence; his persona is what one would expect from an accomplished monk. He is composed and speaks quietly and articulately, with an aura of concern. He smiles readily and offers a light sense of humor that is at times self-deprecating and arresting. I expected that it would be exceedingly difficult to get an interview with him, especially after the manner in which he has been excoriated by Western journalists.

The first time I meet Wirathu, in the summer of 2015, comes about through the quiet intercession of a Burmese Mandalay lawyer known to my journalist friend Wai Moe (1: "The Stringer"). When the timing of the interview is confirmed, I recruit a translator through the efforts of a helpful hotel manager where I am staying in Mandalay. When the translator arrives punctually an hour beforehand, he is somewhat aghast when he learns that we will be speaking directly with Wirathu. In preparation, I discuss the specific questions I want to pose so that we can avoid confusion during the interview itself. When we finally arrive at Wirathu's monastery, fifteen minutes early, the translator is far more nervous than I! He says he has never been involved with an interview of such an important public figure. I tell him to relax and then say, "Neither have I!"

We are escorted into a modest anteroom adjacent to Wirathu's audience hall, along with about five of Wirathu's monastic handlers. The anteroom doubles as his personal office space and private refuge. Aside from two impressive computers placed on desks in the back of the room, the space is fairly nondescript, though it feels dense, with eight people huddled within. Only Wirathu, the translator, and I are seated. Wirathu speaks little English, only a few phrases to move occasions along politely. I don't think he is seriously prepared to take on my interview, as he begins to read a Burmese newspaper just as I think we are about to begin the conversation. He seems distracted. The translator then begins with the first question, somewhat haltingly and deliberately, but it is a question that definitely catches Wirathu's attention when it is posed. I ask him how he expects to cooperate with Sri Lanka's Bodu Bala Sena in the future. He looks up, somewhat surprised, as if he is not expecting such a reference. He says simply that he wants "to cooperate with the BBS to make our shared problems known to the whole world." As problems, he cites the example that just the day before a Buddhist monk was killed by a roadside bomb in southern Thailand. So he means to say that like the Bodu Bala Sena, he believes that the sangha is currently under great duress and needs to cooperate internationally in the future in order to survive.

I have traced much of the ideology that Wirathu shares with the BBS to the earlier public ministry of the Venerable Gangodawila Soma, a charismatic Sinhalese nationalist monk in Sri Lanka who climbed to unprecedented notoriety in the 1990s and early 2000s by working through the media to advance his claims about international conspiracies fronted by the Christian and Muslim communities against Buddhism in Sri Lanka. Soma had styled himself as the quintessential modern monk, stressing the preservation of an originally pure, rational form of Buddhism now under concerted pressure from outside religious and political forces. I had studied Soma carefully, insofar as he had mounted an antideity (especially deities of Hindu origins) campaign while I was researching and writing a book entitled *The Buddhist Visnu* in Sri Lanka in the early 2000s. It was, however, Soma's public conflict with the Muslim community in Sri Lanka that became his most famous claim to fame (see "Comparative Contexts of Conflict: Sri Lanka, Myanmar, and Thailand" in the introduction). Historically and philosophically or ideologically, Soma is a godfather to the BBS. The ideology that surfaced within the 969 Movement and Ma Ba Tha in Myanmar in 2012 is uncanny in its similarity to the BBS posture. So I wondered if Wirathu is aware of his intellectual and political predecessor in the Theravada Buddhist monastic world.

It comes as something of a letdown to me when he says simply that he doesn't know anything about Soma or the JHU (Jatika Hela Urumaya; the Sinhala People's Heritage, a monastic political party founded in 2004)! That throws a big wrench into my plan, as I assumed that he was aware of Soma and I have planned a number of follow-up questions based on that assumption. Wirathu's Ma Ba Tha and the Bodu Bala Sena were connected only insofar as monks in both groups perceived a common threat from respective Muslim communities, and not necessarily the result of a transmission from one group to another, at least as far as I could ascertain upon further reflection and inquiries.

I quickly signal my translator in colloquial English that I now want him to ask a different set of questions, and manage to formulate this one on the spot: What differences does Wirathu see in the situations regarding the Muslim problem between the Sri Lankan and Myanmar contexts? Wirathu says that "there is a much bigger problem in Myanmar than in Sri Lanka. Since Myanmar borders Bangladesh, there are many illegal migrants in Myanmar, which is probably the most important difference. If the Muslims lived harmoniously within the country, that would be fine, but not if they try to engage in jihad." Another problem, he says, is that "Myanmar women are sort of naïve and so they are vulnerable to men from other religions and become converted. Some of them are abused by these husbands from other religions. Sri Lanka has a better Buddhist foundation so they are in better shape in this regard."

On reflection, I found his brief comparison quite concise and consistent with what he has publicly averred in the past and his first point rather incisive. No one in Sri Lanka believes that the Muslim community is made up of recent illegal border jumpers who are threatening the country's immediate political stability. While there have been a lot of accusations by Buddhist nationalists about uncontrolled birthrates among the Muslim community in Sri Lanka, there is simply not the kind of demographic concentration in any one geographic area (comparable to nearly a million Muslims in northern Rakhine State) anywhere in Sri Lanka. Muslims form a majority in only a small slice of the east coast of Sri Lanka between Batticaloa and Pottuvil, and even in these locales, they share a presence with a considerable number of Tamils and Sinhala Buddhists. And of course, there is no predominantly Muslim nation bordering Sri Lanka (unless one chooses to consider the Maldives as such!). As for his second comment, the subject of Buddhist women and their apparent vulnerability, making them easy targets for Muslim men, this is an issue that Wirathu has sought to play up consistently in his public proclamations too. Indeed, it looms large in the reasons that seem to have inspired the four race and religion laws that Wirathu championed so vociferously in his public sermons. And, as we shall see, it may also be something of a personal issue for Wirathu, given his own background and upbringing. I will return to this specific issue when I discuss his autobiography later in this section.

Before getting to the main question I want to pose, I have the translator ask, "Do you feel as if your perspective has been accurately reported by Western journalists?" Wirathu responds by saying that the Western media believes the Muslim propaganda and only broadcasts the news that is unfavorable to the Buddhists. For instance, Maungdaw township has six hundred thousand Muslims and only twenty thousand Buddhists, yet they report that the Buddhist majority has attacked the Muslim minority there. Here he has raised a very interesting issue. In the context of Maungdaw and Buthidaung, the Rakhine or Arakanese Buddhists are indeed a minority. But they are a majority (by more than two to one) in Rakhine State as a whole. This signals one of the fundamental distinguishing features of public consciousness: that all three major parties in Arakan (Rohingya Muslims, Rakhine Buddhists, and Burmese Buddhists) regard themselves as minorities. Wirathu goes on to assert that Muslims create very good propaganda that the Western journalists believe. Even though they know right from wrong, since the media is financed by the Muslims, they do the bidding of their masters. On the BBC website, they publish a picture only of suffering Muslims and no Buddhists. Even that very morning when he granted the BBC an interview, he wanted to show the BBC correspondent a DVD about Muslim violence against Buddhists, but the BBC team members were not interested. "They do not have an ethical posture but are only concerned with business." Given his negative experience with them, I ask him, why does he give interviews, then? His response is simply so that he can tell the truth. If he doesn't grant interviews, they will only attack him more.

I decide to zero in on the question I most want to ask: "Can you explain your perspective about Muslims within the context of Buddhist philosophy?" He has some difficulty fielding this and asks for the translator to repeat the question. It is repeated twice more. (I made sure that it was carefully phrased ahead of time. For "philosophy," I had insisted on the term *dhamma*.) Finally, after a pause, he says, "This is not really a religious belief issue. The problem is one of religious colonization. If we do not defend, we will become like Malaysia. Islam is like a religion and political system that cannot be separated. Religion is like a mask with politics behind it. Religion becomes the means through which politics are expressed. This is a subtle but scary tactic. People are entrapped by this formula. And so we have problems like this in Kosovo, southern Thailand, and Myanmar. The UN doesn't understand, nor do the Americans and the EU, all of whom are standing with the Muslims. What they [the Muslims] aim is to make the whole world Islam. They are targeting small countries to colonize first. They go to various countries in various ways. So the UN, Americans, and EU think that these are refugees, but they are really infiltrators, 'fake refugees' who come with real refugees."

I ask where this impetus is coming from. He says, "There are rich people behind the fifty-seven Islamic countries who are really jihadists. ISIS and al-Qaeda are examples of their aspirations. They are providing arms and technology. If people from Bangladesh want to come to Myanmar, about 10,000 dollars are used to train each of them and to bribe the Burmese border patrol. The Rohingya Solidarity Organization is the terrorist organization that provides funds to enable the infiltration of Myanmar. Bangladesh is very poor and the OIC [Organization of Islamic Cooperation] seeks to use money to enable more Bengalis to come to Myanmar." Knowing the conditions of the Sittwe IDP camp and those who have been rounded up from Sittwe and placed there for a period of more than three years by the time of this first interview with Wirathu, I say to myself, "This man seems misled at best, deluded at worst, regarding the on-the-ground situation out in northern Arakan." At the time of this first interview, Wirathu had not yet been to northern Arakan. Yet he seemed to imagine that all of the Rohingya were basically illegal Bengalis and insurgents.

Since elections are to be held in less than a year's time, I ask, "What will be the ramifications for Buddhist-Muslim relations in the impending election?"

He says, "This will be a different election—this will be clean. If the NLD [National League for Democracy] wins, the Muslims will take advantage of this to engage in more colonization. They will colonize unfairly." By this he means the imagined forced conversions to Islam that he objects to, especially those of women. Nothing of the sort transpired. As indicated in my conversations with Rohingya leaders, the situation for Rohingya actually deteriorated further once the NLD came to power.

The interview has been going on for about an hour and half. Wirathu starts to fidget, and I worry that I have taxed him after a long day that included a tough BBC interview. Moreover, with the translations from Burmese back into English for my benefit, it is taking quite a while to move forward. So I decide to wrap up the interview while the meeting remains cordial. I hope to talk with him again in the future, and it was difficult to gain access to him through the firewall of his monk handlers. I say, "My book is being written for Americans, especially students and teachers. What message would you like to send to them?" He says that he wants to correct the media image of Buddhist people and invites people who really want to know to come to Myanmar and learn directly for themselves. "The whole world is saying that Muslims are an oppressed minority. In fact, minority people are harming the majority. It is the Buddhist people who are suffering from this Muslim minority. Buddhist people are at a disadvantage at police stations and in the courts whenever a crime is being investigated. In Myanmar we have over 130 minorities, but we've never had any of these rape our women. Only Muslims do that." I make a note to myself that the raping of women continues to be a consistent theme in his Buddhist discourse about the "Muslim problem."

Finally, I ask if he would like to ask any questions of me. He asks if I am an American and says that Americans are treating Muslim terrorists cruelly. "We are also afraid of the Muslim terrorists. Just like Americans are attacking the terrorists with drones, we are just like that." He predicts that in the future there will be more jihad, and so that is why he is preaching to the people to be prepared. If we are just like America, he says, why are Americans trying to criticize this situation here? "Remember how Americans were first supporting Ho Chi Minh? And then he turned against them? That is what will happen with the Muslims." He goes on then to assert that there really are no Rohingya people—they are all just illegal immigrants. "We like Americans, but it is not worth envying them. Do not make enemies of your friends! Do not bully our small country and side with the OIC. Please remember we are a small and poor country, but we beat the British for independence too."

Wirathu then proceeds to show me photos from *Time* and another magazine with their sensational covers of him. "They report unfairly and don't write about the good things that Buddhists are doing. Obama is responsible for the ethics of the media." I reply that even President Obama can't control the media in the United States. He counters that "America is an 'undisciplined democracy.'" I leave it at that and decide to beg my leave. Meanwhile, one of his attendant monks has been busy on the internet and has discovered that I have written several books about Buddhism. He informs Wirathu about this and Wirathu's face suddenly brightens. He asks if I can bring copies of my books with me next time for the monastery library. I am heartened by this final exchange and promise to return in some months' time.

August 2016. A year and half later I am back in Mandalay. In the meantime, the NLD has registered its resounding landslide victory over the military's proxy Union Solidarity and Development Party (USDP). Wirathu and the Ma Ba Tha had campaigned heavily for the USDP and many observers both within and outside the country have commented on how the Ma Ba Tha may have been the contrivance and strategy of the military and the USDP per se. Meanwhile, the NLD government, through the formal organizational hierarchy of the sangha, had been able to disestablish the legitimacy of the Ma Ba Tha. The Ma Ha Na had issued a statement indicating that the Ma Ba Tha had no legal status within the sangha. This was seen as a serious blow to Wirathu and his cohorts.

This time the interview is conducted with two translators (mine and his). Neither of them, however, has a complete or idiomatically fluent command of English. Between the two, I think we managed fairly well. The interview is conducted in Wirathu's audience hall, with as many as twenty or twenty-five monastic onlookers. It seems much more formal than the first, and it is video recorded. After thanking him for indulging me for a second time, I begin, "Last year, you said that an NLD victory would be an advantage to Muslims. Has that come to pass?" Wirathu responds, "The NLD victory is very dangerous for the religion [Buddhism] and country. So this has been an advantage insofar as the Muslim aim has been to blow up the Ma Ba Tha. There has also been an advantage given to the Muslims in that the government has given them economic opportunities. The new government has never been on the Buddhist side."

By now, Wirathu has been feeling the beginning of mounting pressure on the Ma Ba Tha. Either the previous USDP government was approving of his efforts to rally Buddhist nationalists, which seems a credible assumption given the Tatmadaw's history of discrimination against Muslims and the USDP's intrinsic links to the Tatmadaw, or it simply cast a benign eye in his direction. The NLD had its own fair share of nationalists in its ranks, but a combination of progressive monks, international pressures, and more forward-looking NLD politicos seemed to have resulted in a policy decision to try to rein in Wirathu for the sake of the religion's and country's reputation. This is perhaps why Wirathu saw the NLD government as a threat to Buddhism and Myanmar. For him, the two are coextensive. But the fact of the matter is that Muslims I had spoken to do not feel in any way advantaged by the change of government. To the contrary, they consistently pointed to worsening conditions. Aung San Suu Kyii's response to the Tatmadaw's violent siege of Rohingya in the aftermath of October 9, 2016 (that the claims of violence were largely a fabrication), was, of course, the most spectacular example. But that example was to occur later, and at the time I thought it prudent to pursue Wirathu's claim further. So to follow up, I ask, "What economic opportunities did the NLD give to the Muslims?"

He replies, "They've tried to look after the welfare of the Muslims. The USDP did not accept the identity of the minority, but in the case of the NLD regarding the Muslims, this new government has said nothing. The USDP tried to prosecute the border wars, but the new government has stopped that project. The NLD has removed the checkpoints between Arakan and Yangon. So this makes it easier for illegals to make it to other parts of the country, especially Yangon. The earlier government used to require that visitors report to local authorities. The new government has removed that rule. We can clearly see how this government has tried to assist the illegals from Bangladesh. This government has also tried to disenfranchise the Ma Ba Tha by saying it is no longer needed. This statement was declared by the Yangon chief minister. Aung San Suu Kyii has told the Ma Ha Na organization to destroy the Ma Ba Tha. Previously, the Ma Ha Na approved and supported the Ma Ba Tha. But the Ma Ha Na has been under pressure by this government."

Wirathu is getting visibly worked up into a bit of a rant, so I try to switch the focus. "What do you see regarding the future of the four race and religion laws passed by parliament last summer before the election victory by the NLD?" As I mentioned, Wirathu had endorsed the USDP, the party that had passed these four laws in parliament.

"Some in parliament want to destroy these laws."

I press, "Will that happen?"

"The new government will try to destroy these laws." If they start discussing this in parliament, he thinks that the country may witness a riot. "If they try to remove these laws, the government will lose support from the people. Their main target is Sayadaw [the leading monk of the monastery, meaning himself] and the Ma Ba Tha." I think he is not far wrong here. But, in fact, there had been no moves in parliament as of then to dismantle Wirathu's signature legislative achievement. The laws are formulated in such an arcane manner that their applicability to specific circumstances seems somewhat remote, in any case. Perhaps Suu Kyii and her NLD strategists figure that raising these issues in parliament is just not a good strategy, simply not worth the trouble, instead leaving them on the books for now and living to fight for a better cause, rather than risking the mayhem that may result from trying to erase them.

Since President Obama twice visited Myanmar, there is a more heightened awareness of American politics and its significance for Myanmar domestically. So I ask, "Will it make any difference to the situation here in Myanmar if Hillary Clinton or Donald Trump wins the American presidential election?"

He responds, "If Trump is elected, the new government will have a more difficult time putting pressure on the Ma Ba Tha. If Clinton wins, that is more dangerous for our country." Given that Trump, a favorite of Wirathu's because of his stance toward the Muslim world, won the election, it must be surprising to Wirathu that the pressure put on him and Ma Ba Tha had only been ratcheted up. I tell him that I think Trump would be hard-pressed to locate Myanmar on a world map and that his knowledge of this part of the world, like it is for any part of the world where he has not conducted his real estate business, is likely pretty minimal, at best.

Next I ask him, "Are you still in contact with the Bodu Bala Sena in Sri Lanka? Do you have any further plans for cooperating?"

"Last month in July," he replies, "the BBS secretary came to visit here and he performed *bana* [a sermon] here and in Meiktila." Wirathu says that he had been invited to go again to Sri Lanka.

I ask him if he would provide a sketch of his background. He says that there is a written autobiography in Bamar and that he will send it to me via e-mail. I say okay, but I still want him to summarize his background for me, especially in case he neglects to send his autobiography. He says he was born in 1968 in Mandalay. His father was a staffer for the agricultural department. (Notice that his mother is not mentioned in connection with his origins.) He became a *samanera* (novice monk) when he was seventeen. At that time, he had received only an eighth-grade education. He began his time in the sangha by meditating for three months. After that, he made a decision to become a fully fledged monk. In 1988 he took *upasampada* (full ordination) at the minimum age of twenty. He came here to this monastery in 1991. At that time, he wrote one book "without permission," called *Theravada pada* (The Path of the Theravada). The main point of the book is that he tried to show that the system of a local meditation center did not work. It was too focused on emotions. This book was read by a lot of people and made his name, Wirathu, well known. Then in 2001, he began to preach about the "Muslim problem." Two reasons motivated him: in 2000, a young Buddhist woman had married a Muslim and had been killed by the family because the girl simply had placed a flower on the desk where she was operating a sewing machine, the presence of the flower being understood as worship of the Buddha. Then in 2001, another girl had married a Muslim, and her father had died sometime after the marriage. The girl was prohibited from attending the funeral. For these reasons, Wirathu began preaching about this kind of anti-Buddhist behavior. The main thing he wanted to preach is that people should understand their religion. Anyone who marries a Muslim would encounter trouble of this nature. This affected him not so much personally, but he could see its ramifications for Buddhist society and the nation. He did not know these women personally.

I ask specifically, "Why were you sent to prison in 2003?"

He jokes that it was because of the military's love. "This was their way of keeping in close touch!" The main reason was because he had become famous for his anti-Muslim preaching.

I ask, "What was life like in prison?"

"Life was upside down. Normally people bow to Sayadaw [again, he is referring to himself here], but he had to suffer punching from others instead. I was not able to eat good food and was forced to wear the prison blue dress rather than the monk's robe. They put me in a small brick room. Prison didn't affect my health because I took care of myself mentally and physically." In prison, the political prisoners were separated from the common criminals.

"Did you make some good friends there?" He smirks as if to say no.

I ask him if he writes another book, what it will be. He says he doesn't have time to write another book. He already has a number of books that need to be printed.

Wirathu seemed more subdued to me (aside from his rant about the government undermining the Ma Ba Tha) than he was a year and half earlier, and maybe he had had the wind taken out of his sails somewhat, owing to the recent events. It had not been easy to get an interview this time, as he was clearly being protected by his coterie. I had been asked several times why I wanted to speak with him. He has had such a difficult relation with the Western press that I was immediately suspected as an antagonist. But he recognized me when we came into each other's view and I knew then that the situation would be all right.

I saw Wirathu again, for the third time, in **January 2017**. He had been in Yangon for several days, and twice I visited his monastery in the hope of arranging an interview through his handlers. Only by means of the intervention of a young monk who persistently pleaded my case to his handlers did I gain an appointment during the evening of my last night in Myanmar, just after he had returned to town.

I had read the translation of the short autobiography he had sent to me via e-mail. The translation had been prepared by my Muslim conversationalist, Jezima Akyabi, in Thandwe (2: "The Teacher"). How it was translated into English is an interesting story. Jezima had translated it by hand, but I did not realize this and had asked her to prepare a Microsoft Word document to be sent to me as an e-mail attachment. So she had gone to a local internet shop to have the translation typed on a word processor, leaving her manuscript with the shop owner. When she returned three hours later, the script was typewritten, but legions of errors had been made, a crucial section that described Wirathu's anti-Muslim activities had been omitted, and her original handwritten translation was nowhere to be found! I asked her if she thought that this was sabotage, and she responded with a "who knows" gesture and said simply, "This is Myanmar." We spent about five hours working on the mangled translation. It was still not suitable for reproduction, but I provide a summary in the following pages to include details that Wirathu left out of his own summary during my second interview with him.

Wirathu wrote his brief autobiography when he emerged from prison in 2012. I can't judge the quality of the Burmese since I had it translated into English, and that translation got rather garbled when it was being typed up. In total, it is only fourteen typewritten double-spaced A4 pages. Three things in general impressed me about the piece, or I should say emerged from the text as I read and digested it. The first is the rather difficult life that his family experienced, about which I'll elaborate shortly. Wirathu comes from no privileged background. Second is the considerable amount of meditation that he claims to have pursued. And third is a strongly developed self-conscious awareness that gave me the impression that it borders on the narcissistic. For instance, Wirathu makes bold claims about his meditation pursuits, his mastery of "all the Pali texts," and his ambition to be a great monastic leader in the sangha. That is, he writes in a way that signals an awareness of his future importance as leader, as if he was somehow destined. Maybe I am overstating this a bit, but the sense of self-importance, or, better, self-aggrandizement, is palpable in the work. And yet, there is a sense in which it is also very morally informed, or assumes that his path is fundamentally the morally correct path in an age of degeneracy and decline.

What follows for the next several pages is a summary of the fourteen pages of roughly translated autobiography written by Wirathu upon his prison release. There is also a section in which I am fairly confident of the translation. That part has been put within quotes.

Wirathu was born Mg Win Khine Oo, the second of eight children (four boys and four girls) born to U Khine Mg Win and Daw Tin Tin Oo. His father was a tractor operator, and the family moved from place to place depending upon his work in and around the Mandalay region, which explains in part why Wirathu started school late, as a nine-year-old, and had completed only the eighth grade by the time he took up robes at seventeen under the auspices of an uncle. He originally intended only to spend a rain-retreat season as a *samanera* (novice monk), but after learning the tradition of *vipassana* (insight meditation) as it had been taught to his uncle for twenty-five years by one Webu Sayadaw, he writes that his decision to stay in the sangha and to become an "outstanding monk" was met with a mixed reaction by members of his extended family, some of whom, including his father, wanted him to come out of the sangha, finish his education, and help support the family, since he was the eldest son. After three more months of contemplation on the matter, he decided he wanted the life of a monk, since in juxtaposition to the lay life, "the *sasana* [tradition of the Buddha's teaching] was a peaceful domain without worry."

At the teaching monastery, he quickly excelled in preparing for the standard examination on the Vinaya (rules of monastic discipline), and he was greatly influenced by a book entitled *Arahants and Outstanding Persons* written by Dhammacarya U Htay Hlaing. He also began the practice of *dutin* (which I think is a derivative of the Sanskrit *dhutanga,* designating the life of austerity), which he describes as the practice of eating just one meal a day, as established, he says, by the famous early-twentieth-century monk Ledi Sayadaw. He then proceeds to describe how he always stood first, second, or third in various monastic examinations. In 1988, just months before the 8888 Uprising, he took *upasampada*. He is careful to mention his monastic mentors and lay sponsors.

Very soon after his ordination, he learned of his father's death while he was working in a gold mine. He says he did not see the cremation, nor was a photo of the body provided to him. His father had died soon after a divorce from his mother, who had promptly married another man who was not liked by the four remaining children living within the nuclear family. In his autobiography, he says that "he had to swallow the hatred and anger he bore toward his mother" owing to her remarriage. Even as a monk, he "had to cry tearfully" at the situation that had developed in his family. Though the onus of somehow providing for his younger siblings was now upon him as the oldest male in the family, he did not want to disrobe. He prayed and meditated on the matter, and soon a telegram arrived from his father's brother, who indicated that he had tried to come to take care of the remaining children but had been unable to proceed because of the 8888 chaos in the country. Through great difficulties, Wirathu himself made the journey to meet his uncle and aunt and thereby established the future well-being of his younger siblings while yet remaining in robes, though the occasion ended up costing him another year in terms of preparing for examinations.

Following this, he passed further examinations and developed an ambition not to be simply the abbot of a monastery, but to become a leading transmitter of the *dhamma* within his lineage of the sangha. His mentor sent him to the Masoyein Monastery in Mandalay only after he had completed his promise to learn by heart "all Pali texts." When he arrived at the monastery, he impressed the lead abbot with his knowledge of the Pali texts but was not readily accepted by the other monks, as they denounced him as a slacker, which made him feel as if he should leave. Even his mentor had begun to think of him as such. Indeed, he did not pass a difficult exam on the first attempt, but later was one of four out of one hundred who succeeded, in 1993.

He writes then about his continued successes with Pali exams, his participation in the compiling of a Pali dictionary, his own continued practice of meditation, and his rise in seniority at the monastery. His first two books were about the proper way to engage in meditation and a critique of other methods that had to do with a focus on too much emotion. He says that the first book sold fifteen thousand copies and with its second printing was called *The Theravada Struggle.* His second book, apparently a sequel, was entitled *Pariyatti Gold Balance* but was not approved by the government censor, or director of religious affairs, Dr. Myo Myint. Yet Wirathu published it independently because "it was very good for Buddhist readers." The second book gave him wide notoriety. "The hand of Virasu [his epithet] was to be gold coated. He became 'Theravada Hero,' 'front line fighter,' and 'the savior of religion.'"

At this time, however, during the early 2000s, the Tatmadaw very harshly tightened its grip on the country, leading to a decline in the quality of life for many. Wirathu believed that Muslims were bribing the military government to suppress Myanmar Buddhists and that Buddhist women were being raped regularly by Muslim men. He says that every day these persecutions against Buddhists were taking place in various ways. He did not like to see this developing situation, so he traveled around the country to get better educated about it. He decided to move against the government, and "the whole country was happy because they got a national leader." When Aung San Suu Kyii was under house arrest, he became very famous throughout the country as he preached against the declining situation being caused by the Muslims. The military arrested him in the fallout of a *kalar*-Bamar riot in Lunkwa village in Kumel township. He had written a book entitled *Let Us Be Ready* before he was arrested on October 25, 2003, and subsequently sentenced to twenty-five years. He was beaten and tortured, but while under interrogation he used the occasion to practice meditation. He was not given the right to a lawyer. In prison, he practiced *dutin,* which helped purify his mind, "though it was the winter of my heart." He says that many monks in Mandalay rallied for his release. At one point during his incarceration, he wrote a letter of protest to the prison director and local government minister about the conditions in the prison. As a result, he was transferred to another prison, where he was provided with a "Pitaka laptop" (a laptop computer with the Buddhist Tripitaka loaded on it). After that, he was able to be more proficient in writing many articles and poems.

When he was finally released, he began to dedicate himself to various charitable causes to raise the standards of the people. He saw the government as responsible for impoverishing the intellectual life of the country and its living standards, its culture being denigrated every day. He exhorted Buddhist monks to address this situation of decline, to save the country, its religion and culture. For the benefit of monks, he had worked to establish the Bawa Ahlinyaung library at the Masoyein Monastery in 2001, and after release from prison he redoubled his efforts in its support. He also established a blood-donation society, in addition to a foundation in support of impoverished children badly in need of education. He also founded a monastic education school with one hundred thousand lakhs of kyats that he raised. He sees the endeavor to upgrade the economy, education, health, and religion as all interrelated to the well-being of the nation. That is why he says he is a nationalist.

Wirathu ends his autobiographical sketch by citing the models of Sariputra, who took poor stray children into the monastery, where they eventually became *arahants,* and Jatila, who, though born poor, became a billionaire and then a gifted *arahant* working on behalf of the educational development of the poor. The final touch is simply a statement about his "political status," of being a supporter of the "democratic path."

I mentioned at the outset three things that immediately had impressed me about this account. But there are others. The first is how Wirathu aligns himself with austere religious practices beyond the observance of meditation. Indeed, he cites himself in the tradition of the great monk Ledi Sayadaw. Moreover, he emphasizes his academic achievements to indicate that he has acquired a superior knowledge of the Buddha's *dhamma.* He is also very concerned to take good care of his family. In this context, I need to discuss the remark concerning his feelings for his mother at the time she remarried and the consequential fate of the younger siblings. When I first read this, I felt that perhaps I had found the key to Wirathu's rather patronizing at best, misogynist at worst, disposition toward women. It seemed a perfect explanation. And perhaps it is. But when I questioned him later about his mother, he indicated nothing of the sort and went on to say that he now supported his mother into her old age. So I hesitate to pile on in any way regarding the causes of his disposition toward women. It may be due to the divorce of his parents and his mother's remarriage, but I do not think that he would admit to this. Finally, there is also his strongly articulated effort to help the poor. In these ways, Wirathu has touched bases with both traditional monastic orientations, the more austere life of renunciation associated with the meditative tradition, and the "wander for the welfare of the many" orientation associated with the selfless and often scholarly village monk. He's been careful to complete a profile that appeals to many dimensions of the Buddhist monastic vocation.

After reading this autobiographical information, I was much better prepared for my third interview. I found Wirathu a bit more tight lipped than in the past, though I am not sure why this was the case. He may have been simply tired.

To begin, I mention that I gained a lot of respect for him by reading his autobiography, especially about all the philanthropy, hard study, and meditation he has done. "When was your autobiography written? Did you write it or did you dictate to someone?" I ask.

He says, "I wrote it myself in 2012 when released from prison."

"Two books made you well known: Can you tell me briefly what *Theravada Struggle* and *Pariyatti Gold Balance* are about?"

He replies briefly, "The first book is about meditation taught by the Buddha, especially the four methods of practice." Here I think he was referring to the four *brahmaviharas* (abidings) of *metta* (loving-kindness), *mudita* (sympathetic joy), *uppekha* (even-mindedness), and *karuna* (compassion). "People complained about the complex nature of the first book, so I wrote the second. They complained that it was the wrong teaching."

"You talk about a problem you had with Myo Myint in publishing the second book. Can you describe this problem?"

"The book was not published because of Myo Myint. I was critical of a wrong form of meditation being practiced at the meditation center, about this type of meditation. Breathing wrong, walking too fast, too much emotion (crying, laughing, etc.), and not being allowed to move for four hours at a time." I had been especially interested in this detail because I had been introduced to Myo Myint through the intercession of Juliane Schober. He had been my principal contact when I came to Myanmar in 2010 to write a book chapter about *kathina* (an annual robe and gift-giving rite to the sangha) to be included in my *Theravada Traditions* (Holt 2017). He had arranged my fieldwork site in Yangon and also provided an excellent fieldwork assistant. Myo Myint was an established historian in his own right, having received his PhD from Cornell University. I suspected that he had some political sensitivities in mind when he refused to endorse Wirathu's book, but I can't say that for sure. Or it may have been that Myo Myint, as director of religious affairs, was aware of a variety of religious approaches and practices across the spectrum and simply did not want to endorse the condemnation of a popular meditation center.

"Can you describe the content of your preaching 'Be Ready'?"

"This preaching was about the Muslims. I was critical about the Muslim relation with the military government."

"Did the army think this book was one of the reasons for the *kalar*-Bamar riot? Why did they accuse you of desecration of the sangha?"

"Yes, they said this. At that time, Aung San Suu Kyii was also under arrest. I had preached that in 2003, Muslims were bribing the military and suppressing Buddhist people."

"When you were released from prison, you preached peace with Muslims. What changed your mind?"

"The main ambition was peace among all the religions to unite against the military government. Later when the Rakhine violence [in Sittwe in 2012] took place, the NLD party did not stand for the Buddhist people. Only the USDP government stood for the people at that time in 2012. The NLD party did not support the people but the Thein Sein government did. At that time, I stopped being political in that sense and shifted to a nationalist stance to protect against Islamicization." This is a critical statement, for it pinpoints Wirathu's return to an anti-Muslim stance after he seemed to have evolved away from it following his release from prison.

"In our earlier interviews, you told me that the situation for Muslims would improve under the NLD. In the last three weeks, I interviewed three Rohingya leaders, all elder statesmen who have Myanmar citizenship, who say that they have lost all faith in the NLD government and that the situation for them is now far worse than under Thein Sein. How do you respond?"

"This government has rejected Rohingya claims to citizenship rights. It does not regard them as a Rakhine people. That is why they are unhappy."

"The first time I talked with you, a year and half ago, I asked you to compare the situations between Sri Lanka and Myanmar regarding the Muslim problem. One of the things you said was: 'Another problem is that Myanmar women are sort of naïve and so they are vulnerable to men from other religions and become converted. Some of them are abused by these husbands from other religions. Sri Lanka has a better Buddhist foundation so they are in better shape in this regard.' Did you mean to say that there is a problem with the Buddhist education of women in Myanmar?"

"Burmese women cannot take care of themselves. Burmese women are afraid and shy and that is why they cannot protect themselves. They don't have enough education and knowledge of the Buddha's *dhamma.*" I interject here and ask if he regards his own sisters and mother in the same way. He replies that his siblings live far away and his only contact is through phone calls. He says that there is no friendship between him and them. His "youngest sister also died because of poverty and lack of knowledge. She died of influenza."

I come right out and asked the brutally personal question about his mother and father. "Nineteen eighty-eight was an important year for you: you took *upasampada* and your father died in a gold mine, and there was great unrest in the country. I have two main questions: (1) Did your father die by accident? Or by influenza? (2) Why did your father divorce your mother? You write about being very angry with her. Was this because of the divorce? Why did your four siblings not go with her when she remarried? Did she remarry after your father's death? Did she have more children in her second marriage?" I realize here that I have asked too many questions at once, and indeed his answer is directed only to the last part of my queries.

"The four younger siblings did not like my mother's second husband. Neither did I! As for my father, he left for the gold mine after the divorce and died of influenza."

I decide to persist because his answer seems to indicate his dissatisfaction. I ask, "Is your mother still alive and do you stay in touch with her?"

Wirathu says that he supported her until she died and does not go into the matter further. I couldn't have realistically hoped that he would, given the context of the interview and the very personal nature of the question. I felt I was lucky to have gotten what I did in response. He did not deny what had been written about his feelings in the autobiography. Though I wanted to pursue all of this more deeply, I dared not trespass further into this terribly personal territory in the presence of so many others. I had some indications for the source of his misogyny, but I could not get him to come right out and say in this context that he had been deeply disappointed in his mother's remarriage, though he had said clearly in his autobiography that he resented her for it.

"Meditation has been an important part of your religious practice. In your understanding, how does *samadhi* [concentration] relate to *panna* [wisdom] and *sila* [morality]?"

"*Sila* is the foundation of human life. *Sila* is like a body of the building. *Panna* is the root of the building, a lifestyle leading away from guilt. *Panna* is peace of mind for the human beings." He looks at my diagram of a triangle showing a reflexive relation among all three cornerstones of the path, and he agrees.

Finally, I raise the question of the significance of the American presidential election, since he had been so expansive about his feelings regarding Barack Obama during our first interview. "I heard you were pleased with Donald Trump's victory in America. Exactly what did you say?"

"When Trump won, I wrote in Facebook I am happy that Trump won. I believe that Trump will protect against Islamization for the American people and all of the world." I tell him I voted for Hillary Clinton and he laughs! I say that for me the results of the American election were not a laughing matter. It is time for me to take my leave of Wirathu.

As my taxi wended its way back to my hotel in downtown Mandalay, I realized I would not see Wirathu again. I felt a bit of pity for the man, trapped as he was in his own infamy, not especially well prepared for the onslaught of attention he commanded on an almost daily basis, especially beleaguered by the media and by people like me (though he had told me that I was something of an exception in terms of the types of people who sought him out). I came back to the thought that his hostility and disdain for Muslims were born from the *raga* [passion], *dosa* [hatred], and *moha* [delusion] that discolored his *cetana* [intention]. That is, Wirathu's disposition was affected by a raging hatred born of ignorance. He symbolized, for me, something of Myanmar's tragedy—that so much of the suffering occurring out of Arakan was the result of misconceptions that have inhibited an ability to generate concord.

The Anti-Nationalists

July 2015. I visited with Ven. Jotika at his Oo Yin Monastery at the base of Yankin Hill a few kilometers northeast of Mandalay on numerous occasions beginning in the summer of 2015 and extending through December 2017. Of all the Burmese monks I engaged with from 2010 to the present, indeed of all the Buddhists with whom I communicated since resuming my visits to Myanmar in 2010, I was most comfortable and least intimidated by this genial, affable, poised, straightforward, mindful, unpretentious, and almost entirely progressive cleric. We seemed to hit it off almost from the first moments and then got along extremely well subsequently. Part of our congenial relation, no doubt, issued from the fact that when I originally introduced myself during our first encounter, I referred to my academic degrees in the comparative study of religions (history of religions) and my long-term scholarly focus on the Buddhist religious culture of Sri Lanka. His face immediately lit up at this and he proceeded to tell me of his two years of study leading to a master's degree at the Postgraduate Institute of Buddhist Studies in Colombo, Sri Lanka, and his unfolding plans to build a University of Global Peace, in which the religions of the world would be studied comparatively in order to emphasize their respective aspirations to create peace internationally. I'm sure that in response, my own face must have lit up too, when he told me about his background and plans. We spoke a little Sinhala, exchanging pleasantries, and then inquired of each other about Sri Lankan scholars whose friendships we might have shared. He even politely invited me to lecture at his university after it opened formally in late 2018. More specifically, he asked me if I could help in supervising the building of the collection of library holdings in English for the university. I was honored by these invitations and plan to return again to Mandalay to help out however I can.

Ven. Jotika is something of a visionary who is not afraid to undertake a major project of this nature. More important, he told me early on that he believes that truth speaks to power, that power can never resist the force of truth's embodiments. I first met him just six weeks or so after he returned from Oslo, Norway, where he was presented with a World Harmony Award by the Parliament of the World's Religions in recognition of his efforts to establish harmonious relations between the religious traditions in Myanmar. He is a well-known public figure, especially in the Mandalay region, not only because of his monastery of more than 450 monks, but also because he writes frequently for newspapers and magazines and is sometimes interviewed for publications with a national reach.

Though it was the fourth time we had engaged in extensive conversation, it was **August 2016** before I learned more details about his background. I'll begin with what he told me at that time.

"At age twelve, I started taking up the robe. My parents donated me to the *sasana* [the tradition of the Buddha's teaching]. In my family, I had two brothers and two sisters. All are married now except for me. My mother, siblings, nephews, and nieces often come to see me at the monastery. Fifteen years ago, my father passed away. My mother lives nearby with a nephew and I support her (she is seventy-nine years old).

"After I took up the robe, I spent thirteen years in a teaching monastery, where I came to learn Pali and was then able to read Buddhist literature. But I really started serious study about thirty years ago. I followed all the monastic exams I could, one after another. I took *upasampada* [full ordination] at age twenty [the minimum age according to the Vinayapitaka] and began attending a university, a *sasana* university in Bago, and continued studying Pali. After four years, I graduated with a degree in Pali. When I came back to my monastery, I became a teacher. My 'monk-mother' [*upajjhaya,* monastic mentor] then wanted me to study Sanskrit. I started to study that language with a Hindu Brahmin, but his location was very far and so it became quite inconvenient, so I could not finish the course. After that, I devoted my energies to learning English instead. My English teacher was an old man who had recently ordained as a Buddhist monk. He was an expert because he had taught English grammar in high school for many years. So I started studying English with him, mostly grammar and not so much speaking. After studying with this monk, I then took up studying more English with a monk who had a master's degree from Nalanda University in India. I read and found Shakespeare to be very compelling despite its difficulty. The sentences were beautiful. I now actually prefer American English because I think it is easier to learn to speak it.

"During the 1988 student crisis, we all had hopes for the coming of democracy, but it didn't happen until just now [2016]. A lot of people demonstrated publicly back then for democracy. I demonstrated with my disciples. The whole country had been shut down for a long time [since 1962] and our people did not really know about democracy. The agitation was something new for the country.

"After that time, my teacher, when I was thirty-one, brought me here to Mandalay and I started this Oo Yin Monastery. My teacher had given me twelve *samaneras* [novices]. I took them to the jungle up on Yankin Hill. It was a very simple monastery. By 1990, I had turned it into a teaching monastery, meaning that it was almost exclusively an educational institution. More and more novices took up residence here. Now it is twenty-seven years old and has 450 students. There are no *thila shin* [unordained nuns]. Almost all monks in residence are *samaneras.* I had two monk friends from the previous monastery who helped me to get started. All of the teachers here now are my disciples. I have sent some of my monk-teachers to Sri Lanka to obtain MA degrees. Now twenty-four of my disciples have finished the MA. Three monks have studied for the

PhD in Sri Lanka at the Postgraduate Institute of Buddhist Studies in Colombo. Slowly, the monastery has expanded."

At this moment, I interrupt Ven. Jotika and ask, "How do you know which students to accept?"

He answers, "At first, it was a matter of my former students simply sending their students to me. *Parampara* [lineage]! They know my ability. I have gained a reputation for really working hard to educate many people. This is how I got support from the laity for my needs. *Dayakas* [lay supporters] believe in me. Now I can support everyone eating some rice each morning because of the level of support I have from *dayakas.* Also, medicine and robes are provided for all of the students here. Many *dayakas* want to support us." In a later conversation I discovered that Jotika had the support of many *dayakas,* indeed. Ten buildings were being put up as part of his university and he had a *dayaka* supporting each one. I ask him if he gained so much support because he is viewed as a virtuous *punya ksetra* (field of merit), that acts of giving are regarded as more potent because the object of the generosity is morally superior. To this he gives his modest assent.

"We had grown to about three hundred students by 1997. My students demonstrated against the military government outside of the monastery with the protection of laity who shielded them with their bicycles. They were demonstrating against the fact that the military had not honored the results of the 1990 national elections and had imprisoned many of the people who had been elected. When they returned to my monastery, they climbed up to the top of Yankin Hill. The bicyclists could not follow the monks. The government said it was unhappy with my monastery.

"In 1990, Aung San Suu Kyii came and gave a speech at my monastery. My teacher was also here with us. He has now passed away. After that, every night the army kept watch on my monastery. I had given a lot of speeches at a nearby monastery. So the military government always watched me. In 2004 or 2005, Aung San Suu Kyii and the National League for Democracy were agitating and Aung San Suu Kyii was assaulted. She was taken by airplane with the help of a general. That year, I had been in jail. I was sentenced to two years in jail, but I got out after one year and eight months. The International Committee of the Red Cross [ICRC] always watched our jail. My *dayakas* and pupils kept the ICRC informed on my behalf. So the ICRC, especially a Japanese lady who spoke some Burmese, helped me in the jail by asking the authorities if I could be visited by my family, *dayakas,* and pupils. Yes, I was able to meet them. I was okay. I brought many people together while in jail. Nobody in jail hated me. I was arrested because the local police had come to my monastery and had asked me to settle a dispute between some laity and monks. I had helped to settle the dispute, but when I came back I was photographed and charged with being an instigator of the problem. I had simply tried to settle the dispute that had to do with an ownership issue of a monastery, as requested by the police. There were two opposing monk and laity groups. Allegedly, someone had complained that I had caused the problem. In fact, I had been set up by the authorities. While trying to get the people to stop their feud, it was said that I had stoked the argument. But I have no problem with the authorities now. Even though my students, along with so many other monks, publicly demonstrated in Mandalay during the so-called Saffron Revolution[1] [in 2007], the security forces have left us alone."

It seems as if his monastic life as a lead teacher and administrator of his well-regarded monastery has been going smoothly now for many years, since he served his time in prison. He feels confident that he was a de facto political prisoner because of his obvious progressive views and backing of democratic forces. In any case, he had the time to tackle a graduate program leading to a PhD at Abhidhamma University in Mandalay. In Myanmar, there is a preponderance of monastic intellectual interest in the Abhidhammapitaka. There is no other Theravada country that rivals Myanmar in this way. Indeed, it is unique to Burmese Buddhism. Jotika's doctoral dissertation, at the time I originally drafted this, was being examined by his supervisor. The process was finished sometime in late 2017, when Jotika was fifty-nine years old. The focus is on how to study the Abhidhamma in light of understanding of the function of the six senses and their contact with corresponding phenomena. It is written in English.

When I engaged Ven. Jotika substantially for a second time, in **August 2015**, his University of Global Peace was due to open provisionally the following Saturday. More than one hundred students would be attending the inaugural sessions, which, for the first year at least, would concentrate on teaching English because the curriculum was to be taught fully in English. To be admitted, students must have at least finished high school.

I ask him about the curriculum and he hands over a summary of the syllabus. I notice that the first term is pretty much given over to studying Walpola Rahula's *What the Buddha Taught* (1959). I have used that book for thirty-five years in my own classes, but increasingly as a foil, or a setup for how *not* to understand Theravada. While the book contains admirably clear explanations of fundamental Buddhist concepts such as *dukkha* (suffering), *anicca* (change), *paticcasamuppada* (the twelvefold conditioning process leading to rebirth and redeath in samsara), *anatta* (without self), and so forth, it contains many sweeping generalizations (such as "Buddhism has never been involved with bloodshed") that are entirely misleading historically. I had also witnessed Rahula leading an anti-Mahayana campaign in 1990 in Sri Lanka, when he deliberately distorted the character of Mahayana for immediate political gain. He had also opposed my efforts to establish a comparative study of religions program at the University of Peradeniya, initially funded by the Asia Foundation, in the mid-1980s. Because of his reinterpretation of the monastic vocation in the late 1940s and 1950s, which included the necessity for making a militant (read, violent if necessary) defense of the *sasana* (see his *Heritage of a Bhikkhu*, 1974), I see Rahula as

1. A monastic uprising that originally had to do with protesting a gargantuan rise in the price of petrol but morphed into a demand for democracy. Massive monk protests in Yangon eventually led to a brutal crackdown by the Tatmadaw.

one of the forces helping to give rise to the contemporary spate of Buddhist militancy in Sri Lanka and Myanmar. One of my teachers, S. J. Tambiah, wrote an exposé of Rahula in his famous and banned–in–Sri Lanka book, *Buddhism Betrayed?* (Tambiah 1992). I aired my grievances to Jotika about Rahula later, during the summer of 2017, on a subsequent visit. Jotika expressed surprise. The remainder of the curriculum involved a lot of Abhidhamma study, but not very much focused on the other religions of the world. This was his tentative curriculum that he put into place for the period of time he was emphasizing the teaching of English.

"Where will the students come from?" I ask.

He replies, "Mandalay and everywhere else in Myanmar."

"When do you hope to complete construction? Have you raised the funds?" He says he hopes to formally open the university in February 2018. In the summer of 2017, he moved the projected opening to August 2018. Now he was focused on the teaching of English to prepare the students. He planned to have seven instructors. The buildings were to be completed by 2018. "I had no difficulty raising the money because I have only one donor per building. Ten thousand lakhs of kyats [about 7.5 million US dollars] have been donated so far. I have no worries about funding. If Myanmar people believe, they will give." I mention to him how, in observing all the fund-raising that takes place during the *kathina* (robe-giving season following the three-month rain-retreat season), I have come to understand that there is no other place in the Buddhist world in which so much of the people's wealth is given over to the sangha. He nods in agreement and says, "My *dayakas* like brick and mortar in supporting the Buddhasasana." He surveys the construction site and notes that the upper floor of the building in the back will be a library. Since many of the books on Buddhism are in English, he mentions the need to acquire them and again invites me to teach here if I can. "This work is going to be for all people of the world." He wants to discuss whether I can be an adviser for his library.

By the time of my third set of interviews with him, in **August 2016**, he had broken ground for the construction of his peace university. Three buildings were under construction: one for ordinations, one for dining, and the other for classrooms. I had gone to see him to set up a time for us to speak late on a Monday afternoon. Workers busied themselves about the huge construction site, which was now being cleared with heavy earth-moving equipment—giant Caterpillars from Peoria, Illinois, I noted. There was lots of rubble about and a cacophony of sound from all the work taking place. A middle-aged couple (a *dayaka* and his wife) arrived with a huge stack of 10,000-kyat notes. I estimated that stack to be at least 5 million kyats, if not more. I excused myself, as we agreed to meet the next morning. Jotika had been very pleased to see me, in stark contrast to the manner in which I had been gruffly received at U Wirathu's monastery earlier in the day, where I had been asked pointedly by a scowling monk why I wanted to see Wirathu. (I had noted that Wirathu's attitude toward the Western media is a bit like Donald Trump's view of American mainstream media!)

The next day I begin our conversations by asking about the status of Ven. Jotika's University of Global Peace. As noted earlier, more than one hundred students had been enrolled and he was still busy making provisions to improve their English. He explains further the rationale for the fact that the curriculum will be taught in English. Not only are there now so many books written about Buddhism in English, but his ambition is to teach about peace for people all over the world. He wants to send his graduates to other countries. Now he has begun publishing his own journal (*Voice of Peace*) as well.

As I mentioned earlier, I found Jotika to be a very engaging monk who was not afraid to talk Buddhist philosophy in a very politically relevant and compelling manner. One of his favorite applications of Buddhist thought is to argue the importance of nonattachment to concepts of nation and religion. He argues that this nonattachment is essential, because attachment to nation or religion has the effect of narrowing one's perspective and leads one to make exclusive claims to truth and power. Attachment can also give rise to nationalism. He gives the same advice to Rohingya Muslims and to Buddhists: give up attachment to the terms "Rohingya" and "Buddhism," respectively, in order for everyone to remain harmonious in Myanmar. "All the problems arising in the world are due to clinging. My goal of founding a university dedicated to the pursuit of peace and justice is to eliminate clinging to particular religions. I want to establish a comparative study of peace and nonviolence as these are articulated within the religious traditions of the world."

He had written an article for a Mandalay newspaper recently, arguing to the effect that "we who are Buddhist monks cannot be nationalists because we do not mix nationalism and religion. The nationalist vision is very different. It's a very narrow vision: we are Myanmar people and cannot oversee other people if we are nationalists. Religion transcends nationalism. The religious view is wider than the nationalist view. They cannot be combined." This statement was somewhat of a response to a prompt I had put forth. I had referred to a popular adage in Sri Lanka for many nationalists that "the country exists for the sake of the religion." He had recognized this perspective, given his own time in Colombo, and knew of the dangers it presages.

Jotika had recently given an extensive interview to a prominent Buddhist nun, one Yogi Nanda Mala, in a Yangon Buddhist publication that centered much on his views about nationalism. He gave me a copy of the interview, and I then had it translated from the Burmese by an aspiring young Burmese academic in Mandalay. I quote extensively from it here, as it fills out his view a bit.

Jotika: I don't believe that nationalism and religious fundamentalism would bring peace to humanity.

Yogi Nanda Mala: First can you please explain why it [nationalism] is against [the monkhood].

Jotika: Our Lord attained Buddhahood to bring well-being for all living beings. He had no intention to divide and benefit one particular group of people or creatures to the exclusion of others. Anybody who follows his teaching will attain peace. No matter what race, religion, color, or gender group you belong to, you will be benefited equally. Distinctions can only be made in accordance with one's wisdom. Monks, as the sons of the Buddha, are supposed to preach sermons that bring peace to humanity without discriminating on any basis. If [we are] discriminating based on religion and race, how could peace to all of humanity be possible? That's why nationalism and religious fundamentalism are directly opposed to the intention of the Lord Buddha.

Yogi Nanda Mala: Can you also explain why you don't believe [nationalism and religious fundamentalism] would bring peace to humanity?

Jotika: It's very simple. The one who accepts nationalism and religious fundamentalism and the one who doesn't are different in terms of peaceful-mindedness and anxiety, worries and calmness, et cetera. To elaborate more, first, the ones who accept nationalism and religious fundamentalism would know that their minds are not in peace and have been ruined [or wounded]. Especially when they compare the status of their minds before and after they accept nationalism and religious fundamentalism, they would know which one is more peaceful. Second, when you recruit others and you propagate nationalism and religious fundamentalism in their minds, these ideologies take root in the minds of the recruits; their minds can no longer be in peace and would be wounded. You must admit it honestly. If you're a nationalist and discriminate against others, you'd be happy to see your own people become rich and you'd be jealous to see another group become rich. You don't want to see other people become rich, but only yours. The same goes for the ones who accept religious fundamentalism; they only want to see the same religious group members doing well but not others. These types of unwelcoming, unfavorable attitudes emerge. Your mind and body narrow up your own space to live. Freedom is much more limited. You will start to worry about security. This is the nature of normal human beings as laymen.

Yogi Nanda Mala: All nations in the whole world nowadays exist due to nationalistic minds. Ancient kings founded their kingdoms with nationalistic minds too. And also General Aung San recruited [the public] with nationalistic minds and gained independence. Aren't these things true?

Jotika: Correct. I want everyone who is marching for the goal of democracy to follow the spirit of General Aung San. General Aung San united various ethnic groups who had differences with the "Burmese" and used them as [a single united] force. Democracy means uniting differences and using them as a single force. Today nationalism and religious fundamentalism arise all because the steps marching toward democracy are not taken as [one] force. That's why it has been delayed and we have divisions. If you divide diversity by means of nationalism and religious fundamentalism, the goal of democracy would always be far away and true peace and stability shall never exist. I want monks, the sons of the Buddha, to work as refuges not only just for Buddhists, but for other religious groups as well.

The discussion of nationalism provides a natural segue into further discussions regarding the Ma Ba Tha, the Burmese acronym for the Association for the Preservation of Society and Religion, the group of ultranationalist monks who had seized public prominence following the relative successes of the 969 monastic-inspired Buddhist boycotts of Muslim businesses in 2012–2014. Jotika says that U Wirathu is probably the most outspoken and well known of the Ma Ba Tha monks, but they are to be found throughout not only Bamar regions of the country, but among the Karen, Mon, and Arakanese Buddhists as well. He goes on to say that the Ma Ba Tha began when a monk in Mawlamyine (formerly Moulmein) protested publicly that the central Muslim mosque in town had been built over the *sima* (ritual boundary) stones of a preexisting Buddhist temple. Whether or not this incident was true, the story very much illustrates Ma Ba Tha's central message that Islam poses a threat to overrun the country by displacing Buddhism, that Myanmar stands in danger of following the examples of Malaysia and Indonesia, once Buddhist countries that have now become thoroughly Muslim.

Jotika agrees that the Ma Ba Tha has close ideological affinities with the Bodu Bala Sena Buddhist militants in Sri Lanka. Both assert that there is an international Muslim conspiracy to dominate these Buddhist countries. They have both often claimed that currently there are jihadist movements afoot in each country, actively working to disestablish Buddhism in each state. They emphasize and exaggerate Muslim birthrates. They claim that Muslims engage in unfair trade practices in the business world and that Muslims are trying to convert Buddhists, especially Buddhist women.

In 2015, in the months before the national election that saw Aung San Suu Kyii sweep to an overwhelming victory, the Ma Ba Tha seemed have reached the apex of its public influence. It had succeeded in advocating for the passage of the four race and religion laws by the then sitting parliament, which was dominated by the military and its proxies. These laws, in effect, make religious conversion extremely difficult by declaring it mandatory to spend 90 to 180 days in studied preparation for adoption of the new religion before submitting to a local committee that will approve or disapprove of an application to convert. They make marriage to more than one partner illegal and outlaw extramarital affairs, regulate interfaith marriages to protect Buddhist women from coercion to convert, and regulate birthrates to one child every thirty-six months in regions where economic sources are deemed insufficient to support uncontrolled population expansion. These laws were the signature campaign of the Ma Ba Tha and were pushed through parliament, abetted by the Union Solidarity and Development Party (USDP), a political party of, by, and for the military.

In the summer of 2015, when these laws were being passed, it was difficult to ascertain the exact nature and extent of power that the Ma Ba Tha had gained in public. The Ma Ba Tha would actively support the USDP's campaign in the impending election only to see them lose in resounding fashion. But at the time there were few voices, monastic or otherwise, that challenged the Ma Ba Tha in public, much like the situation in Sri Lanka before the nationalist Rajapaksas were voted out of office in January 2015.

Jotika had lectured as one of the main speakers at the national Ma Ba Tha conference held in Yangon during the early summer of 2015. He says his speech had been intended to aid in decreasing tensions within the sangha regarding views on Islam. When recounting his experience, he says, "Ma Ba Tha should be regarded as a refuge for people of every religious tradition, not just Buddhists. Lord Buddha is a refuge for all human beings! His *metta* [loving-kindness] spreads everywhere. Every citizen of Burma should rely on this group." But he did not attend the next year (2016) because he learned that most of the monks at the Ma Ba Tha conference had not liked his talk after all.

As I mentioned earlier, in the summer of 2016, the state's monastic supervisory commission, popularly known as Ma Ha Na, made a public statement that the Ma Ba Tha was not to be regarded as a sanctioned unit of the Burmese sangha. This was the first of the broadsides that the movement would suffer during the ensuing year. In the **summer of 2016**, I ask Jotika if he thinks that the Ma Ha Na's statement was a harbinger of the Ma Ba Tha's future. He says, "Ma Ba Tha is now down a little because of the Ma Ha Na's statement regarding its status. Myanmar people, at least the wise, educated people, do not want to support Ma Ba Tha's actions. It is really a question of education. We have problems with the ineffectual Myanmar education system. Uneducated people tend to be nationalist. Educated people disdain nationalism. During the First and Second World Wars, nationalism arose. Hitler and the Khmer Rouge are products of nationalism gone awry. 'My country! My nation!'" Jotika is pounding his chest. I recall for him how during the Vietnam War we had many people responding to protesters in America with the slogan "My country right or wrong." He nods in agreement with the example and says, "This is against the Buddha's teaching. Educated monks know this and therefore do not subscribe to nationalism." He goes on to say that "this year I did not attend Ma Ba Tha's annual meeting because last year, they did not like my presentation. The leaders had commented negatively."

I decide to ask him, "What about the graphic disjunction between the progressive 2007 Saffron Revolution and the regressive 2014 Ma Ba Tha? What happened between 2007 and 2014?"

He says, "The leaders of the Ma Ba Tha, including Wirathu, were all in jail at that time. The military government used these monks to help to create the Ma Ba Tha. The hard-liner politician Aung Thaung, a former general, helped to create the Ma Ba Tha by recruiting these jailed monks like Wirathu. He was very close to Than Shwe [the Tatmadaw dictator who preceded Thein Sein], the general who had become the first 'civilian' president back in 2010." Than Shwe had some influence on the Rajapaksa government in Sri Lanka to adopt a military approach to its civil war or ethnic conflict.

I decide to ask Jotika his views regarding the race and religion laws. He responds, "I like how the Christians can marry as they like. But Ma Ba Tha wants Buddhist people to marry only Buddhist people. I dislike that law. That law is not in conformity with the Buddha's teaching and I think that most Buddhist people do not like that law. Buddhist monks should not interfere socially. The Buddhist monk should be concerned with *lokottara* [ultimate] matters."

"What will the new parliament do?" I put forward in open-ended fashion.

"The new parliament seems to have accepted the new laws." He outlines the four laws for me (as earlier). "With regard to the question of having more than one wife, it seems as if the practice, as seen from a study of the Jatakas ["birth stories" about the Buddha in his previous lives], is that many men, including the Buddha, had as many as four wives. So the Buddha never said that one man must marry only one wife. This is what a senior monk has argued. And I agree."

"What about women? Can they have more than one husband?" He laughs. I tell him about the practice of Kandyan polyandry in the sixteenth through eighteenth centuries in upcountry Sri Lanka. His view is that Buddhist monks should not interfere in the mandates of society. He notes again the worry in Sri Lanka about Muslims taking over. I explain the reality of the situation to him, that Muslims are only 9 to 10 percent of the population and that the money from Middle Eastern workers is somewhat conspicuous in raising the proverbial strains of jealousy. I go on to explain the bifurcation of Muslims in Sri Lanka between the traditional forms and the new Wahabi emphases. Jotika expresses worries about birthrates both in Sri Lanka and Myanmar and then goes on to say erroneously that most Muslims in Sri Lanka are Shia. When I correct him, he says that U Ei Win, a famous Muslim leader in Myanmar, had told him so. I stand my ground. I can see that Jotika isn't used to being questioned!

These discussions about the Ma Ba Tha and the four race and religion laws also include comments about U Wirathu and his public leadership. Jotika thinks that Wirathu is very much a creature of Aung Thaung's creation, that perhaps it was Aung Thaung himself who orchestrated Wirathu's early release from prison. He says that Wirathu was originally given twelve years for inciting hatred against Muslims with the publication of a small book, yet he was released after eight years of prison time. Jotika says that Wirathu is in Aung Thaung's "hip pocket." In fact, he refers to Facebook and YouTube postings of them talking in a friendly manner. "Wirathu told me personally that he and Aung Thaung are very close." This would seem to corroborate the government connection with the Buddhist nationalists, he says. Others have told Jotika about this close connection too. "Wirathu doesn't discuss these matters with me because he knows how I disagree with him. I heard from my friends about the relation between Wirathu and Aung Duang."

"Don't you ever communicate with Wirathu?" I ask.

Jotika says he has written to Wirathu telling him that the problem in the Middle East has come about due to extreme views and that he should abandon his own extreme views for the sake of Myanmar's future.

I ask if the government census figures recently released that show the Muslim population of Myanmar at 4.3 percent will affect Wirathu's argument about Muslims taking over. Jotika responds that U Wirathu doesn't believe the census figures. Most people, however, do give credit to the government census figures. Wirathu has been saying that Muslims are now about 20 percent of the population.

"What question would you put to Wirathu if you had a chance to query him publicly?" I inquire. Jotika says that he is eager to meet Wirathu and discuss issues with him publicly. He thinks for a long time about what he would ask and comes up with this: "Is nationalism in conformity with the Buddha's teaching? Do you believe nationalism can make peace among the people?"

Discussion of the Ma Ba Tha and Wirathu often leads to talk about hardliners in general, and sometimes about the extreme positions taken by Rakhine Buddhists. I share some of my brief experiences with Rakhine Buddhists in Sittwe and mention their virulent demonstrations against UN secretary-general Ban Ki-moon and then, of course, Wirathu's off-color railing against the special UN rapporteur Yanghee Lee.

Jotika then says, "There are some Bengalis in Mandalay and they have no problem. There is no problem here like in Rakhine State. Leaders of Rakhine State see things very narrowly. Sometimes I would like to advise them that problems have emerged because of their narrowness. The previous president, U Thein Sein, constituted a Rakhine State study group to address the outstanding issues, but that group only included Myanmar scholars. It did include Saginah, a famous monk from the 2007 Saffron Revolution who has now disrobed, to find a solution. Now we have the Kofi Annan Commission. Rakhine State leaders are against both of these commissions. They say they do not trust foreigners. Rakhine State leaders are very difficult. Now Myanmar people are beginning to see that the Rakhine leaders are very bad. They are not scholars." I mention that the emergence of the Arakan Army insurgency is further complicating the situation. They do not accept Aung San Suu Kyii either. "The basic problem is their leaders," he responds. I mention their separatist aspirations. Jotika says, "Yes, they have always hated Burma." Then I mention the legacy of the Mahamuni image. He laughs at this and says, "Yes, that's what started the problem!"

Jotika hasn't been to Rakhine yet. I encourage him to think about that possibility. I give him the contact information for U Kyaw Hla Aung in the hope that he will get together with him in a visit to the IDP camp outside of Sittwe. I encouraged U Kumara (3: "The Rector") at Sitagu's International Buddhist Academy to do the same. I gave both of them a copy of my book *Buddhist Extremists and Muslim Minorities: Religious Conflict in Contemporary Sri Lanka* (Holt 2016), and I sent both of them copies of the UN report compiled from interviews with more than 220 Rohingya refugees of the seventy-five thousand who fled to Bangladesh following the Myanmar army's post–October 9, 2016 "search-and-clear operations" in Maungdaw (OHCHR 2017).

Even a progressive Buddhist monk like Jotika has a particular take on the Rohingya that critical Westerner observers like me take issue with. When talking with Jotika about the Rohingya issue, I became ever more aware of just how biased the government and Myanmar media have been in representing the facts. A lot of my reading beyond scholarly books and articles had been done online from the *Irrawaddy, Frontier,* and *Myanmar Now* websites, which are not representative of mainline perspectives. It is impossible not to be affected by the constant misinformation disseminated about the situation on the ground out in Arakan. This only compounds the sense of hopelessness for the plight of the Rohingya as a community.

Jotika tells me that he has talked with high-level officials who point out that Rohingya in their diaspora have committed crimes all over the world. "If we accept the term 'Rohingya,' then we'd be responsible for all of the crimes that these people have committed. So it's a practical and a philosophical argument to refer to them as Bengalis." I push back at this, saying that the Rohingya are not Bengalis in the sense of being former citizens of Bangladesh. Bangladesh was founded only in 1971 and East Pakistan in 1948. Many of the people we are referring to have been, in large measure, a community within Myanmar, specifically Arakan, well before those times. Besides, I say, the Rohingya speak a language that is somewhat different from the Bengalis, different from the Chittagong dialect. Jotika makes no response. I'm not sure he is listening to me at this point. He then tries another tack and suggests that Rohingya should just give up attachment to the term. He repeats that a government official told him that a lot of Rohingya in the international scene have committed so many crimes that by recognizing this group as a coherent community, the Myanmar government would become responsible for all those crimes that have been committed!

In a later discussion that took place in the **summer of 2017**, Jotika asserts to me that "all violence comes from their teaching in the Qur'an." He points out that the president of Belgium has declared that all of this violence comes from this one book. So I ask, "Have you read the Qur'an?" He says, "A little bit in Sri Lanka when I was studying a course on Buddhism and other religions." Seeing my facial reaction, he hastens to add that he sees no problem with the Muslims in Mandalay who have disavowed ISIS, al-Qaeda, and the Taliban.

Jotika floats an idea in the **summer of 2016** in which he mentions sharing the 1 million Rohingya of Arakan throughout the country. He refers to an article he wrote to this extent, and gets up to retrieve it. It's in Bamar. I tell him that his idea to distribute the Rohingya population throughout the rest of the country would be very popular among the Rakhine Buddhists in Arakan—he could run for chief minister there on that platform! I push him further on the issue of the hopelessness that has now assailed the Rohingya community. But he feels that the situation will work itself out. He says, "Aung San Suu Kyii will check all the people according to the 1982 law. I want them all to participate with the government in this process. It's a beginning at least. The government doesn't want to reject all Muslims, but will accept them on a step-by-step basis. I would advise them to engage the Aung San Suu Kyii government." I mention Abu Tahay's historical argument in relation to the 1982 law. But Jotika says history is not important right now. What's important is to start communicating. "One day, definitely all will be accepted: first white card, then blue card [*sic*], then green card. I've heard that the present government will try to accept all but will try to keep others from coming anew from Bangladesh." He says he heard this news recently. "I would advise them to tell their people to please participate in the verification process." I ask if he thinks the Tatmadaw will agree to this. "The army wants to protect the border from more Bangladeshi Muslims coming. They will also accept the Bengali Muslims within Rakhine State on a step-by-step basis. Some Muslims have already accepted the 1982 law."

As much as I am fond of Jotika, he seems not to be aware of the realities on the ground in Arakan. The UN report concluded that the Myanmar army was using killing, rape, and torture as means to cause trauma among the Rohingya, as methods for getting them to leave Arakan. Jotika believes that the NLD will definitely win the upcoming election and it will ameliorate the situation for all minority peoples. In **January 2017**, I tell him that I have been speaking with Rohingya recently and that they say the situation for them has gotten worse under the NLD government. All of them expressed the feeling of hopelessness. And they feared that with hopelessness, the Buddhist fear of an insurgency would become a self-fulfilling prophecy. I got that sense even more powerfully from both Abu Tahay (1: "The Historian") and U Kyaw Min (1: "The Elder Statesman") six months later. But a person as good as Jotika still believes that the Rohingya broadcast fake news that the American and European media uncritically imbibe. He points out that the UN was so severely chastised by government spokesmen, as a source, they simply are not believed by most Myanmar people. Even Aung San Suu Kyii appeared to believe what her army chiefs and internal fact finders were telling her about the situation out in Arakan post–October 9, 2016, rather than what the UN and international NGOs have claimed.

For Jotika, the Oslo conference sponsored in part by the Norwegian Nobel Institute during which he received an award from the Parliament of the World's Religions was a pro-Rohingya exercise. When he says this, I ask him if he felt used. In fact, he says he wondered how they would use the granting of awards to these monks for their purposes. Jotika is not clearly distinguishing between the organizers of the conference (Norwegians, Norwegian Nobel Institute, Parliament of the World's Religions on the one hand, and Rohingya on the other). At one point, he says he objected to the use of the term "genocide," saying that he had not seen this happening in his many years of being a monk in Burma. I offer that Jotika has never been to Arakan, nor have many progressive Buddhist monks. Wirathu himself only began to visit this past year when he made a scene of distributing rice and goods to destitute Rakhine. I ask Jotika if the term "apartheid" was discussed at the Oslo conference, but he doesn't remember the term being introduced. Does this seem to describe the situation in Rakhine State? I ask him. He thinks for a moment and says yes.

Jotika is not about to simply accept my word about the condition of the Rohingya. He says that *New Light of Myanmar,* the government newspaper, has reported that the Rohingya received more aid from the international community than they need (and refers to photos he has seen of piles of goods being sold in the market). This is in response to my statement about how poor the Rohingya are. Government officials report that schools are provided for Rohingya but that they don't attend and that last year a female teacher was raped by Muslims out in Arakan. I say, "Are you aware that the army now has stopped all educational activities in the IDP camps because they believe (wrongly) that the youth are being indoctrinated into 'radical Islam'?"

I tell him that the previous week (in February 2017) I visited with U Kyaw Hla Aung, the seventy-eight-year-old lawyer and spokesperson for the Rohingya in the IDP camp outside of Sittwe (2: "The Spokesman"). I explain how he was a government servant for twenty-four years and had always been a citizen. Why insist on asking him to use the self-reference "Bengali" when he has never regarded himself as such? His grandparents were born in Arakan.

I continue by saying briefly that one of the basic problems seems to be that there is a dearth of fundamental factual information available to the public. Jotika gets up and begins rummaging through a file, then comes back with a page of statistics that includes the following: Rakhine State has Muslims numbering 944,837 (28.6 percent), Christians 12,752; Hindus 5,245, Buddhist 2,303,348 (69.8 percent). The total population is 3,299,182. These figures had been put out by Ma Ba Tha in 2014 and had been taken from different government departments. They are significant because one commonly hears among the Rakhine Buddhists that they are being overrun. In fact, according to these figures, there are two and half times the number of Rakhine Buddhists than there are Rohingya in Rakhine State.

Jotika seems to be reading my mind and says, "According to my view, regarding the Rohingya in Rakhine State, I would accept them all. Other people are afraid to accept them. If we accept the Rohingya, not many more Rohingya would come to Myanmar. If we accept them as 'Bengali,' then we have to face the possibility of that huge population in Bangladesh having a foothold. By accepting Rohingya, there is a separate identity from Bengalis."

Though Jotika acts benevolently when he ponders the collective plight of the Rohingya in Arakan, I find his view of Islam surprisingly innocent. It is indicative of the normative perspectives found among Burmese Buddhists throughout Myanmar. In his interview with Yogi Nanda Mala, he offered this:

> Among today's [world] religions, Islam is the last religion to be founded. Different from the other three main religions, Islam takes some ideas from Judaism. Islam has been described as a religion that discriminates against women. To make Islam distinct from the other three main religions, the styles of men, women, meals, the Sabbath, good deeds, and bad deeds are made different from others. When Islam was being founded, it was not started by gentleness. It's the kind of religion that waged war and recruited by means of killing everybody who didn't accept Islam. That is why nearly all extremist organizations nowadays have come out from Islam. Today, although the world doesn't hate the Islamic people, it despises the fundamentalism and extremism of Islam. [In other words,] Islam is now being punished by its own ideologies of narrow-mindedness, bigotry, and extremism. Buddhist monks in Burma should preach to the Muslims who grow up here to eliminate their bigotry and discrimination [against others]. You can't just

> counterdiscriminate against them by saying Islamists here are same as those outside of Burma. You must teach unity, integration, and harmony only. If you act like them [extremists] you would simply become one of them. The majority must be magnanimous. Like I said previously, Buddhist monks should not only be refuges for one particular religious or racial group. If you love Burma, you must be a refuge for the whole nation.

Jotika's statement reveals what might be regarded internally as a compassionate stance. But in fact it is skewed by persistent stereotypes and articulates a perspective that might allow for the presence of Muslims, but only as a result of the magnanimous generosity of Buddhists. Nowhere does it appear that Muslims would have an intrinsic right to live where they have been born and raised and where their ancestors have trod.

I press him again on his views of Islam in **August 2017** but do not get very far. He thinks that a lot of the Rohingya news is exaggerated. He cites the photo of the Cambodian child (also mentioned by other interlocutors, e.g., 1: "The Commentator") and goes on to talk about how dogmatic the Muslims are—how only their religion is correct. So wherever the Muslims are, they are against other people: in the Philippines, southern Thailand, Myanmar, Pakistan/India/Kashmir. Immigrants in Europe have become a problem in Germany, France, and Britain. "Where there is Islam, there is a problem. Where there is no Islam, there is no problem. They don't seem to know how to cultivate harmony with other people."

I ask him then about differences in play now that the NLD has come to power. He recalls telling me the previous summer that "things were going to get better. It is. Some people want quicker changes, but the government can't effect changes quickly because senior officers coming from the previous government are consciously blocking change. The new government doesn't have the expert staff to implement its new ideas yet. There is a need to grow a new political culture to replace the old. Most of the people really support Aung San Suu Kyii and believe that she can gradually, through her cleverness, effect change."

"The NLD government brought great hope in terms of the economy, art, education, et cetera, but it has not turned out as people hoped." I ask, "Why was the USDP successful economically and the NLD not?"

He responds by saying he's not sure but there was a lot cronyism under USDP and the Tatmadaw. "The cronies have stopped their activities. Their money is not being invested in development. Yet foreign investment has doubled in the past year. It has been stable domestically despite this economic slowdown." He goes on to add that he thinks that the NLD will prepare a new constitution when they feel it is the right time.

I ask Jotika if he thinks it is fair of the NLD to have excluded Muslims (like his friends Abu Tahay and Kyaw Min) from running for parliament in the November 2015 elections. He mentions how the previous government would not even allow Abu Tahay to travel all over Myanmar, despite the fact that it allowed him to travel to Norway. He says that the NLD can win the next election as well because most people would continue to support them, including most Myanmar monks. The previous government tried hard to get the vote from the monks and poor people. In any case, he thinks that maybe the NLD will allow Muslims to run for parliament next time. "U Win Te, an important NLD leader, had declared that this is not the time for Muslim candidates, even though they have abilities. According to the current situation, we could not select any Muslims. But next time, maybe next time we can have Muslims and other ethnic minorities as well. Most Bamar people would not like Muslims to be in the cabinet or head of a ministry, though, because they are afraid that Myanmar would become like the Middle East."

With this, I ask if he follows American politics and he nods yes. I ask him if would be fair to say that Donald Trump might win in Myanmar. He laughs and says, "As of now, probably. This is because of the shared anti-Muslim sentiment."

During my first visit with Jotika back in the **summer of 2015**, he suggested that I meet a monk from Meiktila, U Wisuddha, at his Yadana Oo Monastery. Wisuddha had accompanied Jotika to Oslo and was one of three Burmese Buddhist monks given World Harmony Awards on that occasion. Jotika was one of the others. This particular monk had actually protected a thousand Muslims from attacks by a Buddhist mob in June of 2013 when tensions between Buddhists and Muslims seemed to have reached an apex. These were not Rohingya Muslims under attack, but Muslims from central Myanmar who had been part and parcel of the local society for centuries. Jotika happily called his colleague and provided an introduction for me. I was expected in Meiktila in two days' time! In the meantime, I hustled up a driver, car, and translator and two days later eagerly made the two-hour trip down to Meiktila, known more historically for its strategic location of military importance during World War II, and still a town with strong military affinities, owing to nearby bases. It is also one of the most conservative regions of Myanmar. Perhaps because of its military leanings, it voted for USDP candidates, who decisively defeated the NLD competition in the November 2015 national elections.

The translator and I meet the monk following his eleven thirty lunchtime. His temple is modest by any standards. There are, in fact, no significant grand meditation or sermon halls or image houses. It does not seem to be a thriving venue. There are only four monks residing at the temple. I introduce myself briefly through the interpreter and quickly add my congratulations for the Parliament of the World's Religions award. I mention that I was also in Oslo one week before him, giving talks at the Peace Research Institute Oslo and the University of Oslo. I say that in the midst of hearing about ongoing interreligious mayhem that was occurring in Myanmar, reading about his decisive action to protect these Muslim lives was an inspiration to many people. I say that I am very honored to meet him. He replies by saying that he's happy that he had the opportunity to show the kindness of the Buddha to the world! He says that he attended another conference in February sponsored by the Sri Lanka Foundation and that he was very pleased to meet many monks there who shared a kindred spirit with him. I ask him if he is aware of the Yogyakarta Resolution made public in the summer of 2015 in which twenty-six representatives from the Buddhist, Muslim, Christian, and Hindu traditions pledged to work for inter-communal peace in their countries of origin. He has not heard of this but he definitely welcomes hearing about it and heartily approves of its intention.

I quickly made an observation that leads to my first question. His temple is located on the outskirts of town. Did the Muslims flee specifically to his temple for help? Were they on the run? We are three and half kilometers from the downtown Meiktila area that was destroyed in the rioting. About forty people officially are said to have been killed in the riot, though the BBC has said possibly as many as eighty. He begins his response by saying, "This monastery was established after 1990. Twenty-five years before 1990, I had lived in the downtown area where the recent riots occurred. In the downtown area, I had spent twenty-seven years and so I know many people there. When the riots occurred, because of my connections downtown, these people came to this monastery looking for safety. Since we had spent so much time together, these Muslims understand me and I them. We are friends and because the monastery exists on the outskirts of the city, it would be difficult for the mob to come out here. They had not been followed yet. This was the situation on the first day of the riots. But by the second day, the riots had spread to this area as well. Since the Muslims had always come here, they had contacted their friends in other areas of Meiktila and told them to come here as well. The number increased to about eight hundred to nine hundred. There were other monasteries doing the same thing for fewer people (they did this quietly so they wouldn't be called 'betrayers,' but I didn't do it quietly and people knew my disposition, so the number eventually climbed to over one thousand). There were also Buddhist households who protected Muslim friends. The reason I became well known is that I was open about what I did."

I point out that there is a police station just a hundred meters or so away. "Were the police entirely passive as this situation unfolded?" He says, "In Burma if they don't have orders from above, they don't do anything." This is clearly his way of saying that the authorities in the region were colluding with the violence.

For how long and for how many did he provide protection? (The whole scene as he describes it reminds me of 1983 riots in Sri Lanka, when people were seeking shelter desperately in the midst of chaos instigated by outsiders.) "Riots occurred on March 20. Around one thirty in the morning, some Buddhists came to the temple looking for the Muslims involved in the alleged murder of a Buddhist monk. I told them that if they were going to take these Muslims, then they'd have to kill me as well." (These people, who were troublemakers, had come to the monastery for the Muslim suspects.)

How did he manage to feed so many people? "The rest of the Buddhist population in the neighborhood provided for us and provided protection as well as food. The Muslims stayed for four days.

"The nature of relations between Muslims and Buddhists in Meiktila has always been good and it's just been this one section of Buddhists who created the problem. People are interrelated by marriage in this town; some have converted across traditions.

"The troublemakers actually moved on to other areas and created problems there once they realized I would not let them get at the Muslims. I do not have hard evidence, but I think that these troublemakers were from the military. I heard the news later that there were about forty people who instigated the riots using four light trucks and that they spread the riots in other places too, rather systematically. The people who are supposed to uphold the law were breaking the law. In short, they [the Buddhist nationalists] are the opposite of what Buddhism is about. Buddha's *dhamma* [teaching] is about *metta* [loving-kindness], but they are the opposite.

"The Muslim refugees left only because there were just four toilets here."

I ask him, "What is your view about how relations between Buddhists and Muslims may change as a consequence of the upcoming national elections?"

He replies, "A set of time bombs (political, economic, and social) have been set by the military-dominated government, so that when things go chaotic they will institute a coup d'état to take over again. So I'm doing my best to protect the local situation from going chaotic."

I continue to probe, as I had come to realize that I had only about two hours to spend with this monk. "Do you think the power of the Ma Ba Tha will increase or abate in the near future?"

He says, "Actions have their own consequences! To begin, Ma Ba Tha was a good idea, but now they've been coopted by the government by protecting only the Burmese. Racial preservation leads to segregation among the religions. It's kind of absurd for monks to be proposing these laws. This is going to lead to segregation among the people. As long as the law operates as it does in Myanmar, there's not going to be justice or even a fair application of what already exists as law."

I had heard that Wirathu was actually present in Meiktila when the riots occurred. I ask U Wisuddha if he has had any contact or communication with Wirathu since the event. He says, "I've had no direct contact with Wirathu. But Jotika does and since we are part of the peace-building group, we let the militant monks in the Ma Ba Tha know what our views are about. Jotika attends Ma Ba Tha so they know our opinions. Jotika is building a peace college that will have an international presence with monks from other countries. There is no hatred between us and the militant monks, but we have a different agenda. We look forward to peace among humanity, but Ma Ba Tha has its own agenda."

I ask, "Who will outlast the other?"

He replies, "Precious gems are always outnumbered by useless stones, in the same way that good drinking water is becoming ever so precious."

December 2017. I have some trepidation about meeting Jotika this time, as well as his friend U Kumara. Mandalay is my last stop on this trip to Myanmar, and it may be my last time around in the country, period. In our previous meeting, he indicated his unwavering support for Aung Sa Suu Kyii, and I fear that now that she has been so robustly criticized, he may not be so open to discussing matters "on a level playing field" with me. I am also thinking about how my Australian journalist acquaintance, Sean Gleeson, who was a digital editor for *Frontier,* had said that a "sea change" had occurred since we met the previous summer. "Perspectives have really hardened, boundaries have risen higher, sentiments have sharpened." Yet, I have some hope that the tension I have felt in Yangon will not be present in Mandalay and that my conversations with these two leading monks, progressive in so many ways, will be fruitful and cordial. I am hoping that the most difficult part of my visit emotionally is past and that perhaps I will hear some wisdom from these two venerable Buddhist monks.

This time when I arrive at the still-under-construction University of Global Peace at the base of Yankin Hill, Jotika is not ready for me and I need to search for him amid the huge construction project. After ten minutes or so, I spot him and he warmly welcomes me as usual. He takes my arm genially and we make our way back to his expansive personal quarters and sit down on plastic chairs opposite each other. We exchange affirmations of our friendship. He offers me three different types of libation, two of which are energy drinks. This afternoon, he says he will be seeing a group of Korean Baptist Christians "about making peace." I ask him how he will do this. He says, "They want to come here to study Buddhist, Christian, and Muslim scriptures in detail. They told me that even though every religion wants peace, war is the consequence of people fighting in the name of religion. I also believe that 80 percent of the conflicts leading to war are due to nationalism, from clinging to religion. So we want to undertake an analysis of all of the teachings of the religions. At the opening of this university, we will undertake an analysis of every religion and they will send some of their own people for this purpose." In my own mind, I am feeling pretty skeptical about how constructive it would be for Jotika to have evangelical Korean Baptists at his university from the start. I can only imagine the confusion that will result by adding this mix of fundamentalist Christians.

"When are you hoping to open?" I ask.

"November–December 2018." He says rather proudly, "I will invite Aung San Suu Kyii for this occasion. I want to find a free date for her time during that time." I ponder whether or not this is a possible segue into a difficult discussion and decided to take the dive.

"What do you think of the international criticism of Aung San Suu Kyii these days?"

"Most of the Myanmar people think that the international media has been misled about the current situation. Aung San Suu Kyii is really a very good person and Myanmar people like her. Especially the American media has been very, very bad. Because America does not support us, now we believe in Russia and China." I tell him that I think that the US and European diplomats have actually been very soft on Aung San Suu Kyii because they don't want to lose the little bit of democracy that has been achieved so far.

Jotika believes that the OIC (Organization of Islamic Cooperation) is behind the UN moves being made to bring Myanmar to book. "Why do you think that?" I ask.

"Because most of the UN countries are Islamic." I try to correct him by saying that the OIC is comprised of 57 countries and that the UN is made up of 193. He thanks me for correcting him but continues with this: "The Buddhist areas of this country are peaceful, and only the Muslim areas are experiencing violence."

"But who's responsible for the violence?" I respond.

He says, "The UN doesn't seem to understand that the Bengalis started this violence. It is difficult for us to believe the United Nations. Aung San Suu Kyii has tried hard to get peace in Rakhine State in many ways, chiefly through economic and political development, but the UN does not talk about that, nor do they report about the Muslim attacks that occurred in August." He says that Aung San Suu Kyii is following the Kofi Anan Commission's recommendations. I tell him that the UN also supports the recommendations of the Kofi Annan Commission and that in almost every summary description of how the situation in Arakan has devolved, the ARSA (Arakan Rohingya Salvation Army) attacks of August 25 are referenced. At this point, I don't dare advance the theory put forward by Abu Tahay, the person who first put me in contact with Jotika, and seconded by Kyaw Min, that the army was really involved in orchestrating these attacks. I do say, however, that while the Rohingya, the UN, the United States, and Aung San Suu Kyii have accepted the recommendations of the Kofi Anan Commission, it was the army leader, Min Aung Hlaing, who publicly said that the commission had not understood the history of Arakan properly, meaning that the Rohingya were essentially recent interlopers and invaders usurping Rakhine land.

"Myanmar people are very disappointed in foreign media," he says emphatically. He asserts that Myanmar allows people to be free religiously. "OIC people do not like other religions to be practiced in their countries. They always attack other religious people in their countries." I tell him about the Muslims in Thailand who say they are free to be Muslim however they want. He says that human rights groups never criticize the Muslims, especially sharia law, that Islamic law is the opposite of human rights. I point out that human rights group do, in fact, criticize Muslim nations or movements very often. ISIS, the Taliban, and al-Qaeda are examples of groups that have been heavily criticized, and military action has been undertaken against these militant groups in part because of their oppressive impositions of what they construe to be sharia law. I can tell he feels a bit surprised at my reaction and even a bit chastened because my examples are so obviously the case. I get the feeling that he has been part of discussions where a lot of unwarranted ranting has taken place, and I feel very disappointed at the lack of critical thought now so apparent in what he has to say, an absence of what I have observed in previous conversations.

I find myself getting a bit agitated, and I persist rather than giving up. "Some Westerners would like to know why Myanmar people do not believe what has happened in Rakhine State." As I say this I realize that for him this is a really loaded question because it is clear that in his own mind nothing very untoward has happened in Arakan. He says that the United States, in the UN context, has slandered Myanmar. "Aung San Suu Kyii had tried hard to cooperate with the army, but the American government wants to differentiate the army from the people." I press the question again because I really want to know if he wholeheartedly believes that no violence has occurred in Rakhine. Again, he begins off the point: "Myanmar people like what Aung San Suu Kyii has done in working for peace with the Kofi Annan Commission. We don't believe the on-the-ground news being reported by the Western media. Bengalis are leaving because their husbands participated in the fighting; they have left without facing any real problems." I ask how he knows this, and he says, "The Myanmar media, TV and newspaper, have reported this. Even the Rakhine government has asked them not to leave. They don't listen and want to emigrate. Family in Bangladesh have asked them to go to Bangladesh. At that time, there was no problem with the army. Now people are leaving because of the army. Aung San Suu Kyii wants to bring the army and the people together!" At this point I am so exasperated that I write in my notes that Jotika seems brainwashed by the lies that the army and government have fed through their sycophantic press corps! I don't like writing this down, but I have to find a way to release some frustration.

I recover my inward composure and ask in a genuine-sounding way, "Why would the Western media report what is not true? What is their interest in doing so?"

His answer is very simple and straight to the point: "They are dependent on Islamic state news."

We are not done yet. Jotika is also starting to get worked up, and I am determined to respond forthrightly to what I know to be untrue. I am a bit torn in doing this because I do not want to provoke him and I remember that my primary aim here is to give voice to his perspective. I realize more and more how I have become invested in this conflict. I bite my tongue when he says that "Myanmar people think that international NGOs have supplied the terrorist insurgency. Also, they only support the Muslim people and not the Rakhine Buddhists."

I counter with: "Why do they think that?"

He answers, "We look at the Myanmar newspaper so we all know. By reading our own Burmese newspapers, we know that the wrong news is being reported by the international media." I say to myself that with all I have heard earlier from Jotika about nationalism, that he now seems to be smitten by the same disease. His phone rings and supplies a break to a conversation that is headed nowhere productively, it seems. What is apparent to me is that Jotika has been radicalized by the events of the past four months. He no longer is critical of the army and has closed ranks with the dominant majority opinion among the Burmese. He feels aggrieved by American diplomacy and UN efforts at accountability. I decide to shift the conversation toward the controversial sermon that Sitagu recently delivered to an all-army audience in which he invoked the saga of Dutthagamini from the *Mahavamsa*.

When Jotika gets off the phone, I mention Sitagu's telling of the story and summarize it briefly to refresh his memory. Jotika says that the meaning of the story is that the monks are forgiving the king of his sins. I respond by saying that maybe the story has that meaning, but it is also frequently enlisted by nationalists in Sri Lanka to legitimate violence against Tamil people. By telling the king that only one and half persons have been slain, the *arahants* (arhats; perfected practitioners) are actually saying that the Tamils are less than human. Often in the *Mahavamsa*, the Tamils are referred to as *yakkhas* (demons) rather than humans. The story is a way of illustrating the adage that the "country exists for the sake of the religion." I say to Jotika that this is the motto of Sinhala nationalists. I choose to frame it that way not only because that is indeed the case, but also because Jotika has been such an inveterate enemy of nationalism in the past that I want to drive home that point about Sitagu as powerfully as I can.

Jotika then responds by saying, "I don't agree with what Sitagu has said here. In this situation, we should 'broadcast life.'" By this he means to say that we should not belittle death.

Jotika takes another phone call and says he has to go. Usually he has given me at least two hours of his time. But this time it is a little more than one and I'm beginning to feel as if he wants to escape from me. But he invites me for lunch. I can't stay. I suggest meeting in two days' time, but he has a ceremony to attend then. We agree that I will come the next day at eight a.m. I am simultaneously grateful that I have not alienated him completely and very disappointed at what the sea change seems to have done to his perceptions about the troubles in Myanmar.

Our first day of conversation this time around in **December 2017** was quite rocky. I fretted about how the conversation would go on the second day. He had asked me to come at eight a.m. following his class in Chinese, which began at seven a.m. I was determined to stay even-minded while also trying not to put him on the defensive. I did not want our conversation to end in acrimony.

I let him begin the conversation after pleasantries. I can tell he was also a bit troubled by our sharp exchanges of the day before. He begins by saying that the Italian prime minister had come to Myanmar and at a press conference had explained that Western countries want Aung San Suu Kyii to do what they want. But she is doing what she thinks is best to get peace for the Myanmar people. I think he says this in order to let me know that he realizes that all Westerners do not have a bad opinion of Aung Sa Suu Kyii.

He follows this by saying that the Myanmar people like Aung San Suu Kyii because she is working for reconciliation between the army and the people. I ask if that effort is working. He responds that gradually people are reconciling to the army now and goes on to mention that the USDP, the party of the previous government, does not want to see this reconciliation. They prefer to keep the army separate from the people. I am a bit puzzled by this since the USDP is the party of the military. Jotika explains that the USDP needs to keep the army separate from the NLD party because it could never ascend again if the NLD is close to the army. There would be no need for them, as they function as the political surrogate of the army. The NLD is usurping their place if it reconciles with the army. He points out that in this effort Aung San Suu Kyii still has the great support of the people. I say that Sitagu has also said in sermons that he would like to see a united country with the sangha, the army, and the people as one. What does Jotika think about this?

"Aung San Suu Kyii is trying to do this. Now the USDP has its own newspaper, which is critical of the NLD for being sympathetic to Islam and biased in favor of other religions, and a party that doesn't really practice Buddhism. But people don't believe them." I tell him that some critics of Sitagu and presumably of Aung Sa Suu Kyii fear an alliance of this sort, as it resembles something like Iran. He takes this to mean an understanding indicative of the position of the Ma Ba Tha. "Not all of the sangha is Ma Ba Tha oriented. Most scholarly monks in the sangha don't like the Ma Ba Tha. If the USDP and the Ma Ba Tha were ascendant and combined with the army, then we would have a different situation, one similar to Iran. But they do not want to reconcile the people with the army." I don't want to pursue the dangers of this with him at the moment because I know where it will lead. It seems to me that Khin Zaw Win (1: "The Activist") was right when he said that the army and the NLD want the people to basically believe their version of what has happened out in Rakhine. By reconciling the people with the army, any possible critical opposition would be thwarted.

I ask Jotika, "What kind of constitution would you like to see formulated here in Myanmar?" I explain how there are two types of secular constitutions that could be models. The American version is the one that sees the government with a hands-off policy on religion, trying to avoid establishing religion or advocating religion of any kind to the people. The other model is the Indian approach, which encourages the state to support all religious traditions. Then I contrast these two with the Sri Lankan constitution, which is schizophrenic in that its Article 9 declares all people are free to pursue their own choice of religion, but that Buddhism is given a special status of state support. Jotika has been to South Korea recently, where he learned about how there were pressures from either American companies or companies with strong American ties to convert to Christianity. So he wonders if the American model is really so "hands-off." I tell him that it is true that the situation is not completely hands-off, that some Americans really believe that America is a Christian country and that the government courts have to continuously assert that that the constitution does not advocate or support any particular religious orientation, and that the law does not infringe upon people's freedom to be religious as well. It has become something of a difficult balance to achieve. He seems to think that Buddhism will have to be given some special attention and he worries about Christian missionaries invading the country, particularly the rural areas like Chin State.

He mentions that he has an interfaith meeting that day with Christian priests and pastors, Muslim imams, and Hindu priests. I ask, "What do you talk about during these interfaith meetings?"

"We talk about what is in our scriptures. We choose a topic every month. Today we will talk about the end of time." I ask if he will speak about Metteyya. He says, "Yes! I talk about the decline in time and how it is dependent on morality." I ask if he will cite the *Agganna Sutta* and his face lights up. "Yes, that's the basis for my comments." I learn that their conversations will take place in Bamar.

He asks if I can come to the opening of his university and speak a bit about the importance of peace in the teachings of the world's religions. I say I'm not sure when I might come to Myanmar again. He then asks if I can be an adviser to PhD students. His idea "is to teach a six-month course on how to do research, how to select a topic of study. The nature of these dissertations will stress how to make peace for the people. These dissertations also will involve comparison. How to preach *dhamma* that results in peace." Our conversation then moves on to a brief discussion about the function of comparison in terms of identifying similarities and differences. While he has thought a lot about similarities, I respond by saying that I think understanding difference is the key to generating respect between different types of religious people, and between people who are religious and those who are not.

We've ended on a constructive note. Later, Jotika would e-mail me asking when I can come to Myanmar again, that he hasn't forgotten our conversations, and that he hopes that we can experience peace in our lifetimes. I hope so too.

The Rector

Sitagu Sayadaw has also become something of an icon among many Burmese Buddhists in Myanmar. With the possible exception of U Wirathu, who is more well known, as much for his notoriety as for his piety, it is difficult to imagine a monk whose public profile is as ascendant as Sitagu's. His Sitagu International Buddhist Academy, begun in the early 1990s, is now flourishing. Located in the beautiful Sagaing Hills amid scores of other monasteries, nunneries, and meditation centers, it is the flagship site among his growing international network of religious institutions. There are two other branches of his academy, in Mandalay and Yangon, and three centers of study for the understanding of Theravada Buddhist thought and practice, in Texas, Minnesota, and Florida. There is a missionary zeal to his enterprise and a global vision. For Sitagu, Buddhism is the answer to the world's complex problems.

It is something of an understatement to say that Ven. Sitagu maintains a high public profile. His followers are legion. Photos of the charismatic monk with Aung San Suu Kyii on the one hand, and the radical nationalist Ashin Wirathu on the other, are not difficult to locate. He has sponsored at least two international conferences since the serious conflicts between Buddhists and Muslims broke out in 2012. Immediately following the first conference, held in Yangon in October 2012, Sitagu and a leading Muslim imam jointly visited Thandwe, trying to encourage Rakhine Buddhists and Kaman Muslims to begin a process of healing in the aftermath of the Rakhine attacks on Muslims and their homes in 2013. Sitagu is seen as a great promoter of the Buddha's *dhamma,* a *dhamma* that he understands as a panacea for all types of social woes. In January 2017, he delivered a sermon publicly in which he urged the Myanmar military, the sangha, and the laity to unite to preserve the country. My original hope was to meet Sitagu, since he is regarded by many as the most important or influential, if not the most visible, Buddhist monk in Myanmar. I tried on several occasions to make contact with him through several sources, but to no avail, despite the fact that I had excellent means of introduction at my disposal. But he is an extraordinarily busy religious figure who seems to move relentlessly from one high-profile campaign to another. He was either out of the country or in remote parts of Myanmar whenever I tried to secure an interview. Two of my good friends in the academic world of Buddhist studies speak very highly of his personal warmth and genuine compassion, which they have witnessed in the manner in which he conducts his professional vocation as a monk. Others, whose opinions I have come to respect on a number of other matters, but who do not seem to know

Sitagu personally, see him as a political presence who bends like a reed with the prevailing political winds. Reluctantly, I finally settled for meeting the rector of his international academy in Sagaing, Dr. Ashin Kumara, and in the end, I was very pleased to have made his acquaintance.

I met Kumara four times in 2016 and 2017. He agreed to spend two to three hours with me each time in the privacy of his quarters: a beautiful reception room replete with hardwood floors, lovely floral drapes, oriental rugs, glass chandeliers, recessed carved teak decorative ceilings housing the main chandelier, and wonderfully detailed carved teak doors. In addition, the reception room was adorned with beautiful inlaid wallpaper on the ceiling and walls. Adjoining this splendid and expansive room was a large private bedroom with a wide-screen TV. My description may give a sense of extravagance, and perhaps that is the case, but I think "tasteful décor" is a more respectful description of the rector's accommodations.

Ashin Kumara is a poised, articulate, and thoroughly serious presence. When we first met, he spent his own time slowly sizing me up. I tried to ease into a conversation by asking him questions about the academy and his own research and writing. I had first visited the academy briefly in 2010 and remembered how a photo gallery adjacent to the Sanchi-like stupa in the center of the campus had contained many photos of Sitagu in the presence of important political figures in Myanmar and from abroad. I also remember spotting my friend Myo Myint's presence in some of these photos. Myo Myint had died in 2015, much to my sense of loss. In several of these photos, I was able to ascertain that Myo Myint was functioning as an interpreter for high-level dignitaries meeting with Sitagu. (On another occasion, I spotted Myo Myint in a group that included President Barack Obama during his first visit to Myanmar.) In any case, I had known that the academy was a burgeoning and highly respected institution, so much so that it was often an important stop for visiting foreign dignitaries. There was a fair share of Tatmadaw generals to be seen in some of these photos as well, a phenomenon not uncommon to important temples throughout the country.

Ashin Kumara was born right in Sagaing with five brothers and sisters, just five kilometers away from the academy. "I can visit my family anytime and they can visit me. When I was five years old I went to monastery, studied Bamar and the Buddha's teachings. When I was fourteen, I came to Sagaing Hill and studied. At twenty [in 1988], I took *upasampada* [full ordination]. Two months after ordination was the 1988 uprising. In 1994, I completed my Pali Buddhist education. In 1996, I taught in northern Shan State among the Wa people and other tribes for two years. It was at this time that I was told that I should learn English. But I didn't have a good teacher then. I was advised that I should meet a good monk-teacher to learn English. I met my old teacher here at the Sitagu Academy and he taught me English in a three-year diploma course. I then studied Buddhism in English-medium sources. After three years, I went to Delhi University to study Buddhist philosophy, and there I met many different people from different cultures with different attitudes. I learned a lot outside of the university from the people's daily activities." To illustrate this, he tells a story about how Buddhist monks were not searched at metro security points in Delhi. They were not searched because the authorities "respected" Buddhist monks. "I advised them to search all people in the future because of the chance of impersonation. People should not make judgments simply on the basis of appearance." He completed his PhD at Delhi University in 2010. His doctoral dissertation was entitled: "Analytical Study of *Kamma* in *Patisanthitt* Based on *Abhidhamma* Literature." "In 2011, I came back to Sagaing and I met my master from time to time. Our rector was getting elderly and could not walk much. So I became the acting rector and he sort of just retired. We now have two more campuses, one in Mandalay and one in Yangon. There are between nine hundred and one thousand students altogether. We still need more qualified teachers." He tries to teach his courses in English and he hopes he does so effectively. "They don't understand so much for the first month, but they gradually learn and by the end of the course some of them are fluent."

In response to my questions about the academy, Ashin Kumara begins by telling me that "there are three hundred students at the [home-based] academy. About fourteen are from abroad including nine from India. It is difficult to provide accommodations for all. We have a hostel for about eighty students; thirty more students are accommodated over on the next hill. And all the *thila shin* [nuns] stay outside. *Thila shin* are about fifty percent of the student body."

Like so many scholarly monastic academics in Myanmar, U Kumara is a scholar of the Abhidhamma. He sees it as "a teaching that goes beyond cultural belief." For example, he cites the prohibition of women from getting close to Buddha images, as is the case at the Mahamuni temple in Mandalay, as a practice not advocated in the Abhidhamma. I add, nor is it found in other national Theravada cultural traditions such as in Sri Lanka and Laos. As if to respond to this in a way that would render keeping a distance from women a good idea, especially lay women, he says, "From the Abhidhamma point of view, abstinence from sex is a way to reduce *raga* [passion], *dosa* [hatred], and *moha* [delusion]."

When he has ascertained the central reason for my visit, that is, to discuss with him his views on the Buddhist-Muslim conflicts in Myanmar, he declares, "We believe that the new NLD government can handle the Buddhist-Muslim conflict in Arakan." Four months later, when I meet him in **January of 2017**, after the October 9 attacks and Tatmadaw response, I follow up this statement by asking, "Do you still think that the NLD government is handling the current situation effectively? All three Rohingya leaders (each elected to parliament at various times) that I have interviewed recently have told me that they have now given up hope in the NLD government. They say that their own situations, including the situation in general in the IDP camp outside of Sittwe, is worse now than it was under the previous USDP [Union Solidarity and Development Party] government. In fact, they have pretty much given up all hope in Aung San Suu Kyii. What can they do now?"

I don't think Ashin Kumara is overly thrilled to hear me make that statement and raise that question. In fact, he is still a little uncomfortable with the fact that I use the term "Rohingya." He says, "They [Rohingya] will need to respect the 1982 law or have the law changed. As for Aung San Suu Kyii, she cannot speak loudly now. Whatever she says, action will follow. But she has been mostly silent. I think she will help both [Rakhine Buddhist and Rohingya] communities. There are other communities who are also suffering too. Why do the foreigners only want to help the Bengalis when the Kachin, Chin, Shan, et cetera, are also suffering? Aung San Suu Kyii is going to try to help by providing education and infrastructure for all. If both communities can accept this approach, then both will benefit. The Bengalis have to give up using Islam as an excuse for why they are persecuted. The Rakhines, on their side, need to learn to trust the UN. Both Bengalis and Arakanese have extremists among them and so we are all suffering because of the problems between them. We are ready to help them. I want to help both because they are both human beings. But I cannot help just one side because the other will abuse me. This is actually the Burmese problem in relation to these communities. We have to help both. Education, health, and business are the means of needed development. After twenty years of hard work, the problem will eventually pass."

I respond to this with two comments. The first is that the reason many foreigners are paying more attention to the Rohingya is that it is the Rohingya who have been rounded up and put into camps or who are completely confined to their villages and not allowed to travel outside. Their situation smacks of apartheid. I also mention—and this was before the appearance of the sensational UN report on the extent of violence unleashed by the Myanmar military on the Rohingya after the October 9, 2016, attack on border posts—that there is increasing evidence that many defenseless villagers have been either killed or sexually assaulted by the Myanmar military. This is the kind of news that warrants an international response. The second comment I make is in response to Kumara's optimism about how education and economic development will eventually ameliorate the conditions in Arakan. I mention that with the recent American national elections, in spite of how widespread education is developed in the United States, we have now something like bigotry embedded in our presidency, because around 46 percent of American people who voted simply were not bothered by the racist and misogynist character of candidate Donald Trump. I'd like to think that education is a great answer, and I believe it is imperative too, but I also worry that conditions in Arakan have a very long way to improve before these communities can live together in concord. Kumara responds, simply nodding and saying that "where there are human beings, there are bound to be problems of this kind." I'm afraid that I don't find his response very prosaic, nor does he find mine. Sensing a lack of consensus, he explains further his perspective on the current problem.

"Arakanese complain about how fifty years ago they had so many more religious structures and now the Bengalis have destroyed them." To myself I wonder if he doesn't mean that the Rohingya have lost so many of their mosques over the past fifty years since Ne Win had come to power. "Also, they complain about illegal migration leading to the expansion of the Bengalis. On their side, the Bengalis complain that they have been ignored, but in fact all of Myanmar's governments for the past fifty years have ignored us all!" Kumara then goes on to talk about "how [before] we did not have free speech, all of us. It's absolutely different now. We can criticize. The NLD is very tolerant. Look at Wirathu's criticisms! There is a lot of interreligious dialogue also taking place. Before, those types of meetings [interfaith dialogues] were suspected by the government. I can visit a mosque now with no problem. This highlights the fact that the current problem is basically only in Rakhine State these days." Unfortunately, Kumara made this statement just days before Ma Ba Tha supporters harassed Muslims celebrating Muhammad's birthday in Pyay; before demonstrations led by Ma Ba Tha Buddhist monks in Yangon about the arrival of a boatload of aid from Malaysian Muslims intended for Rohingya in Arakan; and before Ko Ni, a Muslim constitutional lawyer for the NLD, was assassinated inside the new international air terminal in Yangon. I don't mean to be overly critical of Kumara by mentioning these instances. I gather from Kumara that local relations between Buddhists with Muslims in Sagaing are very good. And Kumara, because of his master's (Sitagu's) efforts at interfaith dialogue, wants to remain optimistic because he has seen a lot of goodwill expressed on those occasions. Yet, I also think that there remain some serious issues lurking beneath the surface, especially in central Burma, that could lead to further eruptions of violence between Buddhists and Muslims, and that these eruptions would likely be a result of Buddhist instigations. The military-backed USDP party, with the support of the Ma Ba Tha, actually won the popular vote in the November 2015 election in places like Meiktila, the site of great violence between Burmese Buddhists and Muslims in 2013 (see "Setting the Recent Context: A Résumé of Conflict since 2012" in the introduction and 3: "The Anti-Nationalists").

I am convinced that Ashin Kumara is genuinely concerned about ascertaining the truth of the matter regarding what is now happening in northern Arakan, especially in the aftermath of the October 9 attack on Burmese border guards. He says, "I think we should send different groups each month to Maungdaw and Buthidaung just to find out the truth." I say in response that this might be a good idea because it seems to many, especially outside of the country, that the Tatmadaw's stories about what has happened out there are simply not credible. He agrees that that's a problem and that the army does not want to give up its power. "Some of the soldiers are very ignorant people and not well trained. We need to send only well-trained soldiers to that area. Aung San Suu Kyii is trying to bring the country slowly into a better situation and has to be careful, because if she moves too quickly we'll be under military control again and many educated people will flee this country. We still have to keep silent if we see something askew with the military." Emphasizing the Tatmadaw's continuing hegemony over the current situation, he says, "We have to move in a clever way. We may have the power to remove corruption in the government. We can complain about the parliament. But we still cannot openly complain about the military. They have the weapons. There is some hope that the military top brass is getting the sense of democracy. Aung San Suu Kyii has made it clear to them that there is no return to past ways. And I also think that the army does not want to disturb the welfare of the people."

I turn the conversation to relations between Arakanese and Burmese. I do this first by referring to an encounter I had with two young Arakanese monks I met in Chiang Mai, Thailand, who were studying for their doctorates. Both of them were well versed in English and very articulate about the *dhamma.* But when I raised questions about the Rohingya, as is so often the case with Rakhines, their demeanor immediately darkened. They proceeded to tell me that the Rohingya were really a very dirty people with no sense of hygiene or sanitation, that they bred continuously thereby causing population explosion, that they were almost completely uneducated and thereby untrustworthy, and so on. I then asked them if the problem that they had with Rohingya was more a matter of class than religion. They answered in the affirmative. In response, Kumara talks about how people often live in isolated fashion and that they tend to exaggerate on the basis of limited or no experience. "People like these two young monks need to be invited to work for the welfare of the people. This is more important for young people to engage in—they can play sports, and they can help the refugees. The main purpose is to work together, to understand each other's hearts. We have to respect each other's customs and beliefs, and the country's rules and regulations. Arakanese believe that because the population of Bangladesh is exploding that they will spill over into Arakan, especially since it is very easy to cross over. News about ISIS from CNN and BBC has made them afraid that Muslim extremism will happen there as well. European countries have space for refugees, but our country is poor. It is very difficult for a country like ours to solve a problem like the one facing Bengalis."

Kumara continues by talking about Arakanese monks he met while studying in India. "They do not always accept Burmese monks and feel a special kinship with India instead. Some have migrated to India and have become Indian citizens. Others even assert that Burmese monks have colluded with the Burmese army in order to repress the people of Arakan. In India, there are two groups of monks from Myanmar: (1) monks who are Arakanese, and (2) others who are from the various Buddhist national groups throughout Myanmar. We hear their stories about being the 'real Buddhist descendants.' Most of the time we keep silent when we hear their claims, even though I know in my mind that it is not true, or that there is no solid truth to their claims. So what if the Buddha ever visited Arakan or not?" I mention the myth of the Arakanese descending from the Sakya race and how this establishes a kind of primordial ownership over Arakan for them that makes the Rohingya seem like recent interlopers from their perspective. He nods.

We talk about the great difficulties that will be involved in the development of Arakan. He says that Arakan is a lot like Bihar in India, insofar as it is so difficult to raise up people with low aspirations. He says that there are many instances in which the Bihars have even sabotaged Indian federal attempts at development, implying that the same problem occurs with the Rakhine and Rohingya.

In terms of what can be done practically to defuse the situation in Arakan in the short term, he says, "First we need security, and then the present government should invite good-hearted and well-educated Muslims from Indonesia or Malaysia to help with reestablishing schools, including a medical school. Government should provide the infrastructure to make it possible to transform their lives. Rehabilitation will need to take place for both communities. If we deport Bengalis, it will not be the real solution. The real solution, in the long term, is education and economic development. If we can sustain both, after two or three generations, the whole society will be educated and the problems will be reduced. If we want them to become Buddhist, we have to give them the right understanding about justice. It's okay if they don't convert. We cannot divide among ourselves. The world has become one village. In this world village, the Buddhist population is a minority. So we need to understand our situation is as a minority people in the global village." He goes on to cite the power of the *Metta Sutta* and making the mind without "boundary consciousness." "If there is a border in our minds, we cannot deploy our loving-kindness and it becomes limited. We should stop using these categorical terms only in respect of describing people who do not behave properly. Yes, we are Buddhists and we've been taught not to use intoxicants, et cetera. But there are a lot of drunks and addicts who claim to be Buddhist too. Only behavior is what determines what a person is. Indeed, an educated person who is not kindhearted is a dangerous person."

Kumara says that he has never been to Arakan, but that he would like to take his students with him for a visit. He mentions that he has taken students to the Thai and Chinese borders, and to the Tatmadaw's defense academy. He also took 160 students to the Naypitaw parliament houses, upper and lower. I encourage him to think about taking some of his students to Sittwe and to the IDP camp. I tell him that very few could pull this off but that he is in a rare position to do so, given his academy's and his master's eminence. I give him U Kyaw Hla Aung's personal phone number and tell him that Ven. Jotika is also interested in going to Arakan. Later that night, I send Jotika similar contact details, hoping that these two monks will work together. A lot of perspectives could get impacted, I hope.

The conversation turns again to the personal and the local Sagaing scene. During our first two conversations in the **summer of 2016**, Kumara made the statement that he and his master were certainly not in positions to solve the Buddhist-Muslim problem out in Arakan or nationally. But what they could do practically is work to sustain good relations in their local area. He talks about the goodwill that obtains in Mandalay in general, and how the Buddhist and Muslim leaders averted what could have been a bad riot in July 2014, one he feels was instigated in part by U Wirathu. He says, "There is no fighting in our area here in Sagaing. There are some villagers who have their kids quit school after the sixth standard because they are so poor. This is a bad sign and so even here there is a problem with education and its consequences. I browbeat my brothers and sisters to allow their children to stay in school. Fortunately, they follow my advice." He talks about how he maintains very good relations with Muslims in Sagaing (admittedly a very small community). "I talk with the local imam often and we want to keep the peace here." Kumara wants not only to promote good relations, but also to educate people about Muslims not being of just one kind. He cites the example of a doctor coming from Malaysia to treat people as an example of a good Muslim and how this was posted on Facebook. "We always have to encourage people to turn away from cruelty to kindness. We should not try to convert people from one religion to another but encourage them to convert from being bad to being good people. That's the real conversion. Good religious people of all religions should strive to cultivate moral consciousness. The Buddha was interested in correcting misunderstanding and wanted others to respect their own religions first."

Kumara begins to reminisce about his experiences in India again and talks about meeting Muslim imams in Delhi "who tried to make friendship with me and were very helpful in all ways"—when he was sick or got lost. "I came to realize that religion is just religion, but what we really we need is a good heart of kindness." He then recalls, "Two Muslims from Kyrgyzstan who lived in our hostel got drunk one night and came back around eleven p.m. and knocked at my door. They said they were very hungry. I cooked noodles for them. They ate very quickly, within five minutes. They didn't wash their plates because they were so drunk. One of them went to his room and slept it off. Next day around one p.m., he came by and thanked me profusely for the food the night before. Whenever I had a problem after that, he was always ready to help me. He would ask me about Buddhist culture and ethics. And I realized that everybody, regardless of religion, needs to learn about cultivating kindness. And I knew that since I had been kind to him, he would be kind to me. This I think is the key to growing a civil society."

I ask him, confidentially, if he can relate to me what he understands Sitagu's perspective to be on the Buddhist-Muslim problem. He pauses and ponders. "Not much different from my view. We walk on the same platform, walking on the platform for the welfare of the people. My master was recently invited to speak to the Ma Ba Tha's big convention. But so many of his disciples asked him not to attend. But he went anyway. The main purpose of Ma Ba Tha is to be against Muslims. They think Muslims and terrorists are one and the same. The reason he went is that Ma Ba Tha is also a part of the country. He had said, 'As a teacher I need to try to help balance the situation, to try to have both sides keep quiet.' Sitagu Sayadaw sees himself above the disagreement, like a father trying to control quarreling brothers. He criticizes both sides when they go to excesses. He knows that monks should not be involved politically. But he also says that the politicians should respect religious persons and should not use harsh language against monks. When he gave the speech to the Ma Ba Tha, he said he preached for the welfare of the people. Both sides became quiet and calm. Some Muslims in Yangon said that his speech made them relax. He is a great teacher for all citizens in the country. From time to time in his *dhamma* talks, he expresses the need for each community to respect the other, to follow the universal laws [*parajikas*]. He always stresses the *pancasila* [fivefold morality]. We have also invited Catholic priests to teach a course on biblical studies here to stress moral teachings. These priests were quite liberal and were often pressed by our students, who posed many ethical dilemmas. We also engage in a peace dialogue group organized by Korean Baptist missionaries."

I decide to question him more about militant Buddhists. He's says he's not very familiar with Arakanese monks in Myanmar, so I ask him what he thinks about Wirathu's views on Muslims as a threat to the country. He begins by telling me how he first met the secretary of the Bodu Bala Sena (BBS) and its lay CEO when they first came to Mandalay looking for Wirathu. "We let them stay here and they asked us about what they should see in Mandalay. They inquired about how they could find Wirathu's monastery and if we could arrange a meeting. We did that for them." I made sure that when I returned four months later I gave him a copy of my *Buddhist Extremists and Muslim Minorities: Religious Conflict in Contemporary Sri Lanka* (Holt 2016). I wanted him to know what the BBS was up to in Sri Lanka. In any case, the subject of Wirathu is put on the table and I sit back to hear Kumara's perspective. "With regard to the Burmese problem with Muslims, Wirathu always highlights the criminal cases of Muslims on Facebook, sometimes with false information. For example, there was the famous rape case in 2014 that he posted that almost inspired a big riot in Mandalay. He highlights only Muslims rather than the fact that rape occurs with men in every religious tradition. Wirathu doesn't really appreciate how sophisticated some of the current politicians are. He simply hasn't studied other cultures. He holds that only his view is right. The main purpose of his activities is to oppose the Muslims and he seems to speak only to his own community of like-minded people." Kumara says he was born near a Muslim community and perhaps Wirathu hasn't had much exchange with Muslims, or somehow maybe had a difficult time with them. "We need to support women in their attempts to gain education and succeed economically, but they are not the weaklings that Wirathu seems to think they are. Often people convert to another religion for economic reasons. And sometimes Buddhist men are not taking care of their families and become alcoholics or drug addicts and leave their families destitute. So the wife tries to find a way out and sells out to provide milk or education for her children." Kumara says that he doesn't think most women are weak, maybe only 10 percent or so. "Women who are eighteen to twenty years old may want material stuff and some girls take on a Muslim boyfriend to fund their materialistic desires. If the Muslim man is an educated person, there will not be a problem. But once a Buddhist woman marries a Muslim man, no one is going to help her from the Buddhist side. Wirathu has stepped into this situation, and on the basis of the stories he's heard, he makes a generalization such as this."

I mention that Wirathu was a supporter of the USDP and seems to have had significant connections with the previous government, especially the notorious Aung Thaung, who may have been responsible for Wirathu's release from prison.

Kumara says, "The previous government was corrupt and the businessmen took advantage. They always won by bribing the police and judges. According to my own experience, this is what had been happening. I appreciate the democratic framework now because we have a chance to choose a new government. In some nondemocratic states, there is no hope for change. In the new democratic setup, Buddhists are free to express their religious perspectives." I speak, however, about the danger of the tyranny of the majority, but it doesn't stick. Instead, he says, "In India, the people have freedom of speech and religious practice. There also is a right to complain. The Buddhist population in India has steadily grown within this setup even though the majority are Hindus. We can change the government now every five years if we don't like it. We now can criticize. Buddhism is conducive to democracy and not just monarchy. Like ordination, we take the agreement of all sanghas. If you agree, keep silent, we continue. If you disagree, speak up."

He then goes on to talk about Vesali as a kind of proto-democratic order versus the kingdoms such as Magadha during the time of the Buddha. I mention how the *Mahaparinibbana Sutta* seems to prefigure democratic caucuses by encouraging frequent communal meetings not only for republican political contexts but for the sangha as well.

Kumara is optimistic because he believes that the ascendant NLD government is going to make a significant difference in due time. I describe what happened in Sri Lanka with the BBS and the tacit support it had received from the Rajapaksa government, but how things changed after the election of January 2015. After that, the BBS receded and no longer could act with impunity. They no longer had official support. Kumara nods and begins to talk about the USDP and Ma Ba Tha connection and then says that "with the NLD coming to power, there is no revenge, but that the best revenge is the freedom to speak, and freedom from corruption. The NLD has not arrested anyone for political purposes and have not gone about destroying the businesses that gained so much during the previous government. They want to help grow a good-hearted USDP, a USDP that understands the *dhamma*. This is a positive sign for our society. Some USDP people have realized that they have been mistaken in the past and the NLD is giving them an opportunity to correct their past mistakes. Some people say there are no changes since the NLD came to power, but I see freedom to criticize in the press, radio, et cetera. In the past, the military were cheaters and liars when they did not hand over power to the winners in 1990. I mentioned this at a seminar while the USDP was still in power about how this was an example of how *satya parami* [the perfection of truth] was not realized. Many monks feared that I would get arrested and be sent to jail for ten years. But nowadays, we are free to speak. The NLD does, of course, like to gain the favor of Buddhist monks but also tolerates monks who are critical of them. The chief minister of Yangon has said that Ma Ba Tha is not necessary. The state sangha council [Ma Ha Na] has said that the Ma Ba Tha is not a regulated social body. There is a reminder that no one will be arrested, though. Many refugees gone to other countries are now free to return. They can meet their relations and go to their native places. I am also thankful to Thein Sein [the president of the previous government] because he could control his people, to hand over power to the new government. If they had refused, our country would have faced a big problem, maybe civil war. But he handed over power peacefully. Maybe after three or four years, the NLD can control the military. Already the army chief has said that if the political situation is stable that it will gradually reduce its representation in parliament.

"Another good sign is that the 'ethnic armies' are coming to the table for discussion. Most of the military supports Aung San Suu Kyii's effort to find a federal peace. The new government has recognized the 'legality' of (or is taking seriously) so many (perhaps a hundred) different resistance groups, and that has made them pleased that their voices will be heard."

I ask what has happened to the progressive monks of the so-called 2007 Saffron Revolution. Where are they now and am I wrong to think about how different they are from Ma Ba Tha? "The 2007 monks have kept quiet and do not involve [themselves] in the Ma Ba Tha activities. If the Ma Ba Tha activities put the country at risk, the 2007 group will speak out. If the Ma Ba Tha makes a mistake, the Ministry of Home Affairs would take action against them. If the Ma Ba Tha wants to complain about the NLD government, they'll have to do so without using harsh statements. Some of the Ma Ba Tha monks are actually liberal, but some of the younger monks are really fundamentalists. They don't have a scope wider than what they have seen domestically. They need to find out how people of other religions respect their beliefs, how they maintain themselves and what are the problems between religion and politics, as in Russia, where the communists attempted to destroy all religions until 1990. I tell my students we need to learn a lot from the rest of the world. We need to understand that our situation is just a tiny part of the world."

Kumara laced many of his comments with normative statements about how important it is to cultivate a wholesome disposition that results in beneficial qualities of action. In that way, he is very much in sync with Ven. Jotika. While this is a fundamental understanding in the Buddhist theory of action, neither understands it as an essentially Buddhist teaching, but rather as a universal truth. They also agree that there is a universal pattern to the criminal mind, one rooted in selfish dispositions generated by greed, hatred, and delusion. Of course, this is the fundamental teaching of the Buddha in the early Pali literature, especially the Vinaya.

After my third meeting with Kumara, in the **winter of 2016–2017**, I had sent him a copy of the UN report compiled from interviews with more than two hundred Rohingya refugees who had fled Maungdaw and Buthidaung after the Tatmadaw had attacked them in their villages (OHCHR 2017). I didn't receive any response from him, and he did not reply to my several requests to meet with him again in the **summer of 2017** until the day before I was leaving Mandalay. I was speculating about why he had decided to keep his distance. Perhaps he could ascertain my perspective from reading *Buddhist Extremists and Muslim Minorities* (Holt 2016) and worried about being associated with me.

But that was not the case. When we meet, he says, to my chagrin, that he has only "read a few words" of my book. But what does transpire in our two-hour meeting is a spirited discussion about the Tatmadaw, the UN, and the Rohingya.

U Kumara says that he just can't decide about what is right or wrong in the news reports about the Rohingya. He had not read the UN report that I had sent. He says, "The UN people do not know the long history here." He then relates to me how "Bengalis" came slowly across the border for many years, gradually to occupy land from generation to generation, over fifty to seventy years, and in the process displaced the Rakhine Buddhists. So, he says, the Rakhine are not happy with the situation as it has developed. They believe that the villages of their ancestors have been overtaken by the Bengalis.

"More than ten lakhs [1 million] of Bengalis have tried to leave, telling stories about how bad things are in Rakhine," he continues. "This is what the Westerners believe. The Bengalis who have been here for generations feel that this is their place too. The majority lived here peacefully. They've played political games for benefits being manipulated by some of their leaders living abroad. They teach their women how to give answers to foreign reporters or UN interviewers. They've been told to say they were raped, but they didn't even know the meaning of the term 'rape' when examined. The UN people will only show a hyped report.

"Bengalis are killing Burmese people in Malaysia. The Burmese don't threaten Rohingya here. We can't depend on the UN because for fifty years they did nothing while we suffered. The army ruled mercilessly from 1962 to 2010." He then becomes very forceful in arguing that the Rohingya are not telling the truth. He equivocates and says that it is difficult to believe either side.

I find this disconcerting because I feel it is a way of denying the brutality that the Rohingya have suffered at the hands of the Tatmadaw. I argue that the fact that seventy-five thousand Rohingya have left Maungdaw itself is evidence that something terrible has happened. I tell him that I have seen videos (but I do not say from whom) about the army burning down villages and killing old people, but he will have none of it, saying that the burning of villages was staged by the Rohingya to gain international sympathy. I give up and try to hide my exasperation, though I don't think I do this effectively. I am about to say, "Do you think that the Rohingya dressed up in Tatmadaw uniforms to burn down their villages?" I am also frustrated that he has not bothered to read the UN report and that the UN could be so easily dismissed. But then again, it seems that the UN is so easily dismissed in many other contexts as well, and has become a ripe target in American politics, especially from the right wing and current president, Trump, as well. All I can say at this point is that the truth at some point will need to be respected and that it must have the opportunity to speak to power.

As if he reads my growing frustration, U Kumara begins to talk again about how "the Bengalis" need to be provided with education, health care, and economic development assistance and have some trained elders perhaps from

Malaysia or Indonesia leading the way. But "they also need to respect rules and regulations of the government." Several times during our conversation he mentions the need to follow rules and regulations. (I suppose that is to be expected from the rector of an academic institution!) He goes on to say that the problem will never be solved with violence. He also thinks that perhaps drug groups were involved as a catalyst in the October 9 border attack fiasco. And if that is the case, that's another example of why law and order needs to be imposed.

"We want to follow Aung San Suu Kyii. We don't want to follow the UN's account of our problem. There is a lot of disgust with the UN because we do not want to do like in 'master's [the British] time.' We need time and a step-by-step process. If we do things quickly, the army will take the power again. If Aung San Suu Kyii is seen as dealing directly with the Rohingya, this would be seen as [adverse] propaganda giving in to them. And she might lose the next election because of that." I tell him at this point that I think that the Rohingya just want to be part of the process leading to a solution, to have access to the process per se.

Just when I think we have reached a point where he understands the need for Rohingya to be included in the discussion about their future, he begins to talk about the famous rape of an Arakanese girl by Bengalis in which first they stole her gold, then they raped her, before they killed her. This was, of course, the beginning of the narrative from the Arakanese perspective that led to the 2012 mayhem in Sittwe. (In my notes, I write down that U Kumara doesn't bother to mention how following the rape, ten Muslim men, none of them "Bengalis," were pulled off a bus and murdered.) He goes on to talk about the Gujerat violence back in the early 2000s that was allegedly started by two Muslims who firebombed a train car. Eventually that led to the killing of eight hundred Muslims, in part because then chief minister (now Indian prime minister) Modi let the violence go on for four days before intervening with the police. U Kumara says this is what went on in Arakan. But he says it in a way to emphasize that it was the Muslims who started the problem.

We part amiably, but I am chastened. I think that if a monk with this level of education and experience can sustain such a hostile view and refuse to even consider the possibility that his government's military is guilty of unspeakable atrocities, then the realities for Rohingya in this country can be considered as nothing less than completely grim, and the history of the Buddhasasana (Buddhist tradition or teaching) will eventually contain an unhappy and blemished chapter of callous indifference to brutality.

I do my best to encourage U Kumara to join Ven. Jotika and make a visit for himself to Sittwe. I tell him that we're talking more fundamentally about the welfare of human beings than about the alleged proclivities for violence of the Islamic religion. It strikes me as ironic that, in fact, the bulk of the violence committed in the conflict has been committed by Buddhists, and yet so many Buddhists uniformly insist on tarring Islam with the brush of violence. Of course, this is a result of downloading the geopolitical to the local, or uploading the local to the geopolitical. (When I use the term "geopolitical," U Kumara acts quite amused and says he has never heard that term used before.) Finally, I mention something that the older Rohingya political leaders all said to me in passing, and that is that the younger people are beginning to feel desperate, and that the Buddhists' fear of some kind of insurgency with international backing could easily become a self-fulfilling prophecy.

In the months that follow, before our next meeting during the final days of **December 2017**, I thought maybe our "spirited discussion" had marked the end of a good exchange between us and that perhaps Kumara would find reasons not to meet with me again. Clearly, I had made him feel uncomfortable, and I, for my part, had felt very disappointed in what he had to say in August 2017. He had blurted out almost verbatim some of the propaganda that the military had funneled through Myanmar TV and their state-supported newspaper. I had thought that he had a better handle on the situation than that, especially because he had taken a dim view of the military's history in terms of what they had done to the country. So I approached my appointment with him with a bit of trepidation, prepared for a blowout or a quick demise to the conversation.

When I show up to meet him at four p.m., he doesn't answer his doorbell. I try three times and then head for the academy's reception area, only to find that office empty. I trudge back across campus and am surprised to run into another American about my age with a cell phone whom I judge is a frequent visitor or regular in Sagaing. It turns out that he attended the University of Chicago Divinity School for two years and had left Chicago a couple of years before I had arrived. We know many of the same people from that time and so we enjoy a few moments of reminiscence—the usual "back in the day" stuff. With what seems a stroke of luck, he actually has Kumara's cell phone number and calls it but gets no answer. He begins calling other monks, but they do not know Kumara's whereabouts. My new American friend speculates that Kumara has probably met up with a young Burmese American who had come out of nowhere to the academy that day and was likely "hijacked" by the fascination of a potential student recruit. I start to think that I have been stood up and that it is time to ask the American to call my taxi so I can head back to Mandalay. But his phone rings, he hands it to me, and I find myself speaking with Kumara, who explains he will see me in five minutes' time. I am greatly relieved.

When Kumara finally surfaces, he explains that he fell asleep while reading and didn't hear the doorbell or phone. I shrug it off and thank him for agreeing to see me again. I tell him I have just reread my account of the substance of our previous conversations and am quite pleased with the ground we covered, even with the spirited discussion that we concluded with the last time we met. I feel it is only honest to begin acknowledging our differences. In that way, maybe I can avoid the awkwardness I experienced in a previous conversation with Jotika, two days earlier. Actually, I think I had come prepared for a fight. When reading about our previous conversations, I noted how he had emphasized free speech under the NLD regime in contrast with the old military-dominated regimes, including the recent USDP government that preceded the NLD. I was going to ask him what he thought about the fact that since the NLD had come to power, more than twenty journalists, including two Reuters journalists during the past two weeks, had been detained or imprisoned. The detaining of the Reuters journalists had become an international story, generating official statements from the United States, the United Kingdom, and the European Union that the Myanmar government ought to release the journalists immediately, or this would be taken as a further erosion of free speech culture in ostensibly democratic Myanmar. I was also going to recast what I had been told by Sean Gleeson, the Australian editor for *Frontier,* about the surveillance and intimidation that many reporters for nongovernmental news sources were now experiencing in Yangon. If he denied or claimed he was unaware, I was prepared to give him links to the *Irrawaddy, Frontier,* and *Myanmar Now* websites. All of this would be to counter his earlier claims about free speech under the NLD government. I was also going to quote to him his own earlier words that "violence will not solve the problem" before bringing up the issue of the Tatmadaw's unrestrained and totally disproportionate brutality perpetrated against innocent Rohingya villagers after August 25. My final punch would be concerned with Sitagu's November sermon delivered to a military audience on the Dutthagamini saga from the *Mahavamsa,* a sermon that implied that the soldiers need not fret about negative karma as a consequence of the violence they had committed against the Rohingya. That had been my agenda, and I figured our relationship and conversation were about to go up in a blaze. But as it turned out, and to my surprise, Kumara gives me a warm welcome and keeps to something of his own agenda that he wants to discuss with me. I find myself almost immediately in my stenographer mode, furiously typing his words almost verbatim. I decide to let him run with his opening thoughts and see what develops.

He begins by noting the crucial moment when the Kofi Annan Commission announced its recommendations. I am about to jump up and say, "Yes, and the only quarter that publicly denounced the recommendations was the military. General Min Aung Hlaing had immediately said that the history of the context had not been well understood." But before I can get there, Kumara gets there first, and when he gets started, he lays out a rather comprehensive understanding of what he thinks transpired after August 25. He must have known that I would come to our discussion wanting to understand his perspective. What surprises me is that he does not deny the army outrages but instead seeks to explain how their mistake was the result of miscalculations. "The people who did not like the Kofi Annan Commission were the human traffickers. There are a lot of diasporic Rohingya [he actually uses the word for the first time in our conversations!] who also do not like the report. Some may have the idea of an independent state—any people of this persuasion would not like the report either. I am not sure about Rakhine people on this score, but their leaders also condemned the report. The majority of Rohingya are simple farmers, and probably had little or no awareness of the commission, let alone its findings, which were largely beneficial to them. The army thought that ARSA [the Arakan Rohingya Salvation Army] was a well-armed group. They were worried about the scope of an impending attack. Myanmar newspapers had reported that ISIS was losing in

Iraq and Syria, so the army may have thought that some of their fighters had come here. There had been recent reports of some of them fighting anew in the Philippines. There were some training camps they had found which also led the army to suspect something big was up. The army did not listen to the government's suggestion, which was to talk about what had happened [the attack on thirty border guard posts] to find a way forward. They felt there was no need to pay attention to the government's suggestion. They should have waited on parliament, but they didn't. There was a rift or difference between the NLD government and the military, as I am sure that this government did not want to attack any ethnic group. Instead, they would have advocated discussion. Maybe after ten years and a lot of patience we could get an agreement. We'd fight in the meantime if necessary. I would have asked the military just to leave some areas alone and leave the locals to sort out their differences. Some of these fighters are fighting for business purposes, not for their people or the country. The military simply could not tolerate any attacks because they are always ready to fight."

I mention how some are saying something similar in Thailand: that the army should just pull out of the deep south and let the local peoples sort out their differences. And that the army seems always to be interested in engagement as a way of justifying their continued presence and role as the defender of the people. Kumara agrees that the army could do the same in Rakhine State: just leave the people alone and let locals settle the differences. "But if the government suggests such a policy, the army would remove the government from power. Sometimes it is better to be quiet and slowly undertake the right action. We don't have a full democratic government and we are still somewhat under military control. A lot of ministers from the previous government have a lot of properties that they want to protect through coming to power again. If we lose this democratic government, we'll have to wait another twenty to twenty-five years or maybe even longer. Maybe I won't see another democratic government in my life. Aung San Suu Kyii knows this problem very well. She keeps quiet because that is better for the whole of the people. She can solve the Rohingya problem, but she cannot change the military mind-set. Another thing is that the Burmese are really afraid of terrorism. They don't want the Muslim community to get bigger because they think that the factor of terrorism will grow. There was an isolated event of Muslims feeling that there had been a Qur'an burning and so they attacked. This had a multiplier effect. Sometimes the *mawlawis* [Muslim spiritual masters] preach a lot of anger in regard to the plight of Muslims. People see pictures in the newspapers of violence in southern Thailand where Muslims have attacked monks.

"On the other side, the OIC [Organization of Islamic Cooperation] is only concerned with the Muslim community, while in a place like Myanmar there are problems among the Kachin and Shan and other peoples as well. Therefore, Burmese people don't trust the OIC because they do not speak to the entirety of the problem at hand. Some people say that religion and politics should not mix, but it is inevitable.

"Another problem is how Burmese understand jihad. Some Burmese people understand it as killing non-Muslims, even though there are four meanings of jihad and this is only one of them. Christians here never preach about violence with other people. Hinduism, Buddhism, Sikhism, also do not teach such violence. But some *mawlawis* in the Rakhine area have motivated violence. Rakhine people also do not trust the NGOs. If the international community, especially the OIC, keep up a lot of pressure on the government, that is not a good way to solve the problem. They should let Brunei, Indonesia, or another friendly Muslim country make presentations looking for solutions to the problem. Is there a way for the Muslim countries and the international community to provide health care, food, education, roads, et cetera? If they can do this, that would be great. This would be a good way of assisting our government."

Kumara sees the NLD government as squeezed between the international community and the military. He thinks that perhaps the long view of the situation is to provide education for the young people so that when they join the military their mind-set will be different than what is the case now. "We need to change their mind-set. This will take time. The mistake that has been made before is punishing the civilian masses by sanctions that affect them rather than just the military. If we can change the military mind-set, we can change the situation. It would be a good idea to take some officers from the army to democratic countries and keep them there for five or six years and their mind-sets would be changed by the environment. They would support the democratic system in that eventuality. As for the government, it needs to have patience with the local people and their frustrations. If some group tries for separatism, that will be a big problem. So the government should try to address their problems to keep them within the union before the situation deteriorates and they want to leave."

So far in this discussion, which has been more of Kumara's monologue, I am feeling as if some healthy thoughts are being generated. But then I am taken aback again by the emergence of the majoritarian complex: "If the Bengalis are going to live in Burma, they have to learn and live in Burmese culture. They need to speak our language and observe our laws. They must not live separately." So even here within the context of a progressive monk's attempts to be liberal-minded, the assumption of Burmanization assumes its primary position. Yes, apartheid is a problem, but essentially becoming Burman is yet another. We are a long way here from the Canadian mosaic, a model for how a very diverse population can be sustained with differences intact.

I decide not to follow this up, to let it lie and to take another tack. Since Kumara seems to have accepted the fact that the army has run amuck in northern Arakan, I mention that there may be very serious repercussions in the future. Unless the current situation is addressed very quickly, I say, my greatest fear, as I saw over the years in Sri Lanka, is that seriously violent attacks may begin to take place at the most sacred of Buddhist places in Myanmar, such as the Mahamuni Temple in Mandalay and the Shwedagon Pagoda in Yangon. Kumara's face turns ashen. I don't think the idea of such an attack has ever crossed his mind before because he is almost in shock at the very suggestion. Finally, he says that this would be his great fear too and would "signal the end of any possible peace."

I say, "All the more reason for getting on to a solution."

He replies, "I think Bengalis should accept the verification process but then demand education, health, and basic needs. They should understand that our government is just a baby learning how to walk. They should understand who are their friends. Who is the real leader of the Rohingya? They should be thinking about how to choose their leader. They will have to choose their own leaders beginning at the village level. There is for sure mutual doubt about the verification system as the situation moves forward. But this can be worked out. The deep problem is that the government will never accept the term 'Rohingya.'"

With this last comment about how the term "Rohingya" will never be acceptable, Kumara seems to slip back into articulating some prejudicial statements about the Rohingya. I myself slip into a passive mode, determined to let him articulate his voice without arguing the merits of his statements for the time being. Kumara has just said that in comparison to the Muslims, "the Christian community does not create a problem by using the religion for political purposes. They respect others' religious beliefs. Even though they get angry they do not physically attack others on the basis of religious identity. Sometimes the Muslims will intentionally kill other minorities or Burmese. Fortunately, in Mandalay and Sagaing, there are not any attacks between communities. The problem in northern Arakan is that the Muslims are a majority in those areas and so they want to maximize their positions. They don't want to cooperate with the government. Their thinking is that eventually they will have an autonomous situation because they have distanced themselves from the government."

I think about how hoping for a little autonomy is not such a bad ideal, like the Tamils in Sri Lanka who form a majority on the Jaffna Peninsula and in the northern Vanni region. Here in Myanmar, the proverbial "double minority complex" also seems to be in play when it comes to considering the situation in northern Arakan. The Rohingya, only 1 million out of more than 50 million, are a little minority within the entire context of Myanmar. And they are a significant minority in the Rakhine State population of 3 million. But in northern Arakan, the Rahkine Buddhists cast themselves as an overwhelmed minority and resent any possible stipulations of autonomy for the vast majority of Rohingya in the northern parts of the state. The Rohingya are not even allowed to refer to themselves in the manner they choose. Instead, they are expected to self-identify as "Bengali," as foreigners in what they have considered to be their own lands.

As if he has read my mind, Kumara says, "Rakhines are so nationalist. I have a joke in which I sometimes say, 'We have to thank the Rohingya people, because if there are no Rohingya, the Rakhines would be attacking us.'" He giggles, but I'm typing and forget to laugh. As I mentioned before, Kumara, like almost all Burmese monks, has never been to Arakan. His experience with Arakanese monks comes from the time he spent in India while pursuing his PhD in philosophy. He often lapses into reminiscing about his days in India and the impressions he formed of Arakanese at that time. The impressions are largely circumspect. "There are Arakan monks who live on the borderlands and eventually make it into the heart of India. Senior Arakan monks will accept younger Rakhine for the monasteries, but not Burmese. Though the Arakanese use the Myanmar Monk Association title, they don't want to share the association with the Burmese. After 1997, the number of Burmese monks in India grew because of the liberalization by Myanmar's military regime. So Burmese monks supported another organization, named the Union of Buddhist Monks, in order to provide a platform for educational support. This is an association which is now eighty years old and the number of members is now over six hundred. It was four hundred when I was there. I attend the three days of conference every year. The first time I attended there were only sixty-one, but by the time I left it was four hundred because so many more monks were coming to India for higher education. In India, there is no cooperation between the Rakhine and Burmese [which includes Shan and Kachin] organizations. They have a lot of monastic lands in India since they've been there since the time of the British. They will accept Burmese laypeople's donations, though. Sometimes the Burmese feel that the Arakanese are really racist. Those of us who have studied in India know about this point." His comments make me realize I am hearing the flip side of the coin of what I was told by U Thar Pwint in Sittwe about how the Arakanese had continued to be alienated from the Burmese. I imagined that the Arakanese monks in India felt somehow free not to be under the majoritarian hegemony of the Burmese.

Kumara goes on to talk about how religion has become such a divisive factor in the current context of crisis. He tells me that recently "the Bangladeshis refused helped for Rohingya from Israel." Kumara's point here is that the Rohingya are human beings in dire need of help, and religion, of all phenomena, should not get in the way of ameliorating their suffering. Indeed, perhaps the essence of Buddhism, given the first of the Buddha's Four Noble Truths, is that existence is permeated with *dukkha* (suffering).

Time is passing. It has gotten dark outside and we've been at it intensely for about two and a half hours. I haven't asked him yet about his views regarding a new constitution. So I ask him what he would like to see for Myanmar, and I outline the secular options of the American (hands off religion), Indian (support all equally), and Sri Lankan (freedom for the individual but a special recognition for Buddhism) models. Kumara says that he is skeptical about the reality of secularism in the first place. "No one can be separate from religion. Even the Americans can't escape it," and he cites the swearing-in ceremony of the president with his hand being placed on the Bible, and then the motto "In God we trust" found on all American currency. His fundamental observation comes across in the following statement: "If Muslims and Christians give first place to those religions in other countries, Buddhists think that Buddhism should be given a prominent place here." I can understand why he is saying that, but I point out that in the American context there is an ideal regarding separation that constantly needs observing. Yes, I acknowledge, there are tacit recognitions of Christianity that come through within customary ritual routine, but the 1962 Supreme Court case about banning prayer in public schools is seen as a landmark decision that has continued to push the United States in the direction of maintaining separation. I say that, yes, there are many Americans who regard the United States as a Christian country, but in terms of our constitutional ideals, our government cannot establish religious practice, nor is it supposed to place a burden on it. I try to explain that the American situation is ever evolving and tensions about religion in public will probably always remain. I then point out that America is not a country that constitutionally recognizes one race or ethnic group as historically dominant and therefore deserving of pride of place. While it has suffered from its own forms of nationalism, it is essentially, at base, a collection of ideal abstractions that we struggle to put into practice, and not to be identified with any race or religion. He smiles and understands where I am coming from. He seems to both admire what I say but also doubt the reality of it.

Finally, I want to get his stance on what I recently heard from Ven. Jotika about how Aung San Suu Kyii is attempting to bring about a reconciliation between the people and the army. I am keen to get his view on this because his master, Sitagu, is on record, as I mentioned at the outset, of urging the sangha, the military, and the government to unite. I expect that Kumara will support this. But I am anxious to know if it is actually taking place. Kumara agrees that there is now an attempt at reconciliation. "The army should understand that they are the servants of the country, not the other way around. Step by step, Aung San Suu Kyii is trying to get the military to understand this. This may take ten years or so to happen, to change their disposition. And I am not sure completely that this will actually happen. If it does happen, it will be good for all parties. If it does not happen and the military doesn't want to go along, it would not be good for the future of Aung San Suu Kyii's emerging policies."

I ask, "How is the relation between the military and the people now?"

He responds, "The military could not take over right now because even though the Russians and Chinese might support them as long as they would get some advantages from the move, it would definitely lead to the economic atrophy of the country. I'm trusting the NLD not to take revenge against the corruptions of the previous [military-dominated] governments. For example, in the past roads were built here in Sagaing and in other places where lands had been allocated to military individuals. People know about this. The military people are not quite ready to withdraw from their advantageous positions. The relation between the general and the lady is cold. Aung San Suu Kyii is committed to peace. General Hlaing is not like that. There is fighting here and there going on during what is supposed to be 'the peace process.' This is a state army still empowered by the constitution and they should be more tolerant of the aggressiveness of the respective rebel movements. Let them [the ethnic minorities] be free in their areas and just keep watch on them [to make sure that matters do not get out of hand]. Let the peace process have a chance. A lot of people ask why we have to spend money on so many weapons. Instead we could spend [that money] on transportation, food, et cetera, and it could be given to the ethnic needy people to help them."

I couldn't have agreed more with Kumara on this point, especially because my country is perhaps the worst offender on this score. I can remember President Obama during his last year in office lamenting the fact that the United States spends more on its military than the next five countries combined. As a committed Buddhist monk, Kumara is very serious about this matter. He says, "Eighty-five to 90 percent of the people in this country really want peace. Stop the fighting and just start discussing. As a Buddhist monk, I don't understand why these politicians and army people are so stupid about this."

At this, I think we've found a good bridge to walk across together. Kumara is not ready to see me go, but it is running pretty late and I have an hour of mad Myanmar traffic to endure, across a bridge of my own on the way back to Mandalay in the darkness of night. I came to Sagaing a bit worried and anxious, but I leave with some peace of mind. Isn't that what a Buddhist monk is supposed to help generate?

Afterword

I opened this book by saying that this had been a difficult project to undertake, that its story was by no means uplifting, and that it upended stereotypes that Euro-Americans hold about Buddhism as pacific and Islam as aggressive or violent. While all that is veritably so, in the interactions I experienced with my conversation partners over the years, I also came away with a deep admiration for the manner in which calamities of dehumanization often elicit responses from the profound depths of humanity. For example, U Kyaw Hla Aung (2: "The Spokesman") has recently been cited with a well-deserved international award for his valiant selfless efforts to help his Rohingya brothers and sisters who continue to languish in the massive camp for internally displaced people just north of Sittwe, where he himself is also detained. Abu Tahay (1: "The Historian") and U Kyaw Min (1: "The Elder Statesman") continue to work tirelessly against the proverbial odds within the nascent Myanmar political culture to establish a space for representing the needs and hopes of their people, with the hope that they can be regarded equally with others, to have a share in the nation's political process moving forward. The Venerable Jotika (3: "The Anti-Nationalists") is building a University of Global Peace with the aim of cultivating perspectives within the Buddhist sangha that recognize the fundamental ethical integrity of teachings within each of the major religions of the world. His colleague in peace building, U Wisuddha (3: "The Anti-Nationalists"), is a genuine hero who sheltered and then protected a thousand desperate Muslims by putting his own life on the line in standing up to menacing thugs in the midst of a riotous insanity. Khin Zaw Win (1: "The Activist") is working very hard to establish a foothold within Myanmar's academic culture for the free and open discussion of issues related to ethnic identity, political conflict, and religious tolerance. Wai Moe (1: "The Stringer"), in the face of serious intimidation from a variety of sources, continues bravely with his on-the-ground reporting to inform the wider world of the ever-evolving political dynamics in contemporary Myanmar as they unfold. Khine Kaung Zan (2: "The Social Worker"), with his Wan Lark Rural Development Foundation in Sittwe, is trying to address the gaps left by the government in addressing the needs of the displaced and severely impoverished in northern Rakhine State. My other conversation partners also exhibit extremely fine qualities of the human spirit when engaging the problems that they have encountered. For as depressing as the substance of our conversations became, each of these people gave expressions of hope and perseverance that are testimonies to an indomitable human spirit. That said, eight of my fourteen interlocutors, six of those just described, paid a stiff price for the genuine expressions of their humanity. They were all sentenced to time in prison by the Tatmadaw on spurious charges. While registering admiration for their expressions of humanity in the face of calamitous inhumanity is the first point I want to emphasize in this afterword, noting their unjust and unwarranted incarcerations in the past, and the Tatmadaw's despicable assaults on the Rohingya of northern Arakan, brings me to the second point.

In many of my conversations, a consistent concern that was raised, one that became so tragically apparent in the aftermaths of October 9, 2016, and August 25, 2017, is the awesome danger posed by an unreformed, unrepentant, and uncontrolled Tatmadaw. The impunity with which the Tatmadaw has continued to operate was not only often in the minds of many of my interlocutors, but has often dominated the thoughts of some of those working with the fledgling NLD Myanmar government. After UN representatives were denied access to the northern Arakan problem area, a United Nations fact-finding report filed in August 2018 has recommended that the Tatmadaw's leading generals, including the most senior commanding general, Min Aung Hlaing, be held responsible for acts of genocide against Rohingya villagers in their disproportional response to the Arakan Rohingya Salvation Army's August 25, 2017, failed uprising. Still, in the face of widespread international condemnation including Facebook's somewhat late decision to ban Tatmadaw access to its platform because of its dissemination of false and inflammatory messages that may have encouraged violence, there is reticence throughout Myanmar to poke the Tatmadaw bear too hard for fear of its reactionary power to lash out and punish, including the possibility of disestablishing the recent birth of democracy in Myanmar. Aung San Suu Kyii has remained silent, if not largely indifferent and often defensive as well, postures that also led the UN report to say that her NLD government has been complicit. The Tatmadaw has yet to demonstrate that it can be a military force working for the genuine security of all people living within the country. Rather, it remains a military power operating in its own self-interest, trying to bend the will of the people through its forceful and frequently violent means, buttressed by a shamefully rigged constitution that guarantees its right to control the direction of most government initiatives. In my own view, the Tatmadaw remains the single greatest obstacle to the future well-being of the country. Indeed, I would go so far as to say that this has been the case since it established its dictatorship in 1962. And that is why the purported recent effort to "reconcile" the government, the sangha, and the Tatmadaw is such a difficult proposition to support. If such a "reconciliation" led to the reform of the Tatmadaw so that it became a nonmalignant instrument loyally serving and protecting a truly representative democratic government, then the people of Myanmar would be relieved of a fear that hovers in the background. But if such a "reconciliation" means that the will of the people and the purpose of the Buddhist religion will continue to be manipulated to legitimate the power of a hegemonic nationalist military-backed agenda, then the future of an inclusive, pluralistic, and federal form of government responsible to the aspirations of all ethnic communities will be beyond grasp. We are left pondering the questions: Which direction would such a "reconciliation" take? Would reconciliation transform the Tatmadaw? Or would the Tatmadaw impress its recalcitrant-until-now vision on the sangha and the government? Some of my interlocutors in Myanmar have stressed that, so far, the Tatmadaw has gotten much more from the NLD government and Aung San Suu Kyii than the other way around. However, as of June 2018, there have been some signs that the NLD government may be backing off from the reconciliation prospect a bit and may begin to cooperate more with the United Nations, having allowed the UN to open an office in Naypitaw with a new rapporteur on the scene. In the short term, then, how the Tatmadaw behaves remains the question of the hour. How its leaders and its sympathizers within the NLD government have consistently spewed forth baseless propaganda, acted with impunity, and denied the reality of its out-of-proportion perpetrations of violence upon the Rohingya community in northern Arakan does not inspire confidence in the hope that the Tatmadaw is now ready to assume a constructive role in a genuine partnership coming from a process of "reconciliation." If the NLD begins to open itself up more to cooperating with the international community, this may force the Tatmadaw leadership to reassess its posture. But that possibility is by no means certain.

Third, virtually all of my conversation partners, including "The Teacher," "The Social Worker," "The Anti-Nationalists," "The Rector," "The Activist," "The Gadfly," "The Spokesman," "The Stringer," "The Elder Statesman," "The Historian," and "The Commentator," have identified education, along with economic development, as the chief long-term need of the country in order to promote amity among its people. Many are themselves products of the power that education can transform understanding to transcend the parochial beyond chauvinistic and self-interested dispositions. "The Rector" spoke explicitly about a new generation of educated people that could include even those who opt for military service. "The Historian" and "The Activist" spoke hopefully about how elements in the Tatmadaw have already shown some signs of understanding that a new era is dawning. "The Rector" and "The Activist" also spoke, on the basis of their own personal experiences, about how living abroad and learning from the experience of engaging other cultures had widened their horizons of understanding, especially the place of Burmese culture and society within a global context, thereby putting more fully into perspective the deleterious powers of parochial points of view. "The Rector" surmised what a beneficent effect it might have on military officers if they could spend some time abroad living and learning in other democratic societies. While education is a long-term hope in terms of possibly altering the mind-sets of the military and those prone to jingoism, it is also seen as the long-term need in fostering understanding between the Buddhist and Muslim communities and between all other communities in Myanmar as well.

Yet this long-term hope based on the success of education remains such a challenging and distant goal, given the anemic condition of education within the country at large in the present day. For fifty years, the public educational system, like the sidewalks of Yangon, was fundamentally neglected. Universities were more often closed than open and hardly promoted the value of independent research and critical thought. The effects of being in such a state of isolation from the rest of the world have been powerful and will not be surmounted easily, perhaps for generations, even if new efforts are made to galvanize new forms of education in Myanmar in the near future. In the Rohingya context, it is a bit far-fetched to hope for the development of critical thinking and rational discourse when the literacy rate is currently at about 20 percent, and two-thirds of its people are living in IDP camps without the benefit of any means of formal education, where very few can even hope for an opportunity to study at a university, a university setting itself that remains seriously challenged in terms of its quality as judged by international standards. I make these disheartening comments because even though I agree with my conversation partners who stress that there is a hope for the country as a whole, and the Tatmadaw in particular, because of the constructive and sometimes transformative function of education, I am also aware that reforming education and eventually seeing its beneficial consequences remains a very distant reality, generations away even if the work began immediately. Here, in this connection, I also think about conditions in my own country, the United States, which has such an extensively developed educational system, and yet we continue to do battle with some of the same types of demons that now plague Myanmar: questions about inclusion, belonging, cross-religious understanding, immigration, and interracial or interethnic harmony or conflict. This makes me realize that Myanmar's issues may never go away completely, as they certainly have not in America. But perhaps they can be better managed by more enlightened forms of political leadership, including a reincarnated Tatmadaw that serves the interests of the people and does not form a political force of its own.

Fourth, a remaining large elephant in the room: how to understand the place of Buddhism in the contemporary context? In the summer of 2017 at a Thai studies conference in Chiang Mai, I had a personal meeting with a distinguished political scientist who has written rather definitively about the Buddhist-Muslim conflict in the deep south of Thailand. In the course of our conversation, which ranged over the situations now developing in Sri Lanka and Myanmar as well as in Thailand, he asserted that he believed that the fundamental problem basic to each of these national contexts was the nature of intolerance intrinsic to Theravada Buddhism. At the time, I blanched at his assertion but shied away from taking him on directly because, as a historian of religions, realizing how the bluntness of the charge completely bulldozed over the complexity and nuances of the issues involved, I could not even begin to introduce the various subtleties of history and religion that need to be brought to bear on the question. But I can't avoid that entirely here in this afterword. The issue was always on my mind during my time in Myanmar.

To begin, aside from the issue of my colleague essentializing Theravada Buddhism into a uniform abstract reification, Buddhist civilizations across Asia have included many moments of suppressing or excluding others and of being suppressed or excluded by others, sometimes even suppressing other Buddhists or being suppressed by other Buddhists. Moreover, on the one hand, one can identify any number of paradigmatic Buddhist icons of inclusivity in Asian histories, such as the great third-century-BCE Indian emperor Asoka and the eighteenth-century Sri Lankan king Kirti Sri Rajasimha, leaders who seemed to have espoused ideologies of tolerance and inclusion, leaders who emphasized that every community can have a place within a Buddhist-guided kingdom. At least this is how they are remembered within Buddhist circles. On the other hand, there have also been kings, such as Dutthagamini in the first and second centuries BCE, or Parakramabahu I in the twelfth, who have served as contemporary symbols bolstering Buddhist nationalistic and exclusive claims to hegemony, whose purported victories in battle over encroaching enemies have seemingly enshrined a special place for Buddhists within the history of national political landscapes, in these cases Sri Lanka's. It is not difficult to identify others of these persuasions in the political histories of Laos and Myanmar. And it is also difficult to argue, on the basis of a perusal of Pali Buddhist canonical literature, that either a normatively inclusive or a normatively exclusive posture politically predominates. There is no one clear profile that obviates the issue.

Rather than fingering some element that might be intrinsic to an abstract and reified construction of an essentialized Theravada Buddhism per se, I think it is much more worth our while to focus on the emergent nineteenth- and early-twentieth-century presence of nationalism in the late colonial experiences (or encounters of Theravada-dominated cultures with colonialism), an emergent nationalism that was part of a more broadly impacting social experience of "modernity," contributing to an understanding that linked the birth or rebirth of new national conceptions of identity with the history of the religion. That is, how the identity of the new nation incorporated the legacy of Theravada Buddhist religious culture so that a self-understanding emerged in which the two were difficult to separate: to be genuinely Burman meant to be Buddhist, to be genuinely Thai meant to be Buddhist, and to be genuinely Sinhala meant to be Buddhist. (This inchoate understanding of communal identity is why attacks on the saffron robe or on Buddhist women are so highly potent or catalytic: they register as attacks on religiocultural politicized identity.)

It is this particular understanding that gives rise to the notion that the country (Myanmar, Thailand, or Sri Lanka) exists, primarily or in part, for the sake of the religion (Buddhism). It is this dictum that seems to underpin the basis for privileging Buddhists to assume a preeminent position of belonging that they feel cannot be completely shared with others. It is this assumption, one that is often in play among the majoritarian Buddhist communities in Sri Lanka, Thailand, and Myanmar, that begs the question regarding a need for a secular constitution, whether that constitution is of the American type that seeks to keep separate the concerns of government apart from either establishing or burdening the exercise of religion, or whether that constitution follows the Indian model of providing governmental support for all religious communities. Whether or not the American or Indian constitutions can serve as models, it is clear that some fresh thinking is now needed constitutionally to obviate the problems of intracommunal or religio-ethnic conflict that exist in each of these three countries, but especially in Myanmar, where the nature of conflict has now evolved into a spectacular crisis. "The Activist," "The Historian," and "The Gadfly" seemed especially attuned to this specific need to reset the country constitutionally in a secular vein, while "The Rector" and "The Anti-Nationalists" have hoped for more Buddhist-inspired modes of governance that espoused an ethic of tolerance and inclusion. In any case, I think that the Kofi Annan Commission recommendations regarding the need to rethink the 1982 Citizenship Law and the 2008 constitution, both promulgated with Tatmadaw and Burmese nationalist interests in mind, are now the legal need of the hour in order to clear the way for the emergence of "the Burma that Burma wants to be" (Barack Obama in a speech during his second trip Burma in November, 2014). That means that the root question in this context is whether enough Bamars (or Thais or Sinhalese, for that matter) want a country in which each of its constituent religious or ethnic communities share equally in the rights and privileges guaranteed constitutionally. Theravada Buddhism will continue to predominate, but there is nothing intrinsic to the tradition that makes exclusive claims to truth and power. Even U Wirathu ("The Nationalist") could not answer my question when he was asked where in Buddhist philosophy he finds justification for his view of Muslims.

Finally, related to the fourth issue concerned with law and constitutional guarantees, is the degree to which any form of local autonomy can be instituted. All of my Rohingya and Rakhine conversation partners consistently mentioned the problem of their communities being excluded from the process by which solutions or recommendations were being formulated by various commissions. The fact that it was precisely their own destinies that were being decided by "outsiders" clearly rankled them, and justifiably so. These exclusions were read again as examples of Burmese national hegemony over local parties, or "Burmanization." And the style of governance adopted by Aung San Suu Kyii, who has proven herself to be something of an autocratic micromanager loath to delegate many responsibilities, has only exacerbated this problem. At some point in the future, when a new constitution is finally entertained, a serious conversation about devolution of power to the local and regional levels will need to occur, if now marginalized communities are to cultivate any sense of belonging to a larger whole. (This very same problem, devolution of power, has bedeviled the Sri Lankan historical political experience since its independence, and questions about whether the unit of local power should be at the district or provincial level continue without any arrival at concord. It is also an issue for Muslims of the deep south in Thailand.) But Myanmar especially needs this conversation sooner rather than later, so that its various constituent ethnic communities can hope to exercise some control over their own local governance and participation in their own economic destiny. Such a formula of power sharing between the federal union government and the state, or lesser units of jurisdiction (e.g., municipal), would take an initial step in the direction of arresting the tide of domestic colonialism (Burmanization) that is so deeply resented by minority peoples. Whether or not a special space for a Rohingya majority can be designated in Arakan (in the Maungdaw, Buthidaung, and Rathedaung townships) will no doubt prove to be an especially vexing issue, to be sure. But some form of self-rule would obviate the acute alienation that is now plaguing minority communities and go a long way toward settling the situation in northern Arakan for both Rakhine Buddhists and Rohingya Muslims.

This discussion about devolution of power is relevant for another crucial reason. There is much trepidation in the Rohingya community at present regarding repatriation from the Bangladesh refugee camps back to Arakan. Rohingya are insisting not only on guarantees of safety, but also on rights to their villages and lands that have been confiscated, as well as the recognition of citizenship. On the whole, and for good reasons, most don't trust the Myanmar government. Further, they fully understand the primordial claims and hatred borne against them by the Rakhine Buddhists, and they understandably fear another round of wrath from the Tatmadaw; so the immediate future does not bode much optimism. Perhaps many Rohingya will never return.

But in May 2018, the Myanmar government agreed to allow teams of UN personnel to survey the northern Arakan region to determine what conditions would be like for returning Rohingya. Among the Rohingya, and from the perspective of many UN personnel, there is resistance to the idea of establishing temporary holding camps for the returning refugees, because these camps have a way of becoming permanent. The situation really does demand a constitutional solution in which the rights of the Rohingya to live on their own lands can be guaranteed. One first step, or interim way, of facilitating a beginning would be the establishment of safe spaces. And then eventually, the next step would be the establishment of some form of self-determination mechanism that provides for oversight or control of local security, education, and perhaps even powers of municipal taxation, while at the same time remaining within the orbit of Rakhine State and the Myanmar Union. While such a proposal is anathema to many Rakhine Buddhists and Burmese nationalists, it is not an unreasonable ideal, an ideal that might be replicated in other contested regions of the country that have chafed at the bit of Burmanization. It would require an act of bravery by someone of no less than Aung San Suu Kyii's stature who is willing to sacrifice short-term political expediency for long-term peace. Will there ever be a cooperative political will among the Burmese and Arakanese to accept such a possibility? Perhaps some, like "The Rector," "The Social Worker," and "The Activist," will ultimately realize that such a constructive arrangement of this type can be understood as a reasonable price for peace. Perhaps.

GLOSSARY

Abhidhamma (Pali)	the "higher *dhamma*"; one of the three "baskets" of texts constituting the Theravada Pali canon; focused on analyzing various states of consciousness
anatta (Pali)	without self
anicca (Pali)	change
arahant (Pali)	arhat; perfected Buddhist practitioner who has experienced *nibbana* and personally ended the cycle of karmic rebirth
Bamar (Burmese)	Burmese language and people
bhumi putra (Sanskrit)	"son of the soil/earth"; indigenous person
brahmaviharas (Pali)	four "abidings" or dispositions (*metta, mudita, upekkha, karuna*) to be cultivated through meditation
Buddhasasana (Sanskrit, Pali)	Buddhist tradition or teaching
burka (Arabic, Urdu)	head covering of Muslim women
cetana (Pali)	intention (karma)
Chettiars (Tamil, Telugu)	revenue collectors and loan sharks
dayakas (Pali)	lay supporters of the sangha
dhamma (Pali)	dharma; teaching or truth of the Buddha
dosa (Pali)	hatred
dukkha (Pali)	unsatisfactoriness; suffering; the problematic nature of existence; the first of the Noble Truths preached by the Buddha
dutin (Burmese)	ascetic monastic lifestyle restricting meals to once a day; probably derived from Sanskrit *dhutanga* specifying rigorous, personal, or independent renunciation
gamavasi (Pali)	monastic vocation oriented to the village
Harket-al Yakin (Arabic)	"faith movement;" predecessor to Arakan Rohingya Salvation Army
imam (Arabic)	Muslim cleric
Jatakas (Pali)	"birth stories" about the Buddha in his previous lives

jihad (Arabic)	struggle within; struggle for the defense of Islam
kalar/kala (Burmese/ Arakanese)	foreigners "from the West"; South Asians; Muslims, especially Rohingya
kalpa (Sanskrit)	eon of time in traditional Indian lore
Kaman (Burmese)	small (population of about forty-five thousand) indigenous Muslim community in Myanmar, primarily Arakan
karma (Sanskrit)	intentional action; results of intentional action
karuna (Sanskrit, Pali)	compassion
kathina (Pali)	annual robe and gift-giving rite to the sangha
lokanibbana (Pali)	nirvana in this world
Ma Ba Tha (Burmese)	acronym for Association for the Preservation of Society and Religion
Mahamuni (Pali)	"great sage"; the Buddha image that was the palladium of the Arakan kingdom, taken by Burmese to Mandalay in 1785
Mahaparinibbana Sutta (Pali)	biographical text in the *Digha Nikaya* recounting the final three months of the Buddha's "ministry" and his attainment of *nibbana* at death
mawlawis (Turkish)	Muslim spiritual masters
metta (Pali)	loving-kindness
Metteyya (Pali)	Maitreya, the future Buddha
moha (Pali)	delusion
mudita (Pali)	sympathetic joy
mujahideen (Arabic)	Muslim warriors of the struggle (jihad)
nathalar (Burmese)	indigenous peoples' development program
nibbana (Pali)	nirvana; extinguishing of desire; transcendence of rebirth
pancasila (Pali)	"fivefold morality"; not to kill, steal, lie, engage in improper sex, or take intoxicants
panna (Pali)	wisdom; enlightened knowledge
parajikas (Pali)	four cardinal principles of behavior (not to kill, lie, steal, or have sex), violation of which leads to expulsion from the sangha
parampara (Sanskrit)	lineage
paritta (Sanskrit, Pali)	ritual chanting of suttas to engender power of purification and renewal
paticcasamuppada (Pali)	the twelvefold conditioning process leading to rebirth and redeath in samsara

patimokkha (Pali)	227 rules of monastic discipline chanted every new and full moon
perahara (Sinhala)	annual ritual of processions; specifically in Kandy, Sri Lanka, where the Dalada (tooth-relic of the Buddha) is caparisoned on an elephant for circumambulation of the old city
punya ksetra (Sanskrit)	field of merit
puranas (Sanskrit)	genre of Hindu mythic literature regarding exploits of the gods
purdah (Arabic, Urdu)	confinement lifestyle of Muslim women in domestic quarters
putthujhana (Pali)	person
raga (Pali)	passion
Sakya (Sanskrit, Pali)	name of Gautama Buddha's clan
samadhi (Pali)	mental concentration; meditation
samanera (Pali)	Buddhist monastic novice
samsara (Sanskrit and Pali)	six realms of rebirth; world of karmic retribution
Sanchi (Sanskrit)	major stupa complex in central India
sangha (Pali)	Buddhist monastic community
sasana (Pali)	tradition or lineage of the Buddha's teaching
satya parami (Pali)	perfection of truth
Sayadaw (Burmese)	leading monk of the monastery
sharia (Arabic)	Muslim law
sila (Pali)	morality; ethical consciousness
sima (Pali)	boundaries in an ordination hall within which monastic rites sustaining the purity and lineage of the Buddha are performed
sutta (Pali)	sermon of the Buddha
swabasha (Sanskrit)	"own language"; indigenous language medium
taindar (Burmese)	recognition of national ethnic community
Tatmadaw (Burmese)	Myanmar military forces
Theravada (Pali)	way of the elders; school of Buddhism predominant in Sri Lanka and Southeast Asia
thila shin (Burmese)	Burmese "nun" who usually undertakes a tenfold vow
thugyi (Burmese)	village headman
Tripitaka (Sanskrit)	the "three baskets" of texts constitutive of the Theravada Pali canon
upajhaya (Pali)	monastic mentor
upasampada (Pali)	full or "permanent" monastic ordination

upekkha (Pali)	even-mindedness
Vaddas (Sinhala)	indigenous people of Sri Lanka likely antedating Sinhalese
Vajrayana (Sanskrit)	esoteric Buddhist tradition; the "third wheel" in addition to Mahayana and Theravada, primarily in Tibet and Mongolia, but historically in China and Japan as well
vanavasi (Pali)	monastic vocation oriented to the forest
Vesali	ancient language spoken in what is now Arakan or Rakhine State
Vinaya (Pali)	the "Book of Discipline"; code of monastic behavior; one of the three *pitakas,* or "baskets," making up the Pali canon of Theravada texts regarded as Buddhavacana, or sayings of the Buddha
vipassana (Pali)	preferred Theravada method of meditation
yakkha (Pali)	demonic force
yuga (Sanskrit)	measure of time; four *yuga*s constitute a *kalpa* (eon) of time in Hindu *purana* (mythic) literature
zakat (Arabic)	Muslim "tax" for charity
969	Buddhist monastic nationalist boycott of Muslim businesses

BIBLIOGRAPHY

Berlie, Jean A. 2008. *The Burmanization of Myanmar's Muslims.* Bangkok: White Lotus Press.

Brass, Paul. 1997. *Theft of an Icon: Text and Context in the Production of Collective Violence.* Princeton, NJ: Princeton University Press.

Callahan, Mary P. 2004. *Making Enemies: War and State Building in Burma.* Singapore: National University of Singapore Press.

Chakravarti, Nalini R. 1971. *The Indian Minority in Burma: The Rise and Decline of an Immigrant Community.* New York: Oxford University Press.

Charney, Michael. 2009. *A History of Modern Burma.* Cambridge: Cambridge University Press.

Crouch, Melissa. 2016. "Myanmar's Muslim Mosaic and the Politics of Belonging." In *Islam and the State in Myanmar: Muslim-Buddhist Relations and the Politics of Belonging,* ed. Melissa Crouch, pp. 9–35. New Delhi: Oxford University Press.

Crouch, Melissa, and Tim Lindsey, eds. 2014. *Law, Society and Transition in Myanmar.* Oxford, UK: Hart Publishing.

de Mersan, Alexandra. 2012. "'The Land of the Great Image' and the Test of Time: The Making of Buddha Images in Arakan (Burma/Myanmar)." In *The Spirit of Things: Materiality and Religious Diversity in Southeast Asia,* ed. Julius Bautista, pp. 95–110. Ithaca, NY: Cornell University Southeast Asia Program Publications.

Eaton, Richard. 1996. *The Rise of Islam and the Bengal Frontier, 1204–1760.* Berkeley: University of California Press.

Elverskog, Johan. 2010. *Buddhism and Islam on the Silk Road.* Philadelphia: University of Pennsylvania Press.

Frydenlund, Iselin. 2018. "Buddhist Islamophobia: Actors, Tropes and Contexts." In *Handbook of Conspiracy Theory and Contemporary Religion,* ed. Asbjorn Dryendal, David Robertson, and Egil Asprem, pp. 279–302. Leiden: E. J. Brill.

Fuller, Paul. 2018. "Narratives of Ethnocentric Buddhist Identity." *Journal of the British Association for the Study of Religion* 20:19–44.

Gravers, Mikael. 1999. *Nationalism as Political Paranoia in Burma.* 2nd ed. Richmond, UK: Curzon Press.

Green, Penny. 2013. "Islamophobia: Burma's Racist Fault-line." *Race and Class* 55 (2).

Haniffa, Farzana. 2016. "Stories in the Aftermath of Alutgama." In *Buddhist Extremists and Muslim Minorities: Religious Conflict in Contemporary Sri Lanka,* ed. John Clifford Holt, pp. 164–193. New York: Oxford University Press.

Holt, John Clifford, ed., with an introduction and glossary. 1992. *Anagatavamsa Desana: The Sermon of the Chronicle-to-Be.* Translated by Udaya Meddegama. Delhi: Motilal Bansarsidass.

———. 2015. "Militant Buddhists and Minority Others: Ethnic Conflict in South and Southeast Asia." In *Ethnic Conflict in Buddhist Societies in South and Southeast Asia: The Politics behind Religious Rivalries,* ed. K. M. de Silva, pp. 1–24. Kandy, Sri Lanka: International Centre for Ethnic Studies.

———, ed. 2016. *Buddhist Extremists and Muslim Minorities: Religious Conflict in Contemporary Sri Lanka.* New York: Oxford University Press.

———. 2017. *Theravada Traditions: Buddhist Ritual Cultures in Contemporary Southeast Asia and Sri Lanka.* Honolulu: University of Hawai'i Press.

Human Rights Watch. 2013. *All You Can Do Is Pray: Crimes against Humanity and Ethnic Cleansing of Rohingya in Burma's Arakan State.* New York: Human Rights Watch. http://www.hrw.org.

Ibrahim, Azeem. 2016. *The Rohingyas: Inside Myanmar's Hidden Genocide.* London: C. Hurst and Company.

International Crisis Group. 2013. *The Dark Side of Transition: Violence against Muslims in Myanmar.* Asia Report no. 251. Brussels, Belgium: International Crisis Group.

Jones, Lee. 2017. "A Better Political Economy of the Rohingya Crisis." *New Mandala,* September 26, 2017. http://www.newmandala.org/better-political-economy-rohingya-crisis/.

Larsson, Tomas. 2015. "Monkish Politics in Southeast Asia: Religious Disenfranchisement in Comparative and Theoretical Perspective." *Modern Asian Studies* 49:40–82.

Lee, Ronan. 2014. "A Politician, Not an Icon: Aung San Suu Kyii's Silence on Myanmar's Muslim Rohingya." *Islam and Christian-Muslim Relations* 25.

Leider, Jacques, 1998. "These Buddhist Kings with Muslim Names: A Discussion of Muslim Influence in the Mrauk-U Period." In *Etudes birmanes en homage a Denise Bernot,* ed. F. Robinne and P. Pichard, pp. 189–215. Paris: École Française d'Extrême-Orient.

———. 2005. *Le royaume d'Arakan, Birmanie: Son histoire politique entre le du XVe et la fin du XVIIe siècle.* Paris: École Française d'Extrême-Orient.

———. 2008. "Forging Buddhist Credentials as a Tool of Legitimacy and Ethnic Identity: A Study of Rakhine's Subjection in Nineteenth Century Myanmar." *Journal of the Economic and Social History of the Orient* 51:409–459.

———. 2013. "Rohingya: The Name, the Movement, the Quest for Identity." In *Nation Building in Myanmar.* Yangon: Myanmar EGRESS/Myanmar Peace Center, pp. 204–255.

———. 2018. "History and Victimhood: Engaging with Rohingya Issues." *Insight Turkey* 20:99–118.

McCargo, Duncan. 2008. *Tearing Apart the Land: Islam and Legitimacy in Southern Thailand.* Ithaca, NY: Cornell University Press.

———. 2011. *Mapping National Anxieties: Thailand's Southern Conflict.* Copenhagen: Nordic Institute of Asian Studies Press.

Mendelson, E. Michael. 1975. *Sangha and State in Burma.* Ithaca, NY: Cornell University Press.

Nilsen, Marte. 2012. *Negotiating Thainess: Religious and National Identities in Thailand's Southern Conflict.* Lund Studies in History of Religions, vol. 31. Lund, Sweden: Lund University.

Nuhman, M. A. 2007. *Sri Lankan Muslims: Ethnic Identity within Cultural Diversity.* Colombo, Sri Lanka: International Centre for Ethnic Studies, 2007.

Sarkisyanz, E. 1965. *Buddhist Backgrounds of the Burmese Revolution.* The Hague: Martinus Nijhoff.

Saw, Khin Maung. 2016. *Arakan: A Neglected Land and Her Voiceless People.* 2nd ed. Yangon: Kha Yee Phaw Publishing House.

Schissler, Matthew, Matthew J. Walton, and Phyu Phyu Thi. 2015. "Threat and Virtuous Defence: Listening to Narratives of Religious Conflict in Six Myanmar Cities." M.MAS Working Paper 1:1, University of Oxford, St. Antony's College, Myanmar Media and Society Project, July.

Schober, Juliane. 2011. *Modern Buddhist Conjunctures in Myanmar.* Honolulu: University of Hawai'i Press.

Seekins, Donald. 2011. *State and Society in Modern Rangoon.* London: Routledge.

Skidmore, Monique. 2006. "Scholarship, Advocacy and the Politics of Engagement in Burma (Myanmar)." In *Engaged Observer: Anthropology, Advocacy and Activism*, ed. Victoria Sanford and Asale Angel-Ajani, pp. 42–59. London: Rutgers University Press.
Skidmore, Monique, and Trevor Wilson, eds. 2008. *Dictatorship, Disorder and Decline in Myanmar.* Canberra: ANU E-Press.
Siddique, Mohammad Mohibullah, ed. 2014. *The Rohingyas of Arakan.* Dhaka, Bangladesh: Ali Publication House.
Tambiah, S. J. 1986. *Sri Lanka: Ethnic Fratricide and the Dismantling of Democracy.* Chicago: University of Chicago Press.
———. 1992. *Buddhism Betrayed? Religion, Politics, and Violence in Sri Lanka.* Chicago: University of Chicago Press.
———. 1996. *Leveling Crowds: Ethnonationalist Conflicts and Collective Violence in South Asia.* Berkeley: University of California Press.
Taylor, Robert. 2006. "The Legal Status of Indians in Contemporary Burma." In *Indian Communities in Southeast Asia*, ed. K. S. Sandhu and A. Mani. Singapore: Institute of Southeast Asian Studies.
Thant Myint U. 2001. *The Making of Modern Burma.* Cambridge: Cambridge University Press.
———. 2007. *The River of Lost Footsteps: A Personal History of Burma.* London: Faber and Faber.
———. 2012. *Where China Meets India: Burma and the New Crossroads of Asia.* New York: Farrar, Straus and Giroux.
Turner, Alicia. 2014. *Saving Buddhism: The Impermanence of Religion in Colonial Burma.* Honolulu: University of Hawai'i Press.
United Nations Office of the High Commissioner for Human Rights (OHCHR). 2017. *Report of the OHCHR Mission to Bangladesh. Interviews with Rohingyas Fleeing from Myanmar since 9 October 2016.* February 3. https://www.ohchr.org/_layouts/15/WopiFrame.aspx?sourcedoc=/Documents/Countries/MM/FlashReport3Feb2017.pdf.
Wade, Francis. 2017. *Myanmar's Enemy Within: Buddhist Violence and the Making of a Muslim Other.* London: Zed Books.
Walton, Matthew J. 2016. *Buddhism, Politics and Political Thought.* Cambridge: Cambridge University Press.
Walton, Matthew J., and Susan Hayward. 2014. *Contesting Buddhist Narratives: Democratization, Nationalism, and Communal Violence in Myanmar.* Policy Studies no. 71. Honolulu, HI: East West Center.
Yegar, Moshe. 1972. *The Muslims of Burma.* Wiesbaden: Otto Harrassowitz.
———. 2002. *Between Integration and Secession: The Muslim Communities of the Southern Philippines, Southern Thailand and Western Burma/Myanmar.* New York: Lexington Books.
Yusuf, Imtiyaz. 2018. "The Rohingya, Rising Asian Islamophobia and the Tenuous State of Muslim-Buddhist Relations in Contemporary Southeast Asia." In *Oxford Islamic Studies Online*, ed. John L. Esposito. Oxford: Oxford University Press. http://www.oxfordislamicstudies.com/Public/focus.html.

Media Citations

Within the text, sources are cited by name of media and date. Specific articles can be located within the archives accessible through the following webpages:

AFP (Agence France-Presse). https://www.afp.com/en
Associated Press. https://apnews.com
BBC (British Broadcasting Corporation). https://www.bbc.com/news/world/asia
Christian Science Monitor. https://www.csmonitor.com
Frontier. https://frontiermyanmar.net/en/category/news-feed
Guardian. https://www.theguardian.com/world/asia
Huffington Post. https://www.huffingtonpost.com
The Irrawaddy. https://www.irrawaddy.com
Myanmar Now. http://www.myanmar-now.org
National Public Radio. www.npr.org
New Mandala. http://www.newmandala.org
New York Times. https://www.nytimes.com
Prachatai/English. https://prachatai.com
Reuters. https://www.reuters.com/news/world

Page numbers in boldface type refer to illustrations.

ABOUT THE AUTHOR

John Clifford Holt is William R. Kenan, Jr., Professor of the Humanities in Religion and Asian Studies at Bowdoin College in Brunswick, Maine. He is the author of many books, including *Discipline: The Canonical Buddhism of the Vinayapitaka* (1981); *Buddha in the Crown: Avalokitesvara in the Buddhism Traditions of Sri Lanka* (1991), for which he was awarded an American Academy of Religion Book Award for Excellence; *The Religious World of Kirti Sri: Buddhism, Art, and Politics in Late Medieval Sri Lanka* (1996); *The Buddhist Visnu: Religious Transformation, Politics, and Culture* (2004); *Spirits of the Place: Buddhism and Lao Religious Culture* (2009); *The Sri Lanka Reader: History, Culture, Politics* (2011); *Buddhist Extremists and Muslim Minorities: Religious Conflict in Contemporary Sri Lanka* (2016); and *Theravada Traditions: Buddhist Ritual Cultures in Contemporary Southeast Asia and Sri Lanka* (2017). He was awarded an honorary doctor of letters from the University of Peradeniya in 2002 and selected as the University of Chicago Divinity School Alumnus of the Year in 2007. He has received four National Endowment of the Humanities Fellowships for College Teachers, two Fulbright Fellowships, and a John Simon Guggenheim Foundation Fellowship for research and writing about Buddhist-Muslim conflicts in Sri Lanka, Myanmar, and Thailand. He has also taught at the University of Peradeniya, the Hong Kong University of Science and Technology, the University of Calgary, the University of California, Berkeley, and the University of Chicago.